ROYAL HISTORICAL SOCIETY
STUDIES IN HISTORY

New Series

THE MORAVIAN CHURCH AND THE MISSIONARY AWAKENING IN ENGLAND
1760–1800

Studies in History New Series

Editorial Board

Professor Martin Daunton (*Convenor*)
Professor David Eastwood
Dr Steven Gunn
Professor Colin Jones
Professor Peter Mandler
Dr Simon Walker
Professor Kathleen Burk (*Honorary Treasurer*)

IN MEMORY OF MY LATE AUNT MARJORIE
AND OUR LA TROBE FOREBEARS

Qui la cèrca, la tròba

Baptism of Greenlanders. Woodcut reproduced from *Kurze, zuverlässige Nachricht von der, unter dem Namen der Böhmischen-Mährischen Brüder bekantent, Kirche Unitas Fratrum Herkommen*, n.p. 1757, by kind permission of the Unitätsarchiv, Herrnhut.

THE MORAVIAN CHURCH
AND THE MISSIONARY AWAKENING
IN ENGLAND

1760–1800

J. C. S. Mason

THE ROYAL HISTORICAL SOCIETY
THE BOYDELL PRESS

© J. C. S. Mason 2001

All rights reserved. Except as permitted under current legislation no part of this work may be photocopied, stored in a retrieval system, published, performed in public, adapted, broadcast, transmitted, recorded or reproduced in any form or by any means, without the prior permission of the copyright owner

The right of J. C. S. Mason to be identified as the author of this work has been asserted in accordance with sections 77 and 78 of the Copyright, Designs and Patents Act 1988

First published 2001
The Royal Historical Society, London
in association with
The Boydell Press, Woodbridge
Reprinted in paperback and transferred to digital printing 2011
The Boydell Press, Woodbridge

ISBN 97 0 86193 251 1 hardback
ISBN 978 1 84383 640 7 paperback

The Boydell Press is an imprint of Boydell & Brewer Ltd
PO Box 9, Woodbridge, Suffolk IP12 3DF, UK
and of Boydell & Brewer Inc,
668 Mt Hope Avenue, Rochester, NY 14620, USA
website: www.boydellandbrewer.com

A CIP catalogue record for this book is available
from the British Library

Library of Congress Catalog Card Number 2001035335

This publication is printed on acid-free paper

Contents

		Page
List of illustrations		ix
Acknowledgements		xi
Abbreviations		xiii
Note on terms		xv
Introduction		1
1	The Moravian Church and its missions: Zinzendorf to Spangenberg	5
2	Moravians in England: the Labrador affair, 1764–1784	28
3	Moravians and evangelical Calvinists, 1770–1790	59
4	Bishops in England and Moravians in the West Indies	90
5	The 1788 enquiry into the slave trade	114
6	Moravian missionary teaching and its influence, 1792–1800	143
7	The beginning of the modern missionary movement, 1800	176
Conclusion		193

Appendices

1.	The numerical strength of the Moravian Church, 1822	199
2.	A comparison of texts	200
3.	Distribution of the Moravian *Periodical Accounts*, Feb. 1797–Mar. 1801	202
Bibliography		205
Index		223

List of Illustrations

Frontispiece/jacket illustration: Baptism of Greenlanders
1. View of New Herrnhut, Greenland   22
2. The Moravian mission station at St John's, Antigua   102
3. Exorcism of four negro candidates for baptism   154
4. After baptism   155

Map

1. The South Midlands: founders of the Baptist Missionary Society   85
   and the Moravians

Photographic Acknowledgements

Plate 1 is reproduced from David Cranz, *The history of Greenland containing a description of the country*, London 1767; plates 3, 4 and the frontispiece/jacket illustration are reproduced from *Kurze, zuverlässige Nachricht von der, unter dem Namen der Böhmischen-Mährischen Brüder bekantent, Kirche Unitas Fratrum Herkommen*, n.p. 1757, by kind permission of the Unitätsarchiv, Herrnhut; plate 2 is reproduced from a watercolour by J. H. L. Stobwasser, also by permission of the Unitätsarchiv, Herrnhut.

Publication of this volume was aided by a grant from the Scouloudi Foundation, in association with the Institute of Historical Research.

Acknowledgements

Although this book is not its direct sequel, I hope that it will live alongside Colin Podmore's *The Moravian Church in England, 1728–1760*, which ended when it appeared to Geoffrey Nuttall that 'the Moravian dream was over' (*Times Literary Supplement*, 25 Dec. 1998, 22). Podmore, rather than look forward himself to a new era in the Church's history, generously drew attention to my then incomplete London PhD thesis, 'The role of the Moravian Church during the missionary awakening in England, 1760 to *c*. 1800', leaving it to me to demonstrate how the Moravians 'regained public esteem', largely through the reality of their foreign missions. This book is a revised version of that thesis.

Beginning in the eighteenth century and for three generations my La Trobe forebears were members of the Moravian Church in Britain. In the words of Mrs Janet Halton, until recently archivist of the Church's British province, they appeared to have a 'dynastic hold' over the Moravian missionary society in London. I am indebted to Mrs Halton and to the British Provincial Board which gave me a free run of the archive at the Church's headquarters in London. In particular I should mention Bishop Geoffrey Birtill and the Revd Fred Linyard from whom I also learnt much about the Moravian Church past and present.

I also wish to thank other members of the Church who have shared their knowledge with me: the Revd John McOwat who was at Fulneck in Yorkshire when he allowed me access to the archive there, Miss Margaret Connor of Fulneck, and Mrs Edna Cooper who edits the *Moravian History Magazine*. I am also most grateful to Lucy Torode for allowing me to refer to copies of James La Trobe's letters in her private collection.

A brief visit, after I completed my thesis, to the Moravians' great archive at Herrnhut in Saxony enabled me to fill one or two gaps. I greatly appreciated the assistance of Dr Paul Peucker and his staff there, both at that time and later, in making available to me the pictures from the Church's collection which are reproduced by permission. I am also very fortunate to have obtained the good services of Mrs Bridgitte Burkett who translated some passages from *Handschrift* for me. However, it should be noted that all the manuscript material in Britain, to which I refer, is in English. My research was also assisted by a grant from the University of London's central research fund for microfilm.

I acknowledge the kind permission of the earl of Clarendon to quote from the Barham papers which are part of the Clarendon deposit at the Bodleian Library, Oxford. Grateful appreciation is expressed to the Baptist Missionary Society of Didcot for permission to consult and select my own quotations from their archive material which is housed in the Angus Library at Regent's Park College, Oxford. In this connection I wish to thank Mrs Susan Mills, the library's archivist, for her assistance over several visits. I also acknowledge Dr Daniel Potts's permission to quote from his draft typescript of the almost indecipherable journal kept by William Ward, the Baptist missionary.

I have benefited greatly from the friendship and constructive comments of many other scholars, most notably Penny Carson, James Hiller of Memorial University, Newfoundland, who allowed me to copy his thesis on Moravians in Labrador, Bruce Hindmarsh and Colin Podmore. It is to Professor Hindmarsh that I owe references to John Newton's papers at the Firestone Library at Princeton. The map of the South Midlands of England was created by Mrs Jane Pugh and it was at her suggestion that we found an appropriate source for the roads. I must also thank the John Rylands University Library, Manchester, and the Mitchell Library, State Library of New South Wales, for permission to quote from microfilms which were made available to me from manuscripts in their collections. I particularly wish to acknowledge the assistance of Christine Linehan in preparing this book for publication: she is surely one of the kindest and most tolerant of editors.

Chapters 3 and 6 began as seminar papers given under the auspices of the North Atlantic Missiology Project, co-ordinated by the University of Cambridge and financed by the Pew Charitable Trusts. The opinions expressed in these chapters are those of the author and do not necessarily reflect the views of the Pew Charitable Trusts.

Finally, I owe an enormous debt of gratitude to Professor P. J. Marshall who supervised my thesis. It is a privilege and a pleasure to have been one of his research students. Professor Marshall is always generous with his time and he has encouraged me to complete this book. Any mistakes or errors of judgement that remain are mine alone.

'Heureux, qui comme Ulysse, a fait un beau voyage.'

John Mason
London 2000

Abbreviations

AL	Angus Library, Regent's Park College, Oxford
APC	*Acts of the privy council of England: colonial series*, v–vi, ed. James Munro, London 1912
BCD	[Moravian] Bristol congregation diary
BDEB	*Blackwell dictionary of evangelical biography*
BL	British Library
BMS	Baptist Missionary Society
BOT	Board of Trade
BPA	*Periodical Accounts Relative to the Baptist Missionary Society*
BQ	*Baptist Quarterly* n.s.
BRO	Bedfordshire Record Office
BUL	Bristol University Library
CFWC	Cheshunt College Foundation, Westminster College, Cambridge
CMS	Church Missionary Society
CWM	Council of World Mission [London Missionary Society]
DNB	*Dictionary of national biography*
EM	*Evangelical Magazine*
FLD	Fetter Lane [London] congregation diaries
HMC	Royal Commission on Historical Documents
IPC	*In the privy council: in the matter of the boundary between the dominion of Canada and the colony of Newfoundland in the Labrador peninsula* [London 1926–7]
JRUL	John Rylands University Library
LPL	Lambeth Palace Library
LMS	[London] Missionary Society
MCH	Moravian Church House
ML	Mitchell Library, Sydney
PA	*Periodical Accounts Relating to the Missions of the Church of the United Brethren Established among the Heathen*
PHC	[Moravian] provincial helpers' conference
PRO	Public Record Office
PWHS	*Proceedings of the Wesley Historical Society*
SFG	[Moravian] Brethren's Society for the Furtherance of the Gospel among the Heathen
SPCK	Society for the Promotion of Christian Knowledge

SPG	Society for the Propagation of the Gospel
TMHS	*Transactions of the Moravian Historical Society*
UA	Unitätsarchiv, Herrnhut
UEC	[Moravian] Unity Elders' Conference (the directorate in Germany over the Church world-wide)
UF	*Unitas Fratrum*

Note on Terms

The international Moravian Church
By 1760 the Unitas Fratrum was generally known in Britain as the Moravian Church. It is an international, Protestant evangelical denomination.

Moravians
British Moravians usually described themselves collectively as the Brethren, or more formally as the United Brethren. Similarly their Church and its missions were known as the Brethren's Church and missions. These terms or the abbreviations Brn/Brns. appear in documents quoted, but elsewhere members of the Church worldwide are referred to as Moravians. Individuals were described as Brother or Sister, shortened to Br/Sis. followed by their surname.

Evangelical/evangelicals
The term 'evangelical' describes a member of any Protestant denomination in England who held an evangelical belief. In instances where it is essential to discriminate between faiths, evangelicals within the Established Church are referred to as Church Evangelicals. It is assumed that all Moravians were evangelicals.

The three new missionary societies
'The Particular Baptist Missionary Society', founded in 1792, is referred to as the Baptist Missionary Society (BMS), the name it adopted in 1795.
'The Missionary Society', established in London in 1795 as an interdenominational society, is referred to by the name it adopted in 1818 – the London Missionary Society (LMS).
'The Society for Missions to Africa and the East', formed in 1799 by members of the Established Church, is known as the Church Missionary Society (CMS), the latter title being already in use by 1812 when it was formally adopted.

Introduction

This book is about the contribution to the missionary awakening in England made by the Moravian Church between 1760 and 1800. The significance of the period arises from the formation in the last decade of the century of three new missionary societies. This was a turning-point in the long awakening which is now seen as the beginning of the modern British missionary movement, the movement that led to the expansion of Protestant Christianity to all parts of the empire and beyond.[1]

It is generally agreed that by 1760 the Moravian Church had influenced the course of eighteenth-century English Protestant evangelicalism. The part which it had played has been described in the past and most recently by Colin Podmore in *The Moravian Church in England, 1728–60*,[2] a work which describes the interaction between the Moravian Church, leaders of the evangelical revival, bishops of the Established Church and men prominent in public affairs. Podmore also explains why the Moravian Church attracted many more 'ordinary' people. His account draws to a close, however, at a low point in the Church's history caused by a very public and damaging crisis of confidence: the Church had lost both its good name and was severely financially encumbered with debt. The effects of this were to reverberate for the rest of the century.

Whilst other scholars have examined the involvement of Moravians in the religious life of the British Isles during the eighteenth century,[3] their role in the missionary awakening in England is a field which lies wide open. But why begin in 1760? What of those earlier Moravian missions to the heathen to which the Church already attached the greatest importance?

The revival of the Moravian Church in 1727 at Herrnhut, in Saxony, on the estate of Count Nicholas von Zinzendorf, its effective founder, was followed by the launch, five years later, of the Church's foreign missions. They soon aroused much interest, if only for a brief period, among prominent British Christians. It was, indeed, the intention of the Associates of Dr Bray to employ two Moravians as missionaries to slaves in Georgia that led to the

---

[1] A. N. Porter, *Religion and empire: British expansion in the long nineteenth century, 1780–1914* (inaugural lecture, King's College London), London 1991.
[2] Colin Podmore, *The Moravian Church in England, 1728–60*, Oxford 1998.
[3] For example, R. T. Jenkins, *The Moravian Brethren in north Wales: an episode in the religious history of Wales*, London 1938; Clifford W. Towlson, *Moravian and Methodist: relationships in the eighteenth century*, London 1957; Geoffrey Stead, 'European Pietism in Yorkshire: the origins and early development of the Moravian settlement at Fulneck, 1742–90', unpubl. PhD diss. Leeds 1994.

archbishop of Canterbury's personal endorsement of the Church in 1737.[4] Bishop Wilson of Sodor and Man was also attracted to the Moravians mainly on account of their missionary endeavours. Among Dissenters, Philip Doddridge of Northampton was associated with the Moravians' newly formed missionary society in London before he called on his fellow ministers in 1742 to support the conversion of the heathen abroad.[5]

However, there was no effective follow-through to these missionary stirrings. Doddridge's call went unanswered for another fifty years and there were no further similar initiatives in pursuit of the Associates' objective of the 'Conversion of the negroes in the British plantations'[6] after 1739 when the Moravian mission they sponsored was abandoned.[7] Moreover, by the middle of the century the societies for the Promotion of Christian Knowledge and for the Propagation of the Gospel had lost that zeal for missions to the heathen overseas displayed by an earlier generation of members.[8]

Nor was the initial interest among evangelicals in the Moravian Church itself sustained. Doubts, principally about the Church's doctrine, soon surfaced on both sides of the Atlantic and leaders of the evangelical movement withdrew from their association with Moravians. In 1741 the breach with John Wesley became final and George Whitefield's hopes for a union with the Moravians ended four years later in a similar manner. In the American colonies Presbyterians were hostile and at home Doddridge broke off his contacts.[9]

Doctrinal differences and an atmosphere of mistrust meant that in the longer term Moravians, although active in England from the 1740s, were bypassed by the two main streams of British evangelicalism. Nevertheless, the Church retained a small but ardent following which led to the formation of congregations of British Moravians on a permanent footing, first in London in 1742 and then in Yorkshire. Their number increased after 1745 when John Cennick, then a great lay-preacher, deserted Whitefield for the Moravians by whom he was ordained. The Church was and remained very cautious indeed

---

[4] D. Benham, *Memoirs of James Hutton: comprising the annals of his life and connection with the United Brethren*, London 1856, 24, 158.
[5] E. A. Payne, 'Doddridge and the missionary enterprise', in Geoffrey F. Nuttall (ed.), *Philip Doddridge*, London 1951, 87–93.
[6] *An account of the designs of the associates of the late Doctor Bray: with an abstract of their proceedings*, London 1789, 4.
[7] J. Taylor Hamilton and Kenneth G. Hamilton, *History of the Moravian Church: the renewed Unitas Fratrum, 1722–1957*, Bethlehem, Penn.–Winston-Salem, NC 1983, 84–5.
[8] For the decline by 1740 of the SPCK's support for mission in India see Daniel L. Brunner, 'The role of Halle Pietists in England (c. 1700–c. 1740) with special reference to the SPCK', unpubl. DPhil. diss. Oxford 1988, 165, 254. For the failure of the SPG's plans of 1711 for its Codrington estates in Barbados see J. Harry Bennet, *Bondsmen and bishops: slavery and apprenticeship on the Codrington plantations of Barbados, 1710–38*, Berkeley–Los Angeles 1958, 2–5.
[9] J. E. Hutton, *A history of the Moravian Church*, London 1909, 333–4. For Doddridge see Payne, 'Missionary enterprise', 93–5.

in accepting new members, but small Moravian congregations did develop in various parts of the British Isles, and of these a few became settlements on a larger scale to which the great eighteenth-century terrace of buildings at Fulneck in Yorkshire bears testimony.

The potential for these promising developments was not, however, realised. In 1755 Zinzendorf, who had been living of late in England, returned to Germany, most probably in disgrace. When he died five years later Moravians seemed such a marginal factor in English religious life that it was as though they were 'in retreat'. Their Church, engulfed in troubles, had lost credibility and drew in upon itself. Its missions, up to this point, and for some years afterwards, had not received anything like the same publicity in England as the Church itself.

Congregations with around 200 members nevertheless remained pockets of influence. In addition to the congregations in Yorkshire, there were important communities in Bedford, Bristol, a more recent development, and London, the Church's provincial headquarters, where the Fetter Lane congregation and community around the chapel in the City added to the Moravian presence in Britain.

By 1760 it seemed most unlikely that in the future religious leaders would allow themselves to be associated with the Moravians. This was not, however, to be the case. Confidence was gradually restored and before the end of the century founders of new missionary societies in England were to turn to the Church for a missionary model.

Historians have long recognised that the Moravian Church had some influence on these men. The Moravian J. E. Hutton, for instance, had no doubt that this was so in the case of the Baptist and London missionary societies. But since he originally made this point in 1909 and again in the 1920s,[10] the only study known to have been attempted has been of the Baptist pioneer, William Carey, a work considered inadequate by his co-religionists.[11] Recently, however, Brian Stanley has confirmed that the Moravians had a powerful influence on Carey,[12] while Graham McKelvie, has concluded that in 1794 Beilby Porteus, bishop of London from 1787 until 1808, 'hoped to model' the missions which he attempted to have established in the West Indies on those of the Moravians.[13]

---

[10] Hutton, *Moravian Church*, 251–3, and *A history of Moravian missions*, London n.d., 107, 202 (preface dated 1922).
[11] 'Principles of the missions of the Pietists, especially of the Moravians', in A. H. Oussoren, *William Carey, especially his missionary principles*, Leyden 1945, 219–69. For a recent judgement on this work see Brian Stanley, *The history of the Baptist Missionary Society, 1792–1992*, Edinburgh 1992, 39 n. 14.
[12] Ibid. 39–40.
[13] Graham D. McKelvie, 'The development of official Anglican interest in world mission, 1783–1809, with special reference to Bishop Beilby Porteus', unpubl. PhD diss. Aberdeen 1984, 1000–3. An earlier and similar conclusion appears in Elsa Goveia, *Slave society in the*

This study has two main aims: first to explain the importance of the example of the Moravian Church's foreign missions for the missionary awakening in England; and second to examine the influence of the Moravian missionary model on the thinking of the founders of the Baptist, London and Church missionary societies. Particular attention is given to the first two of these societies; the Church Missionary Society, being the last of the three to be established in the 1790s, is examined in less detail.[14]

A thematic approach has been adopted which means that the story does not unfold entirely in a chronological order. The first five chapters, covering the years between 1760 and 1790, describe how the Moravian Church regained its reputation in England. They show how it became known and respected above all for its foreign missions which by 1790 had come to be highly regarded by evangelicals, who went on to establish the new missionary societies, by statesmen at home and by government officials overseas. The final chapters explain why the example of the Moravian Church was important to founders of the Baptist and London missionary societies and identify features of the Moravian missionary model which in the beginning were of particular significance for these societies. After a separate examination of the Church Missionary Society, all three societies are brought together in an analysis of the situation in 1800, establishing the influence of the Moravian Church on the modern missionary movement as a whole. In order to explain how perceptions in England were effected by progress overseas, excursions are made from time to time into the mission field, in particular to the Moravian missions to the Inuit of Greenland and Labrador and to the slaves in the West Indies.

The story begins in Germany where, after the death of Zinzendorf in 1760, the Moravian Church took crucial decisions which in the longer term made it possible for this small Church and its foreign missions to have a quiet but substantial influence on the missionary awakening in England. Inevitably, despite his immense importance, Zinzendorf appears but fitfully and in the background to this study.

British Leeward Islands at the end of the eighteenth century, New Haven, Conn.–London 1965, 285.

[14] For all three societies, titles and years of formation see p. xv.

1

The Moravian Church and its Missions: Zinzendorf to Spangenberg

Count Nicholas von Zinzendorf (1700–60) attributed his own precocious missionary awakening, and hence the beginning of the Moravian missions, to the example of the Pietist-inspired Royal Danish mission at Tranquebar, in India, which began in 1706. Zinzendorf had been raised in a Pietist household where he heard accounts of that mission and then, as one of August Hermann Francke's students, he met missionaries on leave at Halle. It was shortly after this that he made his youthful vow to forward missions to the heathen when he was old enough,[1] a pledge he was to realise through the Moravian Church.

Well before the end of Zinzendorf's life, and under his direction, the Moravians had established a particular approach to the conversion of the heathen overseas to Christianity, which was shaped by some of the Church's most predominant characteristics, although modified by experience in the field. Their missionary activities began in 1732 in St Thomas, one of three islands in the West Indies belonging to the Danish crown, and a year later in Greenland, also a Danish colony. These were the Church's first permanent missions and although by 1760 they had been extended into the British world and beyond, they remained by far the most important. Few Christians in other Churches, however, least of all in Britain, were aware of the scale of the Moravians' work overseas. Little had been done to make the missions generally known and it was too late when in the late 1750s the age of Zinzendorf was drawing to its close. For that was the period when the Moravian Church lost its good name in the crisis which overshadowed Zinzendorf's last years and caused damage to the Church's reputation which was to endure for generations.

After Zinzendorf's death his successors drew up the Church's first formal constitution; its introduction marks the beginning of a prolonged period in the Church's history which has been described as the era of Spangenberg. A. G. Spangenberg (1704–92) was, after Zinzendorf, the Church's most promi-

---

[1] Jüngenhaus-Diarium, 31 Aug. 1753, London, in Hans-Christoph Hahn and Hellmut Reichel (eds), *Zinzendorf und die Herrnhuter Brüder: Quellen zur Geschichte der Brüder-Unität von 1722 bis 1760*, Hamburg 1997, 352. For a relevant biographical sketch see 'Zinzendorf and his context', in Arthur J. Freeman, *An ecumenical theology of the heart: the theology of Count Nicholas Ludwig von Zinzendorf*, Bethlehem, Penn.–Winston-Salem, NC 1998, 21–38. See also A. J. Lewis, *Zinzendorf the ecumenical pioneer: a study in the Moravian contribution to mission and unity*, London 1962.

nent thinker and leader; his influence continued to be felt well into the following century.² In particular, without him it is difficult to imagine that towards the end of the eighteenth century British missionary leaders would have drawn on the example of the Moravian Church and its missions. A Lutheran theologian, trained at the university of Jena and attracted by Pietist thinking, he succeeded Zinzendorf as the exponent of the Church's doctrine and practice of missions. Even before he became a member of the Church in 1733 some of the first Moravians to go overseas consulted him on how their mission should be conducted.³

By 1760 Spangenberg was respected on both sides of the Atlantic. During the 1740s he had established the Church's permanent presence in Britain and had led the Moravians in the American colonies through the testing period of the French and Indian Wars. Recalled to Europe in 1762, with a proven record, he emerged as *primus inter pares* among the Elders who directed the Church from Germany world-wide. A measured and deliberate approach was as characteristic of the man as it was of the post-Zinzendorfian Moravian Church as a whole. But what was the status of the Church to which he returned?

An internationally recognised Church

The revival of the Moravian Church, in the aftermath of the famous religious awakening of 1727 among settlers at Herrnhut, as well as the launch of its foreign missions five years later, would have been inconceivable without the influence of German Lutheran Pietism amongst Protestants world-wide. Moravians during the age of Zinzendorf fall well within Ernest Stoeffler's description of Pietism as 'venturesome, . . . oriented towards life's vital concerns, and vibrant with spiritual and emotional dynamic'.⁴ From the beginning Zinzendorf had channelled their movement into a prolonged period of evangelical endeavour and extraordinary missionary effort. He taught and inspired the Moravians to follow 'The Saviour's instruction; go forth to all the world and preach the Gospel to all creatures.' It was better, he wrote in 1738, to go out to 'all the peoples of the world' than to none.⁵ It is

---

² Hans-Christoph Hahn, 'August Gottlieb Spangenberg (1704–1792)', in Hahn and Reichel, *Zinzendorf und die Herrnhuter Brüder*, 445–7. See also David A. Schattschneider, ' "Souls for the Lamb": a theology for the Christian mission according to Count Nicolaus Ludwig von Zinzendorf and Bishop Augustus Gottlieb Spangenberg', unpubl. PhD diss. Chicago 1975, 35–47.
³ A. G. Spangenberg, *An account of the manner in which the Protestant Church of the Unitas Fratrum, or the United Brethren, preach the Gospel and carry on their missions to the heathen*, trans., London 1788, 60–1.
⁴ F. Ernest Stoeffler, *The rise of evangelical Pietism*, Leiden 1965, 246.
⁵ 'Instruktion an alle Heidenboten, 1738', in N. L. von Zinzendorf, *Texte zur Mission*, ed. Helmut Bintz, Hamburg 1979, 52.

partly for this reason that today most members of the International Moravian Church are non-Europeans residing in its provinces beyond those of continental Europe.[6]

Although Zinzendorf was initially very reluctant indeed to allow the Church or its missions to develop along institutional and denominational lines, other considerations, which even he could not resist, soon prevailed. Governments and officials required a definable entity with which to deal, but above all the settlers at Herrnhut found identity and cohesion in the history of the ancient Bohemian–Moravian Church, the Unity of the Brethren. Thus the revelation in 1727 that the rules of conduct, to which the settlers had so recently agreed, were similar to those of this ancient Church was a vital element in the evangelical awakening and fusion which followed. They 'discovered therein the finger of God', the contemporary account states, and '[we] found ourselves as it were baptized under the cloud of our Fathers, with their spirit'.[7] Ever since then legend and fact have been an important part of Moravian identity: it is, for instance, generally agreed that the Unity was founded in 1457 at Kunwald, the birthplace in Moravia of some of the first settlers at Herrnhut.[8]

Despite Zinzendorf's misgivings, the Moravian Church began to take on the appearance of an institution. In 1735, justified later by the need for missionaries to the heathen to be ordained,[9] their first bishop was consecrated by the last incumbent of the ancient Church. The Church's orders were also introduced and a few years later the Saviour Christ was made head of the Moravian Church. These decisions, which shaped the Church's future constitution, were some of the first to lend credence to the perception that Moravians were members of a separate Christian denomination.

Described later by Spangenberg as 'even the most ancient of the Protestant Religions',[10] the Moravians possessed a rich heritage which had for long been admired throughout the Protestant world. Their *Ancient and modern history*, first published in German in 1771, wove past and present into a 'seamless web'. Festivals, which began to be introduced during the age of

---

[6] The largest concentration of Moravians is now to be found in the Church's provinces of Tanzania, South Africa, Nicaragua and the West Indies. Total membership in 1995 was 764,852. For membership figures see 'Provincial statistics', in 'The Moravian Almanac', *Daily Watchwords 1998*, Moravian book room, London 1998, 7.
[7] *Memorial days of the renewed Church of the Brethren*, trans., Ashton-under-Lyne 1822, 99–100.
[8] Edwin A. Sayer, *These fifteen pioneers of the Moravian Church*, Bethlehem, Penn.–Winston-Salem, NC 1963, 21; cf. Rudolf Rican, *The history of the Unity of the Brethren: a Protestant Hussite Church in Bohemia and Moravia*, trans. C. Daniel Crews, Bethlehem, Penn.–Winston-Salem, NC 1992, esp. p. 28.
[9] This was the only reason given in July 1764 when the constitution was established: MCH, general synods, weekly accounts, 1764–89, fo. 33.
[10] A. G. Spangenberg, *A concise historical account of the present constitution of the Unitas Fratrum; or Unity of the evangelical Brethren who adhere to the Augustan Confession*, trans., London 1775, 27.

Zinzendorf, celebrated landmarks in the history of the Church and its missions. These ceremonies, known as memorial days, had a vital role in cementing a sense of solidarity between members throughout the world.[11]

Moravians of all nations seem to have shared a vision of being a chosen people as well as being part of an international fraternity. In 1777 British Moravians described themselves as 'a peculiar people . . . belonging to the Unity of the Brethren . . . embodied in a folk who have a stamp impressed upon them from ancient times as a company of confessors and martyrs'. They also saw themselves as members of a select family especially chosen by their Saviour for 'His own' to bear witness to 'Christians and heathens' throughout the world.[12]

However, in an age of national Churches, the development of the revived Moravian Church into an international evangelistic movement was highly dependent on the attitude of governments and officials who needed to be satisfied that Moravians were neither sectarian at home nor seditious overseas. The Church issued repeated assurances to this effect in which its evangelical objective was stated in inter-confessional terms, and members were consistently taught to hold in profound respect the laws of the land wherever they found themselves.[13]

Moravians earned the reputation of being good settlers, peaceable and industrious, and by 1750 theirs was an internationally recognised Protestant Church, albeit with qualifications. The British act of parliament of 1749 to encourage Moravians to settle in the American colonies was a defining moment in their history. The Moravian Church was now acknowledged to be an 'antient protestant Episcopal Church' and its members had a legal standing throughout the empire. Moravians were granted the right to affirm, rather than to swear an oath, and they were not obliged to carry arms.[14] Those in Britain, however, remained Dissenters.

The British world was to be of increasing importance for the Moravians and their missions. The act of 1749 gave them grounds for security and proved to be a considerable asset overseas. For instance, parliament's acceptance of the Church's episcopate meant that the validity of baptisms performed by missionaries could not seriously be challenged. It was also significant, surely, that the act's passage was followed in the 1750s by the first attempts to establish Moravian missions in the British West Indies. Missionaries who then went from the Danish to the British islands of Antigua and

---

[11] David Cranz, *The ancient and modern history of the Brethren; or a succinct narrative of the Protestant Church of the United Brethren or, Unitas Fratrum, in the remoter ages, and particularly in the present century*, trans., London 1780. The title and preface make the link clear. I owe this apt expression to Mrs Halton.
[12] MCH, FLD-21, memorabilia 1777.
[13] Guntram Philipp, 'Verhältnis zur Obrigkeit', in Hahn and Reichel, *Zinzendorf und die Herrnhuter Brüder*, 304–5; Spangenberg, *Historical account*, 28–9, 39.
[14] 22 G.II C.30; Podmore, *Moravian Church*, 228–65.

Tortola carried the act as a 'passport',[15] and it remained the document to which Moravians would refer officials whenever they needed to be reminded of parliament's recognition of the Church or of its members' rights.[16]

The Moravians' sense of their history was apparent from their loyal address of 1760 on the accession of George III to the throne, describing themselves as a 'small class of your faithful subjects known to your Majesty's Royal Predecessors'. A further passage disclosed the grounds on which their well-established attitude of deference towards the powers that be were founded: it was part of the 'scripture doctrine embraced by us that we shall always, from duty and inclination, love and revere the father of our country'. Moreover, it was the 'constant endeavour' of 'each' Moravian throughout 'your Majesty's dominions, to exhibit, on all occasions, proofs of our attachment, zeal and obedience to your Majesty's sacred person and government'.[17]

All this was undoubtedly true; what is also true is that in the period between the passage of the act of 1749 and the loyal address the Moravians had lost their good name and credit in a sensational fall from grace.

The crash of 1753 and its long-term effects

By 1750 the Moravian Church was over-extended: it resembled an enterprise that had ventured greatly due to the entrepreneurial spirit of its founder and dominant leader, Zinzendorf. Its expansion, moreover, its land purchases, its great buildings and other initiatives – in which the cost of the missions was no more than a fraction of a much greater problem[18] – was funded mainly by loans. Finances were precarious and expenditure out of control. Reckless expenditure at home and a period of baroque religious enthusiasm, 'the time of sifting', during the 1740s, led, despite a purge beginning in 1749, to the inevitable four years later: a spectacular crash in credit[19] and reputation. The many detractors in Britain of Zinzendorf and the Church pounced, sweeping away their good names in an orchestrated avalanche of books and pamphlets

---

15 For the act being carried by missionaries to Antigua (1756) see Vernon H. Nelson, 'Samuel Isles, first Moravian missionary on Antigua', *TMHS* xxi/1 (1966), 9; to Tortola (1759) see C. G. A. Oldendorp's *history of the mission of the evangelical brethren on the Caribbean islands of St Thomas, St Croix and St John*, ed. J. J. Bossard, Barby 1770; trans. and ed. Arnold R. Highfield and Vladimir Barac, Ann Arbor, Mich. 1987
16 C. I. La Trobe to Sullivan, secretary of state's office, [?] 27 July 1801, MCH, transactions with government; missionary Hofner to [?] C. I. La Trobe, 16 June 1794, MCH, letters from Barbados.
17 *Public Ledger*, i, no. 278, 1 Dec. 1760.
18 Adolf Schulze, *Abriss einer Geschichte der Brüdermissionen*, Herrnhut 1901, 51. See also W. R. Ward, 'Zinzendorf and money', in W. J. Sheils and Diana Wood (eds), *The Church and wealth* (Studies in Church History xxiv, 1987), 283–305.
19 Hamilton and Hamilton, *History of the Moravian Church*, chs x, xii at pp. 107–18, 132–45.

against which Moravians protested in vain.[20] The effect was salutary but nearly ruinous.

Of these works, *A candid narrative of the rise and progress of the Herrnhuters, commonly called Moravians* by Henry Rimius, first published in London in 1753, was by far the most prejudicial. A summary from Rimius' book in the *Gentleman's Magazine* that year included the accusation that 'Herrnhutism, ... has debased Christianity by connecting with it the most detestable absurdities, and expresses doctrines which it has grossly corrupted in figures borrowed from the stews, and terms too gross to be repeated.' The article also implied that the Moravians had obtained by deceit parliament's recognition that theirs was the ancient episcopal Church they claimed.[21] The bench of bishops, the majority of whom had voted for the act of 1749, were among those who cut themselves off from the Moravians.

Rimius was believed on both sides of the Atlantic to have revealed the truth about the Moravians.[22] However, the most long-lasting damage seems to have been to their prospects in Britain. Few Moravians, if any, can have escaped the malign ridicule heaped upon them, or the effects of the prolonged financial crisis; both, as British sources demonstrate, have every appearance of having been an indelible experience. Memories were long during the long eighteenth century. Not only did Moravians have the calumnies of Rimius and his kind to contend with; the imagery from Moravian hymns, the cause of much derision, remained deeply embarrassing. In 1788 the British Moravian, (Christian) Ignatius La Trobe, remonstrated with his and his Church's evangelical friend in London, the Revd Richard Cecil, for 'speaking so freely' in front of his servants against 'Zinzendorf & his hymns'; and at Magdalen College, Oxford, he was 'amazed to find' 'how much Rimius has been taken as the pure knowledge concerning the Brn'.[23] As late as 1808 the evangelical *Christian Observer* reminded readers that Moravians, like the 'Anabaptists' in an earlier period, had more recently 'exhibited a deplorable licentiousness of practice'.[24]

George Whitefield's *Expostulatory letter*, addressed to Count Zinzendorf, followed within weeks of Rimius' first publication and it too was long lasting in its prejudicial effect. To sensational accounts of idolatrous practices in England, Whitefield added well-founded tales of the financial plight of British Moravians. These, they believed at the time, further undermined

---

[20] See 'The crisis of 1753', in Podmore, *Moravian Church*, ch. ix, pp. 266–89.
[21] *Gentleman's Magazine* xxiii (1753), 236–7.
[22] John Penn to Thomas Penn, 6 May 1754, Thomas Penn papers, Pennsylvania Historical Society, Pennsylvania, private correspondence (microfilm), iv (reference kindly provided by Professor P. J. Marshall); cf. Lady Mary to Sir James Stuart, 1 Oct. 1758, in *The complete letters of Lady Mary Wortley Montagu, 1752–62*, ed. Robert Halsband, Oxford 1965–7, iii. 183.
[23] C. I. La Trobe, journal, 17 Jan., 21 June 1788, JRUL, MS Eng. 1244.
[24] *The Christian Observer*, Jan. 1808, 39, cited in C. I. La Trobe to the editor, 23 Feb. 1808, MCH, transactions with government.

confidence in the shaky credit on which the whole edifice of the Church depended.[25]

Contrary to predictions of collapse, however, the international Church survived. But it was a close run thing: the Church and its properties had 'been not once, but several times on the brink of ruin', an official minute of 1762 reads.[26] It is impossible to exaggerate the long-term effect of the crisis. Moravians were haunted both by the allegations made against them and by the burden of debt for which they became responsible. Moreover, a lack of funds constrained the development of the missions.

The era of Spangenberg: reform and the expansion of the missions

As the period of Zinzendorf's inspired but sometimes impetuous leadership came to an end with his death in 1760, the Moravians, chastened by 'so many mistakes', planned for the future.[27] The era of Spangenberg began with measures to revive confidence in the Church and to restore its good name. Above all, much would depend on the Moravian Church gaining widespread respect for its foreign missions. This did not happen by chance; a range of reforms included positive steps which made this outcome possible. Except within the confines of the Church, Moravians had done very little so far to make their missions known: they had developed largely away from the glare of unwelcome publicity.

The end of the Seven Years War in 1763 made it possible for the all-important reforming general synod to be held the following year in Germany, attended by members representing the whole Church whose agreement to the proposed new constitution was essential. This and a form of collective leadership, which synod endorsed, led to stability at the price of direction and control from the centre over almost every detail at home and overseas. Highly centralised oversight, orthodox evangelicalism and cautious determination became dominant characteristics of the post-Zinzendorfian Moravian Church. Three further synods, the last held in 1782, introduced some modifications of an administrative or procedural nature, but it was the first that was crucial:[28] the Church's constitution was not changed from that established in 1764 until 1857 when a provincial structure was adopted.

---

[25] George Whitefield, *An expostulatory letter, addressed to Nicholas Lewis, Count Zinzendorf*, London 1753, 10–16; Benham, *Memoirs of James Hutton*, 265–81.
[26] Extract from interim conference 1762, MCH, general synod 1764, fo. 17.
[27] Ibid.
[28] See Hamilton and Hamilton, *History of the Moravian Church*, ch. xv at pp. 163–75.

Doctrine

The Moravians' sober evangelicalism, which emerged after the excesses of the 1740s, was confirmed and accentuated during the Spangenberg era. Two inter-related decisions and an admission by synod were a formal rejection of all that had gone before. These were the resolution 'to make the heavenly father more an Object of our Doctrine and Liturgy',[29] the withdrawal of the majority of Zinzendorf's works[30] and an expression of deep contrition. Whether or not some of Zinzendorf's most ardent admirers protested, synod admitted in the name of the whole Church that 'we have formerly expressed many private opinions & made such representations of the truth, both in our preaching & in our printed Books, which have no foundation in holy Writ and have given offence'.[31]

This statement referred to Zinzendorf; the Church wished to erase from the public's mind the impression made by his sometimes unorthodox teaching. 'The Holy scriptures . . . shall remain the only standard and rule both of the doctrine and practice' of the Moravian Church, it was asserted in the *Historical account* of the Church's constitution. This work, written for other Christians and first published in 1772 with an introduction by Spangenberg, explained that Moravians were not required to defend Zinzendorf's 'private opinions'. An English edition appeared three years later.[32]

Collective leadership and external relations

Synods appointed Elders who were made collectively responsible for the direction of the Church's affairs and guardians of its doctrine. Through committees they also administered the Church and its missions throughout the world. One, the 'missions department', as it later became known, managed the missions. Although those in the western hemisphere had been controlled for some twenty years from Pennsylvania, even this degree of regional delegation was now withdrawn.[33]

The official explanation given for the Elders' all-embracing vigilance from the centre was the need to foster 'unity of the spirit' among all members of the Church.[34] This meant oversight of a range of issues which might otherwise undermine that essential part of being a Moravian, the sense of fellowship. One of these issues was undoubtedly the control of money and assets, the Church and thus its members now being responsible for the mountain of debt which had accumulated in the past. Although the scale diminished, money, or rather the want of it, nagged away for the rest of the century and created

---

[29] MCH, general synod 1764, resolutions, fos 32–3.
[30] MCH, harmony of the four synods, ii, no. 986.
[31] Ibid. i, no. 32.
[32] Spangenberg, *Historical account*, 35, 38.
[33] 4 July 1764: MCH, general synods, weekly accounts, 1764–89, fo. 21.
[34] Cranz, *Ancient and modern*, 562.

tension between members and with the centre. For example, in 1765 divisions surfaced when British Moravians discussed a levy imposed upon them. Members with outstanding loans to the Church had good reason, they believed, to feel aggrieved owing to the new and less favourable terms now being offered.[35]

The resolution that the Elders should 'appear as little as possible outside of our circle particularly in any negotiations' may have seemed like a welcome degree of delegation. In practice, however, it meant no more than it said.[36] The Elders set the policy and monitored every step; their authority over provinces such as Britain is symbolised by the title 'provincial helper' given to the local leader.[37]

The reforming synods re-emphasised that Moravian characteristic of deference towards the powers that be, although a potential clash of interests was inherent in one series of resolutions. These stated that once directed by the Saviour, 'we overlook all difficulties & only think how to fulfil his commands' and that the Church's evangelical mission should 'absolutely not' be subject to the state's requirements. On the other hand, Moravians were also reminded that they 'must willingly be subordinate' to the civil authorities.[38] This was a delicate balance which was maintained, for example, although not without difficulty, during the protracted negotiations with the British government for the establishment of the Labrador mission.

Resolutions concerning the 'duty of a faithful subject' went beyond what might have been expected. Moravians were instructed to 'study' the interest of governments and 'to the utmost of our power to contribute to the welfare of that land, where the Lord has planted us'.[39] Missionaries overseas would have understood that these general statements applied as much to them as to their brethren at home. From 1776 such avowals of good intent were underwritten by 'brotherly agreements' into which Moravians in all provinces solemnly entered. These established rules of conduct for a godly life to be led in fellowship amongst them and members were warned that failure to observe, 'knowingly', civil laws would result in expulsion from the Church.[40] As these agreements were a revival of those made in 1727 at Herrnhut,[41] they were a forceful link with the Moravians' historic past.

In an age of national or state Churches Moravians made little distinction between secular and ecclesiastical authority. The first they observed and they respected both. Indeed, they had for long been taught to reverence all

---

[35] MCH, minutes of the English provincial synod, 1765, fos 15–18.
[36] MCH, harmony, ii, no. 679.
[37] Hamilton and Hamilton, *History of the Moravian Church*, 168–9.
[38] MCH, general synod 1764, resolutions, fos 4–5.
[39] MCH, harmony, ii, nos 567, 573.
[40] *The brotherly agreement and declaration touching the rules and orders of the Brethren's congregation in London*, London 1776, 18.
[41] *Memorial days*, 115n.

Churches of Christendom and to learn from them.[42] The 1764 synod reaffirmed that evangelising by Moravians among other Christians was restricted to the cure of souls and that they should endeavour to persuade those who wished to be associated with them to remain in communion with their own Churches.[43] These instructions were underlined when the 'brotherly agreements' were introduced. One British agreement, for instance, stated that Moravians 'will not, separate themselves from any child of God in any denomination of Christians'. Moreover, they were warned that making 'proselytes' was 'useless . . . hurtful work'.[44]

Whether or not the Moravian Church was to have any further influence in England would depend in large measure upon it remaining quietly in the background. Least of all would the Church wish to lay itself open to being accused by other denominations of 'sheep stealing'. Moravians seem to have been assiduous in the enforcement of their own guidelines. For instance, in London even a suspicion of proselytising was checked[45] and in Bristol a misguided attempt to preach 'without commission' to the sick at an infirmary was halted.[46]

In England Moravians had always believed that they should enjoy a special relationship with the Established Church. This had been the case at one time, but since 1753 it had broken down totally. Their anxiety to repair the damage is evident in a letter of 1774 from the Elders referring to policies agreed by the general synod ten years earlier. The British brethren were now reminded that they must 'avoid everything whereby the Established Church especially . . . could lose credit'. That some of its members were associated with the Moravians seems to have been of such concern that a further restraint was placed on those who might wish to join the Moravian Church. They were required to remain in communion with their own Church, that is the Established Church, for two years before an application for admission could even be considered.[47] Then there was the hurdle of the Lot, which was a deterrent in itself.

The constitution and the Lot

Zinzendorf is known to have made frequent use of the Lot. The Elders' resort to it for almost every decision required of them, however, was justified, as members were constantly being reminded, by the Church being a theocracy under the Saviour. This is fundamental to understanding one of the most

---

[42] Dietrich Meyer, 'Grundsätzliches zur ökumenischen Arbeit', in Hahn and Reichel, *Zinzendorf und die Herrnhuter Brüder*, 373–4.
[43] MCH, general synod 1764, resolutions, fo. 38.
[44] *Brotherly agreement*, pp. iv–v.
[45] MCH, extracts from the London archives, fo. 119, minutes of the congregational council, 18 July 1771.
[46] BUL, [Bristol] elders' conference, minutes, 21 Aug. 1795.
[47] Barby 1774, MCH, UEC circular letters, 1760–1860.

substantial reasons for the Church's extraordinary degree of authority over members and, for instance, its seemingly inflexible persistence in the mission field. The Elders' corporate authority rested upon their methodical and ritualistic referral of proposals to the Lot by means of which the Saviour's directions to His Church were determined. Questions were posed on separate slips of paper to elicit 'Yes' or 'No' and with these a 'blank' was mixed which, if drawn, left the way open for further consideration. As examples of decisions obtained in this manner, Spangenberg cited all official appointments and the beginning of new missions.[48] All who became missionaries were volunteers, but their appointment was made by reference to the Lot.

The requirement to submit to the Lot was pervasive throughout the Church. Its use, which is apparent at every level at home and overseas,[49] began, for instance, in the provinces with proposals for the admission of candidates into Moravian congregations. This method of deciding upon new entrants became a cause for widespread disquiet, in England for example.[50] Nevertheless, as this unease was recognised by no more than a procedural change, introduced in 1775, the principle of submission to the Saviour, as head of the Moravian Church, was retained.[51]

Similar practices prevailed in the mission field where the baptism of each convert, for example, required prior approval *via* the Lot. While there may have been misgivings among Europeans at home about the Lot, this procedure may have found more favour overseas. Bernhard Krüger suggests that its benefit in South Africa was to turn converts' attention away from the missionaries and to focus it on the Saviour. Candidates seem to have understood that admission into His Church was a privilege that He conferred upon them.[52]

The Saviour's instruction to establish a mission explains, in part, the Moravians' persistent zeal for the conversion of the heathen. However, compared to Zinzendorf's sometimes impetuous approach to a new venture, referrals to the Lot made the Elders much more deliberate. Once the command to begin a mission had been obtained, there was no turning back because results in the field were unfavourable. A formal proposal to withdraw would not be made until 'circumstances themselves render it altogether impossible to maintain' a mission 'any longer'. When permission was given in 1782 to 'discontinue' the mission to the Copts it had been utterly unrewarding and wasteful of good lives and scarce resources for thirty years. So

---

48 Spangenberg, *Historical account*, 48.
49 Karl Müller, *200 Jahre Brüdermission*, I: *Das erste Missionsjahrhundert*, Herrnhut 1931, 293–5. For Zinzendorf and the Lot see also Freeman, *Ecumenical theology*, 223–5.
50 BUL, [Bristol] elders' conference, minutes, 11 Apr. 1775.
51 MCH, harmony, ii, no. 591.
52 Bernhard Krüger, *The pear tree blossoms: a history of the Moravian mission stations in South Africa, 1737–1869*, Genadendal, SA 1966, 107.

that 'all such mistakes may be carefully avoided', Moravians became very cautious indeed before committing themselves, almost irretrievably, to new ventures.[53]

The Church's mission
There could be no doubt of the Moravians' adherence to their evangelical tenets when synod affirmed in 1764 that 'Our whole Brethren's people is destined by our Savr. to show forth His Death.' Despite severe financial constraints and diminished standing, they did not retreat from a world view or from a persistent zeal for evangelising among the heathen. This epoch-making synod proclaimed in the name of the whole Church that 'we have a call to propagate the Gospel not only among Christians, but among all men & the intention is no other than to bring the People to our Savr'.[54]

It was of paramount importance that members' confidence in the Church and its destiny was restored. This surely was assisted by their faith in the Saviour's guiding hand over them and their belief that they were a chosen people. Nowhere is this more apparent than in their intentions overseas. The Moravians were 'convinced', they recorded at a later synod, that 'our missions are the most important work of God, entrusted unto the Brn. by our Lord [the Saviour] himself'.[55] In 1764 the Church had received His direction that missions overseas were not to be 'contracted'; they were to be 'expanded'.[56]

Publications policy
Moravians were determined not to allow anything that they might say in print to be a cause for further embarrassment or offence. On the other hand, positive steps were initiated by the 1764 synod to prepare for publication a few major works about the Church and its missions. In due course some of these would make a significant contribution towards restoring the Church's reputation and making its role in the mission field widely appreciated. This plan, like so much else endorsed at this reforming synod, seems to have been prepared in advance.

Synod ruled that nothing could appear in print without the approval of the Elders and that, as no direction had been received through the Lot 'to answer the Accusations against us', none of the new publications was to be of an apologetic nature.[57] Rather than argue through the press, the Church commissioned drafts on a few nominated topics which were not intended to

---

[53] MCH, conclusions of the synod, 1782, fos 249–53.
[54] MCH, general synod 1764, resolutions, fos 8–9.
[55] MCH, general synods, weekly accounts, 1764–89, fo. 15.
[56] Lot indicated by *, 30 July 1765: 'A short relation of the general synod . . . by Br. Layritz', ibid. fo. 189.
[57] MCH, general synod 1764, resolutions, fos 35–6.

be controversial. The Moravian David Cranz was to be one of the authors, but a greater part of the load fell on Spangenberg's broad shoulders.[58]

When synod assembled one work was available in draft, Cranz's *History of Greenland*, an apparently authoritative account of the country, its people and of the Moravian mission to them. Its author, as part of his meticulous preparation, had spent twelve months from the summer of 1761 in Greenland. The decision to publish his work was made in the hope that it would prove a 'stumbling stone' to those who thought ill of the Moravians and that 'many hundred other Persons' would learn of the Church's 'service to humanity'.[59] The book first appeared in Germany in 1765[60] and an English edition followed two years later.

The authority to proceed with this first publication was obtained through the Lot and only after anxious consideration. It was a new departure for the Moravians and the beginning of a major investment in the future. They also planned the next steps ahead. Spangenberg, for instance, was to sketch out an idea of the Moravians' faith and an instruction was given to bring together material for a history of the mission in the Danish West Indies.[61]

Nothing, it could be said, had been issued about the missions for twenty years. All that then had appeared in print were a few letters and other pieces, including Zinzendorf's missionary instructions, scattered within a rare, short-lived collection of occasional writings on a range of topics published in Germany. This Moravian journal, which was not translated into English, was discontinued in 1745 owing to vicious attacks on Zinzendorf and the Church.[62]

But these had abated. There were now encouraging signs that much might be gained through making the missions known and that this form of publicity was unlikely to spark off a new round of controversy. The most telling evidence came from the internationally respected and scholarly Danish Pietist, Erik von Pontoppidan (1698–1764), a bishop of the Lutheran Church in Norway and from 1755 until his death in 1764 principal of the university at Copenhagen. A 'churchly Pietist', close to the Danish court, Pontoppidan had been one of the most severe critics of Zinzendorf and the Moravians during the 1740s. Like many Pietists, he was also an ardent supporter of the Royal Danish Lutheran missions.[63]

His wider concern for the heathen overseas was one reason why in 1760

---

58 Ibid.
59 'A short relation', fo. 182.
60 David Cranz, *Historie von Grönland*, Barby–Leipzig 1765.
61 MCH, general synods, weekly accounts, 1764–89, fos 21, 75; resolutions, 1764, fo. 36.
62 David Cranz, *The history of Greenland: containing a description of the country, and its inhabitants; and particularly, a relation of the mission carried on for above thirty years by the Unitas Fratrum* . . ., i, London 1767, pp. i–ii: reference to [N. L. von Zinzendorf], *Büdingische Sammlung*, Büdingen 1742–5.
63 R. Skarsten, 'Erik Pontoppidan and his asiatic prince Menoza', *Church History* l (1981), 33–43.

Pontoppidan went out of his way to praise the Moravian mission to the slaves in the Danish West Indies. This was apparent in his introduction to an account of the Guinea Coast, by another hand, published first in Denmark and later in Germany.[64] Pontoppidan wrote that slaves transported to the West Indies:

> are come much nearer to the light of the gospel, than in their own country. And to [for] this, the so called Moravian brethren (whose words and undertakings in Europe, I cannot for the rest entirely approve of) certainly deserve thanks . . ., and are justly commended by many.

A further passage must have encouraged the Moravians to overcome their inhibitions about publicising their missions. To his surprise Pontoppidan had received assurances from gentlemen, who could not be suspected of 'Herrnhutism', that the missionaries' labour in the Danish islands was 'attended with greater evident fruits' than were to be found amongst most congregations.

This was praise indeed; and it was reproduced in the foreword to the *History of Greenland*.[65] Pontoppidan was a director of the *Missions Kollegium* in Copenhagen, as well as an eminent Lutheran churchman, for whom Moravians had seemed like a disruptive force at home. Information from overseas suggested that this perhaps might no longer be so.

Moravian missions in the Danish colonies

Moravian missions began in colonies belonging to the Danish crown. The first, launched in 1732 to slaves in the West Indies, was followed a year later by the mission to the Inuit in Greenland. When the very first pioneers left Herrnhut to make their way overseas Zinzendorf was so very unsure of what might happen that he simply advised them to be guided by the Saviour. Neither then nor later did he envisage that during his lifetime a large number of converts would be made among the heathen. Nor did he wish for those who became Christians to be gathered into a Church in a denominational sense.[66] Nevertheless, by 1760 all this had occurred within Moravian missions in the two Danish colonies.

These missions were not only the most significant; each was also a model for extension into the British world, from Greenland to the Inuit of Labrador, and from the Danish West Indies to slaves in the British islands. In the longer term the favourable impression that they were to make in England played a vital part in restoring the Church's good name.

However, there were serious problems on the way and by 1740, less than

---

[64] L. F. Römer, *Nachrichten von der Küste Guinea*, Copenhagen–Leipzig 1769, trans. from the 1760 Danish edn with foreword by Pontoppidan.
[65] Cranz, *History of Greenland*, i, pp. xx–xxi.
[66] Schattschneider, ' "Souls for the Lamb" ', 77–81.

ten years after their foundation, Moravians had grounds to fear that their missions would no longer be tolerated. The emergence of their Church as a separate denomination in Europe had led to an epidemic of religious strife, infecting relations with Lutheran and Reformed Churches as far afield as the Cape of Good Hope, then a Dutch colony, and Pennsylvania. Largely for the same reason, when Zinzendorf arrived early in 1739 in the Danish West Indies he found the mission at St Thomas on the point of collapse.[67]

Survival of the missions in the Danish colonies was crucial. Whether they did so depended upon the Pietist-inclined Danish monarchy being favourably disposed towards foreign missions in principle and on the conduct of the Moravian missionaries themselves. In the earliest years of the missions the government made a clear distinction between its concern for the spiritual well-being of native peoples under the crown and its distaste for Moravians as an apparently separatist force at home.[68] As a consequence, a question, albeit to a decreasing extent, hung over Moravian missions until 1771 when 'acts against us' (the Moravian Church), such as the Conventicles Act of 1741, '& to the Security of our Heathen Missions' were repealed. It was only then, after a lapse of thirty years, that the Church was permitted to establish a settlement in Denmark.[69]

The missionaries' standing had been far from certain in the Danish colonies and, in Copenhagen, attempts were made from time to time to place the missions under Lutheran supervision.[70] Also, Moravians were pioneers in the West Indies where their position at first was particularly insecure. It was therefore important that from 1739 the crown issued instructions which authorised them to conduct baptisms in the islands and gave them a degree of protection. Nevertheless, these were conditional orders that could be withdrawn at any time.[71]

Missionaries learnt from opposition to them, and from their own mistakes in the field, that they had to undertake their work in a law-abiding manner, which also gave the least offence. From 1740 onwards it became gradually evident that they could be trusted. Moreover, Europeans believed that there were commercial benefits to be gained from that discipline which Moravians exercised over converts for religious purposes. For these reasons a leading trader in Greenland preferred Moravian to Lutheran missionaries,[72] and a pious director of the Danish West India Company claimed that slaves under Moravians' care made better workers.[73]

---

[67] See Zinzendorf at St Thomas, 29 Jan. to 16 Feb. 1739, in *Oldendorp's history*, 357–66.
[68] Cranz, *History of Greenland*, p. xxi. Courtiers with 'Moravian leanings lost their influence': Finn Gad, *The History of Greenland*, II: *1700–82*, trans. G. C. Bowden, London 1973, 166.
[69] MCH, UEC minutes, 1770–4, week 50, 8–14 Dec. 1771.
[70] Gad, *History of Greenland*, ii. 258–60, 334.
[71] Instructions issued between 1739 and 1747, in *Oldendorp's history*, 690–1 n. 1.
[72] Gad, *History of Greenland*, ii. 322–5.
[73] Testimony of John Carstens, director of DWI Co, 14 Feb. 1739, St Thomas, in *Acta*

By 1760, then, although the Church's legal status was yet to be resolved, the missions' continuity in the two Danish colonies seemed reasonably secure. In 1759 the government's order authorising the establishment of a Moravian mission in the East Indies cited the 'laudable example of the Brethren in Greenland and the West Indies'.[74] At the same time it seemed to pious Danes, such as Pontoppidan, that Moravian missionaries were succeeding in making real Christians from among the heathen.

Some twenty years had now elapsed since the Moravians had transferred to the mission field their Christocentric religion of the heart, followed by their own institutions and practices for the care of souls. Beginning with Zinzendorf's perceptive teaching, his 'Blood and Wounds theology' for a period from around 1740,[75] the Church had consistently maintained that success in making converts to Christianity began by preaching the crucified Saviour,[76] while their ideal of Christians living together in fellowship found its living embodiment in the settlement, with its choir houses, ritual, chapel and workshops. In this the choir system was of central importance. First established in 1728 at Herrnhut, and based upon a separation by age, sex and marital status, it provided members of each choir with fellowship and an intimate discipline in order that their faith might grow. (Much, indeed, of the Moravians' dynamic in the age of Zinzendorf can be attributed to this system; it is notable that between 1732 and 1737 fifty-six volunteers for the mission field came from the 'single-men's house', bachelors being the first group of settlers to have their own separate accommodation at Herrnhut.[77])

In Greenland, after six frustrating years, the missionaries' efforts began to bear fruit when the first converts were made in 1739 and two years later the choir system was introduced.[78] Guided by the missionaries, 'the Greenlanders' gradually changed from being a scattered and nomadic people. During his visit David Cranz found a large 'orderly settled' community of more than 400 Christian Inuit. 'Orderly' meant, among other things that these people gave up a way of living that undoubtedly contributed to periods of famine when young and old, unable to fend for themselves, were abandoned. The missionaries were appalled by this seemingly barbarous and unnecessary custom. Under their instruction, Inuit methods of fishing and

---

Fratrum Unitatis in Anglia: report from the committee to whom the deputies of the United Moravian Churches . . . was referred: together with some extracts of the most material vouchers and papers . . ., London 1749, 52. See also the account of von Watteville, 12–13 May, 2 June 1749, described in *Oldendorp's history*, at pp. 450, 454.

[74] Edict of 19 Jan. 1759, cited in Cranz, *Ancient and modern*, 506–7.

[75] Zinzendorf to Geister, 1732. Instruction no. 23 of 1738 preceded adoption of this method of preaching: Zinzendorf, *Texte*, 35, 53, 60–1.

[76] Cranz, *History of Greenland*, ii. 424–5.

[77] Hans-Christoph Hahn, 'Das Chorwesen', in Hahn and Reichel, *Zinzendorf und die Herrnhuter Brüder*, 250–1; Hamilton and Hamilton, *History of the Moravian Church*, 36.

[78] Extracts from diaries, 1740–2, in Cranz, *History of Greenland*, ii. 1–62.

hunting were modified in order that the people could live together and care for one another. Hidden in Cranz's statistics is evidence of the astonishing degree to which converts were persuaded to adopt the Moravians' social organisation for religious purposes. Fifty-five unmarried men and boys and more than seventy single women lived in separate 'choir houses'. A further sixty-two widows also lived apart from families with young children who were not yet old enough to join their respective choirs.[79]

Cranz saw for himself that the Church's principal rituals at home, such as those held at Easter, were being observed in Greenland. He noted with approval that the *Singstunde*, or singing-hour, for which hymns were translated, was a regular occurrence. To his ear the singing, accompanied by a few instruments, compared favourably with that heard at settlements in Europe. As Moravians did not catechise prior to baptism, Cranz's observation that 'hymn-theology' was to be preferred, is notable.[80]

Moravians followed the Lutheran tradition. They were great hymn-writers themselves and they took their hymns and musical instruments with them wherever they went. Their lives were filled with music and for some this was a key to their own spiritual awakening.[81] Finding words and expressions with which to describe concepts and Christian imagery in non-European languages was a challenge to which the missionaries applied themselves from the beginning. Despite Inuit being an exceptionally difficult language for Europeans, Cranz reported that from about 1742 Greenlanders could be heard in their own dwellings singing verses, such as from the 'Saviour's Blood and righteousness', the meaning of which had been explained to them:[82] hymns surely made a great contribution to many a heathen's understanding of Christian doctrine.

The first settlement in Greenland was New Herrnhut. The Danish historian, Finn Gad, wrote of the prefabricated meeting house shipped to Greenland in 1747 that 'No such large or commodious house had ever been seen by the Greenlanders before, and it undoubtedly helped to boost the membership . . . it was in the years following its erection that the large numbers of baptisms were recorded.'[83] (The extent to which the Moravians sought to replicate overseas their ideal of a Christian community can be seen from plate 1.) By 1760, when a second settlement had recently been established, the mission in Greenland was served by fifteen Moravians, six of whom were the wives of missionaries. In 1762 the total number of baptised Inuit was more

---

[79] Ibid. ii. 397–410 ('choir houses' at p. 400).
[80] Ibid. ii. 370–1, 423.
[81] For first and second generation Moravians see, respectively, Oldendorp's '*Lebenslauf*', in *Oldendorp's history*, 633–4, and C. I. La Trobe, *Letters to my children: written at sea during a voyage to the Cape of Good Hope in 1815*, London 1851, 28–9.
[82] Cranz, *History of Greenland*, ii. 31.
[83] Gad, *History of Greenland*, ii. 263.

Plate 1. View of New Herrnhut, Greenland, reproduced from David Cranz, *The history of Greenland containing a description of the country*, London 1767, ii, facing p. 397.

than 500 and the mission continued to make progress over the years that immediately followed.[84]

The mission to slaves in the Danish West Indies was on a much larger scale. In 1757, the twenty-fifth anniversary of the mission, of more than 1,700 blacks who had been baptised almost 1,500 were still living.[85] Mission stations had been established in all three islands where the first, that in St Thomas, was also known as New Herrnhut.

In the Moravians' opinion their mission in the West Indies was similar in its essentials to that in Greenland. Such 'minor points of differences' as existed between the two arose from climate, and 'principally from the slave status' of African peoples in the islands, conclusions which appeared in *Oldendorp's history* of the mission. Oldendorp, himself a Moravian, spent eighteen months in the islands gathering material for this work. Completed

---

[84] Cranz, *History of Greenland*, ii. 442–3. For missionaries and further statistics see Müller, *200 Jahre*, i. 354–5.
[85] *Oldendorp's history*, 530–1.

with editorial assistance, it was first published in 1770 in Germany.[86] An edition in English did not appear until 1987, however.

Although it had never been Zinzendorf's intention that the Moravians should plant a separate Church overseas, this was happening by 1760 in the two Danish colonies and attempts from Copenhagen to place Moravian missions under Lutheran supervision had failed. During the era of Spangenberg the idea of the Moravian Church was cultivated actively in the minds of its converts, for it was 'expedient', the missionaries were advised in 1784, that 'the heathen . . . know something' of the Church's 'history and constitution'.[87]

The Moravian Church and its missions

The 1764 synod could not have taken the decisions that it did, unless Moravians had reasonable grounds for confidence in the Church's destiny. This now rested to a great extent on its foreign missions, which could not possibly have been sustained if members of the Church had not had faith in the cause nor without those men and women who willingly sacrificed their lives for it.

The Church's accumulated experience of the mission field was extensive and was not confined to the West Indies and Greenland. It even surpassed that of the Danish Lutherans whose own work among the slaves did not begin until 1757.[88] Permanent Moravian missions were also under way among North American Indians and in Surinam. Many attempts elsewhere in the past had failed, including in the East Indies where a mission settlement was now being established at Tranquebar, the Danish enclave on the Coromandel coast of the Indian sub-continent. By all accounts Zinzendorf was personally responsible for this latest venture: thirteen Moravians reached there two months after his death.[89]

What all this meant in human terms is indicated by the total of more than 200 Moravians who had entered the mission service by the end of 1760.[90] Some sixty-six missionaries, including their wives (and excluding that large contingent who had just reached India[91]), now had more than 4,000 converts in their care, some four-fifths of whom were in the West Indies. The expression 'care' embraces all those who were receiving some degree of instruction, as well as those who were baptised.

---

86 Ibid. 625.
87 A. G. Spangenberg, *Instructions for members of the Unitas Fratrum who minister in the Gospel among the heathen*, trans., London [1785], no. 60, p. 48.
88 Jens Larsen, *The Virgin Islands story*, Philadelphia 1950, 74–80.
89 Müller, *200 Jahre*, i. 253–9.
90 Hutton, *Moravian missions*, 520.
91 For the number of converts in 1761, and missionaries in 1760, see Müller, *200 Jahre*, i. 354–5.

The decision to expand the missions was followed by volunteers coming forward from nearly every congregation,[92] so that within twenty years the number in the field had more than doubled. In 1782, on the first jubilee of the missions, the total was 165 and this remained the approximate establishment for the rest of the century.[93]

Many factors contributed to this quite disproportionate effort. Of these Zinzendorf's leadership and the theology of mission which he, and later Spangenberg, propounded are considered to be the most important.[94] Another was the economy with which the missions were maintained. Missionaries did not receive a salary and many were craftsmen whose labour was essential for the upkeep of the mission where they served. Men of German birth were prominent from the beginning. This suggests that the role of refugee Moravians from Bohemia-Moravia was of much less importance than the influence of Pietism in determining who became missionaries.[95]

Moravian historians also believe that a key reason for the Moravians' exceptional zeal for service abroad was the extent to which the missions were always an integral part of the whole Church. It was a 'cardinal principle', wrote Bishop Hassé, that 'to be a Moravian and to further foreign missions are identical'.[96] From the very beginning Zinzendorf ensured that the whole community at Herrnhut participated in decisions which led to the launch of the missions[97] and his successors followed similar practices when general synods were held.[98] It is a measure of the Moravians' involvement that a general call for volunteers to serve overseas does not seem to have been necessary until 1780.[99]

The missions were an inescapable part of the Church's ritual. Every Sunday the litany included prayers for missionaries and for each race of converts[100] and edifying extracts from the missionaries' diaries were read at least once a month at services which the public could also attend.[101] Memorial days or festivals were a constant feature of the Church's calendar and of these, the 'heathen festivals' that marked the beginning of the missions, were doubly unique: held twice a year they commemorated the date when the first

---

92 Cranz, *Ancient and modern*, 560.
93 BUL, general synod 1782, weekly accounts from the synods.
94 Schattschneider, ' "Souls for the Lamb" ', 183.
95 Schulze, *Abriss*, 45; Müller, *200 Jahre*, i. 280–1.
96 E. R Hassé, *The Moravians*, London n.d., 122. See also Schattschneider, ' "Souls for the Lamb" ', 61–2; Hutton, *Moravian Church*, 247.
97 *Memorial days*, 139–41.
98 MCH, harmony, ii, nos 750–66.
99 MCH, UEC circular letters, 13 Sept. 1780.
100 Spangenberg, *Account of the . . . missions*, 55.
101 'Diaries read from four mission stations', 7 May 1769, MCH, FLD-24.

missionaries left Herrnhut for the West Indies and for Greenland[102] and collections were made on both occasions at all chapels.

These ceremonies and the total integration of the missions within the Church meant that a separate institution, such as a missionary society, was not required as a focus for members' donations. The voluntary principle, including giving, embraced all aspects of the missions. Nevertheless, such was the Church's overall indebtedness and poverty that urgent and special appeals for the missions did become necessary during the Spangenberg era.[103] 'Weekly Leaves', a newsletter in manuscript, was circulated throughout the Moravian world: information from the mission field ranged from events overseas to movements of personnel and to progress at each station measured by the latest number of baptisms.[104] The 1764 synod agreed to continue these regular bulletins as the means through which 'the History of our whole People of Election is communicated'.[105]

Just as the missions were united at home within the Church, so a similar approach to maintaining union was adopted overseas. The most formal means of achieving this was through official visitations which commenced shortly after the missions began. One of the first was made by Zinzendorf, and by 1797 there had been twenty-three.[106] Zinzendorf was sensitive to the absolute necessity of each side trusting the other. The visitant, he advised a newly appointed bishop, was to approach his inspection as 'the servant of Christ' and the missionaries should receive it as 'a child of Christ'.[107] Later, when Spangenberg discussed the subject, he explained that the aim of visitations was primarily to enquire into consistency in doctrine and preaching, and whether converts had 'actually as poor sinners, sought and found grace'.[108] By then all aspects of a mission's well-being, including its own finances, should also have been examined.

From the beginning the precedent was established that Moravian missionaries should attempt to keep themselves overseas. When the first pioneers left Herrnhut in August 1732 for the Danish West Indies one of the two men was expected to preach to the slaves, whilst the other worked at his trade. Although this did not prove practicable at first, this mission does seem to have been one of those which became largely self-supporting. At the other extreme, that in Greenland depended largely on supplies and materials from Europe.

Once the missions were underway, the Church's central fund, adminis-

---

102 *Memorial days*, iii.
103 See pp. 47–8, 184 below.
104 For example, MCH, 'Weekly Leaves', in UEC 1770–4 (minutes).
105 MCH, general synod 1764, resolutions, fo. 34.
106 Hutton, *Moravian missions*, 225–6.
107 A. G. Spangenberg, *Leben des Herrn Nicolaus Ludwig Grafen und Herrn von Zinzendorf und Pottendorf*, Barby 1773–5, repr. Hildesheim–New York 1971, 2166–7.
108 Idem, *Account of the . . . missions*, 105–7.

tered by the missions department, paid the missionaries' passages and met the cost of building chapels overseas from time to time. Responsibility was also taken for educating the missionaries' children and for the care of the old. In 1790, when the department's financial statements were circulated 'for the first time',[109] centrally funded expenditure of some £3,000 a year was exceeding revenue by up to one sixth.[110] As the department warned that expenditure would surely increase,[111] these accounts and a continuing deficit revealed the absolute necessity of funds being augmented by monies raised from other Christians.

Missionaries were not immune to financial problems at home and their own situation could be exacerbated by bad management. The mission in Barbados, which began as part of the expansion after 1764, is a case in point. With insufficient funds available at home with which to establish the mission, loans were raised locally. By 1771 £300 was owing to merchants on the island. A missionary's widow then attempted to sort out a tangled mess, to secure title to the Church's property, and to pacify what seemed to her an ungrateful missions department at home. Her late husband had begun a tailoring business, she earned a little in the same line, and the poor lady even had to repay the cost of materials which Moravian sisters in England had sent to her.[112]

There should never have been any coercion whatsoever on the men and their wives who offered themselves for service overseas: all were volunteers. Many died soon after arriving in the tropics and Moravians were well aware that they risked their lives. Despite these deterrents, eight volunteers immediately stepped forward when on one occasion Spangenberg told the Pennsylvania congregation of losses in islands in the West Indies.[113] This was not an isolated response; it was the announcement in 1769 of the death of missionaries on the Guinea Coast that 'was . . . the chief motive which induced' two British-born Moravians 'to offer themselves particularly for that Coast'.[114]

By 1771 more than 100 Moravians had died in the field. It was then said of those who went overseas that:

> Indeed we have reason to praise and adore the Grace of our Lord [the Saviour Christ], which has formed a people in the Church of the Brethren, who, knowing all difficulties, and having no prospect before them, but to endure

---

[109] Circular, 9 June 1790, accompanying missions department's 1789 accounts, MCH, missions diacony, 1789–1824.
[110] Ibid.
[111] Ibid.
[112] Elizabeth Bennett (Barbados) to John Wollin (London), 11 June 1772, the first of four heart-rending letters: MCH, letters from Barbados.
[113] Spangenberg, *Account of the . . . missions*, 37.
[114] MCH, SFG minutes, 1 Aug. 1769.

extreme heat or cold, with few conveniences of life, and no hopes of gain, have offered themselves unto the Lord for his service among the Heathen.[115]

The era of Spangenberg had begun with the adoption of a constitution and regulations which confirmed that the Moravian Church had evolved into an international, evangelical denomination. The Moravians' forward role among other Christians continued to be restricted as a matter of principle, even if the reverse was possible. On the other hand, no such constraints inhibited evangelising among the heathen overseas where converts were being gathered into congregations distinctly Moravian in character. Expansion overseas, indeed, was much more likely to be held back by lack of resources than by theoretical considerations. As it was so very difficult for other Christians to join the Moravian Church, the implications must have been obvious: the Church would rely mainly on succeeding generations for its members and missionaries, and a shortfall in central funds meant that an increasing level of financial assistance from non-Moravians for the missions would be essential.

Decisions taken in 1764 established a basis for recovery. Moravians, in choosing to expand their foreign missions, were building from strength. They also had reason to be confident that their missions now had their own contribution to make in restoring the Church's good name at home. The first considered step was taken to make the Church's work of converting the heathen overseas to Christianity generally known.

---

115 B. La Trobe, *A succinct view of the missions established among the heathen by the Church of the Brethren or Unitas Fratrum in a letter to a friend*, London 1771, 6.

2

Moravians in England: the Labrador Affair, 1764–1784

Despite the apparent success of the general synod in 1764 and the decision to expand the missions, British Moravians in London were initially reluctant to promote the Church's cause overseas to other Christians in Britain. It was largely the needs of the important Labrador venture that persuaded them to overcome their inhibitions, and to make approaches in Whitehall and subsequently to influential members of polite society.

Having received the direction in 1764 through the Lot to 'Seek after Esquimaux in Terra Labrador',[1] the Moravians were committed to a course that they would pursue cautiously to the end. Labrador developed into a British-managed affair which, directed from Germany by the Church's Elders, began with a prolonged campaign in Whitehall for a mission settlement on that hostile coast. It was not until 1769 that the government met the Moravians' terms and two further years elapsed before the mission itself was launched.

Two further initiatives were linked directly by the Church's leaders with the Labrador project, the publication in Britain of David Cranz's *History of Greenland* and the revival of the Moravians' long-defunct missionary society in London, the Brethren's Society for the Furtherance of the Gospel among the Heathen (the SFG), which became the platform for the promotion of Moravian missions. For, from the time of the launch of the Labrador mission, Moravians in London were to find themselves thrust into the missionary business with a pressing need to raise funds.

The foundation of the mission in Labrador and its connection with British policy have been the subject of a number of scholarly studies.[2] Nevertheless, in order to explain why the government encouraged the Moravians, discussion begins with an assessment of the attitude of statesmen and officials in Whitehall towards them and their project. It seems that the recovery of the Church's good name, in which the missions were to play such a significant part, may have begun first with men of the world in England rather than among the pious.

---

[1] 'A short relation . . . 1764', MCH, general synods, weekly accounts, 1764–89, fo. 189.
[2] W. H. Whiteley, 'The establishment of the Moravian mission in Labrador and British policy, 1763–83', *Canadian Historical Review* xlv (1964), 29–50. See also J. H. Hiller, 'The foundation and the early years of the Moravian mission in Labrador, 1752–1805', unpubl. MA diss. Memorial University, Newfoundland 1967.

Sentiments of humanity in Whitehall?

James Hutton, the well-known Moravian, was particularly active in Whitehall during negotiations for the establishment of the Labrador mission. A layman and a founding member of the congregation at Fetter Lane in London, Hutton appeared to be the Moravians' most prominent representative in England. Warm-hearted and alert, with a sprightly personality, Hutton made it his business to be acquainted with many of the leading men of the age.

The conclusion in 1763 of the Treaty of Paris enabled the Moravians to consider a mission in Labrador once more. Their approach to this new venture was affected by their earlier ill-founded expedition of 1752 which had ended in disaster. Then none of the party had been able to speak the difficult Inuit language which may have been one of the reasons why seven of its members were lost on the coast, murdered, it was believed, by Inuit. Whatever the circumstances of this tragedy, it inspired the Moravian missionary, Jens Haven, to develop an over-riding desire to take the gospel from Greenland, where he had served, to the Inuit of Labrador.[3]

Early in 1764 Haven was in London, intent on making his way to Labrador, when Hutton introduced him to the newly appointed governor of Newfoundland. By the end of that year the Church knew from Haven that a mission was a practical possibility. He had succeeded in meeting a small group of Inuit who, he confirmed, spoke the 'same' language as the Greenlanders with which he was familiar. They had received him in 'friendship' and his reconnaissance was made under the governor's patronage.[4]

The British objective for Labrador was strategic: development of the fisheries as a blue-water nursery for the Royal Navy through the employment of many thousands of sailors. To forward this policy Labrador was placed conveniently under the governor of Newfoundland by the Proclamation of October 1763 and Commodore, later Admiral, Hugh Palliser was appointed to the post which he held for five years. Palliser, a vigorous officer, proved himself to be as dedicated to the expansion of trade and navigation as he was to the service.

There is no doubt that the Moravians' commitment to extending their evangelisation of the Inuit from Greenland to Labrador complemented British policy for the coast. Commercial advantages were stressed by both sides during prolonged negotiations, but were these the only reasons why statesmen and officials encouraged the establishment of the mission?

In addition to ensuring that the French observed the terms of the treaty, Palliser's instructions presented him with two particular problems. The Inuit had to be prevented from descending on the fishing camps on the south coast of Labrador, where pillaging and murder ensued, and, if the fishery was to

---

3 'Account of the life of Brother Jens Haven', 1724–94, PA ii (1797), 99–115.
4 MCH, general synod 1764, 'Weekly Leaves', 18–24 Nov. 1764.

become a nursery for the navy, sailors should return to Britain at the end of each season.[5] Palliser's attempts to enforce this policy, by curtailing permanent camps, were thus in marked contrast with his wish to have Moravians settle on the coast in order to solve his problems with the Inuit. The Inuit were considered an exceptionally vicious race, but, as the government believed that trade could be developed with them, Palliser was instructed to 'use your best endeavours to conciliate their Affections'.[6]

Before they would launch their mission, the Moravians demanded an inalienable grant from the crown of substantial tracts of land for settlements on the Labrador coast. This precondition became the central issue from early in 1765 when negotiations began in Whitehall. A grant was not made until four years later, by which time the amount of land requested had been reduced. Soon after the mission settlement was founded in 1771, however, the Moravians' work on the coast appeared so promising to British officials that two further large tracts were ceded three years later.

Haven's successful reconnaissance resulted in Palliser advising the Board of Trade that 'friendly' relations might 'be easily introduced' with the Inuit. He also recommended that an 'advanced Post' to the north would inhibit their descent on fisheries on the south coast.[7] It was at this point that British and Moravian interests coincided. Once it was confirmed that the Inuit came from somewhere to the north, it was there that the Moravians wished to make a settlement, well clear of fishing camps in the south. Palliser had commended Haven when he forwarded the missionary's report to the Board of Trade[8] and the outlook for a swift and favourable outcome to the Moravians' negotiations in Whitehall must have seemed promising.

At the Board of Trade the idea of using missionaries as intermediaries in North America had been reinforced by experience during the Seven Years War. The gradual elimination of Roman Catholicism among native peoples in the newly acquired territories was now part of a long-standing policy of encouraging 'the Protestant Religion' in the colonies.[9] Further, in 1764 the Board of Trade had agreed a 'Plan' with Sir William Johnson, superintendent of Indian affairs in North America, whereby missionaries were also to be used to regulate relations between Indians and colonists. The board knew from Johnson that it was 'extremely essential . . . proper missionaries' were appointed, who should 'reside amongst the Indians in their own villages' and speak their languages. The board was endeavouring to find suitable men through the Society for the Propagation of the Gospel.[10]

---

[5] William H. Whiteley, 'Governor Hugh Palliser and the Newfoundland and Labrador fishery, 1764–68', *Canadian Historical Review* l (1969), 141–63.
[6] Instructions to Hugh Palliser, no. 14, 10 Apr. 1764, in *IPC*, ii. 422.
[7] Answers from Hugh Palliser to the BOT, no. 13, BL, MS King's 205, fo. 326.
[8] Palliser to the BOT, 9 Oct. 1764, PRO, CO 194/16 (pt 1), fos 36, 59–63.
[9] *Royal instructions to British colonial governors, 1670–1776*, ed. Leonard Woods Labaree, ii, New York 1967, nos 723, 726, pp. 497, 502.
[10] Johnson to the BOT, 13 Nov. 1763, in *Documents relative to the colonial history of the state*

It can be assumed that the Established Church had no objection to the board's intention of encouraging Moravians to establish a mission in Labrador. Of more significance was the Moravians' impressive record during the late French and Indian War in the American colonies. For instance, when in 1759 the governor of Pennsylvania acknowledged missionary Frederick Post's successful 'Negotiations to secure the Indian Nations' from the French to the British interest, he also praised the example of Moravians more generally among these people.[11] Johnson also recognised the Moravians' contribution. In 1758 he sought their agreement to confer with the Six Nations at the Moravian settlement at Bethlehem, Pennsylvania, and when a further treaty was made in 1761, at nearby Easton, David Zeisberger, who was to become a famous Moravian missionary, attended as an observer.[12]

In all probability John Pownall, the board's experienced and trusted secretary, was well disposed in principle towards the Moravians' Labrador project. Pownall, who earlier had a hand in drafting the Proclamation of 1763, a statement of post-war policy for the American colonies which reflected a proper concern for the rights of the native people,[13] was now advising ministers on its implementation. He almost certainly was aware of the services rendered by Moravian missionaries during the war and may well have read Post's *Remarkable journal*, published in London in 1759 as an appendix to an *Enquiry into the causes of the alienation of the Delawares and Shawanese Indians from the British interest*.[14]

Pownall's considerable influence with the board proved invaluable to the Moravians, who in 1766 quoted him as wishing 'to do us real service in the Labrador matter'.[15] Three years later, when they 'at last succeeded' in obtaining the first grant from the crown, Hutton gratefully acknowledged 'the obligation we all have to you, Sir, for your instructions and assistance through the whole of the affair'.[16]

In the course of some ten years of negotiations Moravians were received frequently and courteously in Whitehall where Pownall was secretary to the Board of Trade throughout this difficult period for the government. There

---

of New York: procured in Holland, England and France, ed. E. B. O'Callaghan, Albany, NY 1856–87, vii. 579. For reference to the 'Plan', see no. 8 at p. 637.
[11] Testimonial and passport for Frederick Post, 1759, in *Pennsylvania archives (1st series): selected and arranged from original documents in the office of the secretary of the commonwealth by Samuel Hazard*, Philadelphia 1852–6, iii. 578–9.
[12] Glenn Weaver, 'Moravians during the French and Indian War', *Church History* xxiv (1955), 247.
[13] F. B. Wickwire, 'John Pownall and British colonial policy', *William and Mary Quarterly* 3rd ser. xx (1963), 546–7.
[14] *Enquiry into the causes of the alienation of the Delawares and Shawanese Indians from the British interest . . . together with the remarkable journal of Christian Frederic Post, by whose negotiations, among the Indians on the Ohio, they were withdrawn from the interest of the French*, London 1759, 130–71.
[15] MCH, PHC, 19, 22 Dec. 1766.
[16] James Hutton to John Pownall, 12 May 1769, in Benham, *Memoirs of James Hutton*, 477.

was also continuity in ministers. Between 1764 and 1766 Pownall served first Lord Hillsborough and then the earl of Dartmouth, while they were presidents of the Board of Trade, and again when they were successively secretary of state of the enlarged and powerful department. The board itself, which had no executive powers, dealt with the Moravians' proposals without unreasonable delay. Dartmouth was in favour of the project and Hillsborough claimed later that he was similarly inclined from 'the Beginning'.[17] The privy council approved the first grant in 1769, on Hillsborough's commendation, and the second in 1774 after he had been succeeded by Dartmouth as secretary of state.

Towards the end of 1764 the prolonged negotiations which were eventually to have this positive result opened with preparatory meetings with Pownall and governor Palliser. In February of the following year the four accredited representatives of the Unitas Fratrum delivered a memorial to the board for the establishment of the Labrador mission. Hillsborough, who was among the Lords of Trade present, had interviewed Haven earlier on Palliser's advice. In its records the board knew the Moravian Church as the Unitas Fratrum,[18] the Church's official title and the name by which it had been recognised by parliament in 1749.

The preamble to the submission recalled the mission to the North American Indians and Haven's successful visit to the Inuit under the governor's patronage. The board was also reminded of its evident 'desire that the Brethren should settle' in Labrador. In their statement of intent the Moravians confirmed that they were resolved, 'after mature deliberation . . . to do every thing in their power towards the Conversion and Civilizing the Savage Natives . . . by the preaching of the Gospel, & by the good example of the Missionaries and others of the Unitas Fratrum'.

Then followed terms to be met before the Church would proceed with the establishment of the mission. The first was for a vessel to be made available; its master's instructions would enable four of the brethren to locate sites suitable for mission settlements. Secondly, the Moravians petitioned for an inalienable grant, sight unseen, of four separate tracts of land totalling almost fifty square miles on the Labrador coast. Finally, so that they were not restricted in the 'means of earning our livelihood', they sought the same rights as all British subjects to trade and fish the length of the coast, and 'full Liberty to send Ships of English Bottom . . . [to Labrador] . . . and back again to any' British port.[19] This reference to trade reinforced a suspicion, which soon gathered strength, that a commercial plan was hidden within the Moravians' evangelistic objective.

The memorial acknowledged what would be the principal objections to

---

[17] MCH, SFG minutes, 31 Jan. 1769.
[18] *Journals of the commissioners for trade and plantations, 1764–76*, London 1936, 111, entries for 20 Nov. 1764, 26 Feb. 1765.
[19] Petition of Moravians to the BOT, 23 Feb. 1765, PRO, CO 194/16 (pt 1), fos 81–5.

the Moravians' conditions, rehearsing arguments that Hutton later deployed in some extensive lobbying. These related to demands for permanent sites and trade. Inuit were a nomadic people, it was explained, but if lasting conversions were to be made they would have to be settled on one spot. This would require large areas of land where they would not be molested by rapacious Europeans. For these reasons government should underwrite the settlements' security. To their assurance that they were not seeking a 'Monopoly', Moravians added that they would not prevent traders, who 'Conform' to their regulations, from using their 'Harbours'.

The Moravians appreciated that their terms appeared excessive. Moreover, the popular perception that they were not British was an additional cause for embarrassment. To counter this issue they suggested in a careful choice of words that 'the natural answer seems to be, that we are the first adventurers and consequently the first Inhabitants & Subjects to the Crown of England in Terra Labrador'. Further, they risked their own lives and funds to establish a mission which would be 'so useful to the English Nation'. In view of this and to clinch their argument, the Moravians proposed that the 'nation should consider our Brethren as faithful, good & useful Subjects & fellow Citizens'. The tenor of this closing section to the first submission was that the British should be grateful to them rather than object to their conditions or nationality.[20] (It will be seen that it took the revival of the Brethren's missionary society and a formula devised in all probability by Pownall to resolve the issue of nationality.)

The meeting closed with the delegation being informed that the proposal would be considered 'as soon as other pressing business would admit'.[21] When, after further representations, the Moravians were summoned before the board again in April 1765 its support for their project could no longer be in doubt. Hillsborough and some of his fellow Lords of Trade were again present at the interview. Although the board could not 'recommend . . . making any grants of lands' until Labrador had been surveyed, the Moravians' most pressing demand was met and on generous terms. Arrangements were made at once with the Admiralty for four missionaries to make a reconnaissance during the summer on vessels of Palliser's squadron.[22] This party was to include Haven and Christian Drachart, a well-educated Danish-born Moravian under whom he had served. Drachart, who had long experience of Greenland and was skilled in its people's language, was well chosen.[23]

Within a week the delegation was recalled to hear the Admiralty's order issued on behalf of the missionaries. Palliser and the Board of Trade undoubtedly wished the Moravians to be under no illusion that a warship could be

---

20 For this and the two previous paragraphs see ibid; see also *IPC* iii. 1311–13.
21 *Journals of the commissioners, 1764–67*, 152, entries for 26 Feb 1765.
22 Ibid. 168, entry for 23 Apr. 1765.
23 For Christian Larsen Drachart see *Dictionary of Canadian biography*, iv, Toronto–Buffalo–London 1979.

expected to regulate its course to suit their objectives.[24] Nevertheless, the Moravians should have been satisfied by the content of 'passports' issued by the Board of Trade and by Palliser. The board's, signed by Pownall, confirmed its support for the Moravians' 'Resolution of establishing' a Christian mission to the Labrador Inuit, and its 'intire approbation of an undertaking so commendsable [commendable] in itself, & that promises so great Benefit to the public'. The 'Society of the Unitas Fratrum' was under the crown's protection and 'all aid comfort and assistance' was requested for the missionaries in their 'Arduous & difficult Service they have so zealously engaged in'.[25]

As the Moravians must have anticipated, Palliser had plans of his own for the missionaries. His 'Order for establishing a communication & trade' signalled his intention of using them as interpreters and mediators. It also carried the warning that the murder of Inuit, one of several 'treacherous' practices by Europeans 'most contrary to His Majesty's sentiments of Humanity', must cease.[26]

Reconnaissance during the summer of 1765 proved so successful, from Palliser's point of view, that he immediately reported upon it to Lord Halifax at the Admiralty. Drachart's ability to speak the language of the Inuit and to gain their confidence left Palliser in 'not the least doubt of these People being soon reconciled, & made useful'.[27] He reported more fully to the Board of Trade to whom he explained that he had kept two of the four Moravians with him on the south coast. Drachart acted as his interpreter in making peace with a large contingent of Inuit who, it was confirmed, came from the north. The other two Moravians went by sea in that direction in an unsuccessful search for Inuit encampments.

Palliser and traders on the south coast benefited from the unique and remarkable degree of trust which developed between the missionaries and the Inuit. His 'many Interviews' and peace-making with the 'Savages', only made possible by Drachart's courage and experience, convinced him that they could be turned into useful citizens by 'kind treatment' and 'fair dealing'. Palliser also commended the Moravians for the 'great Pains' that they had taken to assist him as much as in the 'Business of their Mission': they were 'very worthy of that Countenance and Protection which his Majesty and your Board are pleas'd to Honour them'.[28]

The Moravians presented the board with their own 'Account of the voyage of the four missionaries' to Labrador, which appeared to confirm that they were the only effective intermediary between the Inuit and the British.

---

[24] *Journals of the commissioners, 1764–67*, 169–70, entry for 29 Apr. 1765; Stephens, secretary to Admiralty, to Pownall, 27 Apr. 1765, PRO, CO 194/16 (pt 1), fo. 146.
[25] Certificate from the BOT signed by Pownall, 29 Apr., 1765, in *IPC* iii. 1315; cf. proclamation signed by Palliser, 30 Apr. 1765, ibid. iii. 1316.
[26] Order by Palliser, 8 Apr. 1765, PRO, CO 194/16 (pt 2), fo. 179.
[27] Palliser to Lord Halifax, 11 Sept. 1765, PRO, CO 194/27, fos 102–3.
[28] Palliser to the BOT, 30 Oct. 1765, PRO, CO 194/16 (pt 2), fos 171–2.

The 'Account' records in vivid detail how the missionaries gained the Inuit's confidence and thus were able to promote British interests. The Moravians warned that 'those Barbarians' would only be conciliated to the 'English Nation' when missionaries had a permanent opportunity of 'instilling good principles into their minds'. This should have come as no surprise; the Moravians had not lost sight of their precondition, a secure grant from the crown.

The results of the missionaries' enquiries 'for his Majesty's information & for the Benefit of the Publick' were impressive. To notes on Inuit customs, a long list of manufactures was added which the Moravians expected could be bartered for whalebone and furs. 'N.B.', the report ended, 'Strong Liquors they wont as yet taste. Fire arms they would purchase at any Rate. May they never be seduced to like the first; nor our people so imprudent as to trust them with the latter.'[29] The consequences of this advice being ignored some years later were considerable.

It was evident from their 'Account' that the missionaries thought that they had been used too extensively by officers of the crown. This led to Hutton's protest that they were treated as 'enlisted' men by Captain Sir Charles Adams, who had detained two of their number on board HMS *Niger*, pending Palliser's arrival on the coast.[30] The synodal resolution of 1764 that the Church's evangelistic mission should 'absolutely not' be subservient to the state was reflected in the stance now adopted by the Moravians. Without a grant they remained obdurate in refusing to accept pressing invitations to send missionaries as intermediaries to Labrador. This they repeated 'over and over again' to the board, to Palliser and to others.[31]

Nevertheless, they consistently aligned themselves with British objectives. For instance in 1766, when they reduced the amount of land requested by three-quarters, 'for the present', they expressed their confidence that a settlement in Labrador would 'prove of benefit to the commerce of your Majesty's subjects', and that the Inuit would become 'a Christian and civilized people'.[32]

Within three weeks of receiving this revised proposal, the board made representations to the privy council to the effect that the grant requested could be 'made to the mission of the Unitas Fratrum reserving to his Majesty's subjects the right of carrying on fisheries there'.[33] Perhaps Dartmouth's personal views contributed to this recommendation. An evangelical known for his charity on behalf of the North American Indians, Dartmouth had

---

[29] Account of four missionaries (1765), in A. M. Lysaght, *Joseph Banks in Newfoundland and Labrador, 1766: his diary, manuscripts and collections*, Berkeley–Los Angeles 1971, 193–4, 203, 221 (transcript of PRO, CO 194/16 (pt 2), fos 225–45).
[30] Hutton to Christian Brodersen, 4 Mar. 1766, in Benham, *Memoirs of James Hutton*, 389–90.
[31] Jens Haven to Capt. George Oliver, 18 Apr. 1766, ibid. 409.
[32] Moravian petition to the privy council, 6 Mar. 1766, PRO, CO 194/16 (pt 2), fos 246–7.
[33] Representation of the BOT to the privy council, 27 Mar. 1766, in APC v. 427.

replaced Hillsborough recently at the board. However, although he personally supported the project, he warned Hutton that this could only be to the extent to which it was 'consistent with the interests of the English'.[34] Dartmouth relied on Pownall for advice but he also had Palliser's views to consider.

Palliser was consulted before the council received the board's advice and his only *caveat* was similar to Dartmouth's. It was also apparent from his plan for 'Encouraging the Fisherys' that he wished to secure the services of the missionaries without delay. He proposed settling them 'at any place they may Pitch upon' and to award them one of four blockhouses that he wished to erect on the coast.[35]

Timing, however, was not on the Moravians' or Palliser's side. The survey of the coast was incomplete, Palliser could not be precise about where they would settle and their demand 'for so much land', despite the reduction, still raised suspicions that they were seeking a monopoly on the coast.[36] Even worse, the government's law officers were aware that Palliser had landed himself in 'vexatious Suits and Prosecutions', brought by traders in Labrador whose rights he had curtailed.[37] However, Palliser's thorough mistrust of these men extended to their treatment of the Inuit and he gave priority to obtaining the missionaries' assistance.

The security of the fisheries was not the sole reason for a Moravian mission being considered so favourably. There was in Whitehall a genuine concern for free native peoples overseas. In 1766 Palliser justified his contentious order closing the coast to permanent settlers, other than the Moravians, by the need to prevent 'Horrid massacres' perpetrated against 'the Poor Natives'.[38] A year later, when he confirmed to the Moravians that further atrocities were 'too true', he also suggested a mission to the Newfoundland Indians.[39] He drew the 'barbarous custom' of murdering these people to the attention of Hillsborough who told the Moravians of 'his abhorrence . . . of the English settlers; who . . . shot them on sight'.[40]

Hillsborough had returned to office in 1768 to take charge of the newly formed American Department, incorporating the Board of Trade, and Palliser now had a particular reason to remind him of the Moravians' desire to establish a mission in Labrador. An initiative taken by Palliser led to a 'very intelli-

---

[34] Hutton and J. Hill to UEC, 12 Mar. 1766, in Benham, *Memoirs of James Hutton*, 408.
[35] Proposals for encouraging the fisheries, enclosed in Palliser to Pownall, 22 Apr. 1766, PRO, CO 194/16 (pt 2), fos 283–5: consulted 18 Mar. 1766, *Journals of the commissioners, 1764–67*, 262.
[36] Hutton and Hill to UEC, 12 Mar. 1766, in Benham, *Memoirs of James Hutton*, 406.
[37] Pownall to [?] Charles Yorke, attorney-general, 29 Mar. 1766, Hardwicke papers, BL, MS Add. 35,915, fos 47–9. See also Whiteley, 'Palliser'.
[38] Proposals, 22 Apr. 1766, PRO, CO 194/16 (pt 2), fos 283–5.
[39] MCH, PHC, 9 Dec. 1766.
[40] Palliser to Lord Hillsborough, 20 Oct. 1768, PRO, CO 194/28, fos 25–6; interview with Hillsborough, 31 Jan. 1769, in Benham, *Memoirs of James Hutton*, 465n.

gent' Inuit woman, known as Mikak, being brought over to England with her son. Together they had been captured during a bloody encounter. Palliser wished them to be given 'an idea of the power, splender[our] and generosity of the English Nation' so that 'by means of these People and the [Moravian] Brethren' relations with the Labrador Inuit could be improved.[41]

The boy, who was placed in the Moravians' care in England, died of smallpox. But Mikak was fêted. It was the age of the noble savage: six years later the Polynesian, Omai, brought back from Cook's second voyage, received a princely reception. According to one London newspaper of January 1769 the 'Esquimaux Indians . . . were much talked of in Town' and their 'Dresses' were to be exhibited during a 'Masquerade . . . at the Theatre Royal Dury Lane'. Mikak was presented to the duke of Gloucester, who gave her among other jewels 'Gold Clasps, having the King's arms engraved on them'; from the dowager princess of Wales she received fine clothes.[42]

In the spring of 1769 Mikak was returned to her own country where a year later she helped the missionaries to select the site for their first settlement on the coast. They brought back furs from her for members of the royal family and for Palliser.[43] Without his intervention she would most probably have died in captivity.

In 1769 the Moravians were to make their first successful attempt to obtain a grant from the crown for a settlement in Labrador.[44] However, in January, before it was formally considered, Hillsborough held a preliminary meeting with them at his own house. He was now a secretary of state and a member of the privy council, the body which would decide on the Moravians' application. Pownall, who seems to have arranged the meeting, had advised the Moravians to present Hillsborough with 'the public advantages likely to be derived' from their Labrador venture.[45]

It turned out that Hillsborough wished to satisfy himself about the Moravian Church and to learn about its missions. From the answers which he received he concluded, according to his visitors, that there was 'no real difference, either in doctrine or ordination' between the Moravian and the Established Church. No doubt briefed by Pownall, Hillsborough advised the Moravians on how a secure grant could be obtained. He assured them of his support.

Hillsborough had been impressed by the scope of the missions and astonished to learn that missionaries were not paid. His comment that the bishop of London was unable to find even one clergyman to serve in the Floridas,

---

[41] Palliser to Hillsborough, 20 Oct. 1768, PRO, CO 194/28, fos 25–6.
[42] *Public Advertiser*, 17, 25 Jan. 1769.
[43] Extract of the journal of the Jersey Packet, MCH, Labrador voyages miscellaneous, 1770–1851.
[44] Memorial in the name of the Moravian Church and the SFG, n.d., marked 'read', 11 Feb. 1769, PRO, CO 194/18, fos 43–5. See also memorial, 3 Oct. 1768, in Benham, *Memoirs of James Hutton*, 444–7.
[45] Reviewed 26 Jan. 1769, ibid. 462.

although a salary was offered, was symptomatic of the difficulties encountered by the board in implementing the 'Plan' agreed earlier with Johnson.[46]

Although Hillsborough certainly did not share Dartmouth's evangelistic fervour, which he thought excessive, he appears in a more sympathetic light from the Moravians' records than might be expected.[47] Since 1764, when he first met Haven, Hillsborough had consistently maintained a supportive interest in the Labrador project. Perhaps it was the dedication of Moravian missionaries which made the greatest impression. He is reliably reported as saying, after he met Drachart, 'I protest, you are the only truly public spirited people I know.' It is also recorded that after he left office he attended the chapel in Fetter Lane.[48]

Hillsborough was as good as his word. Immediately after his meeting with the Moravians he raised their renewed Labrador application with the privy council and then instructed the board to submit its advice.[49] In May 1769 the Moravians obtained their first grant from the crown, land sufficient for one settlement. In the two-year interval before the mission was actually established a final reconnaissance of the coast was made; the missionaries sailed this time on a vessel which the Moravians themselves had purchased.

The Moravian Church had achieved all its immediate objectives; a secure grant to a site of the missionaries' own choosing, protection under the crown and freedom for them to gain their livelihood the length of the coast. The board's recommendation to the privy council stated it had no reason to 'dissent' from its previous opinion that there were 'publick and Commercial advantages to be derived' from the Moravians' 'pious and laudable object' of establishing a mission settlement.[50] Thus a further link was created between the British government and the Moravians who consciously, but discreetly, began to use Labrador to 'cultivate' the authorities' 'good will & countenance'. Progress reports, for example, were submitted in the first years of the mission.[51]

An independent report from overseas, however, was of more consequence and this was forthcoming in 1773 when Lieutenant, later Admiral, Roger Curtis, ordered by Governor Shuldam, visited Nain, the first Moravian settlement in Labrador. The missionaries assembled some Inuit before Curtis and a translation of the governor's proclamation, forbidding them to go south where the British fishing camps were situated, was read to them. Curtis was impressed by the settlement, by the missionaries' industry and by the progress

---

[46] Interview with Hillsborough, 31 Jan. 1769, ibid. 462–7n.
[47] S. E. Rees, 'The political career of Wills Hill, earl of Hillsborough (1718–93) with particular reference to his American policy', unpubl. PhD diss. Aberystwyth 1976, 405, 430.
[48] *PA* xxi (1853), 77, 1 May 1770; MCH, FLD-21, 27 Apr. 1777.
[49] *Journals of the commissioners for trade and plantations, 1768–75*, London 1937, 73, 75, entries for 11, 15 Feb. 1769.
[50] Representation of the BOT to the privy council, 3 May 1769, in *APC* v. 182–3.
[51] Reports, Hutton to the BOT, 6 Dec. 1773, MCH, SFG minutes (draft) and papers, parcel C; 6 Dec. 1773, 9 Nov. 1775, PRO, CO 194/19, fos 9–17, 4–7.

which they were apparently making 'in civilizing the Indians' by teaching them 'honest labour' and obedience. His report, warmly endorsed by Shuldam, was forwarded to Dartmouth who had replaced Hillsborough in 1772 as secretary of state for the colonies.[52]

With good timing and now a fair wind behind them, early in 1774 the Moravians petitioned for twice the amount of land already conceded. This was for two further settlements which, seeming 'reasonable and proper' to the board, was promptly approved by the privy council.[53] The Moravians had now obtained three-quarters of the land originally requested.

A draft of part of their petition confirms that they remained mindful that their evangelistic objective was linked to the government's aims for the Labrador coast. Where further settlements were justified, as 'indispensably necessary [if] abiding fruit of the Gospel . . . is to be expected', another hand had inserted, 'or the accomplishment of our wishes in civilizing & rendering the Esquimaux useful to Great Britain'.[54]

The crown maintained its moral support for the mission and honoured its obligation to protect the mission by means of a 'proclamation' circulated by the governor of Newfoundland at the beginning of each season. For example, the first, issued in 1770 when the missionaries sailed to select a site for the first settlement, stated that 'this establishment is undertaken and formed under his Majesty's express direction and authority'. The order also called for 'all friendly assistance for their [the Moravians'] undertaking calculated for the benefit of mankind in general, and for the Kingdom of Great Britain in particular'. The 'proclamation' was signed by Captain John Byron,[55] 'foul weather Jack' (and the poet's grandfather), who had succeeded Palliser the previous year.

The Moravians in London assiduously cultivated the good will of the governors of Newfoundland before these officers sailed each spring. When Admiral Shuldam replaced Byron in 1772 he too was engaged 'heartily in our cause' and two years later he was dined by the Moravians at their impressive London residence, Lindsey House, which fronts the river at Chelsea.[56]

The Moravians continued to represent the interest of their missions to government. Shuldam's comment in the spring of 1774 that he would do his 'utmost' to support the mission was unusually timely. With the reannexation of Labrador to Quebec pending, the Moravians made Dartmouth aware of

---

52 Governor Molineux Shuldam to Dartmouth, 15 Sept. 1773, PRO, CO 194/31, fos 31–4 with fos 56–66. Shuldam succeeded John Byron in 1772 as governor of Newfoundland.
53 Moravians' memorial to Dartmouth and the BOT, 24 Jan. 1774, PRO, CO 194/19, fos 42–3. This was considered on 7 Feb. 1774, and granted on 9 Mar. 1774: *Journal of the commissioners, 1768–75*, 385. For the grant see APC v. 184–5.
54 MCH, SFG, minutes and papers, parcel B.
55 Governor John Byron, proclamation, 21 Apr. 1770, PA xxi. 76; cf. proclamation of Governor Edwards, 29 July 1779, in *IPC* iii. 1334.
56 MCH, SFG minutes, 10 Mar. 1772; FLD-19, 25 Apr. 1774. See also P. Kroyer, *The story of Lindsey House*, London 1956.

their concern that the governor of Quebec's responsibility 'to protect our missions' might be overlooked.[57] Dartmouth's immediate response was to instruct the Admiralty that when the governor of Newfoundland's responsibility for Labrador ceased, he should continue to encourage and to protect the mission 'formed under the King's Authority'.[58]

In January 1775 the Moravians' anxiety for the mission's security was also taken into account when Guy Carleton, governor of Quebec, received his 'Instructions'. The area under his authority included Labrador where the fisheries were 'the main object of your attention', the Inuit deserved 'some attention' and 'it is Our express Will and Pleasure' that the missions receive 'every countenance and Encouragement'.[59] Although muted, the specific mention of the Inuit can be attributed to Palliser and the Moravians having kept sentiments of humanity alive in Whitehall. The government also maintained its policy towards native peoples; the 1764 'Plan for . . . Management of Indian Affairs', agreed with Johnson, was appended to Carleton's instructions.[60]

The crown continued to expect the governor of Newfoundland to honour its obligation to protect the mission on Labrador, an arrangement which was to be tested in 1782 when a small contingent of Inuit went south and returned with muskets and liquor, exactly what the Moravians had warned the Board of Trade about before the mission began. As more than 200 'Esquimaux' followed the next year, the Moravians feared that their people would 'certainly Suffer Hurt to their Souls'.[61] If such expeditions were to become a regular feature, the damage to the mission's prospects would be incalculable.

In 1784 Lord Sydney was at the Home Office and responsible for the colonies when the Moravians gave him their account of this distressing affair. He readily accepted that the Inuit should not be enticed by 'officers and others on the coast' to go south. He commended the Moravians' report without delay to the governor of Newfoundland whom he instructed 'so far as it may be in your power to enforce a compliance with their desire'. Sydney thought it 'essentially necessary' to prevent the Inuit's 'Excursions . . . which have heretofore proved so fatal to them'.[62] Governor John Campbell's proclamation of 1784 consequently required all subjects on the Labrador coast to 'act towards the Esquimaux Indians, justly, humanely and agreeable to those Laws, by which his Majesty's subjects of all classes are bound'.[63]

---

57 MCH, PHC, 25 May 1774; Hutton to [?] Dartmouth, 1 July 1774, in Benham, *Memoirs of James Hutton*, 496–7.
58 Dartmouth to Admiralty, 16 June 1774, in *IPC* iii. 1147.
59 Instructions for Guy Carleton, no. 37, 3 Jan. 1775, ibid. ii. 834.
60 Ibid. ii. 840–6.
61 MCH, SFG minutes, 21 Oct. 1783.
62 Lord Sydney to Governor Campbell, 28 May 1784, in *IPC* iii. 1337, enclosed with Moravians' report to Sydney, 26 May 1784, ibid. 1335–6. For Thomas Townshend, Viscount Sydney (1733–1800) see *DNB* s.v.
63 A proclamation, 15 May 1784, MCH, transactions with government, parcel.

From the very beginning of the Labrador affair, ministers and officials had a number of considerations which told in the Moravians' favour, assuring them of a sympathetic hearing. Their exceptional record in the French and Indian War and the impressive reputation of their missionaries from Greenland were highly relevant to particular aspects of post-war policy. This included a determination to establish stability, order and trade on the imperial frontier and to prevent the abuse and atrocities which free native people under the crown were suffering in North America. The Labrador mission in fact gave sentiments of humanity in Whitehall a rare opportunity of being expressed in practical terms. The Moravians were also fortunate in the men with whom they negotiated and that, as the Labrador submissions made a point of demonstrating, their Church shared with the British that eighteenth-century idea of 'improvement': Moravians identified themselves with a belief that non-European peoples could and should be 'civilized' and thus rendered useful to colonial powers.

The many face-to-face meetings in Whitehall which the negotiations involved had given men of the world reason to have confidence in the Moravians. However, their past was not forgotten. In December 1766, for example, when the earl of Egmont, lately First Lord of the Admiralty, invited Moravians to consider a further settlement in the colonies he is reported as saying: 'I want you to be known to the Government according to your true character.' Egmont, it seems, had been presented with a copy of the newly published *History of Greenland*,[64] the first of the new generation of works to appear since the synod of 1764.

The History of Greenland

David Cranz's *History of Greenland* was to be one of the most significant of the Church's new publications. It helped to break down prejudices against the Church and in due course became a classic of the missionary awakening. This, however, was in the future; in autumn 1766 Moravians in London hurried to use it, hot from the press, as a fresh element in their lobbying on behalf of the Labrador project.

With a return to 'more peaceable times' for the Moravians, the *History* was by far their most substantial publication about the missions to date.[65] It was also their first in English on this subject, and they had great hopes for its reception by a British public on whom a swarm of hostile polemical works had made such a lasting impression. The initial result was not altogether satisfactory.

The book was published at a time when the Labrador negotiations in

---

64 MCH, PHC, 19, 22 Dec. 1766. For John Perceval, second earl of Egmont (1711–70), see *DNB* s.v.
65 Cranz, *History of Greenland*, i, p. iii.

Whitehall were stalled. The Elders of the Church, on being consulted, advised the Moravians in London that before a further application to government was made 'it will be good and necessary that the Greenland history be first in the hands of the public'.[66] When they made this suggestion the Elders undoubtedly hoped that the work would go some way towards mitigating the suspicion, echoed by Lord Egmont at the Admiralty in March 1766, that 'the demand for trade, . . . freighting of ships, and the right of fishing did not altogether, . . . prove to him our evangelical disinterestedness'.[67]

Perhaps the record of the early years of the Greenland mission was expected to serve as a testimonial to the purity of the Moravians' motives. Here was to be found the story of missionary dedication, a life of utter destitution at first, and some six years of patient endeavour before the first converts were made. There were also those independent assessments of the Moravians' achievement, which could be found by readers who looked no further than the preface. Nothing appeared here to suggest that the Moravians' motives might be tainted by commerce.[68]

The English translation of the two-volume *History*, which had been completed under considerable pressure,[69] bore the name of the Brethren's Society for the Furtherance of the Gospel on the title page. It was the end of the year and parliament was in recess, but such was the Moravians' sense of urgency to get the *History* into the hands of those who could do most to advance the Labrador affair that it was advertised and some of the eighty copies of the print run were delivered personally to members of the nobility 'where found at home'. The opportunity was also taken to call on Egmont and on John Pownall.

Before the year was out it was said that the archbishop of Canterbury, Thomas Secker, had read the first volume 'mostly thro'', and Dartmouth was moved to exclaim, 'we must all agree that there is no justification [but] thro' the Merits of Christ'. Dartmouth had so far only read the preface in which Cranz, prayed:

> May He bless . . . this simple account of the congregation out of the heathen in Greenland; and may he let every reader taste somewhat of the grace of our Lord Jesus Christ.[70]

Despite these and other pleasing reports, Moravians were to be disappointed by the wider reception given to the complete work. The first volume, mainly an account of Greenland, its people and topography, appealed to a growing market for readers 'curious in voyages'. It was 'greatly admired by many

---

[66] MCH, PHC, 9 Dec. 1766, 1 Jan. 1767.
[67] Hutton and Charles Metcalf, report on interview with Lord Egmont, 7 Mar. 1766, in Benham, *Memoirs of James Hutton*, 401.
[68] Cranz, *History of Greenland*, i. 352–88, and also preface at pp. xviii–xxii.
[69] MCH, SFG old papers, 27 Sept., 17, 21 Dec. 1766
[70] MCH, PHC, 19, 22 Dec. 1766; Cranz, *History of Greenland*, i, p. xxiii.

people', a Moravian reported, 'but', he continued, 'they say at the same time that they understand nothing of the Second Volume'.[71] This, with its history of the mission and passages from missionaries' diaries, is at best repetitious and in places bizarre for readers unfamiliar with the Moravians' mode of expression.

The author of the review appearing in the *Gentleman's Magazine* shared these sentiments. The description of Greenland, from which extended summaries with illustrations appeared, was commended as 'most valuable', but accounts of the mission were not so well received. Although the perseverance of the 'zealous Moravian missionaries' was acknowledged, the reviewer could not resist a sly dig: as the Greenlanders apparently lived 'so virtuously' before the Moravians' arrival, 'the greater part of Christians would do well to learn to live and think like Greenlanders; while Greenlanders are learning to live and think like Christians'.[72]

Cranz's *History of Greenland* also came to the notice of the *Critical Review* in which it fared no better. Again the first volume was praised for that part through which 'Even our commercial interests might be served'. But as for the mission, 'the rational reader will be amazed at the enthusiasm and wildness which employs the last five hundred and sixty-three pages of these two volumes, and may be puzzled to find such a collection of absurdities in any other work'.[73]

The *Critical Review* had been founded by Tobias Smollett who, no friend of the Moravians, had claimed in his well-known *Continuation* of Hume's *History of England* that those who disagreed with Zinzendorf were expelled either to Greenland or Pennsylvania.[74] This was nonsense, but Moravians were up against something more than just their past: it was more that 'satirical ... bad character of the age, and of human reason' against which synod had warned in 1764. It seemed to the then beleaguered Church that 'the Spirit of the World goes so far that even the most innocent things are looked at in no other point of view but their weakness'.[75]

In 1771 John Wesley published, in his *Journal*, his views on Cranz's *History*, which he had read four years earlier. His thoughts thus probably reached several thousand readers. He took a rather similar line to that of the press. Although the Moravians generally exaggerated, Wesley explained, he did not doubt 'that some of the Heathens were converted'. But his regret that 'so affecting an account' was 'disgraced with those vile doggerel verses; just calculated to make the whole performance stink in the nostrils of all sensible

---

[71] MCH, SFG old papers, 17 Jan. 1768.
[72] *Gentleman's Magazine* xxxvii (1767), 60–6, 209–10, 293–7.
[73] *Critical Review* xxiii (1767), 22.
[74] T. Smollett, *The history of England from the revolution to the death of George II*, Edinburgh 1805, 323. The allegation most probably first appeared when separate numbers were published c. 1761/2.
[75] MCH, general synod 1764, resolutions, fo. 13.

men',[76] referred surely to some sanguinary lines from a hymn reproduced in Cranz's *History*, reminiscent of those for which Moravians were notorious.[77] It may not have been a coincidence that the sensitive Moravians declined to meet 'John Wesley [who] seems yet too full of enmity' at this time, a suspicion supported fifteen years later by 'his method of publishing' being the reason for not then holding talks with him.[78]

The production of the *History of Greenland* was a major investment for the Moravians. Although initial sales were disappointing, various promotional stratagems were turned down because these would leave the second volume unsold. The account of the mission, as opposed to that of the country, it was said, would not be relished by 'the Generality of the People of the World'.[79]

Among the pious, however, there was some evidence of the *History's* beneficial effect. For instance in Bristol, a centre of religious heterodoxy, 'a popular dissenting Minister of this City', greatly surprised by what he had read, discussed the work with an acquaintance who, the Moravians reported, thought that they 'build upon the right foundation'.[80] This proved to be a fair augury for the future. The first volume, in the meantime, became a work of reference for those whom Palliser and the Admiralty despatched in search of the North West Passage.[81]

The Brethren's missionary society in London was moribund when the *History of Greenland* was published with its name on the title page. The Church's Elders could not allow this situation to continue. Attempts to revive the SFG in 1768 were therefore associated with the Labrador negotiations.

The revival of the missionary society

It was Spangenberg who had established the Brethren's Society for the Furtherance of the Gospel among the Heathen in 1741. Its purpose had been to support the missions by caring for and by meeting the expenses of missionaries passing through Britain to posts overseas.[82] A minute of 1748 suggests

---

[76] 25 Aug. 1767, 'An extract of the rev. Mr. John Wesley's journal' (1771), in *The works of John Wesley, journal and diaries*, V: *1765–75*, ed. W. Reginald Ward and P. Heitzenrater, Nashville, Tenn. 1993, 99–100 and n. 39.
[77] Cranz, *History of Greenland*, ii. 115.
[78] MCH, provincial . . . conference, 28 Aug.–4 Sept. 1771, fo. 12: B. La Trobe to Johannes Loretz, 6 Jan. 1786, in William George Addison, *The renewed Church of the United Brethren, 1722–1930*, London 1932, 206.
[79] MCH, SFG minutes, 31 Jan., 14 Feb. 1769.
[80] BUL, BCD, 1 Dec. 1768. See also, MCH, SFG old papers, Sept. 1767.
[81] May 1778, Prince William Sound: *The voyage of the Resolution and Discovery, 1776–1780*, ed. J. C. Beaglehole, pt 1, Cambridge 1767, 349–51. For Pickersgill (1776) see Glyndwr Williams, *The British search for the North West Passage in the eighteenth century*, London 1962, 184–5.
[82] 'Retrospect', PA xvi (1841), 1–4.

that the £7,000 disbursed through the SFG, an astonishingly large sum, came chiefly from Moravians in London. Some of them, and one at least to his embarrassment, had lent as much as £300 before the society collapsed sometime around 1749, a victim, presumably, of the Church's growing financial difficulties.[83]

It was not until 1766 that meetings were resumed, but they were not a success. Members from the old SFG were not of one mind and even so respected a man as Peter Böhler was unable to cajole them into taking some positive action. They declined to involve non-Moravians in the cause and they could not agree upon a secretary.[84] These men were lay members of the Church in London. Their inertia was surely a reflection of the congregation's committee which, it was reported in 1767, 'sit together for Hours & only feed one another dark gloomy thoughts'.[85]

A year later, in a letter to James Hutton, one of the original founders of the society, Spangenberg attempted to inject some life into it. He reminded Hutton that the SFG was not needed for members of the Church who 'cheerfully' made voluntary donations for the missions. Rather he wished to see it re-launched with the intention of making itself known to 'many' other Christians who, he expected, would 'feel called upon to take an interest' in the furtherance of the Gospel. He also gave Hutton an assurance that members would not be 'compelled to make debts' and that the missions department 'will always back them'.[86]

Nothing of consequence happened as a result of this advice until the summer of 1768 when Spangenberg led the Elders on a very necessary visitation to England. At some point earlier they must have decided that a British leader was required for British Moravians and on their arrival the appointment of Benjamin La Trobe as provincial helper was confirmed.[87] He was the first British-born member of the Church to hold this position.

Labrador was the Elders' principal concern at the end of August when the state of the missions was discussed over several days in London.[88] As a result, the Labrador negotiations were reopened and Haven called upon John Pownall who pointedly asked why members of the SFG 'did not appear'. Pownall revised an earlier petition from the Moravians, to his own satisfaction, and requested that members of that society 'should subscribe their names to it'.

The report of these meetings forms part of the minute recording the revival of the SFG in September 1768. Pownall's observations undoubtedly

---

[83] MCH, Pilgrim House diary, 13 May 1748. For loans see, for example, FLD-2, 10 Oct. 1743. The SFG is not mentioned in 1749: FLD-3.
[84] MCH, SFG old papers, minutes, 10 Mar. 1766, 18 Jan., Sept. 1767, 18 Feb. 1768.
[85] MCH, PHC, 16 Jan. 1767.
[86] Spangeberg to Hutton, received 28 Mar. 1767, in Benham, *Memoirs of James Hutton*, 420–1.
[87] BUL, congregation accounts of Unitas Fratrum, 24 July 1768.
[88] Ibid. 18–22 Aug. 1768.

injected a further sense of urgency into its members' deliberations with Spangenberg and his colleagues. It was agreed that as so 'much depended' on the society it could 'no longer remain in a state of Inaction'. The SFG was therefore reconstituted and it was resolved to invite 'such Friends, who wish well of the Aims of this Society, tho' not of the Church' to become 'honoury or corresponding Members'.

This crucial meeting then turned to the 'Renewed' Labrador negotiations and issued a statement concerning the Moravian Church and its missions.[89] This *Candid declaration*, signed by Spangenberg 'In the Name of the Directors of the Missions', was described as the 'same' as that which had 'spoken' on behalf of the missions ever since 1740 when it first appeared. Its purpose was to assure all interested parties, including Church and State, that Moravians were not subversive, that their missionaries would not compete with those of other faiths and that they would be withdrawn if a conflict of principle arose. A new paragraph was added as a catch-all aimed at those in Britain who were opposed to Moravians, who took exception to their foreign connection, or who objected to their commercial intentions on the Labrador coast. 'It is a matter of great importance to us', the paragraph runs 'that the government and the whole nation may not be preoccupied with false ideas, and thereby prejudiced against innocent subjects and useful fellow-citizens of the English dominions.'[90] A list was drawn up of 'proper persons' to receive the document, 'the sooner the better';[91] Hillsborough was probably one of the first.

When the Labrador negotiations first began the issue of nationality was an embarrassment which the Moravians had attempted to put behind them.[92] It was also a problem that the *Candid declaration* had already addressed when in January 1769 Moravians met Hillsborough in private. However, it remained an unresolved difficulty, compounded by the Unitas Fratrum being in effect a foreign institution.

The link between the revival of the Brethren's missionary society and the Labrador project can now be shown in its true light. It would have been inconceivable for fishing rights on the coast to be awarded apparently to foreigners. Thus, when the first grant was made jointly in May 1769 to the Church and to its missionary society, trustees were named whom the crown could be seen to hold accountable. These trustees, who were members of the Church and resident in London, had already subscribed their names, no doubt at Pownall's insistence, to what proved to be the Moravians' first successful petition. They were also members of the SFG, described as a 'Society settled in London' whose members were 'chiefly natural born

---

[89] MCH, SFG minutes, 23 Sept. 1768.
[90] [A. G. Spangenberg], *A candid declaration of the Church known by the name of the Unitas Fratrum relative to their labour among the heathen*, London 1768, 7; 'Einfältiger Aufsatz' (1740), in Zinzendorf, *Texte*, 56–9.
[91] MCH, PHC, 25 Oct. 1768.
[92] Moravians' petition to the BOT, 23 Feb. 1765, PRO, CO 194/16 (pt 1), fos 81–5.

subjects of his Majesty'. The trustees, who were also named in the order in council, included Benjamin La Trobe and James Hutton.[93]

In the meantime the missions department in Germany welcomed the revival of the society, anticipating that it could contribute, for instance, towards 'extraordinary tho' necessary expenses ... such as building chappels' overseas. Noting that 'doors' to Labrador and British India had the 'appearance' of opening,[94] the department looked forward with relief to the prospect of the SFG's further participation.

In 1770 the society met the cost of the final reconnaissance to Labrador that fixed on the site for the first settlement. The vessel on which the party sailed was owned by the SFG's newly formed British Moravian associate, the Ship's Company, a trading company. Moravians accepted the need for trade and ownership of a vessel in order to maintain the mission. The company, which was absorbed before the end of the century by the society, is treated here as part of the SFG.[95]

Unlike the reconnaissance, which had resulted in a 'considerable loss', the actual establishment of the mission in Labrador during the following summer was a much more substantial undertaking. Fourteen missionaries and assistants, some with their wives, were to found the permanent settlement. Their survival in so hostile an environment, where in winter temperatures fell to as low as minus forty degrees Fahrenheit, meant that almost everything had to be provided in advance and, with the coast closed by ice for seven months, there was no guarantee of supplies reaching the settlement from Britain every year. By April 1771 the SFG had met the cost of the missionaries' prefabricated living-quarters, a larger ship had been purchased and the expedition was due to sail around the end of the month.[96]

Early that month, however, an emergency meeting of the SFG was called to consider an urgent plea from the Elders in Germany that the society should meet in full the cost of establishing the settlement. The missions department in Germany had nothing in reserve. Its limited resources were already over-extended, having, in Spangenberg's words, 'too many Irons in the Fire'. Its funds, the department stated when it broke the news, were 'more than exhausted ... so that we are at a loss how to carry this new Mission to Labrador into Execution'. The society was asked to 'take this matter in Hand'.

It is a measure of the Church's embarrassment that Spangenberg, as an associate and founder of the SFG, addressed a personal letter to the society.

---

[93] Memorial in the name of the Moravian Church and the SFG to Hillsborough, 3 Oct. 1768, and order in council, 3 May 1769, reproduced almost certainly from the certified copy obtained by the Church: Benham, *Memoirs of James Hutton*, 447, 475–6. A copy of the order appears in PRO, CO 194/18, fos 143–7. APC v. 184, has an abbreviated version.
[94] MCH, SFG minutes, 17 Jan. 1769.
[95] See also 'The difficulties of trade', in Hiller, 'Foundation', 112–16.
[96] [James Hutton], *A brief account of the mission established among the Esquimaux Indians, off the coast of Labrador, by the Church of the Brethren or Unitas Fratrum*, London 1774, 1–6.

The letter was both a warm-hearted sermon on members' Christian duty and a statement of hard-headed advice based on Spangenberg's own experience as a pioneer in the American colonies, when 'everything almost was wanting'. 'May He make your Hearts warm in Love & your Eyes single', Spangenberg prayed, when he reminded members of 'that great call which is given you, ... to minister to the Lord Jesus Christ, in helping his servants who venture Life & all, to bring the Heathen' to Him. 'What shall we do', Spangenberg asked, if the SFG were not to be 'both able and willing to take the matter in Hand?'

Then came Spangenberg's practical advice: supply only what was absolutely essential and 'Do not borrow money' for, as Moravians in England hardly needed to be reminded, it was much 'heavier' to pay off debts than to raise loans. Spangenberg underwrote his recommendation of a special collection with a donation from his own pocket, adding that, in the event of the SFG following the course he proposed, the society was assured of the Church's prayers in support.

It appears that alternative courses of action arising from these weighty letters were hardly mentioned. Without further ado the SFG resolved to 'take upon itself the fitting out & the voyage of the Brothers and Sisters going to Labrador'. According to the minute, the meeting closed with members' 'Hearts ... full of faith that he in whose Cause they engaged will help them through.'[97] The alternative was almost unthinkable. Had the launch even been postponed, the Moravian Church would have risked its credibility: the government was already impatient for results from the grant awarded two years earlier.

Early in May 1771 the launch of the Labrador mission was celebrated by members of the SFG, their wives and friends who joined in a solemn love feast (*agape*) with the missionaries before they sailed from London. They were also presented with a pair of French horns and some of the *talars* (surplices) which were worn at communion. In November, when a similar feast was held to mark the vessel's safe return, the journal which described the successful establishment of the mission was read.[98]

Labrador gave the SFG the impetus it needed to get underway, and Labrador gave the society's committee, Moravians in London, a much-needed mission. They now had a platform from which to promote the Church's missions and a pressing need to do so.

---

[97] Quotations from Spangenberg's letter to the SFG, 1 Mar. 1771, and (undated) from the 'deputies' responsible for the missions. For these, a similar letter from UEC and minute quoted, see MCH, SFG minutes, 4 Apr. 1771.
[98] Ibid. 3 May, 11 Nov. 1771.

Friends of the missions: first responses to the revival of the SFG

In meeting the cost of launching the Labrador mission and continuing to take particular responsibility for the mission's supply, the SFG was achieving its stated purpose of relieving the Church from 'carrying the whole burden of the missions'. But what of the decision that the SFG should also act as a focus for other Christians?

The intention of giving effect to this resolution was addressed early in 1769 when the society published its rules, together with a brief history of the SFG, in *A letter to a friend*. The Moravians, however, were going to be circumspect in their search for support. The expression 'friend' was chosen with care. It denoted a member of another Church who was known to Moravians personally, and who shared their evangelical faith. The rules made it clear that the SFG was a Moravian society on whose executive committee only Moravians could serve. Other Christians who wished to assist the Church's missions were eligible for admission as honorary or corresponding members. As no subscription on entry or at any time later was mandatory, the Church maintained its principle that giving for the missions was a voluntary act. The society stated, however, that special appeals for donations would be publicised from time to time.

The SFG confessed that, because so little had been published in the past, 'The world in general knows little of the missions.' The Church's intention that this should now change was signalled by a reference to Cranz's *History of Greenland* and by the news that honorary members would be sent, 'occasionally', the most recent reports received from overseas. From time to time extraordinary meetings would also be held for those members at Fetter Lane. Moreover, regular news of the missions could be heard at the Church's monthly 'General public meetings' where 'strangers who behave orderly' were welcome.[99] ('Strangers' denoted Christians unknown to the Moravians.)

Although 1,000 copies of the *Letter* were ordered, its circulation, as might be expected, appears to have been limited. Sixteen years elapsed before a further print run became necessary.[100] During this period there is no record of the SFG itself being promoted beyond the Moravians' circle of friends, except, for instance, on the title page of the *History of Greenland*.

Moravians were so very cautious in nominating candidates to be invited to join the society that up to the end of 1769 fewer than fifteen honorary members were proposed, and even then not all nominations were accepted.[101] Minutes from June 1772 until February 1776 have disappeared, leaving the society's records during this formative period incomplete. Never-

---

99 J. H. [James Hutton], *A letter to a friend in which some account is given of the Brethren's Society for the Furtherance of the Gospel among the Heathen*, London 1769, 9, 11–12 (account and rules of the SFG).
100 MCH, SFG minutes, 20 Dec. 1768, 9 Mar. 1784.
101 Ibid. 25 Sept. 1768–22 Nov. 1769.

theless, sufficient evidence remains to show that some influential members of polite society took an active interest in the missions. Moreover, congregation diaries suggest that attendance at Moravian chapels was an important factor in raising awareness of the Church's foreign missions across a much broader section of the public.

The SFG believed that its supporters ought to receive news regularly from overseas, but preparation of a sufficient number of 'Flying Leaves', or news bulletins in manuscript, proved impractical. This led to a proposal to publish accounts of the missions perhaps 'quarterly'. Old inhibitions and the policy of concentrating on a few large-scale works, however, prevailed. There was also a nagging fear, recorded in 1769, that a printed circular 'might lay' the missions 'open to the Enemy and his Instruments',[102] a reference almost certainly to recent articles in the press mocking the mission in Greenland. Three years later the idea of issuing a financial statement with a list of donors to the Labrador mission was 'Considered too publick a Measure'.[103]

The need for publicity, however, was recognised when in 1771 the society sponsored the publication of an overview of Moravian missionary methods and the status of each of the missions. Known as *A succinct view of the missions*, this was an extended pamphlet. Presented to the SFG's 'friends', it does not seem to have been a cause for further embarrassment.[104] It remained the only comprehensive account of the missions until after 1789 when the Church at last agreed to a regular publication, the quarterly *Periodical Accounts* of the missions.

It was not only the Moravian Church that wished to protect itself from unwelcome attention. The Welsh evangelist Howell Harris at Trevecca had similar concerns. Although Harris was an exceptionally good friend of the Moravians, he declined their invitation to become an honorary member of the SFG on the grounds that he did not think it 'prudent' for him to be associated so 'publicly' with them. Nevertheless, as Harris had the conversion of the heathen 'much at heart', he contributed several guineas to the society on more than one occasion. A note in manuscript concerning the Labrador mission, sent to him by Hutton in February 1771, survives as a rare example of the SFG's attempt to keep friends in the country informed.[105]

It was far easier to accomplish this where there was a Moravian chapel, and in London above all. The SFG also met at 10 Nevill's Court, one of a growing complex of Moravian-owned houses clustered around the chapel at Fetter Lane in the City. London was also the home port of the Labrador vessel. Her departure and safe return continued to be celebrated by those Moravian love

---

[102] Ibid. 31 Jan. 1769.
[103] Ibid. 10 Mar. 1772.
[104] Ibid. 12 Mar., 2 July 1771; B. La Trobe, *Succinct view*.
[105] MCH, SFG minutes, 18, 20 Dec. 1768, 15 Jan. 1770. Report to Howell Harris, National Library of Wales, Aberystwyth, Trevecca letters 2691–2. I am grateful to Dr Boyd Schlenther for this reference.

feasts during which tea was taken and godly conversation ensued. These biannual ceremonies, to which the SFG's friends and other Christians were invited, were always a unique opportunity to focus attention on the missions. It must have been a memorable occasion in 1777 when, after their return from Labrador, Jens Haven and his family appeared in 'Esquimaux Dress'.[106]

The constant traffic of missionaries and others through London undoubtedly played a part in making the missions known. 'It is on occasions as these', the diarist reflected a year later, that the congregation in London 'enjoys the situation as a Central Cong.[regation], thro which so many dear Servants of our Lord pass.'[107] These Moravians were lodged in London, sometimes for an extended period, and members of the SFG negotiated their onward passage.

By 1771 there were twenty-two Moravian 'congregations' in the British Isles.[108] Readings at public meetings from the missionaries' diaries appear to have been a particular reason for other Christians to attend their chapels. For instance, in January 1769 at Bristol:

> There was as many people as this Chappel could hold, yet it is amazing what a Stillness and Attention there was, especially when a conversation w[i]th one of our Indians in N America ... was related.

The occasion was a 'heathen festival', held to mark the beginning of a mission, and the collection 'was very handsome'. A month later an extract from missionary Zeisberger's diary was heard at a further general meeting 'with singular Pleasure', and attendance in Bristol continued to increase. Similar entries can be found in the records of the London congregation.[109]

Most members of the public who attended these meetings were, like the Moravians themselves, from the 'lower middling-sort' and below. In London, however, 'people of Fashion' also came in increasing numbers to the chapel in Fetter Lane to hear the preaching, necessitating the addition of a gallery in 1778 for 'Strangers of Distinction'. On the occasion of the heathen festival members of the SFG's committee sat prominently in the front pew and a collection was made at the door.[110] With two 'Labrador' love feasts being held in addition to the Church's heathen festivals, missions were the object of special attention four times a year in London.

To what extent strangers and friends contributed to the missions is less clear. Most recorded donations from these sources were of between half and five guineas, sums which compare favourably with the level of ordinary giving by members of the Established Church to the Society for the Propagation of

---

106 MCH, FLD-21, 20 Nov. 1777.
107 Ibid. 30 Oct. 1778.
108 John Holmes, *History of the Protestant Church of the United Brethren*, London 1830, ii. 354 (Northampton was closed by 1822 when the list was compiled).
109 Memorabilia for 1772, 8 Jan., 19 Feb. 1769, BUL, BCD; MCH, SFG minutes, 14 Mar. 1769; FLD-15, 7 May 1769.
110 MCH, FLD-18, 3 June 1772; FLD-21, 2 Aug. 1778.

the Gospel.[111] Small donations could soon add up to a useful amount. For example, the 'passage' charged for each missionary going to Labrador was £13;[112] La Trobe and Hutton, who were adept fund-raisers, sometimes deposited larger sums than this. Special appeals for assistance were made from time to time, such as when the cost of launching the Labrador mission proved considerably greater than was anticipated. In this instance the response seems to have come largely from Moravians in Europe and in England: substantial donations of up to £50 were received.[113]

The return from trade in such items as whalebone and oil from Labrador was not sufficient for the mission to be self-supporting year in and year out. There was thus constant pressure on Moravian members of the SFG to turn to their 'friends' for support. From January 1772, when £300 was borrowed to meet bills falling due arising from the launch costs,[114] the SFG does not appear to have been out of debt for another nine years; and in 1784, with revenue 'considerably less than formerly', members were urged to redouble their efforts to obtain 'help' from other well-disposed Christians.[115]

All these activities, from diaries from overseas being read in chapels to fund-raising, contributed to publicising the missions. Moravians were also a skilled and cultured people who attracted the interest of a small but influential cross-section of polite society. The names of Dr Samuel Johnson and Dr Hawkesworth, also well-known in literary circles, and the Revd Henry Venn, who each gave a guinea or two, would not have appeared in the SFG's records of 1771 without the Labrador exigencies.[116]

Dr Johnson was 'so curious . . . as to every language' that Moravians gave him translations used by the Greenlanders. When the SFG again needed assistance, Johnson introduced Hutton to Henry Thrale, the brewer, who donated five guineas.[117] Members of Johnson's circle who were also friends of Moravians included General Oglethorpe, the founder of Georgia, men prominent in the book trade and Dr Charles Burney, the musicologist. Hutton, who began his adult life as a bookseller, seems to have initiated many of these and other connections.[118]

The addition of the name of Joseph Banks illustrates the range of the Moravians' influential friends in the metropolis and that they were not all renowned for their piety. It seems to have been the Labrador mission which

---

[111] *Abstract of the charter and of the proceedings of the Society for the Propagation of the Gospel in Foreign Parts*, London 1771, 3–6.
[112] MCH, SFG minutes, 22 Apr. 1771.
[113] Ibid. 4 Apr.–17 Dec. 1771.
[114] Ibid. 20 Jan. 1772.
[115] Ibid. 16 Jan. 1781, 9 Mar. 1784.
[116] Ibid. 2 July 1771.
[117] Hutton to Boswell, 29 Jan. 1792, in *The correspondence and other papers of James Boswell relating to the making of the 'Life of Johnson'*, ed. Marshall Waingrow, London 1969, 465–8.
[118] J. A. Cochrane, *Dr Johnson's printer: the life of William Strahan*, London 1964, 10; *The letters of Dr Charles Burney, I: 1751–84*, ed. Alvaro Ribereiro, Oxford 1991, 131–4.

first brought the Church's work overseas to their attention. In Banks's case his interest was also almost certainly aroused by his mother, a pious lady, who had lived near the Moravians in Chelsea since 1761. Banks, who came down from Oxford two years later, was about to embark upon a career which extended from gentleman botanist to benevolent imperial promoter.

In 1765 Moravian missionaries collected plants for him in Labrador and in the following year Banks himself sailed to Newfoundland aboard the HMS *Niger*, Adams's warship on which they had been detained. Banks thereafter remained a supportive and influential friend of the missions.[119] Moravians continued to add to his herbarium, Dan Solander reporting enthusiastically in 1775 on an outstanding collection of plants received from them in India,[120] and Banks's library included their publications, of which the *History of Greenland* was most probably the first.[121] The election to the Royal Society in 1780 of the Moravian Philip Hurlock, a surgeon and an active member of the SFG, can also surely be accepted as a considerable compliment to the Moravians. Solander was one of Hurlock's nominees and Banks was president.[122]

Banks was a careful observer, which makes an extract from his 'Journal of a trip to Holland' in 1773 of particular interest. He and his friends had 'looked into' two Churches one Sunday, but they went out of their way to visit the Moravian settlement at Zeist on another occasion. There,

> we were not a little pleased with the simple & unaffected manner of these people: their buildings are extensive & rather beautiful: in them they live as a kind of Brotherhood, each working & exposing his manufactures to Sale . . . for the Benefit of the Community; we attended their Service, & a decency was observed . . . seldom to be met with in other Religions: a Hymn began it, then the History of one of their Brethren, who had travelled far for the propagation of their faith was read . . ., & a Hymn concluded the whole: . . . I confess I was much Edified.[123]

The journal, it should be noted, was edited, most probably, by Banks's sister.

One of Banks's travelling companions and a fellow member of the Society of Dilettanti was Charles Greville, best known today for his mistress Emma whom he passed on to his uncle. Moravian missionaries had discovered Labradorite, a brilliantly coloured felspar, and their brethren in London

---

119 MCH, FLD-30, 14 Jan. 1812. See also C. I. La Trobe's correspondence (copies) with Joseph Banks *re* Greenland, Aug. 1812–19 Apr. 1813, in MCH, transactions with government.
120 Harold B. Carter, *Sir Joseph Banks, 1743–1820*, London 1988, 266. For his Labrador herbarium see Lysaght, *Banks*, 172.
121 BL, press mark, 980.l.24.
122 Copies of the Royal Society index and election paper, 16 Nov. 1780, were kindly provided by Professor George Brownlee. Philip Hurlock (1713–1801) had been a Moravian since 1744.
123 Joseph Banks, journal, 4 Mar. 1773, Wellcome Institute Library, London, MS 1049.

assisted Greville with his collection of minerals. He responded by taking a keen interest in the mission and later, for instance, with political advice.[124] These men of the world, in the widest sense of that expression, were surely impressed, like Palliser, by the Moravians' thorough approach to whatever they put their hand.

Given the Moravians' reticence and their past, personal contact between them and the pious among other Christians was of critical importance. The inclusion in 1771 of the Revd Henry Venn in the list of SFG donors, together with his friend James Stillingfleet of Hotham in Yorkshire, is notable since at this juncture few of the clergy associated themselves with the Moravians. In the period immediately following the SFG's revival only three ministers of the Established Church actually became honorary members of the society.[125] They were most probably all, like Venn, fellow evangelicals.

Henry Venn almost certainly had met Moravians in Yorkshire before 1771 when he moved from Huddersfield to the rectory at Yelling in Huntingdonshire. From Yelling he established a warm connection with the Foster Barhams, a wealthy Moravian family living in Bedford, who sponsored the mission on their estates in Jamaica.[126]

The name of the merchant philanthropist John Thornton, described by Venn as 'one of the saints of Christ Jesus . . . like the family at Bedford', does not appear in the SFG's records of this period.[127] However, he was not a man to have allowed himself to be prejudiced against the Moravians. His friend Berridge's earlier critique of them seems to have made little or no impression[128] and in 1781 he joined Venn for a Moravian service at Bedford.[129] It seems quite likely that Thornton, who is known to have given substantial sums in confidence to the SFG shortly before his death in 1790,[130] made similar gifts earlier, perhaps through La Trobe. Inundated with requests, Thornton hid his bounty through trusted third parties, 'to save myself the trouble of applications'.[131]

---

[124] MCH, SFG minutes, 20 Jan. 1778, 2 Feb. 1801. See also letters of C. Greville to C. I. La Trobe, 1799–1800, Hamilton and Greville papers, BL, MS Add. 40,715, fos 92–124. For C. F. Greville (1749–1809) see Sir Lewis Namier and John Brooke (eds), *History of parliament: the House of Commons, 1754–90*, ii, London 1964.

[125] Election of honorary members: Revd George Thompson of Cornwall, Revd [?] Grigg and Revd [?] Brewer, 25 Sept. 1768, 14 Feb. 1769, SFG minutes. Thompson was a noted evangelical. The pious inclinations of the other two have not been determined.

[126] BRO, MO 351, 354, 27 Aug. 1776, 18–19 Aug. 1779.

[127] Henry Venn to Miss [?] Venn, 26 Aug. 1777, in *The life and a selection of letters of the late Rev. Henry Venn*, ed. Henry Venn, London 1839, 258–9.

[128] See especially Thornton's comment on Berridge's notes cited in the editor's preface to *Bogatzky's golden treasury: a reprint of John Thornton's edition of 1775, with critical notes hitherto unpublished by John Berridge*, ed. Charles P. Phinn, London 1891, pp. xxii–xxiii.

[129] BRO, MO 356, 13 Dec. 1781.

[130] MCH, minutes, 15 Sept. 1789, 27 Apr. 1790.

[131] Thornton to the countess of Huntingdon, 28 May 1772, countess of Huntingdon's papers, CFWC, MS F1/183.

Around 1760 John Thornton's friend, the countess of Huntingdon, had drawn close, but only temporarily, to the Moravians: by 1767 when she received her copy of the *History of Greenland*, that noble lady had gone her own way.[132] Three years later, when she argued with Harris at Trevecca, 'saying they are Jesuits, cunning, artful etc.', her ambivalent feelings towards the Moravians had surfaced once more.[133]

Nevertheless, some pious members of the aristocracy associated with her were better disposed. It is notable that this small group of 'supporters' were all familiar with the Moravians prior to the revival of the SFG. For example, Dartmouth's name appears as a benefactor in the society's minutes,[134] and the circle of ladies around him and the countess included two sisters, Mrs Carteret and Mrs Cavendish, of St James's Place in London. Their letters to her with evangelical gossip form a bridge between Moravians, 'Dear Mr Venn' and this genteel upper class.[135] The sisters were also those 'Sincere friends' of the SFG whose regular contributions are recorded from 1766 until their deaths in 1792.[136] Another to be associated with the Moravians was Thomas Childs of Chelsea, who held the quit rents to that part of the Carteret hereditary land acquired by the Church in 1753 from Lord Granville for its settlement in North Carolina. Childs became one of the first honorary members of the revived SFG.[137]

A further advantage of the Labrador project and the revival of the SFG was that it led to an improvement in relations between Moravians and the Society for Promoting Christian Knowledge. These had for long been less than fraternal due to the SPCK's close association with the Pietist centre at Halle in Germany. Not only had the society's churchly secretary since 1743, the Revd Thomas Broughton, assisted in the campaign against the Moravians,[138] but the SPCK also relied on Halle for the missionaries it employed in British India. It was only natural, therefore, that that society should echo the Pietists' shocked reaction to the arrival at Tranquebar in 1760 of a large party of Moravians alongside their own missionaries. The society's annual report of 1763 states that 'Some Moravians of Count Zinzendorff's [sic] Sect have lately settled among them; but, they hope whatever may

---

132 It was presented on 2 Jan. 1767: shelved at CFWC.
133 Conversation of 27 July 1770: *Howell Harris's visits to London*, ed. Tom Benyon, Aberystwyth 1960, 284. For the countess's brief 'flirtation' with the Moravians see also Edwin Welch, *Spiritual pilgrim: a reassessment of the life of the countess of Huntingdon*, Cardiff 1995, 85–8.
134 MCH, SFG minutes, 10 Mar. 1772, 12 May 1778.
135 Mrs B. Carteret [and Mrs Anne Cavendish] to the countess of Huntingdon, 1777–c. 1782, CFWC, MS F1/374, 427, 1120, 1152.
136 MCH, SFG minutes, 11 Sept. 1792, records their demise and generosity. For these pious sisters and their connections with the nobility see A. C. Hobart Seymour, *The life and times of Selina, countess of Huntingdon*, i, London 1844, 461.
137 MCH, SFG minutes, 23 Sept. 1768.
138 Podmore, *Moravian Church*, 217; Benham, *Memoirs of James Hutton*, 109–10, 128. For Thomas Broughton (1712–77) see *DNB* s.v.

be a Scandal or Hindrance to the Christian Doctrine and Practice will soon be removed.'[139] In spite of Halle's vigorous remonstrance, the Moravians were not removed.

It may have been as a result of an initiative taken by Hillsborough[140] that in 1769 Broughton was induced to pay a friendly call on James Hutton. An exchange of notes followed which included the Moravians' newly published *Candid declaration*. Secretary Broughton responded with a conciliatory 'Billet wherein he certified that the Perusal of these Accounts had given him great Pleasure & that sincere Christians of every Denomination must wish our Labourers among the Heathen good Luck in the name of the Lord.'[141]

Missionary stirrings, patrons and sponsors

Although Labrador and the associated activities of the revived SFG had led to the Moravians being recognised in some quarters as useful in the mission field, the old suspicions about them still remained. This is exemplified in an exchange of letters between William Knox and his first and influential mentor Dr Philip Skelton, the scholarly Irish divine.[142] Knox, who was now a secretary of state working alongside Pownall at the Board of Trade, is known today as the author of pamphlets that incensed the American colonists.

In 1774 Knox told Skelton that he had engaged Moravian missionaries for his slaves in Georgia. Skelton's cautious reply, in which he reminded Knox of the 'many very ugly eccentricities' with which Zinzendorf and the Church stood charged, confirms yet again those deep-seated prejudices that continued to plague the Moravians. Nevertheless, Skelton accepted that Moravian missionaries might, perhaps, be more effective than 'our lukewarm clergy'.[143]

Knox was a member of the Society for the Propagation of the Gospel who, in the words of his biographer, Bellot, 'vented his own frustrated evangelicalism' when he turned to the Moravians for missionaries.[144] However, it seems unlikely that as an ambitious man advising the administration, he would have associated himself with Moravians without the foreknowledge that their Labrador mission enjoyed the government's countenance.

---

[139] 'Some account . . . mission to East-Indies, 1762', in *An account of the Society for Promoting Christian Knowledge*, London 1763, 94, 31. For Moravians at Tranquebar see 'Unpleasant interlude', in E. Arno Lehmann, *It began at Tranquebar*, trans. M. J. Lutz, Vepery, Madras 1956, 163–7.
[140] Interview with Hillsborough, 31 Jan. 1769, in Benham, *Memoirs of James Hutton*, 463n.
[141] MCH, SFG minutes, 11 Apr. 1769.
[142] For Knox and Philip Skelton (1707–84) see Leland J. Bellot, *William Knox: the life and thought of an eighteenth-century imperialist*, Austin, Tx–London 1977, 6–12.
[143] Philip Skelton to William Knox, 25 July 1774, in 'Manuscripts of Captain H. V. Knox', in HMC, *Report on manuscripts in various collections*, vi, Dublin 1909, 444.
[144] Bellot, *Knox*, 112. For Moravians and Knox see MCH, PHC, 25 May 1774.

Knox, in his own way, and the strong-minded countess of Huntingdon in another, are early, but as yet unco-ordinated, examples of that evangelistic urge and frustration which later inspired the founders of the new missionary societies. When the countess despatched her own missionaries to Georgia in 1772, she had assembled such an ill-assorted crew that, even without hindsight, her ambitious project to evangelise among Christians and the heathen was doomed to fail.[145] She might have been better advised to have begun on a small scale and sponsored Moravians, but she is unlikely to have considered such an option.

John Wesley and some of his followers in Bristol, on the other hand, were prepared, on one occasion, to turn to the Moravians, and although the Moravians withdrew at the last moment, the plan remains a rare example of co-operation between the two parties. It is also notable for what is probably the first entry in Moravian records concerning the redoubtable Dr Thomas Coke, founder of Methodist missions.

In the autumn of 1774 the Moravian Church agreed 'to make use of Mr. John Wesley's offer to send Brethren to Old Calabar on the Coast of Guinea, to live with the two Africans'.[146] These men were the 'two African Princes' baptised by Charles Wesley in January that year at Bristol who had escaped from Virginia. Freed by Lord Mansfield's recent ruling, they were to be 'sent honourably back' to their homeland.[147] Shipwrecked, they returned to Bristol, where the Moravians had a lively congregation.

It is quite likely that the idea of a Wesleyan-sponsored Moravian mission originated with John Wesley's followers in Bristol and more particularly with James Ireland, a most respectable sugar merchant of that city. A pious west country philanthropist and patron of evangelicals, Ireland was just the man to attempt to bring the two parties together. Like his friend John Thornton, he strove for reconciliation between evangelicals[148] and a mission, in this instance, provided just the opportunity.

The Moravians' side of this story can be followed in the official diary kept by their congregation in Bristol where the Africans were lodging with a generous supporter of the SFG. In July La Trobe and Ireland called to see them and at a further interview the '2 pretty young men' expressed the wish that 'missionaries could go with them, assuring that they would be well

---

145 Boyd S. Schlenther, ' "To convert the poor people in America" ', *Georgia Historical Quarterly* lxxvii (1994), 225–56.
146 BUL, BCD, 23 Oct. 1774.
147 Charles Wesley to William Perront (postscript), 23 Jan. 1774, *PWHS* xvii (1929–30), 182.
148 Albert Brown-Lawson, *John Wesley and the Anglican evangelicals in the eighteenth century*, Edinburgh–Cambridge–Durham 1994, 330. On John Ireland (1724–1814) see also G. R. Balleine, *A history of the evangelical party in the Church of England*, London–New York–Toronto 1933, 91–2.

received'. In January 1775 the Church confirmed its intention of establishing the mission and called for volunteers.[149]

The Africans sailed for their homeland once more[150] and word eventually reached Bristol from one of them, renewing their appeal for missionaries. A Wesleyan lady in the City urged the Moravians to respond, saying that the Wesleys 'had no prospect of sending missionaries from among their own people', but repeating their offer of assistance. The Moravians nevertheless withdrew their volunteers on the grounds that the master of the vessel on which they were due to sail was not a suitable person. 'Consequently the matter rests in suspense', an entry of April 1776 in the Bristol diary explained.[151]

In August 1778 Dr Coke, who some time over the previous twelve months had allied himself with Wesley, may in discussion with a Moravian minister have attempted to revive the Moravians' interest. The two men may have met[152] the day before Coke attended his first Wesleyan Conference at which it was decided that further attempts to send missionaries to Africa should be abandoned as 'the call seems doubtful'.[153] Expectations for a Wesleyan–Moravian project on limited terms were not therefore realised, but the prospects of a mission overseas and the good offices of John Ireland, had brought the two 'denominations' together.

From 1770 British Moravians had in the SFG a platform from which in their quiet way they could make the Church's missions known in Britain, raise their public profile and gain essential support for work overseas. Crucially, through the establishment of the Labrador mission, the first and the most important of the Church's new projects in the British world and the catalyst for the re-establishment of the society, Whitehall and men of the world had found Moravians to be sound and valuable. There was now no doubt, in these quarters at least, that the Moravians could be accepted as a respectable people. Early responses from other Christians, lay members mainly of the Established Church, were more muted but promising, although with a few notable exceptions the clergy do not appear to have been interested. Pious friends, mainly evangelically inclined members of polite society, already acquainted personally with Moravians, came to the support of the SFG, while a broader cross-section of society attended Moravian chapels and listened to accounts of the missions.

---

[149] BUL, BCD, 4, 15 July 1774, 22 Jan. 1775. For Mr [?] Alison, with whom the Africans lodged, see MCH, SFG minutes, 15 Apr. 1777, 23 June 1778.
[150] John's question to Charles, 4 Aug. 1775, in *The letters of John Wesley*, ed. John Telford, vi, London 1960, 170.
[151] BUL, BCD, 12 Apr. 1776. See also John Vickers, *Thomas Coke: apostle of Methodism*, London 1969, 132. Moravians do not figure in Vickers's account.
[152] MCH, SFG minutes, 4 Aug. 1778. The minister was John Sulger.
[153] Thomas Taylor, diary, entry for 5 Aug. 1778, cited in *The journal of the Rev. John Wesley*, ed. Nehemiah Curnock, vi, London 1938, 206 n. 3.

3

Moravians and Evangelical Calvinists, 1770–1790

Time was needed for the prejudices held in England against the Moravians to subside. The recovery of the Church's reputation would depend upon how other Christians perceived the effect of the reforms and policies which the Church had adopted. Personal contact with Moravians seems to have played a crucially important part in a favourable outcome: it was through face-to-face meetings over the Labrador project that the Moravians became known to ministers of the crown and officials as a useful and reliable people. On the other hand, there was as yet little opportunity for the pious to revise their opinion of the Church and its beliefs. The Church's orthodox evangelical teaching had yet to be revealed and its missions were largely unknown. This situation was to be transformed over the next twenty years, again substantially through personal contacts. By 1790 leaders of the large and growing community of evangelicals in England, members of various denominations but holding Calvinistic tenets to a greater or lesser degree, were among those who admired the Church above all for its labours in the mission field. Many were also attracted by Moravian spirituality and impressed by the Church's doctrine: once evangelicals became well acquainted with Moravians, they found that they had much in common.

The 1780s was a period in the long missionary awakening of the eighteenth century when evangelicals were growing in numbers and influence and were ever more concerned at the failure of their own Churches, compared with the small Moravian Church, to evangelise overseas. As the evangelical movement gained strength so the tempo of the missionary awakening accelerated until in the 1790s some of the most prominent evangelicals of their day established what would become three of the great new missionary societies that launched the modern missionary movement. The formation in 1792 of the Baptist Missionary Society (the BMS), by Baptist ministers in the Northamptonshire Association was followed three years later by the establishment of 'The Missionary Society'. Known later as the LMS, this society was established by members of various denominations on an interdenominational basis. In 1799 Church Evangelicals of John Newton's Eclectic Society and William Wilberforce's Clapham Saints began their own society, known later as the Church Missionary Society (the CMS); its object was the forwarding of missions to Africa and the East. This chapter, and the two which follow, explain how the Moravian Church both stirred the missionary awakening and stimulated those evangelicals who founded the new societies.

The accelerating pace of the missionary awakening

The seemingly providential expansion of the British world by the end of the Seven Years War failed to inspire a new surge in missionary activity. Pious hopes expressed by bishops of the Established Church were not realised[1] and by 1772 it was apparent that the SPG and the SPCK lacked the will, men and funds for a significant extension of their missionary effort overseas. The SPG's requirement that it would only employ men in the field who were ordained was a particular constraint,[2] while the SPCK continued to depend on Lutherans from Germany to supply men for its mission in south India. Much of the money raised in support also seems to have come from Lutherans.[3]

Issues of men and money were addressed in February 1781 by Richard Hurd, bishop of Lichfield, when he preached the SPG's annual charity sermon in London at St Mary-le-Bow. Hurd drew attention to the 'antient and modern missions' of other Churches some of which, he accepted, were conducted successfully by unlettered men, that is by those who had not graduated from one of the two universities, a prerequisite, usually, for ordination. As missionaries required 'heroic virtues', Hurd refrained from describing by 'the disgraceful name of fanaticism' defects inherent in their calling: 'It is enough that the word of the Cross is preached in simplicity and godly sincerity.' He called on all Christians to support the work overseas liberally, and to 'Thus . . . make some amends for those multiplied mischiefs . . . which our insatiable Commerce occasions.'[4]

According to the Revd John Newton (1725–1807), who intended to be at St Mary-le-Bow for the occasion, the sermon was welcomed by evangelicals and Dissenters alike. He observed that 'Many dissenters' were 'even' present, that the bishop 'sent them home full of commendations' and that the sermon's 'whole strain' was 'evangelical'.[5] Later in the year it was read 'with much Pleasure' at a meeting of the Moravians' missionary society.[6]

Sometime between 1784 and 1785 Newton himself preached a missionary sermon, in which he voiced frustration and a sense of national guilt at the

---

[1] John Hume, *Sermon preached before the incorporated Society for the Propagation of the Gospel . . . at their anniversary meeting . . . 1762*, London 1762, 16; Richard Terrick, *Sermon preached before the incorporated Society for the Propagation of the Gospel . . . at their anniversary meeting . . . 1764*, London 1764, 26. These references were kindly provided by Professor P. J. Marshall.
[2] *Abstract of the SPG charter*, London 1771, 3–6, 10–12, 22–6. For finance see pp. 33–7. See also Peter M. Doll, 'Imperial Anglicanism in North America, 1745–1795', unpubl. DPhil diss. Oxford 1989, 37–8, 52–9.
[3] *An account of the SPCK*, London 1772, 131–3, 143.
[4] Richard Hurd, *Sermon preached before the incorporated Society for the Propagation of the Gospel . . . at their anniversary meeting . . . 1781*, London 1781, 11–16.
[5] John Newton to William Bull, 17 Feb. 1781, Bull papers, LPL, MS 3095, fos 92–3.
[6] MCH, SFG minutes, 31 July 1781.

lack of progress overseas. The burden of his message was that, compared with the great prizes secured by her arms and trade in the East and West Indies, Great Britain's efforts to evangelise among the heathen were negligible. Moreover, recent 'discoveries', a reference undoubtedly to Cook's voyages, had 'added almost a new world'. 'None of the commercial nations in Europe', Newton believed, 'have had the propagation of Christianity less at heart than the English', despite being so favoured by providence. Newton reserved his praise among contemporaries for the Moravians whose 'labours . . . compared to their circumstances and resources . . . doubtless excite admiration, and thankfulness to God, in every serious mind acquainted with the subject'.[7]

These were sentiments shared by the growing numbers of the Moravians' evangelical friends as feelings of frustration, contrition and a knowledge of the Church's disproportionate and extensive endeavours overseas quickened the pace of the missionary awakening.

The 1780s marked the beginning of significant and active years for the long missionary awakening. Developments were now taking place which were to have a bearing on the formation of the missionary societies during the following decade and Cook's discoveries in the Pacific added a further dimension to the opportunity and scale of the task. The acrimonious Calvinist–Arminian theological dispute had drawn to a close and a period of relative peace and fraternity between the parties ensued. Evangelicals believed in new birth: a lasting conversion experience caused purposeful individuals to pray for the expansion of Christ's Kingdom throughout the world, to seek useful means of spreading the gospel, and to participate together in benevolent and humane causes. Irrespective of their particular tenets, many shared expectations of a coming millennium and a vital concern for the state of the poor heathen overseas.[8]

It would indeed be misleading to over-emphasise the particular denominational allegiance of evangelicals during this period – although it usually mattered very much indeed. This is well illustrated by the career of John Newton himself and that of Thomas Haweis (1734–1820), clergymen who over their long lives were pivotal personalities in religious and missionary beginnings; although active in different spheres, both were leading advocates of the Moravian Church and its missions. Newton's ' "I am a sort of middle-man" ' appears as typical of his part in the missionary awakening as it is of how he saw himself in relation to other Christians, irrespective of their

---

[7] Sermon XXXII, 'Messiah: Fifty expository discourses, . . . 1784 and 1785', in *The works of the Rev. John Newton*, iv, London 1808, 363–4. I owe this reference to Professor Bruce Hindmarsh.
[8] Roger H. Martin, *Evangelicals united: ecumenical stirrings in pre-Victorian Britain, 1795–1830*, Metuchen, NJ–London 1983, chs i–ii, esp pp. 9–18, 23–33; Stephen Orchard, 'Evangelical eschatology and the missionary awakening', *Journal of Religious History* xxii (1998), esp. pp. 132ff., 139, 144–6.

denomination.⁹ Haweis, who was similarly inclined, joined, mainly with Dissenters, to found the LMS.¹⁰

An example of the crucial effects of a newly found evangelical faith is to be found in the actions of the Northamptonshire Association of Particular Baptists. The adoption, around 1785, of an evangelical–Calvinistic theology by ministers made them look outwards and be concerned for the souls of the heathen world-wide; it was the essential step that made the formation of the BMS a possibility.¹¹ Moreover, when the Society for the Abolition of the Slave Trade was formed in 1787, they joined members of other denominations in rallying to the society's cause.¹²

Stirrings more generally reflected that sense of frustration and unease felt by Church Evangelicals at the lack of missionary zeal displayed by their own Church and its two associated societies, the SPG and SPCK. Thomas Haweis almost certainly had prayed for a mission to the heathen for some time before he made his own attempt in 1789 to send missionaries to Tahiti¹³ and two years earlier Charles Grant launched his campaign from India for a mission in Bengal. Although these initiatives failed, both men persisted. It was Haweis who persuaded the LMS to adopt the South Seas as the site for its first mission and Grant and India were to be associated with the formation of the CMS.¹⁴

That Moravian influence can be detected in these and other missionary beginnings is an indication of the steady improvement in the Church's standing. As early as 1771 British Moravians noted that, despite Whitefield's telling attack of 1753, his followers were inclined to be friendly.¹⁵ The Moravian Church was not party to the religious 'discord' of the 1770s, a reference to the dispute between Wesleyans and Whitefieldites, and its public services were often well attended, sometimes remarkably so. With 'prejudices' against them beginning to abate, Moravians had 'access to the houses and hearts of some, where all was formerly bolted'.¹⁶ For instance, in 1780 when John Newton called on a non-Moravian household in London he found, as he expected, Benjamin La Trobe discoursing before the company on a text from the Scriptures. Mrs Wilberforce, John Thornton's sister and William Wilberforce's aunt, was among ladies present. The head of the household was

---

[9] D. Bruce Hindmarsh, *John Newton and the English evangelical tradition between the conversions of Wesley and Wilberforce*, Oxford 1996, 325.
[10] A. S. Wood, *Thomas Haweis, 1734–1820*, London 1957, 237–8.
[11] Stanley, *Baptist Missionary Society*, 1–9.
[12] T. S. H. Elwyn, *The Northamptonshire Baptist Association*, London 1964, 20.
[13] Wood, *Haweis*, 170–1, 177–80; for Haweis and the LMS see pp. 191–8.
[14] For Grant see Charles Hole, *The early history of the Church Missionary Society for Africa and the East to the end of AD 1814*, London 1896, 7–16.
[15] MCH, provincial conference, 1771, fo. 11.
[16] MCH, FLD-21, memorabilia, 1777. See also BUL, BCD, 1772.

William Cardale, a solicitor and the Moravians' legal advisor, who went on to be a founding member of the CMS.[17]

Benjamin La Trobe (1728–86)[18]

Leader of Moravians in Britain from 1768 until his death in 1786, Benjamin La Trobe made a vital contribution to the recovery of the Church's reputation and to making the missions known. An able man with an attractive personality, La Trobe was a preacher of note and his influence continued to be felt after his death. Founders of all three new missionary societies must at least have heard of him, and some of them, like Haweis and Newton, knew him very well indeed. Born in Dublin in 1728 into a family of Dissenters, La Trobe was raised with the intention that he would enter the Baptist ministry. But he came under John Cennick's influence in 1746 and was ordained a minister of the Moravian Church two years later. Following his marriage in 1756 to Anna Antes, the Moravian daughter of a prominent Pennsylvania-German family, La Trobe was responsible for the very important settlement at Fulneck in Yorkshire. He remained at Fulneck until 1768 when he moved to London on being appointed provincial helper.

La Trobe's nationality was a useful asset at the interface of the Moravian and British worlds. It was undoubtedly helpful to him in establishing an effective relationship with 'persons in eminent situations, both in Church and State'.[19] Whether during this period a German Moravian would have been as successful is questionable. La Trobe was British-born, but as a true member of the Moravian Church he prayed for 'an end of those national . . . prejudices', which he believed had been so damaging to its cause in the past.[20]

When he died in November 1786 at his residence in Fetter Lane, London, by then well known and widely respected, 'a very large company was present' at the funeral. The observation that 'no less than 58 coaches attended exclusive of those that followed the hearse' was surely made to denote the social standing of those within, rather than that it was a very wet day.[21] An obituary in the *London Chronicle* is significant for its content and for the identity of its authors. La Trobe, they wrote, had been 'indefatigable . . . in promoting the laudable purpose' of his Church 'at home and abroad' and through his careful oversight of a 'variety of publications' he had 'firmly established' the Church's

---

17 Newton to his wife, 20 Jan. 1780, Newton papers, LPL, MS 2935, fo. 182. For Cardale see Hole, *Early history*, 624.
18 For Benjamin La Trobe see BDEB. See also John Mason, 'Benjamin La Trobe', in John Mason and Lucy Torode, *Three generations of the La Trobe family in the Moravian Church*, Newtonabbey, Co. Antrim 1997, 3–15.
19 MCH, transactions with government, fo. 3, n.d.
20 B. La Trobe to Johannes von Watteville, enclosed in Hutton to UEC, 25 Oct. 1768, in Benham, *Memoirs of James Hutton*, 457.
21 MCH, FLD-26, 6 Dec. 1786.

'reputation'. The effect of the whole piece was without doubt far too fulsome and personal for Moravians; nevertheless, few men or woman could have dissented from the tenor of these sentiments, or that 'The goodness of his heart, and the affability of his disposition, endeared him to all his connexions'.[22] The Moravian community honoured La Trobe's wish that 'nothing might be said of him, for he thought it wrong to give praise to any man, when the whole was due to God'[23]: the obituary was placed in the *Chronicle* not by James Hutton who then, and perhaps until now, has been suspected of being the culprit, but was 'entirely the doing of Mr Strahan & his Secretary of State as Br. La Trobe used to call him[,] Mr Preston', as a Moravian assured a colleague. These gentlemen had received 'a great deal of consolation with La Trobe'.[24]

The background to this can easily be explained. W. & A. Strahan, the king's printers, with premises in the City of London, had printed two of the Moravians' most important publications. William Strahan, the firm's founder, on whose death eighteen months before that of La Trobe the business had passed to his son Andrew, had thought particularly well of La Trobe.[25] William Preston, an employee of long standing, was manager of the business.[26]

Moravian publications, 1771–89

As a result of the policy adopted by synod in 1764, Moravian publications had made by 1790 a significant contribution to the recovery of the Church's good name, those concerned with doctrine and missions proving invaluable.

La Trobe had been responsible for these publications; and subsequently his successors were urged to 'do everything in their power' to ensure that further new works continued to be introduced without delay.[27] The majority had first to be translated from the German, a very demanding task in itself. They were sold through booksellers, but Moravians in England knew from experience that personal contact, 'friendly intercourse', with other Christians was crucial in the establishment of a sympathetic audience for their works.[28] Publications

---

[22] *London Chronicle*, 30 Nov.–2 Dec. 1786.
[23] 29 Nov. 1816: C. I. La Trobe, *Journal of a visit to South Africa in 1815 and 1816 with some account of the mission settlements of the United Brethren, near the Cape of Good Hope*, London 1818, facsimile edn, Cape Town 1969, 392.
[24] J. G. Wollin to Br George Tranecker, London, 13 Dec. 1786, Moravian archive, Fulneck, Yorkshire, MS FU 86 TCMR. For later suspicions see Benham, *Memoirs of James Hutton*, 545–6.
[25] Hutton to Boswell, 29 June 1792, in *Correspondence of James Boswell*, 468.
[26] Cochrane, *Johnson's printer*, 208.
[27] Appointment of J. G. Wollin, successor to B. La Trobe as provincial helper, Mar. 1787: MCH, UEC, circular letters.
[28] [?] to Br Mathias, 30 July ?1788, MCH, copies of letters and reports, 1787–93 (reports to UEC).

were made available and promoted at the Brethren's chapels throughout the British Isles where attendance by other Christians must have been one of the most important links in the circulation chain.[29]

Two extended pamphlets were issued during the first half of the 1770s which, taken together, presented readers with a comprehensive account of the Moravian Church and its missions. The first, published in the form of a 'Letter to a friend' from La Trobe in 1771, was a *Succinct view* of how the missions were conducted, where they were situated and progress to date. Such extensive detail had not been available in print earlier. The pamphlet was advertised, it included a carefully worded appeal for support through the SFG for the missions and it was presented to 'friends'.[30] It is likely that it made its way into the hands of the future founders of the new missionary societies.

Those reading the work were left in no doubt of the Moravians' zeal for missions. No less than 160 missionaries were in the field, all, it was explained, volunteers, and the survey of missions, spanning islands and four continents, was in itself an impressive record of forty years of persistent endeavour. The number of converts in the Danish West Indies, said to be about 6,000, was a notable achievement, but that progress in the British Caribbean, in Antigua in particular, seemed problematical was not disguised.[31]

The second pamphlet issued during the 1770s was the *Concise historical account* of the Moravian Church and its constitution, the constitution being that of the post-Zinzendorfian Church. This work, with its preface signed by the respected Spangenberg, is a mine of carefully presented history and detail which describes the origin and development of the Church, and its beliefs and rituals. A survey of its establishments, presented by kingdom or nation, left readers in little doubt that the Moravian was an international Church.

La Trobe edited the English version of the *Historical account* to the main text of which he added a further preface and explanatory notes. He drew attention to the respect which Moravians had for all Christians as members of 'The Universal, or . . . catholic church of Christ'. Moravians prayed 'not only for mutual forbearance', but for unity and love between all denominations.[32] (When the *Historical account* appeared the doctrinal dispute over perfection between Calvinists and Wesleyans was raging and the protagonists were members of the same Church.) It was characteristic of Moravians that their British leader should also draw attention to the historic link between the Moravian and the Established Church. The Moravian, Lutheran and, it was stated, the Reformed (Calvinistic) Churches in Germany subscribed to

---

[29] For books and pamphlets published between 1760 and 1800, with full titles and listed by year of publication, see bibliography.
[30] MCH, SFG minutes, 12 Mar., 22 Apr. 1771.
[31] B. La Trobe, *Succinct view*, 8–22, 28–31.
[32] Spangenberg, *Historical account*, p. vi.

the Confession of Augsburg. Moravians 'esteemed' the Established Churches of England and Scotland as branches of the Reformed.[33]

The first substantial book to appear in Britain, after *The history of Greenland*, was the *Ancient and modern history* of the Moravian Church, also by David Cranz. References to John Wesley in the German edition, published in 1771, worried British Moravians; they counselled caution in what was to appear[34] and nine years elapsed before the English translation came out. In the event a short statement, without discussion, that the breach with Wesley forty years earlier was due to a disagreement over doctrine, and to his refusal to 'submit' to Moravian discipline, seems to have passed off without further incident. Wesley, perhaps, was mollified by being described as 'an eloquent man, and mighty in the scriptures, like *Apollos*' in the Acts of the Apostles.[35]

The *Ancient and modern history* was printed by the Strahans, to ensure quality of production,[36] and copies were 'distributed directly'. At the end of 1780 Moravians at Bedford claimed that this new work 'was a Treasure . . . which we have made good use of',[37] but it failed to gain the reputation eventually achieved by Cranz's *History of Greenland*. The *Critical Review*, for example, found it 'too circumstantial and tedious' for readers not 'personally' concerned with the Church's 'affairs'.[38]

Spangenberg's *Exposition of Christian doctrine as taught in the Protestant Church of the United Brethren*, was first published in 1779 in German, under the title *Idea fidei fratrum*. Also available in Danish, Swedish, Dutch and French, it made a good impression in Europe. It was published in Britain in 1784, immense pains having been taken with the translation to ensure that it did not lose the meaning of the German text.[39] It proved to be one of the Moravians' most influential publications and met with a favourable response from the beginning. Its aim, as Spangenberg explained in a preface, was to 'lay before the Public, in a free, clear and unaffected connection [the Moravians'] insight into the Gospel, which Paul calls the mystery of Christ'. As he further explained, Moravians themselves were convinced that it was still essential for them 'to make their mind publicly known, as the perverted tenets, which are charged upon them, are almost innumerable'.[40] The *Exposition* itself is nowhere an apologetic work; this was left to La Trobe who, as editor of the English edition, provided an invaluable preface.

As might be expected of Spangenberg, this work, of nearly 500 pages, has every appearance of being very learned. It was well received by the *Monthly*

---

[33] Ibid. 28, 36 nn. h, i.
[34] MCH, PHC, 27 May 1774; MCH, original letters (copies), A. C. Hassé, I, 216, 30 July 1774.
[35] Cranz, *Ancient and modern*, 227–8; Acts xviii. 24.
[36] MCH, [Fetter Lane] elders' conference minutes, 6 Nov. 1779.
[37] BRO, MO 355, 21 Nov., memorabilia, 1780.
[38] *Critical Review* liv (1780), 372.
[39] Spangenberg, *Exposition*, pp. vii–viii.
[40] Ibid. pp. iii–iv.

Review, which was 'happy to see' the Moravians 'rescued from unmerited obloquy',[41] and, more significantly, by Beilby Porteus, bishop of Chester. Porteus received his copy from La Trobe whom he invited to his house in Westminster for an evening's 'conversazione'. Dr Micheal Lort, prebend of St Paul's, was among the scholarly company present. It was 'something new', La Trobe commented to the Elders in Germany, 'that a Bishop of the Ch. of England is not ashamed to avow friendship for a Br.[other]'.[42]

During the 1780s two further works by Spangenberg were issued in England. They too bear the imprint of the man, authoritative and meticulous in detail and presentation. Each was concerned with how the missions were conducted (see chapter 6) and made no departure from previous missionary doctrine or a change in practice.[43] The first, his *Instructions* for missionaries, first published in 1785 only a year after the German edition, was a pamphlet of fifty-five pages. Its main purpose was to give Moravians at home a sound basis on which to assess for themselves their own conviction and suitability for service overseas. The second, *An account of the manner* in which the Moravians conducted their missions, was primarily an explanation of the Church's mission theology. This relatively substantial work of 110 pages was written for other Christians; new material was introduced and the discussion is more expansive than that in the *Instructions*.

A review of Spangenberg's latest work in the *Gentleman's Magazine* suggested that a considerable change for the better in the Moravians' reputation had occurred since the mission in Greenland was ridiculed in the same journal twenty-years earlier. 'Every one knows', the author claimed, 'the peculiar doctrine of the Moravians; but perhaps every one does not know the happy effect their arduous labours have had in civilizing barbarous and uncultivated people.' As for the Moravians themselves, they were 'mild and benevolent religionists'.[44]

Publications concerned with travel and exploration, foreign lands and peoples, were now being widely read by a public 'curious in voyages'.[45] This had an undoubted part in raising the level of awareness of Moravian missions and in restoring the Church's good name. Evidence for this can be assumed from the success of a major work by Thomas Pennant (1726–98), an internationally renowned naturalist and zoologist as well as a prolific, respected and a very popular travel-writer. Although he was not noted for being an especially religious man, Pennant's scholarly interest in the natural world explains why he concerned himself with the Moravians. One of his most notable and im-

---

41 *Monthly Review* lxxii (Jan.–June 1785), 350.
42 B. La Trobe to UEC, 1 Feb. 1785, UA, R.13. D.47.c. no. 494. Porteus' copy of *An exposition* is in his library: University of London Library, PTAZ Spa.
43 See p. 146 below. For publication see MCH, SFG minutes, June 1784, 6 Jan. 1789.
44 *Gentleman's Magazine* lix (1789), 932.
45 Paul Langford, *A polite and commercial people: England, 1727–83*, Oxford–New York 1992, 90–5.

mediately successful works was *Arctic zoology*. In the first volume, published in 1784,[46] Pennant went out of his way to praise the Moravians in his description of Labrador, and refuted one reason for comparing their approach to missions with that of the recently suppressed order of Jesuits. Citing Cranz's histories of the Church and of Greenland, for Pennant the Moravians were 'These pious people', who,

> like the Jesuits have penetrated almost into every part of the known world. They endeavour to humanize the savages of Greenland, and improve the morals of the soft inhabitants . . . of Bengal. They are not activated by ambition, political views, or avarice. Here my comparison with the once-potent order of the Roman Church fails.[47]

By 1790 a range of Moravian books and pamphlets were thus available of which any two presented a full account of the Church and its missions. Pennant's assessment, and the recent review in the *Gentleman's Magazine*, may also have reassured a public sceptical about missions in general, and still doubtful about the Moravians. Moravians were now being described in favourable terms by independent authorities who had no particular reason to be in sympathy with them on religious grounds. Moreover, their missions were being commended to a public that took an increasing interest in the world overseas. These developments were all part of the missionary awakening. Likewise, what was happening in the broadly Calvinist-inclined evangelical community in England: Spangenberg's *Exposition* of doctrine was being well received by those evangelical ministers of the Established and Protestant dissenting Churches who, in the 1790s, came to be associated with one or another of the new missionary societies, and Moravian doctrine and practice had come to be generally acceptable to that community. Shared beliefs and a network of relationships between evangelicals contributed to this outcome.

John Newton and his circle

Evangelicals tended to give priority to the essentials of their faith rather than to particulars. Newton and Haweis are well-known examples of an older generation of men who thought in this way, as was their friend and contemporary Henry Venn, Sr (1724–97), whose affectionate respect for the Moravians seems to have developed at around the same time and in a manner similar to Newton's.

Even a brief survey of a few of John Newton's connections illustrates the

---

[46] Ronald Paul Evans, 'The life and work of Thomas Pennant (1726–1798)', unpubl. PhD diss. Swansea 1993, i, 63, 66. Pennant exchanged samples with Erik Pontoppidan, 'A keen naturalist', ibid. 362.
[47] [Thomas Pennant], *Arctic zoology*, i, London 1784, pp. cxiv–cxcv; see also pp. clxxviii–clxxx for reference to Cranz, *History of Greenland*.

complex network of links between evangelicals. Newton was rector of St Mary Woolnoth in the City of London from 1780, but for the previous twelve years he had been curate at Olney, in Buckinghamshire. He owed his earlier position to Lord Dartmouth, through the good offices of Thomas Haweis,[48] and his living in the City for the rest of his life to John Thornton. His interest in the Moravians had begun in about 1773 while he was at Olney, a ride of about twelve miles from the Moravian settlement at Bedford, and had soon ripened into admiration. As early as 1774 Newton commended Moravian spirituality to his friend and confidant Joshua Symonds, then Baptist minister of the Old Meeting at Bedford, writing: 'If they have, notwithstanding, some little peculiarities, I apprehend very few of those societies which are ready to censure them, can exceed them in the real fruits of the Spirit.'[49] By 1780 he knew Moravians very well indeed. He was also on good terms with other Baptists in the Northamptonshire Association and he must surely have discussed the Moravians with John Ryland, Jr (1753–1825), son of the Baptist minister in Northampton. From the early 1770s an 'intimate and lasting friendship' developed between the two men.[50] Many years later John Ryland, Jr, was to be one of the founders of the Baptists' missionary society.

The part played by Moravian communities and especially by individual members of the Church in making lasting connections with other Christians cannot be stressed too strongly. Thus it was through the pious and hospitable Foster Barhams of Bedford, and the settlement in that town, that the initial interest of Newton and Venn in Moravian spirituality was stimulated. The Foster Barham family had itself been a remarkable prize for the Moravians in England. Joseph Foster Barham, Sr, and William Foster, his brother, were received into the Moravian Church in 1756 and subsequently settled in Bedford with their families. (Joseph had added Barham to his name on inheriting his portion of their mother's extensive plantations in Jamaica: it was at the brothers' request that the mission based on their estates in the island was launched in 1754.[51]) They were most respectable representatives of planter society in England. Educated at Eton, Joseph Foster Barham is said to have made the Grand Tour with Lord Dartmouth and Lord North, and before he joined the Moravians he was well known in polite evangelical society.[52] He maintained his connection with Church Evangelicals[53] and in 1785 withdrew from the Moravians on his marriage to Lady Hill, second wife of the late Sir Rowland Hill, father of the famous evangelical preacher of that name.[54]

---

48 Wood, *Haweis*, 91–102.
49 Newton to Joshua Symonds, 24 June 1774, in *Letters by the Rev. John Newton . . . including several never before published*, ed. Josiah Bull, London 1869, 174–5. For Symonds see H. G. Tibbutt, 'Joshua Symonds, diarist', *Bedfordshire Magazine* iv (1953–5), 338–42.
50 Hindmarsh, *Newton*, 143.
51 PA xxi (1854), 289, 12 Aug. 1753.
52 F. F. Foster Barham, *The Foster Barham genealogy*, London 1844, 15.
53 [Mrs] B. Carteret to the countess of Huntingdon, 4 Jan. 1777, CFWC, MS F1/374.
54 BRO, MO 360/2, 31 Jan. 1786.

Nevertheless, before his death four years later, he had ensured that his eldest son, also Joseph, kept up the family's support for the Moravian mission on its Jamaica estates.[55]

To Newton the Moravian Foster Barhams were 'perhaps' the happiest family he had ever encountered and, he recorded in 1773, when he only recently had met them, that it was one in which the 'love of God seemed to dwell in every heart'. Two years later he and his wife joined them at chapel for the first time.[56] The family became very much part of Newton's circle and he kept up his connection with them in London.

In 1777 Henry Venn, also a regular visitor, wrote in similar terms. A few years later, when he attended chapel at Bedford with John Thornton they were accompanied by Newton's friend Symonds and by two other 'ministers'.[57] On another occasion Venn's daughter participated in the Church's intimate meetings appropriate to her unmarried state.[58] A rare privilege indeed for a non-Moravian, it certainly met with her loving father's approval. His son John and Charles Simeon, both future founders of the CMS, would certainly have known of Henry Venn's respect for the Moravians. John Venn and Simeon, born in the same year, 1759, were firm friends from Cambridge days; when Simeon was about twenty-three he found in the elder Venn 'an instructor and a most bright example'.[59]

It was almost certainly also through the elder Foster Barham that La Trobe met Newton, although it was in London that this acquaintance grew into one which was to be cherished on both sides. In October 1779 Newton was in London preparing to take up his living in the City where, a month later, he intended to hear La Trobe 'if he preaches'.[60] La Trobe did preach at Fetter Lane on the Sunday in question and that evening 'remarkable accounts' were heard, 'concerning our Mission in the Nicobar Islands. An exhortation was added, warmly setting forth Christ Crucified'.[61] Following La Trobe's death in 1786 Newton was unstinting in his praise of the Moravian leader. He was 'a great man, a useful man, Oh! how he will be missed', Newton told his long-standing confidant, William Bull, but it was impertinent to question God's will for mankind.

'Mon cher ami Mons Taureau' of this[62] and other letters, William Bull, Independent minister of Newport Pagnell, was himself another 'good friend' of Moravians in nearby Bedford. The Church's hand-book of daily texts from the Scriptures, of which a new selection is published each year, was one of

---

[55] Joseph Foster Barham, Jr, to Wedderburn and Graham, 8 Sept. 1789, Barham papers, Bodleian Library, Oxford, MS Clarendon Dep. c.428, fos 1–3.
[56] *Letters by John Newton*, 209; BRO, MO 350, 7 Oct. 1775.
[57] Venn, *Life*, 254–9: BRO, MO 356, 13 Dec. 1781.
[58] BRO, MO 354, 12 Aug. 1779.
[59] Simeon quoted in Venn, *Life*, 345.
[60] Newton to William Bull, 26 Oct., 20 Nov. 1779, Bull papers, MS 3095, fos 61, 63.
[61] MCH, FLD-22, 21 Nov. 1779.
[62] Newton to Bull, 22 Dec. 1786, Bull papers, MS 3095, fos 198–9.

two works that he carried in his 'Pocket Library', and he was a keen student of Moravian literature.[63]

The same can be said of Newton who, on receiving a copy of Cranz's *History of Greenland* from Foster Barham, immediately began to read it. As this occurred in 1774,[64] it was at that critical moment when Newton's interest in the Moravians was beginning to ripen. Many years earlier his study of Rimius' accusations against them had made such a deep impression upon him that he resolved to hold fast to the doctrine of his Church.[65]

By the end of 1780 Newton had also read Cranz's newly published *Ancient and modern history* of the Church, but he was not impressed. In his opinion it displayed a serious lack of candour over past events, those described by Rimius for instance which, he thought, ought to have been explained. Newton made his views known in a characteristically forthright but constructive letter, almost certainly to La Trobe. He began by explaining that:

> Crantz's [sic.] History of Greenland had a marvellous efficacy some years before I knew you, in removing or softening my prejudices against a people of whom till that time I hardly heard anything but evil. Had his history of the Brethren, for which I thank you, found me under like prepossessions I do not think the perusal of it would have had the same favourable effect.

Newton acknowledge that the 'finger & work of God' had led the Moravians, so few in numbers, to establish their extensive missions, and that this and their dedication overseas, 'even unto death is well worthy of notice'. Turning to the *Ancient and modern history* of the Church, he said he found it too long, even worse that 'wrong matters we have often talked of' were described merely as 'misrepresentations' without 'specifying them', and finally that grave errors were not even briefly admitted. In the absence of a frank explanation, he warned, only personal acquaintance with Moravians, such as he had the 'pleasure of knowing', could alleviate 'almost immovable' prejudices against them.[66]

Newton's letter is notable for its advice, its stress on personal contact, his admission that the *History of Greenland* had contributed to a healing process in his generous mind and that it was their missions which made Moravians worthy of notice. They were fortunate in having such an open-minded and influential friend among other evangelicals.

La Trobe seems to have found Newton's provoking letter helpful, for three years later he gave him a translation of the *Exposition* 'to revise with a view to the diction', an amended entry in the diary baldly states. However, they were

---

63 BRO, MO 355, 30 June 1780. See also Josiah Bull, *Memorials of the Rev. William Bull, . . . compiled chiefly from his own letters, and those of his friends, Newton, Cowper and Thornton, 1738–1814*, 2nd edn, London 1865, 106.
64 I owe this information to Professor Bruce Hindmarsh.
65 'John Newton's recorded reading, 1725–56', in Hindmarsh, *Newton*, 335.
66 Newton to [?] B. La Trobe, 23 Dec. 1780, extract, copy, MCH, folder B, A 3.

'very hearty together'.⁶⁷ Newton, whose evangelical Calvinism gave priority to 'new birth' over particulars,⁶⁸ could be counted on as being broadly in sympathy with the Moravians' interpretation of the Scriptures as the way to salvation.

La Trobe's preface to the *Exposition* went to the heart of Newton's earlier criticism, the Church's failure to admit errors. Many leading Christians, to be sure, expected to find in this latest work an *apologia* from the Moravian Church for what had seemed to them in the past to have been a dangerous departure from sound doctrine. Such expectations were met, but only in La Trobe's preface in which the Moravians distanced themselves, publicly, from some of Zinzendorf's works and striking imagery. These were described as 'transient private opinions', having no part in the Church's beliefs. Moravians did not take his teaching 'as their standard of doctrine' and, the preface continued, 'the Bible alone is their standard of truth.'⁶⁹ This was an unexceptionable statement in itself. Moreover, it was now twenty years since the Moravian Church had rejected past excesses in word and deed. This was now evident to all who knew them from the utmost decorum with which its members conducted themselves.

Christians, for whom the essentials of Christianity had assumed transcendent importance, found in the *Exposition* confirmation of the orthodox nature of Moravian doctrine. For example, in a passage taken from 'Of the Church of Christ', one of the most substantial chapters in the *Exposition*, Spangenberg concludes that 'the greatest consequence' of the Reformation, was that

> all the reformers unanimously, and with zeal and energy, urged and inculcated the fundamental doctrines of the holy Scripture; namely, All men are sinners, and cannot deliver themselves from this wretched condition: Jesus Christ is the one and only Helper and Saviour. . . . All men must be directed straitway to HIM: Nothing is of any avail but his blood of atonement: He that finds forgiveness of sins in the blood of Jesus, has life and salvation, and can live holily as a child of God.⁷⁰

By the end of 1785 Moravians in Britain had reason to be pleased with the reception afforded the *Exposition*. In London they claimed that other Christians 'not only admire the Orthodoxy of our doctrine, but reap benefits for their hearts from the practical manner [in] which it is set forth'. The Bedford Moravians reported that their good friend William Bull 'loves the Brethren

---

⁶⁷ MCH, FLD-24, 21 Nov. 1783. The Moravian minister Jan [John] Swertner accompanied La Trobe.
⁶⁸ Newton to Thomas Scott, the Bible commentator, 11 Aug., 17 Nov. 1775, in Bull, *Letters*, 253–66.
⁶⁹ Spangenberg, *Exposition*, pp. iv–vi.
⁷⁰ Ibid. 437.

& delights much in Brother Joseph's [Spangenberg's] book'.[71] From Ayr came news in 1790 that 'many Scotch Divines' had given both the *Exposition* and Spangenberg's *Account* of the missions a 'friendly reception'.[72]

Newton, in a reference to the *Exposition*, felt himself 'free to confess, that of all systems of divinity I am acquainted with, none seems in the main to accord more with my sentiments'.[73] His 'protégé' Richard Cecil (1748-1810), 'the most cultured and refined of all Evangelical leaders',[74] also found much that was truly agreeable to him and remarkable about the Moravians. 'The Moravians', Cecil at some point decided, 'seem to have very nearly hit on Christianity. They appear to have found out what sort of a thing it is – its quietness . . . patience – spirituality – heavenliness – and order.' His only qualification, that 'they want fire', was the opposite of their virtues. Cecil also studied their missionary works from which he concluded that all human beings were depraved, that 'the grace of God operates' universally upon them, and that 'a Christian minister has to deal with just the same sort of creatures as the Greenlander and the Indian, among civilized nations'.[75]

The *Exposition* and the founders of the Baptist and London missionary societies

Compared with Newton, who wore the Calvinistic cloak with which he clothed his evangelistic faith exceptionally lightly, the Baptist minister Andrew Fuller (1754–1815), maintained a 'strict Calvinist' interpretation of the Gospels.[76] Fuller's attitude towards the Moravians probably carried considerable weight. Not only was he the most prominent founder of the BMS, to which as its secretary he dedicated the rest of his life, he was also a widely respected, though self-taught, theologian. Some time before the society's formation he undoubtedly studied Spangenberg's *Exposition*.

Fuller and his fellow Baptist, John Ryland, both as crucial to the establishment of the BMS as they earlier had been to their Church's adoption of an evangelical form of Calvinism, were among a group of evangelical–Calvinistic ministers associated together in the *Evangelical Magazine*. First published in 1793, this influential periodical was aimed at all who held 'evangelical principles' of whom, it was estimated, there were more 'than three-hundred thousand Calvinists, and many others'. As befits its founders' avowedly interdenominational purpose, trustees and contributors were drawn

---

71 MCH, FLD-25, memorabilia, 1785; BRO, MO 360, 25 Mar. 1785.
72 MCH, SFG minutes, 12 Oct. 1790.
73 *Works of the Rev. John Newton*, vi, London 1808, 439.
74 Balleine, *Evangelical party*, 61.
75 *The works of Richard Cecil, MA, with a memoir of his life*, ed. Josiah Pratt, London 1838, ii. 568, 513–14.
76 Hindmarsh, *Newton*, 122–5.

from ministers in both the Established and Dissenting Churches.[77] It seems to have been important to these ministers that they could commend Spangenberg's *Exposition* of Moravian doctrine to their followers; moreover, articles in the magazine suggest that, in all probability, principals of the BMS and the LMS had been familiar with the Church's publications for many years before these two societies were established.

In the events leading up to the formation of the London Missionary Society, the *Evangelical Magazine* acted as midwife through its articles and exhortations. The magazine's founders and principal editors, John Eyre and Matthew Wilks, were deeply involved in the society from its beginnings.[78] Wilks, a Dissenter, was Presbyterian minister at Moorfields' Tabernacle, whilst Eyre, a clergyman in the Established Church, began his ministry as a curate to Richard Cecil; for a brief period before his death in 1803 he was secretary of the LMS.[79]

One of the journal's objects was to present 'a manly and impartial Review of Religious books' whose authors were 'wise and godly ministers, in the Established Church, and among the Dissenters'.[80] The two review articles discussed below appeared unsigned, a common practice, but it is likely that Thomas Haweis at least had a hand in the second. Haweis had been associated with the *Evangelical Magazine* from its launch; in November 1794 he is known to have reviewed Melville Horne's famous *Letters on missions*.[81]

The publication by the Moravians, in 1794, of George Henry Loskiel's *History* of their mission to the North American Indians led to an entirely favourable review. It was also the occasion for a passing reference to the *Exposition* by 'the venerable Spangenberg' and to the range of Moravian publications. Of these, it was claimed that 'Besides smaller pieces [presumably the pamphlets], ... Cranz's History of Greenland ... is in many hands', that the Moravians had 'never been deficient' in publishing their 'constitution' and 'history' and that they had been 'greatly misrepresented'.[82]

The reissue of the *Exposition* in 1796[83] was the opportunity for a full review article which appeared during the following year. It is understandable that Whitefield's name was notably absent from the opening passage in which 'misrepresentations and malignity' of Rimius and others were discounted. These, it was said, 'can no longer prejudice the candid against' the

---

[77] EM i (1793), quotations at p. 2; trustees and contributors appear on the frontispiece.
[78] Richard Lovett, *The history of the London Missionary Society, 1795–1895*, London 1899, i. 11–24.
[79] Ibid. i. 10–11, 13; EM i (1793), 1–4. For additional information on Eyre and Wilks see Geoffrey F. Nuttall, *The students of Trevecca College, 1768–91* (repr. from the *Transactions of the Honourable Society of Cymmrodorion* [1967], pt ii), Denby n.d., 259–65, 277.
[80] EM i (1793), 3.
[81] Wood, *Haweis*, 95, 191. Haweis's review of Horne's *Letters* appears in EM ii (1794), 476–8.
[82] EM iii (1795), 77.
[83] Spangenberg, *Exposition*, repr. Bath 1796.

Moravians. The thrust of the article, however, was that the Moravians should not be ignored on account of past excesses of enthusiasm or differences in doctrine over inessentials. Indeed, they were worthy of considerable respect, a view which had probably been representative of moderate Calvinistic thinking for some years past. One quotation is sufficient to confirm that the Church's doctrine was generally acceptable and that the preface, with its essential *apologia* by that 'worthy servant of our Saviour Mr Latrobe', was well judged. His 'candid' piece, the author explained, 'displays a mind fraught with the spirit of simplicity and truth; . . . manifesting the soundness of the doctrine of the Brethren in all the great essentials of divine truth'. The *Exposition* was highly commended as a work which should 'be read with edification by every body of true Christians throughout the world'.[84]

A reference to the Thirty-Nine Articles in this review is a further indication that Haweis, who prided himself in being something of a theologian,[85] rather than a Dissenter like Fuller, was its author.

Thomas Haweis and the Moravians

Haweis had an exceptionally long-standing and warm relationship with Moravians. It is likely that initial personal contact with them may have been as essential in his case as it had been for Newton. Unlike Fuller, Haweis belonged to that generation who were adults in the fifties when Rimius' prejudicial attacks first appeared. These, to be sure, were in his mind when, some time around 1760, he met Moravians at Oxford: first Hutton's brother-in-law, Abraham Brandt,[86] and then La Trobe. Haweis 'gained' from them, he recalled, 'a full Account of the Brethren & their proceedings who I could not but honor for their works' sake'.[87] Spelt 'Hawes', as it is pronounced, his name and that of his wife first appear in the SFG's minutes of 1781.[88]

In the same year, after a long illness from which he did not expect to recover, Haweis 'considered how I might do the most good'. He made a will in which he left his estate on the death of his wife, 'to Mr LaTrobe for the benefit of their [the Moravians'] Heathen Missions, so strongly was I prejudiced in favour of this desirable Work, and knew of no other denomination to whom I could as conscientiously commit what the Lord had given me'. Although Haweis subsequently altered his will, this was not because he had lost his admiration for the Moravians and their missions overseas.[89] He

---

84 EM v (1797), 348–9.
85 For Haweis's defence in 1801 of a Calvinistic interpretation of the Thirty-Nine Articles see Wood, *Haweis*, 231–2.
86 From December 1759 Abraham Brandt was frequently in Oxford: MCH, FLD-11.
87 Thomas Haweis, 'Autobiography', i, ML, MS B1176, fos 30–1.
88 MCH, SFG minutes, 16 Jan. 1781.
89 Haweis, 'Autobiography', fos 30–1.

referred to their example in glowing terms in May 1788 when he drafted a proposal for 'an Institution for a Mission among the Heathen Nations',[90] and he was to do so again and again both before and after the formation of the LMS.

It was not only their missions that attracted Haweis to the Moravians. For instance, he believed that their Church represented his ideal of the true or primitive Church of apostolic times.[91] In his *History of the rise, . . . and revival of the Church of Christ*, published in 1800, he also singled the Moravians out for exceptional praise: 'No name of professing Protestants in our day has displayed more fervent zeal for the Lamb of God, and the characteristic principles of Christianity, as connected with his blood-shedding for us, than the Moravian Brethren.'[92]

The origin of Haweis's own determination to be active himself in forwarding foreign missions seems to owe more than a little to the Moravians. It was the usual turn of events; he was sufficiently impressed by his first personal contacts with Moravians to make his own appreciation of the Church and its work overseas.

La Trobe's connections

The improvement in the Moravians' reputation was due to a significant degree to that network of personal relationships between evangelicals in which La Trobe's part was so apparent. The contribution made by his sympathetic personality and abilities as a preacher was of considerable importance.

It was not the Moravians' practice to draw attention to themselves, and least of all in matters concerned with pastoral care. Although not of La Trobe's choosing, it worked out differently for him, however, in 1777 in the case of the 'unfortunate' Dr Dodd. Dodd, a London society divine, had obtained money by forging Lord Chesterfield's signature for which he was sentenced to death. His fate became a *cause célèbre* which, as La Trobe himself acknowledged, resulted in the Moravian leader becoming something of a public figure. 'Never was any delinquent so much lamented by all ranks of people as this poor gentleman [Dodd]', the good Moravians in London believed. They may have exaggerated the depth of sympathy for Dodd, but his was a very public cause. Many of the Fetter Lane Brethren had added their names to a petition,[93] drafted, most probably, by their neighbour, Dr Johnson, who estimated that in all some 23,000 signatures were collected.[94]

La Trobe's constant attendance on Dodd at Newgate, as he prepared for

[90] Thomas Haweis, miscellaneous papers, ML, MSS 1961/2: Y839.
[91] Wood, *Haweis*, 224.
[92] Thomas Haweis, *An impartial and succinct history . . . of the Church of Christ*, iii, London 1800, 183.
[93] MCH, FLD-21, 27 June 1777.
[94] *Boswell's life of Johnson*, ed. G. B. Hill, New York n.d., iii. 137.

death, 'made me more public, although I absolutely protested'. La Trobe wrote his own account of his ministrations that led to Dodd dying a seemingly evangelical death and James Hutton presented their majesties at Kew with a copy, which they passed on to the bishop of Lichfield and others.[95] La Trobe's sympathies with the pious are illustrated by copies which he is known to have circulated personally: one reached the countess of Huntingdon and another he sent to Mary Bosanquet, an ardent Wesleyan lady who later married the saintly Fletcher of Madeley.[96]

La Trobe was an impressive and a persuasive preacher. For the sermon he preached in 1770 at ceremonies opening the Brethren's chapel at Northampton he chose St Paul's admonition to the Corinthians 'not to know anything among them, save Christ and Him crucified', the central tenet of Moravian doctrine. 'There were', the resident Moravian minister, Francis Okely, observed, 'at least three hundred persons within and without the chapel. All were still . . . whilst he [La Trobe] showed them the true object of all preaching and hearing with an energy and fullness not to be described.'[97]

1783 proved to be a memorable year for the Moravians. At its close the Fetter Lane diary drew attention to further 'proofs that enmity & prejudices have abated greatly among the religious'. La Trobe had received invitations 'to preach in several of Mr. John Wesley's chapels, in Lady Huntingdon's & by some dissenting ministers'. Only a 'want of time obliged' him to decline further opportunities.[98] It is testimony to La Trobe's reputation that he preached twice in the spacious Wesleyan chapel at Birmingham and that 'above 1000 people' came on the second occasion to hear him.[99]

There could now be no doubt of La Trobe's personal standing. It was a great compliment to all concerned that in February he preached a charity sermon at Fetter Lane, at the 'request of certain Gentlemen' who had recently formed a society to distribute Bibles 'among Soldiers & Sailors'. Described by the Moravians as 'A Society of Worthy and respectable Persons of the various Denominations',[100] this was the Naval and Military Bible Society, as it became known, founded in 1780 by two Wesleyans assisted by John Thornton. The names of well-known evangelicals can be found among those respectable gentlemen who later associated themselves with it.[101] The

---

95 Benham, *Memoirs of James Hutton*, 508–10.
96 It can safely be assumed that [Mrs] B. Carteret's undated note (CFWC MS, F1/1120) was to the countess. For Mary Bosanquet see R. E. Kerr, 'A letter from the Rev. Benjamin La Trobe to Miss Mary Bosanquet', *PWHS* xx (1935–6), 88–92.
97 [Francis Okely], *Supplement to the short sketch of the work carried on by the Moravian Church in Northampton . . . respecting the erection of the chapel . . .*, London–Aylesbury 1888, 8–9.
98 MCH, FLD-24, memorabilia 1783.
99 B. La Trobe to UEC, 22 July 1783, UA, R.13.D.47.c. no. 388.
100 MCH, FLD-24, 18 Feb., memorabilia, 1783.
101 *Memoirs of Mr George Cussons of London . . . extracted from his diary*, London 1819, 71–6; *Account of the Naval and Military Bible Society, from its institution in 1780 to Lady-Day 1804*, London 1804, 18–21.

event having been advertised in advance, 'the Auditory ... was Extraordinary numerous'. La Trobe took his text from Timothy, 'From a child thou hast known the holy scriptures' and the ensuing collection of some £23 'exceeded also our [the Moravians'] expectations'. Growing public support for good causes, and notably for Moravian missions, is also suggested by the collection, 'almost £20', made at Fetter Lane in January 1783 when the fiftieth anniversary of the Greenland mission was celebrated at the first heathen festival that year.[102]

A further tribute to La Trobe's reputation came in July of that year when, 'after some hearty interviews', he was 'chosen a member of a small Society consisting chiefly of clergymen of the Established church ... who preach our Saviour'. Soon to be known as the Eclectic Society, Newton, Cecil and some of their evangelical associates in London, all of whom were known to La Trobe,[103] had held their first meetings earlier in the year at the Castle and Falcon, a tavern in Aldersgate later made famous for its association with the origins of the LMS and CMS. La Trobe was soon 'much pleased and edified by the Conversation'.[104] By the time he joined it the Eclectic Society included amongst its members the clergymen Henry Forster and William Abdy and the sculptor John Bacon RA who, in addition to Newton, were to be among the founders and first directors of the Church Missionary Society. Cecil, too, was to be nominated as a director but he appears to have declined on grounds of ill health.[105]

The future founders of the Church Missionary Society

Botany Bay, 1786–92

Meetings of the Eclectic Society in the 1790s, at which missions to the heathen were the topic for discussion, led eventually to the formation of the CMS in association with William Wilberforce's Clapham Sect. However, the Eclectics almost certainly had turned their attention to ideas for missions overseas by the end of 1786,[106] the year in which they had been involved in finding a chaplain for Botany Bay. Prospects of an evangelical nature in the southern hemisphere seized John Newton's fertile mind and in due course serious consideration was given to a Moravian mission. At the same time links began to the forged between the Moravians and Wilberforce.

In August 1786 Pitt's administration announced a 'Plan' to transport

---

[102] MCH, FLD-24, 19 Jan. 1783.
[103] B. La Trobe to Br Henry (28th) Reuss, 30 Sept. 1783, UA, R.13.D.47.c. no. 403. The Revd Henry Foster and the Revd William Jarvis Adby are among those named.
[104] MCH, FLD-24, 20 Sept., Nov.–Dec. 1783.
[105] Hole, *Early history*, 38.
[106] Ibid. ch. i, esp. pp. 29–34. See also Michael Hennell, *John Venn and the Clapham Sect*, London 1958, 220–3, 229.

convicts to Botany Bay. A year had elapsed since Wilberforce's evangelical conversion and Newton's advice to him to be useful in public life. It was almost certainly owing to Wilberforce's influence with Pitt that provision was made in the 'Plan' for a chaplain to the penal colony. The Eclectics found a suitable candidate for this post in the Revd Richard Johnson who, following an interview with Captain Sir Charles Middleton (1726–1813), comptroller of the navy, received his commission in October that year.[107]

Middleton, later Lord Barham, a renowed naval administrator,[108] was party to the 'Plan' from the beginning. Pitt later told Wilberforce that he was 'the best man of business I know, but he will do anything for a Methodist'.[109] (To a man of Pitt's disposition a Methodist was anyone who said 'his prayers'.[110]) Middleton and his wife were dedicated evangelicals and he became a founding member of the CMS.[111] Moreover, since his first meeting with La Trobe in May 1785 he had been keenly interested in the Moravian missions and a generous supporter.[112] Wilberforce already knew the Middletons and he became an intimate of their circle.[113] He most probably first learnt of Moravian missions through them and Newton.

Botany Bay created much excitement among Church Evangelicals. Once Johnson received his appointment, Newton, it seems, was his principal mentor in England and correspondent for a period thereafter. The Eclectics anticipated that the appointment of their man would open the way for a missionary enterprise to the South Seas. Newton, for instance, wrote to Wilberforce in November of ' "the pleasing prospect of an opening for the propagation of the Gospel in the Southern Hemisphere" '.[114] This was just two days after a meeting on 13 November when the Eclectics had discussed 'the best method' of achieving this desirable end. Although invited to the meeting, the newly-appointed chaplain to Botany Bay did not appear.[115]

Newton, believing that the 'Gospel, sooner or later *must be* preached in the South Seas', had linked the Moravians' inspiring missionary zeal with Johnson taking 'glad tidings into the southern atmosphere. . . . Perhaps this is

---

[107] This discussion follows Neil K. Macintosh, *Richard Johnson: chaplain to the colony of New South Wales: his life and times, 1755–1827*, Sydney 1978, chs i–ii. Macintosh does not appear to have known of the link between Johnson and the Moravians.
[108] I. Lloyd Phillips, 'The evangelical administrator, Sir Charles Middleton at the Navy Board, 1778–90', unpubl. DPhil. diss. Oxford 1974.
[109] Ibid. 31, citing Robert I. Wilberforce and Samuel Wilberforce, *The life of William Wilberforce*, London 1838, ii. 212.
[110] Ibid. iii. 365.
[111] Hole, *Early history*, 622.
[112] B. La Trobe to Br Henry (28th) Reuss, 3 May 1785, UA, R.13.D.47.c. no. 507; MCH, SFG minutes, 3 May 1785.
[113] John Pollock, *Wilberforce*, London 1977, 17, 52–3.
[114] Newton to William Wilberforce, 15 Nov. 1786, in Robert I. Wilberforce and Samuel Wilberforce, *The correspondence of William Wilberforce*, i, London 1840, 15, cited in Macintosh, *Johnson*, 26.
[115] Hole, *Early history*, 6.

the time', he wrote, but Newton was not sure of his man.[116] To his doubts can be added the sheer practical question of what one man acting alone could reasonably be expected to achieve.

Did the Eclectics expect Johnson to be accompanied or joined by Moravian missionaries later? This suggestion is supported by what he told Moravians in London and his words add credence to the suspicion that he was to some extent 'press-ganged'. Moravians, unwittingly, seem to have been a reason for Johnson accepting the post overseas.

Early in December La Trobe was buried at Chelsea. Later that month Johnson, 'recommended by our friend Mr Newton', called 'several times' at Fetter Lane 'with a view to learn how our [Moravian] Missionaries proceed in preaching the Gospel to the heathen'. Johnson told the Moravians that he had 'hesitated for some time to accept his vocation', but on hearing that they were to send missionaries, 'he accepted the call without scruple'. On being informed 'by us' that he was mistaken, Johnson is reported as having replied: 'I go to Botany bay in hopes that the Brethren will soon send Missionaries after me and if this should be the case, I will receive them with open arms and look upon them as my Brethren.' 'He has repeatedly desired us', the note continues, 'to pray for him that he may be a blessing both to convicts and savages.' Discussion of his visits ends with the words: 'we were deeply sensible how much we had been deficient in our call in this respect, which caused deep bowedness before our Lord and Head'. This suggests that around the end of 1786 the Moravians were perhaps invited to consider sending missionaries to 'New Wales'.[117]

When the Church did receive a formal request to do so in 1789 it was signed by Middleton and Wilberforce, and they wished to know how they could 'promote so laudable [an] undertaking'. Johnson's duties as chaplain made it 'impossible for him to pay any attention to ye Heathen'.[118] The Church, however, had too many demands upon its scarce resources and this was to be the reason given to Wilberforce and Middleton for the proposal not being considered further.[119] Moravians in London continued to hear from Johnson; and in 1792 he wrote to the effect that, as much as he personally wished for their assistance, there was 'as yet no prospect of success' for their missionaries.[120]

It is now clear why the Revd Thomas Palmer, one of the 'Scottish Martyrs' transported, described Johnson, whom he met at Sydney, as 'a Moravian Methodist'.[121] Johnson himself seems to have been an early example of how

---

[116] Newton to Bull, 27 Oct. 1786, Bull papers, MS 3095, fos 196–7.
[117] MCH, FLD-26, 28–31 Dec. 1786.
[118] Memorandum (original) signed by Middleton and Wilberforce, London, 18 July 1789, UA, Beilagen zum Protokoll des Synodus II, 1789, R.2.B.48.e. no. 47.
[119] Protokoll des Synoclus, 1789, R.2.B.48.b.2, fo. 708.
[120] MCH, SFG minutes, 6 Nov. 1792.
[121] Thomas Palmer to the Revd T. Lindsey, 15 Sept. 1795, in *Historical records of New South Wales*, ed. F. M. Bladen, ii, Sydney 1893, 881.

Moravian influence affected men from other denominations who served abroad. He no doubt had the Moravians' recently published *Instructions* for missionaries with him in 1787 when he sailed with the first fleet. Middleton and Wilberforce thought sufficiently well of the Moravians that they wished to promote the services of their missionaries in the British world overseas.

Charles Grant and the Moravians in India

Whilst the Eclectics and Wilberforce were finding a chaplain for Botany Bay, Charles Grant in India was preparing a missionary proposal of his own. Newton and Wilberforce were among those to whom it was despatched in 1787 and it was read by Moravians in England the following year.[122]

From 1760 until 1787, when they began to withdraw their missionaries, Moravians themselves had focused considerable attention on the sub-continent,[123] and their experience with the East India Company was a portent of the difficulties which the new missionary societies were to encounter. Before he drew up his own missionary plan, Grant must have known that the Church had failed to obtain sanction from the Company to send missionaries to Bengal.

The connection between Grant and the Moravians began sometime around 1775 through Grant's friendship at Calcutta with one George Livius. Grant, whose religious conversion dates from this period, held a senior position within the government of Bengal. His circle of pious friends at Calcutta included John Shore, later Lord Teignmouth, and William Chambers, an interpreter at the Supreme Court. Chambers was an admirer of Schwartz, the Lutheran missionary, whom he had known in Madras.

Grant's intimate friendship with George Livius is well known,[124] but it has escaped notice that Livius was a pious man, attracted to the Moravians even before he left England. He was their 'good friend' when he sailed at the end of 1773 for India, with 'our hearty wishes'[125] and he became an outstandingly generous contributor to Moravian missions.[126] Two years after he returned to Britain in 1783 he married into the Foster Barham family and was soon received into their Church. He and his wife made their home at Bedford where Grant was among their visitors.[127]

More than a year before he left for India Livius discussed with Moravians

---

122 MCH, SFG minutes, 19 Aug. 1788.
123 A letter . . . concerning the missions . . . in the East Indies, MCH, archive material relating to Bristol, packet 4, circular, 7 Aug. 1787. See also Hamilton and Hamilton, *History of the Moravian Church*, 305–6.
124 For this and Grant's friends in the paragraph above see Ainslie T. Embree, *Charles Grant and British rule in India*, London 1962, 44–5; Henry Morris, *The life of Charles Grant*, London 1904, 43.
125 MCH, FLD-19, 1–20 Nov. 1773.
126 MCH, SFG minutes, 6 Aug. 1776, 28 Oct. 1777, 4 June 1782.
127 BRO, MO 365, 8 Aug. 1791. For George Livius himself see MO 361, 9 Sept. 1785, 26 Nov. 1786.

in London the prospect of his finding an opening for their missionaries in British Bengal.[128] A satisfactory outcome then seemed promising. Livius had in Edward Wheler, his brother-in-law, who had been chairman of the court in London and was now appointed to the council in Calcutta,[129] an influential connection with the Company.

In 1776 the Moravians prepared the way by stationing missionaries at Serampore, the Danish enclave surrounded by British territory, only fifteen miles up-river from Calcutta. About a year later heartening news reached London: Livius had offered the missionaries 'his country house near Calcutta for a mission settlement'; moreover, 'some of the principal people', who undoubtedly included Grant, would welcome their presence.[130]

The outlook in London, however, was not so promising. It was soon apparent that whether or not the Moravians obtained permission for their missionaries to go to Bengal would depend on the chairman of the court of EIC directors, George Wombwell MP, who was not likely to be well disposed. La Trobe learnt this from Richard Holt, deputy secretary to the Company. Holt thought well of the Moravians and their project, but he warned La Trobe that, without authorisation, their missionaries could be expelled from Bengal on the directors' orders as 'vagrants'. The fact that they were welcomed by 'gentlemen' in the country and might even be successful would not alter this.[131]

La Trobe's ensuing lobby of directors found them by no means personally opposed to the mission, but they deferred to Wombwell who was not in 'favour' of introducing 'sects' into the East Indies. 'Thus far have we proceeded', La Trobe concluded his second report, 'none see any reason to doubt its [petition] being granted, and yet we cannot say how it will go. . . . There is a vast difference in treating with the Ministry [cf. Labrador] & these Gentlemen. The Directors seem to know that they are petty Sovereigns and the Chairman Emperor among them'.[132] Nevertheless, in June 1778 a memorial was presented to the court seeking permission for three Moravians to 'proceed in one of the Company's ships bound to Bengal next year'. Their only purpose was stated to be the establishment of 'a protestant mission among the heathen in the neighbourhood of Calcutta' where 'Gentlemen' who had met the missionaries from Serampore were 'persuaded . . . of their usefulness', and, moreover, that it was they who had desired the Moravians to apply for a 'Licence'. A postcript to the document attempted to meet those objections that La Trobe had encountered. With reference to the Moravians being a 'sect', it was reaffirmed that they 'never interfere' with other Chris-

---

[128] MCH, SFG minutes, 24 Jan. 1772.
[129] Embree, *Grant*, 45.
[130] MCH, SFG minutes, 5 Aug. 1777.
[131] B. La Trobe to Johannes Loretz, 14 Jan. 1778, UA, R.13.D.47.c. no. 1.
[132] B. La Trobe to UEC, 16 June 1778, ibid. fo. 11. For George Wombwell MP see Namier and Brooke, *House of Commons, 1754–90*.

tians. As for 'vagrants', there could be no question of the missionaries being a liability; many were 'handicrafts men' who would support themselves, although 'never', of course, become traders.[133]

Despite these assurances, in March 1780 Moravians recorded with 'pain ... that all attempts for procuring a Passage to Bengal ... in one of the English Indiamen has been unsuccessful'.[134] A new opening, however, this time through a Danish trader, and the absence, apparently,[135] of a definitive veto from the Company at home, enabled the Church to station two missionaries at Patna for a period during the early 1780s. Nevertheless, in 1787, sometime after their withdrawal, the Church explained that they had 'little hopes' of being 'at full liberty to act as missionaries in that part of Bengal belonging to the English E. Company'.[136]

James La Trobe, Benjamin's half-brother, was one of the two Moravians at Patna. In 1784 he replied to enquiries from him about Charles Grant: 'Mr Grant is a Methodist, & has an excellent character', but they had not met, for he was up country when James passed through Calcutta. Grant 'frequently dines with Mr Livius' and often met John Grassman and Br Schmitt, the missionaries from Serampore.[137]

Grassman and his colleagues remained quietly at Serampore waiting in vain for an entry into the hearts of the heathen. According to his letters they also kept up 'a constant friendly intercourse' with the Revd David Brown, a Company chaplain who arrived at Calcutta in 1786.[138] Brown in fact contributed to Grant's missionary proposal before its despatch to England a year later. This was a modest proposal for one or two clergyman to go to Bengal and Bihar as missionaries. The governor-general's approval and the goodwill of the government at home, Grant thought, were absolutely essential and to put pressure upon them his plan was circulated widely, Wilberforce and Beilby Porteus, by now bishop of London, being among those to whom it was sent.[139] Neglect, however, was its fate at the hands of Church and State.

In 1790 Moravians in London recorded that: 'Mr Grant lately returned from the East Indies where he has shown much friendship to our Brethren, paid us a friendly visit, & was afterwards visited again. He has it much at

---

[133] James Hutton and B. La Trobe, memorial to the court of directors, 8 June 1778, BL, Oriental and India Office collection, miscellaneous letters received, E/1/62 pt 3, fos 317, 321; copies of the 1749 act and Labrador orders in council, ibid. fos 318–20.
[134] MCH, SFG minutes, 14 Mar. 1780.
[135] No reference to the memorial of 1778 appears in Oriental and India Office collection, MSS (photocopies), index to court minutes, 1774–85.
[136] MCH, 1787, remarkable occurences extracted from 'Weekly Leaves', 1768–1831.
[137] James to B. La Trobe, May 1784, manuscript extracts from Br James La Trobe's correspondence during his residence in the East Indies, Lucy Torode collection, Leominster.
[138] MCH, SFG minutes, 30 Mar. 1789. For Brown see Hole, *Early years*, 7–11.
[139] Morris, *Grant*, 107–14. See also Penelope S. E. Carson, ' "Soldiers of Christ": evangelicals and India, 1784–1833', unpubl. PhD diss. London 1988, 39–47.

heart to promote the Gospel in the east Indies, under the countenance of the Government.'[140]

Grant, India and frustration with the East India Company all went into the making of the CMS. But long before this Grant met Moravian missionaries in India with whom he discussed, no doubt, the Church's missionary methods. He surely also knew of the Moravians' failure to obtain the Company's approbation before he made his own proposal. Back at home, Moravians benefited from his goodwill.[141]

The course of the missionary awakening would have been different had Moravians succeeded in establishing a mission in British Bengal. Their departure from Serampore in 1792 was followed by William Carey's six frustrating years in Bengal. Krishna Pal, the Baptists' first convert, was not baptised until after Carey moved to Serampore in 1799 and formed with Joshua Marshman and William Ward the famous trio. Pal, they only 'found out' later, had been in Grassman's service for four years.[142]

The founders of the Baptist Missionary Society and Moravians in the Midlands

The formation at Kettering in 1792 of the Baptist Missionary Society is unimaginable without first William Carey, a pioneer of the modern British missionary movement, and then three other ministers in the Northamptonshire Association: John Sutcliff of Olney, the younger John Ryland of Northampton and Andrew Fuller of Kettering. These three men were in the forefront of the movement which caused Baptists in the south Midlands to embrace a more evangelical form of Calvinism; they were also Carey's mentors.[143] Sutcliff, for instance, assisted Carey between 1785 and 1787 in preparing himself for the ministry, Fuller was secretary of the BMS from the beginning until his death in 1815 and from around 1798 Ryland and Sutcliff prepared candidates for service overseas.[144] With the publication of Carey's *Enquiry into the obligations of Christians to use means for the conversion of the heathen* in May 1792 – before which time his influence had been limited to his immediate associates – it was apparent that the example of the Moravians had contributed to these Baptists deciding that their Church should play a part in overseas missions.

Baptist historians have noted the influence of Moravians upon Carey and

---

[140] MCH, FLD-27, Dec. 1790.
[141] For Grant's first recorded donation see MCH, SFG minutes, 23 Apr. 1793.
[142] AL, William Ward's journal, 1/2, entry for 15 Jan. 1801, MSS transcribed by E. Daniel Potts, 135.
[143] See, for instance, Michael A. G. Haykin, *One heart and one soul: John Sutcliff of Olney, his friends and his times*, Durham 1994, chs iv (Ryland), vii (Fuller), ix (Carey).
[144] George Smith, *The life of William Carey, shoemaker and missionary*, Everyman edn, London–New York n.d., chs i–iii, is the Baptist source for Carey used in this section.

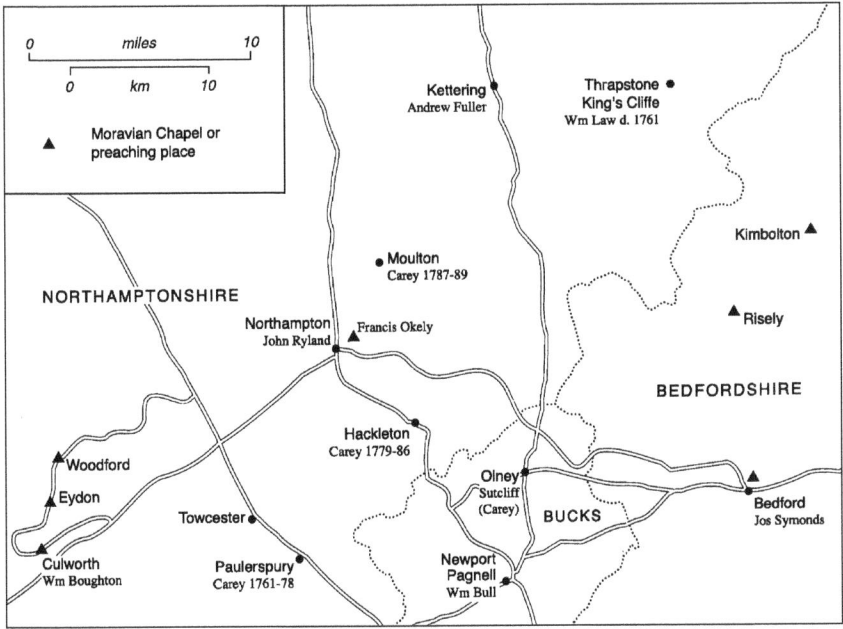

Map 1. The South Midlands: founders of the Baptist Missionary Society and the Moravians. Based on Carey's new map of England and Wales 1794, and old Ordnance Survey maps.

have urged that it is 'desirable that Carey's contacts with the Moravians be more closely investigated'.[145] How indeed did he and his mentors acquire their well-informed respect for Moravians and their missions? Part of the answer is almost certainly through John Newton, one the Calvinistic ministers not of their own denomination most highly esteemed by the Northamptonshire Baptists.[146] It is likely that they consulted him, but it has not been possible to prove this for the period before 1792.

There is, however, considerable evidence for direct contact between these Baptists and Moravians in the south Midlands. Although some of this is circumstantial, it is certain that from the early 1780s Baptists had ready access to Moravian sources. Bedfordshire lies within the wide area that was covered by the Northamptonshire Association of Baptists (see map 1). From about 1745 Moravians from their centre at Bedford had added their presence to the religious revival in the south Midlands. By the 1780s the community around Bedford had grown to some 180 souls. The Church was also very

---

[145] E. A. Payne, ' "William Carey, especially his missionary principles", by Dr A. H. Oussoren', BQ xii (1946–8), 166.
[146] Roger Hayden, 'Evangelical Calvinism among eighteenth-century British Baptists with particular reference to Bernard Foskett, Hugh and Caleb Evans and the Bristol Baptist Academy, 1690–1791', unpubl. PhD diss. Keele 1991, 345–55.

active in parts of Northamptonshire. When their chapel, with resident minister, was opened at Northampton in 1770, Moravians had well-established and thriving societies in villages to the south-west of the town where preaching places were licensed. From around the end of the century barns and rooms in private houses were replaced by newly built chapels.[147] Contact between Baptists and Moravians was thus inevitable.

Francis Okely had settled at Northampton by 1770 as Moravian minister. He was about seventy-five in 1794 when he died on a visit to Bedford. A former 'Cambridge Methodist', Okely was one of the leaders of the revival, most especially at Bedford. A scholarly man on whom William Law and the German mystics made a profound impression, a preacher of note and well known in evangelical circles, he also translated and published devotional works.[148]

In 1761 William Carey was born at Paulerspury into the Church of England, but at the age of eighteen in 1779 he was attending Dissenters' meetings in the vicinity of Hackleton where he was living and working as a cobbler's apprentice. In an autobiographical note written many years later in India, Carey thought that some of these meetings were conducted by followers of William Law, the mystic. These had a particular attraction for him. He also recalled that a decisive moment in his conversion occurred when at this time he read verses based on a work by William Law.[149] The author of these affecting pieces in *Seasonally alarming and . . . exhilarating TRUTHS*, published in 1774, was Francis Okely. Okely's purpose was to 'set forth Jesus Christ the *Crucified*' in the hope of 'leading all his fellow-sinners to the Selling All for this Most Excellent Treasure'.[150] His wishes were realised in Carey.

Perhaps while he was searching for that evangelical expression of faith, which he found among Dissenters, Carey had encountered followers of the Moravians rather than of Law. A glance at the map suggests that this is quite possible. Not only had Law, a recluse, died in 1761 near Thrapstone, but Okely discussed works by mystics with, among others, one Thomas Boughton of Culworth. His house was a licensed preaching place and he was the leading Moravian presence in Northamptonshire. Boughton, a layman, was also a

---

[147] *The Northampton group of Moravian chapels and preaching houses*, London–Aylesbury 1886. Although not included in this work, Towcester was on the itinerary from Bedford during the 1770s.
[148] Ibid. 8a–11. For Okely's spiritual odyssey see J. D. Walsh, 'The Cambridge Methodists', in P. Brooks (ed.), *Christian spirituality: essays in honour of Gordon Rupp*, London 1975, 252–83.
[149] For the identification of Okely as the author see Smith, *Carey*, 11.
[150] [Francis Okely], *Seasonally alarming and humiliating, animating and exhilarating truths respecting the nature of Christ's passion; . . . in a metrical version . . . from the works of . . . William Law*, London 1774, p. vii.

'respectable shoe manufacturer';[151] Carey, a cobbler's apprentice, may even have attended a Moravian meeting in the area. From around 1780 Moravians may also have contributed to Carey's precocious interest in the world overseas. He continued to live at Hackleton for the next five years, Okely was the most prominent of the Moravians who made regular preaching tours in the vicinity, but the brethren also came from Bedford and during their visits often lodged with Boughton at Culworth.[152]

When John Ryland baptised William Carey in 1783 in the river Nene, at Northampton, he was in a position to fuel his apparent concern for the heathen overseas. Ryland had read the exemplary *Life* of David Brainerd, the missionary to North American Indians, now being commended to younger Baptists, and he was on friendly terms with Okely. According to Okely, a casual encounter in 1782 had led to the two ministers developing an 'amicable' relationship. Baptist and Moravian 'forgot all Differences of Opinion and fastened upon Essential Truth', when they 'Drank tea' together for the first time, and at Ryland's 'request' Okely read Brainerd's *Life*. This was the first of two key works by Jonathan Edwards, the New England divine, to have a catalytic effect on the Baptists' receptive minds. It was crucial for their future relationship with the Moravians that Okely did not disagree with it on 'some points', as Ryland had feared. Okely passed the test when they next met and discussed Edwards's classic of the revival. Compared to a 'Sense of Fall, and a Sense of Redemption . . . let other Non-Essentials be as they may', Okely reassured his Baptist friend. Brainerd, the Moravian wrote, was 'an extraordinary dear man out of the Calvinistic School'. By the end of 1782 the two ministers were exchanging 'a few long Billets upon this and that'.[153] It would seem, therefore, that the Northamptonshire Baptists' interest in the Moravian Church and its missions almost certainly began with Ryland. It is then quite likely that in due course Ryland passed on to Carey Moravian missionary works which were surely among those that Okely had given him to read.

In 1784 the Northamptonshire Baptists issued their 'Call' to rally their members, in particular, to join them in prayer for the ' "spread of the Gospel to the most distant parts of the world" '. The Baptists' 'Call' and prayer more generally had an immense influence on the missionary awakening.[154] It was also from around this time that Carey began to develop his missionary ideas. However, as these matured a period of uncertainty for him followed. This only began to be resolved from about 1788 when his three mentors encouraged him to complete a draft of his *Enquiry*. Even then a further three years

---

[151] Okely to Bull, 12 Oct. 1782, Bull papers, MS 3097, fo. 65. This quotation is from Boughton's obituary in the *Northampton Mercury*, 26 Apr. 1817; he died aged 97.
[152] For example, BRO, MO 352–5, 1777–80; MO 363, 13–18 June 1788, gives an unusually full account of a Moravian's tour.
[153] Okely to Bull, 9 Aug., 12 Oct., 26 Nov. 1782, Bull papers, MS 3097, fos 61–5.
[154] E. A. Payne, *The prayer call of 1784*, Edinburgh 1942, 6.

elapsed before Fuller, for one, was convinced that the Baptists should form a missionary society with the intention that they, themselves, would enter the mission field.[155]

Surely, as Fuller and his colleagues, now joined by Carey, pondered what was practical, the example of the Moravian Church weighed on their minds. Moreover, they could see within their own area that Moravians were people like themselves and mostly in humble circumstances. The subsequent appearance in January 1789 of Spangenberg's *Account of the . . . missions* was undoubtedly timely. In March the SFG 'Read . . . extracts of letters from Br. Okely at Northampton, in which he mentioned several testimonies from persons' who had read Spangenberg's authoritative work.[156] Unfortunately these reports have not survived, nor is it known what transpired a few weeks later when John Ryland called on the Moravian minister at Bedford, except that he was 'very friendly & expressed his regard for the Brethren'.[157]

When in November 1790 John Sutcliff paid a similar 'friendly visit' to Bedford the first number of the Moravians' influential *Periodical Accounts* of their missions was available.[158] A year later the final steps were taken which led to the formation in 1792 of the Particular Baptist Missionary Society, soon to be known as the BMS. Carey then, it is said, tabled copies of the *Periodical Accounts* at the meeting.[159] ' "See" ', he might well have said, ' "what Moravians are doing, and some of them are British like ourselves, and many are only artisans and poor!" '[160] Although these words are apocryphal, they remain as appropriate to what is known of the occasion as they were to the Baptists' circumstances. Their author, Pearce Carey, used his imagination, but 'never did he alter facts'.[161]

Whatever was actually said, the good relations that had developed earlier between Moravians and founders of the BMS were soon confirmed. In the course of 1793 Okely opened a subscription to the BMS and the society voted a gift of five guineas to the Moravians' SFG, 'merely as an expression of friendship . . . and fellowship'.[162]

Connections between the Moravians and the founders of the BMS can therefore be traced with some certainty. Moravians were very active in a part of the area covered by the Northamptonshire Baptist Association, a Moravian played an indirect but vital part in Carey's religious awakening, and beginning in 1782 friendly contacts developed between his mentors and Moravians. It is also reasonable to assume that Moravian literature was part of

---

[155] Stanley, *Baptist Missionary Society*, 9–11.
[156] MCH, SFG minutes, 3 Mar. 1789.
[157] BRO, MO 364, 4 Apr. 1789.
[158] BRO, MO 365, 15 Nov. 1790. The first PA was published in March 1790.
[159] Payne, 'William Carey', 166.
[160] S. Pearce Carey, *William Carey DD*, London 1923, 90.
[161] E. A. Payne, 'Carey and his biographers', *BQ* xix (1961–2), 8–9.
[162] Donation recorded, 13 Mar. 1793, AL, cash account in BMS committee minutes I; quotation from minute, 12 Nov. 1793, ibid. See also *BPA* i (1800), 49–50.

the Baptists' missionary awakening, while later, personal contact and the evangelical faith they held in common with the Moravians surely helped Fuller and his closest colleagues, Ryland and Sutcliff, to realise that it was entirely practical for Baptists to establish their own foreign missions.

According to the testimony of Haweis, Newton and, in the case of the Baptists, Okely, personal contact seems to have created a situation in the 1770s and 1780s in which Moravians came to be seen in a more favourable light. Their books, pamphlets too, and perhaps most of all Spangenberg's *Exposition* had contributed to the recovery of their good name. Moravians could no longer be dismissed as dangerous enthusiasts and their spirituality, in association with an orthodox expression of evangelical faith, attracted the attention of a growing body of like-minded Calvinists. Though few in numbers, they had an effective presence in England, ably led by their British-born leader, Benjamin La Trobe, and 'moved easily between denominations'. Well before the 1790s, Haweis and Newton were each advocates of Moravian missions and there can be no doubt that Carey's mentors, Ryland and Sutcliff, were on friendly terms with Moravians. Thus firm links between each of the nascent missionary societies and the Moravian Church were in place. As the pace of the missionary awakening accelerated the example of the Moravian Church added a real and practical force to that sense of guilt felt by evangelicals and inner compulsion that they ought to do something for the conversion of heathens to Christianity.

4

Bishops in England and Moravians in the West Indies

That the mission to slaves in the West Indies contributed more than any other to the prominence which the Moravians achieved in Britain was due not only to the evangelicals. Towards the end of the 1780s slavery became the cause around which the serious-minded and evangelicals of various denominations were to unite. What made Moravians of much wider interest was the realisation that they already had substantial and well-accepted missions to slaves in the West Indies. The example of these missions, and that on the British island of Antigua in particular, was praised by those who on one side sought reform and by those on the other who opposed it.

The Moravian example

As, during the eighteenth century, bishops of the Established Church became increasingly alarmed at the enormity of West Indian slavery, it was one of their number, rather than the Moravians themselves, who made the public aware of their missions in the West Indies and appreciated that they were showing a way forward. Bishops had long hoped for the conversion of the slaves, but they had been unable to bring it about. As the Society for the Propagation of the Gospel owned the Codrington estates in Barbados, expectations for its slaves were a particular focus of the bishops' attention and later frustration.

Leaders of Georgian Britain prided themselves in holding a patriarchal and a benevolent view of their obligations to society. Their belief in rank and obedience was supported by the Church's teaching. Concern for free peoples under the crown overseas was evident from the expansion of empire, in the discussion of the Labrador affair for instance, but anxiety for enslaved Africans at first manifested itself less powerfully. It was assumed that Africans, in their homelands, had been captured in war and British opinion accepted that in the colonies they were their masters' property. The Established Church also maintained that slavery was not contrary to Christian teaching. Even before these assumptions began to crumble, however, bishops were gravely perturbed by the implications of West Indian slavery, though their pious expressions of concern had little effect on Christians at home or overseas.

In 1783 Bishop Beilby Porteus began what was to develop into a personal campaign to have something practical done by his Church for the slaves.

Porteus believed that the Society for the Propagation of the Gospel should set an example on its plantations in Barbados. He was the first to suggest that proof of this being an entirely practicable proposition was to be found in Moravian missions in the Caribbean.

But what of his well-meaning predecessors? In 1727 Edmund Gibson, bishop of London, in a published letter told plantation owners that as 'Christian Masters' they had an obligation to do all in their power to 'enlarge the Kingdom of Christ'. Gibson acknowledged that fears for their property may have inhibited proprietors but assured them that baptism did not 'make the least alteration' to the slaves' status.[1] Despite this assurance, it was not long before he conceded that opposition from planters and City merchants made it inadvisable for missionaries to be sent to the West Indies.[2]

Then, in 1741, Bishop Wilson of Sodor and Man issued a prophetic warning. Wilson believed that the only 'righteous recompense' for enslaving Africans was to 'endeavour to bring them' to Christianity. He continued: 'And indeed, if this is not sincerely endeavoured, it will be very difficult to justify the trade of BUYING, TRANSPORTING, and SELLING them as beasts of burthen.' Having reminded those who forgot that 'THEY THEMSELVES HAVE A MASTER IN HEAVEN', Wilson called on all concerned to assist the Society for the Propagation of the Gospel in its work in Barbados. Wilson also assured planters who permitted their slaves to be converted that it was 'the best way to secure their fidelity'.[3] Perhaps this advice was based simply on the Christian doctrine of obedience to authority. Wilson, however, would have known from his Moravian friends that they already had independent evidence to this effect from a prominent Danish planter. Wilson admired the Moravians, he was impressed by their missions, and he greatly respected Zinzendorf for the visit that he had made to the West Indies in 1739.[4]

Nothing of consequence happened as a result of these pleas and warnings until, more than twenty years later, in 1766, Bishop Warburton of Gloucester delivered a challenging sermon before the Society for the Propagation of the Gospel. His statement that all mankind was rational and intended by nature to be 'free', and that the slaves were stolen from their homelands, introduced a new and a humanitarian dimension into the bishops' argument. Warburton believed that the cruel treatment and the neglect of the spiritual needs of the

---

[1] (Edmund, Gibson), *The bishop of London's letter to the masters and mistresses of families in the English plantations abroad; . . .* May 19, 1727, London 1727, 26–9.
[2] Gibson's advice to the Associates of Dr Bray, 5 Mar. 1734–5, HMC, *Manuscripts of the earl of Egmont, Viscount Perceval: diary of the first earl of Egmont (1730–47)*, II: 1734–8, London 1923, 157.
[3] Preface to 'The knowledge and practice of Christianity . . . essay towards an instruction for the Indians', in Thomas Wilson, *The works of . . . Thomas Wilson*, in *The life of . . . Thomas Wilson, D.D., lord bishop of Sodor and Man*, ed. C. Crutwell, Bath 1784, iii. 15–16, 23.
[4] Testimonial of John Carstens, St Thomas, 14 Feb. 1739, reproduced in *Acta Fratrum*, 52–3. For Wilson and the Moravians see Podmore, *Moravian Church*, 214.

slaves were 'a general scandal'. The society's Codrington estates, he reminded members, meant that they had an obligation to set an 'Example . . . to the Colonies at large'.[5]

A year later the Quaker Anthony Benezet attempted to open a new front when he respectfully urged the SPG to 'consider at least endeavouring to put a Stop' to the traffic in slaves. This drew from the society the answer that it could not condemn keeping slaves on scriptural grounds, and if it did so, their masters would become 'more suspicious and cruel', and even 'more unwilling' for them to 'learn Christianity'.[6]

This response was drafted, according to William Knox, the Moravians' friend, by Archbishop Secker with the assistance, in all probability, of Beilby Porteus, then his devoted chaplain.[7] It soon emerged that the SPG had abandoned whatever attempts it may have made in the past at evangelising among its own slaves in Barbados. The society, which by now had no confidence that they could be instructed in the Christian faith, did however order that their treatment should be improved.[8] In 1783, when it was announced that the Codrington estates had been leased, owing to their 'very unprosperous condition', the society had neither a missionary nor a schoolmaster on the island.[9]

That February Porteus, who had been raised to the bench of bishops, preached the SPG's annual charity sermon in London. His subject was 'the civilization & Conversion of the Negroes' in the West Indies. Porteus was well prepared. Discussions at home, correspondence with a 'gentleman' in the islands and study of the literature had convinced him that something had to be done; some half a million slaves 'were in a most deplorable Situation both Temporal and Spiritual'. Porteus also condemned the record of the SPG in Barbados. Its several hundred slaves were 'absolute Heathens . . . totally destitute of every Principle of Morality & Religion'.[10]

It is notable that Porteus' library included the Moravians' *Succinct view*; it was almost certainly he who marked passages concerning the conversion of slaves in the Danish West Indies and two in particular may have influenced his thinking. These were that 'many thousands' had been converted and that they were 'proof that a genuine reformation in principles and practices is always inseparable from true conversion, and the Proprietors . . . acknowledge

---

[5] William Warburton, 'A sermon preached before the incorporated Society for the Propagation of the Gospel . . . at their anniversary meeting . . .', 1766, in *Proceedings . . . Society for the Propagation of the Gospel*, London 1766, 26, 29.
[6] Benezet to SPG, 26 Apr. 1767, and SPG to Benezet, 3 Feb. 1768, Friends House Library, London, MS Box 5.22 (1) (copies).
[7] Knox to Lord Chancellor Thurlow, 26 May 1789, in 'The manuscripts of Captain H.V. Knox', in HMC, *Various collections*, 203. See also William Knox, *A letter from W. K. Esq. to W. Wilberforce, Esq.*, London 1790, 16–17.
[8] Bennet, *Bondsmen and bishops*, 90.
[9] (Reports), in *Proceedings . . . Society for the Propagation of the Gospel*, London 1783, 41, 61.
[10] Porteus notebooks (transcript), 11 Feb. 1783, Porteus papers, LPL, MS 2099, fos 57–9.

this to be the Fruit of the Gospel'. Baptised slaves made reliable workers, the second passage concluded.[11]

All this, so different from the SPG's experience, was to be reflected in Porteus' sermon. His theme was that slavery could be reformed, that laws were required for the protection of the slaves in the West Indies, and that these should include provision for religious instruction. That 'slavery' could cease one day, Porteus suggested, was 'far . . . from being a visionary idea'. He set to to 'confute the various objections that have been made to the conversion of the African slaves', adding in a footnote:

> That such a real and general conversion of the Negroes as is here proposed is no romantic project, but a thing perfectly practicable; and that it would be highly beneficial both to the slaves and their proprietors, is evident from the progress already made in this work by the Moravian missionaries.

Porteus backed up this statement with independent and first-hand evidence to confirm that conversions were real, numerous, and that the missionaries' work was encouraged by planters. He cited nearly 6,000 Moravian converts in the Danish islands and 'several hundreds' in Antigua. Porteus had received an assurance from Antigua that the slaves' conduct at worship was 'remarkably serious, attentive, devout, and edifying. And they so greatly surpass all other slaves in sobriety, diligence, quietness, fidelity and obedience, that the planters are anxious to have their Negroes put under the direction of the missionaries'.

Porteus' objective was to persuade the SPG to develop its estates in Barbados as a Christian model for the British West Indies. In the course of his sermon he announced that, in the event of the society accepting his ideas in principle, he would present proposals for what he thought should be done. These were submitted twelve months later by a colleague.[12]

Described in an article in the *Gentleman's Magazine* as an 'admirable discourse', it seemed at first as though Porteus' sermon was well received. The author of this article also endorsed his ideas that the society should set an example on its estates, and that a code should soon be introduced for 'the encouragement, the improvement, and the conversion of our own negroes'. It is a sign of the authority with which Porteus had spoken that readers were informed 'That a general conversion of the negroes is practicable, the success of the Moravian missionaries . . . has evinced.'

Discussion of the sermon in the *Gentleman's Magazine* opened with a pointed reference to the 'diabolical' slave trade, a trade which 'many serious

---

[11] B. La Trobe, *Succinct view*, 16–17, University of London Library, shelved 12 mo. B.P. 54. Although the pages are cropped, traces of Porteus' marking can still be discerned.

[12] Beilby Porteus, *A sermon preached before the incorporated Society for the Propagation of the Gospel . . . at their anniversary meeting . . . 1783*, London 1783, 29, 31 at pp. 29–30n. For further information, including Porteus' *Plan*, see McKelvie, 'Anglican interest', 174–296, 1000.

people, have thought . . . is alone sufficient to draw down, and to justify, the severest visitations of Heaven on this devoted kingdom'.[13] This observation illustrates a particular reason for that sense of national guilt already associated with the missionary awakening. The recent loss of the American colonies, only two years before Porteus' sermon, would surely have concentrated those eighteenth-century minds, with their strong belief in providence.

The belief in divine retribution was taken up in July 1783 by the *New Spiritual Magazine; or Evangelical Treasury* which chose Porteus' sermon as the subject of an article in its very first number. The authors considered that all aspects of slavery '[so] contrary to the laws of God and the dictates of humanity, has proved a main cause among others, of bringing down on this nation the judgements lately inflicted on it'. This new journal, a forerunner of the *Evangelical Magazine* launched a decade later, stated on its title page that it was produced by 'A real Society of Gospel Ministers', that is by evangelicals, on 'Moderate Calvinistical principles'. The article continues 'We are assured that the Lord Bishop of Chester [Porteus] . . . is indefatigable in his efforts to rescue the negroes in our West Indies.'[14] There was to be no doubt about this.

Over the next twelve months Porteus prepared his *Plan*. The auguries for its acceptance by the SPG were not altogether favourable, although it met with the approval of some of his colleagues on the bench, including the archbishop of Canterbury, the society's president, but others did not even agree that the conversion of the blacks was one of the SPG's objectives. Worse, Porteus suspected that lay members of the society, with interests in the West Indies, were 'adverse to any improvement in the situation of the Negroes'.[15] Present most probably in the original, 'education of the young Negroes' was at the centre of a later published version of his *Plan*.[16] When in 1784 the 'Barbados committee' of the society laid aside his proposal, its plea of 'Circumstances' was 'mere pretence', wrote an indignant Porteus who, in a private note, returned to the Moravians. 'Will anyone . . . assert', he demanded, that 'Civilization & Conversion' of the blacks on the SPG's estates 'is a thing in itself impractical? The Moravians have actually civilized & converted Thousands of them in the Island of Antigua, & they have done the same with the Greenlanders who are still more stupid than the Negroes.'[17]

Porteus had received further reliable information with which to reinforce his argument. He raised dramatically his estimate of the number of Moravian converts in Antigua from hundreds to 'several thousands' and added that the planters 'greatly encourage' the missionaries. This further testimony, coming as it did from a British island, was an answer to those interests within the SPG

---

[13] *Gentleman's Magazine* liii/2 (1783), 859–60.
[14] 14 July 1783: *New Spiritual Magazine* i (1783), 50.
[15] 19 Mar. 1784: Porteus papers, MS 2099, fos 82–5.
[16] Beilby Porteus, *An essay towards a plan*, London 1789, 11.
[17] 1784: Porteus papers, MS 2099, fo. 92.

whom Porteus believed were responsible for the rejection of his proposal. A frustrated Porteus considered these facts so telling that they appeared in a revised edition of his SPG sermon, published in 1784.[18]

Porteus turned to the example of the Moravians for evidence that conversion of the slaves and reform of slavery were not a chimera. Without their example he could only have repeated the pious aspirations of his predecessors. He also went out of his way to link the planters' interests directly with his belief that Moravian missionaries were making real converts to Christianity. His confidence was not misplaced. At the same time it could be said that, by referring to the progress being made by Moravians in the West Indies, a bishop of the Established Church was attempting to shame its members into action. Moreover, for Porteus 1783 was only a beginning; advanced to the see of London in 1787, he then resumed his crusade, but no longer alone, and continued to give prominence to the Moravians and their missions.

The development of doctrine

Long before Porteus preached his sermon Moravians had adapted their doctrine of mission and built themselves into West Indian slave society.

Their missions to the islands had begun in 1732 when the first missionaries to leave Herrnhut reached the Danish West Indies. These men sailed without definite instructions. By 1756, when the work was extended to Antigua, the Church had established its doctrine of mission and introduced regulations which took into account the particular circumstances of the slaves. Without these developments Moravians could not have made the many thousands of converts which were to make such an impression on Porteus. Indeed, at one time it seemed very unlikely that this could happen.

The problem was Zinzendorf's 'First fruits idea', a doctrine which he introduced around 1740, based on his conviction that only a very select number of potential true converts to Christianity existed among the heathen. Zinzendorf always had a horror of mass conversions and his millenarian belief that the time of the heathen had not yet come was but part of his eclectic thinking.[19] The degree to which his restrictive 'idea' was taken up in the Danish island of St Thomas, in the Caribbean, brought that seminal mission close to collapse. It was crucial for the future of Moravian missions that the issue be resolved.

In 1749 the application of Zinzendorf's 'idea' in the West Indies ceased and a formal change in doctrine took place. Regulations for the conduct of the mission were also introduced. The result of these decisions was so signifi-

---

18 Beilby Porteus, *A sermon preached before the incorporated Society for the Propagation of the Gospel . . . at their anniversary meeting . . . 1783*, London 1783, rev. 1784, 30n.
19 Schattschneider, ' "Souls for the Lamb" ', 68–78. For discussion of the 'idea' see ibid. 78–81.

cant and long lasting that they marked the effective beginning of the Moravian Church in the region. When Zinzendorf died in 1760 there were more than 3,000 converts and catechumens in the Danish islands alone.[20] Had his teaching prevailed, this significant number would have been inconceivable.

An official, but apparently frank, version of the story can be followed in the first account of the mission in the Danish islands, known as *Oldendorp's history*. Sometime around 1742 missionaries in St Thomas adopted Zinzendorf's 'First fruits idea'. They ceased evangelising and transferred all their efforts to their first and most promising converts. The missionaries, unwilling, apparently, to compromise in their search for the evident depth of religious conversion and faith that might have been expected of Moravians at home, 'nearly gave up the effort entirely, considering it almost impossible to establish a genuine Christian community'. They came to believe that blacks did not have the capacity to become true Christians, nor did circumstances allow it.

The dramatic effect of Zinzendorf's 'idea' on the mission's progress is clear: ninety converts were baptised in St Thomas in the year before its introduction, but over the next four years only ten baptisms occurred, and these were of the dying. The evidence of faith expected of candidates was too demanding, missionaries ceased visiting the plantations, slaves lost interest and in due course the missionaries themselves grew disheartened. It was as well that one of their number, Frederick Martin, refused to accept the interpretation which his colleagues placed on Zinzendorf's teaching. Martin, although not one of the very first pioneers, is considered by Moravian historians to have been a founder of their mission in the Caribbean. In 1747 he went back to Europe where he attended a synod at which the dispute was 'discussed in detail', and resolved.[21] His intervention seems to have been crucial. Synod instructed Johannes von Watteville, a bishop of the Church, Zinzendorf's son-in-law and a man of considerable influence, to make a visitation to the West Indies.[22]

Martin returned to the islands and, pending von Watteville's arrival, missionaries in St Thomas prepared candidates for baptism. Von Watteville's visitation of 1749 marked a new beginning. First he secured the missionaries' agreement to the proposition on which everything that followed hinged: 'to offer salvation only to a few first fruits among the heathen had no basis in the holy scriptures and was, therefore, false and harmful. The Saviour's command was universal, namely, to preach the gospel to all people and to baptize all

---

[20] Müller, *200 Jahre*, 355, gives a figure of 3,555 in 1761.
[21] For this and the previous paragraph see *Oldendorp's history*, 414–17, 433–42, quotations at pp. 438, 440. The synod of 1747 was held at Hernhaag in Germany. For Frederick Martin (1704–50) see PA xvi (1841), 323–33, 371–5
[22] For Johannes von Watteville [Johannes Langguth] (1718–88) see *BDEB* s.v.

those who embraced it without exception'.[23] This marked the formal abandonment of Zinzendorf's 'First fruits idea'. Von Watteville also introduced guidelines for the conduct of the mission. The effect of these on the missions' progress was almost as significant as the change in doctrine. Preaching to the slaves on plantations was resumed, regular communion revived and infant baptism was allowed for the first time. Rules were also introduced which took into account the realities of the Africans' enslavement and that it was impossible for them to have a stable family life. Issues resolved included those which arose from polygamy, the consequences of forced separation of couples whom missionaries had married, and the status of children born to converts out of wedlock. Baptism of these infants was permitted and a polygamous association prior to conversion was not to be a reason to withhold baptism from partners.[24]

During the visitation baptisms were performed at large impressive ceremonies, witnessed by leading members of the European community. A general awakening among slaves on all three Danish islands followed and a year later the missionaries had some 1,000 catechumens on their lists. Particular attention began to be given to children who were brought into the Moravian choir system, which was soon introduced at every level.[25]

Ten years later Bishop Nathanael Seidel, also on a visitation, seems to have been concerned that too much was still being expected of 'the poor slaves'. He advised the missionaries not to apply to the same degree those rigorous standards of discipline which were enforced among Moravian communities at home. He urged them to 'show much more patience' with back-sliders and 'compassion for the fallen'.[26]

The great and continuing increase in the number of baptisms following these visitations is explained by a retreat from Zinzendorf's 'idea' and by the Church coming to terms with the slaves' harsh circumstances. The missionaries seem to have been encouraged to make a more sympathetic allowance for these unfortunate people than they might have done for those who were free, in Greenland for instance. A reduction in what was expected of converts added impetus to the missions' progress.

But what of the qualitative effect of the new policies? Although written long after their introduction, an extract from a missionary's letter of 1813 gives an impression of the result in Antigua: 'I see more & more the differences. . . . If we would expect of a converted Negroe so conspicuous fruits, as we do of a true Brother and Sister at home, we would find ourselves very often disappointed.' Although most African Moravians were 'thoroughly converted', they had not felt, he explained, a similar 'deep experience of their

---

[23] *Oldendorp's history*, 445–6.
[24] Von Watteville's 'Visitation', ibid. 443–55.
[25] Ibid. 458, 477, 494.
[26] Ibid. 535.

sinfulness'.²⁷ This surely was a reference to that sense of new birth experienced by Moravians and other evangelicals raised in the Christian tradition. Earlier, another missionary noted that 'real awakenings are rare' among individual members of the congregation in Antigua.²⁸ These observations from the perspective of Europeans, however, did not preclude that final evidence of faith so dear to evangelicals known to Moravians as a 'happy' death or departure. One missionary wrote from Antigua that 'I have seen many departing happily out of this world',²⁹ and testimony to this effect also appears in *Oldendorp's history*.³⁰

The change in doctrine and regulations introduced by von Watteville in 1749 established the basic principles for the conduct of Moravian missions to the slaves. Later, when Spangenberg put a gloss on Zinzendorf's 'First fruits idea', he praised von Watteville's part in the resolution of what must have been a doctrinal dispute. 'From that time', Spangenberg explained in his *Account . . . of the missions*, 'the work was carried on with more alacrity, and more and more were added to those that were gained by the gospel'. Nevertheless, readers were informed, 'it must be presupposed that all and everyone in particular were to be carefully attended to by the brethren'.³¹

This assurance, linked to the missionaries' teaching, is a clue to why planters accepted Moravian missions. To what extent it was practical for 'all and everyone' among converts to be as closely supervised at all times, as Spangenberg cautiously implied, is open to conjecture. It must have depended on circumstances, particularly when a large mission was shorthanded. What is undeniable, however, is that Moravians were themselves a disciplined people and that the framework was in place. Over the long term Spangenberg's word can therefore be accepted.

The Herrnhut model in its entirety was rejected as being inappropriate for the West Indies, a settlement for the converted, for instance, being impractical. But Moravian practices for the care of souls and discipline were adopted. The choir system, 'speakings' and 'helpers' were mobilised in an attempt to ensure that all members of the congregations, and even potential catechumens, were 'carefully attended to'.

'Speakings' were those formal occasions when missionaries and their wives separately exercised pastoral care over individual men and women in a manner similar to that at home.³² In the West Indies a start was made with all those who wished to be considered candidates for baptism. Those who persevered experienced Moravian discipline from the beginning. For instance, on the completion of a series of 'speakings' a missionary reported that: 'There is a

---

[27] Lewis Stobwasser to C. I. La Trobe, 27 Apr. 1813, MCH, letters from Antigua.
[28] F. W. Bardill to C. I. La Trobe, 25 June 1798, ibid.
[29] Henry Tschirpe to C. I. La Trobe, 28 Nov. 1799, ibid.
[30] *Oldendorp's history*, 525.
[31] Spangenberg, *Account of the . . . missions*, 52–3.
[32] Idem, *Instructions*, nos 36–8 at pp. 30–3.

great desire for Holy baptism. . . . But we keep to our rule to administer this favour only to such that we have reason to believe will prosper to the joy of our Saviour.'[33] A conscientious conduct of these personal interviews was not only demanding, it left missionaries exhausted on a large mission.[34] As a result of the sheer necessity of having to deal patiently with back-sliders, some missionaries in Antigua became 'very cautious' before admitting new candidates for baptism or communion.[35] Their caution is understandable. Earlier, during the 1770s, missionaries were concerned that they may not have been able to screen candidates for baptism as carefully as they wished. On occasion as many as thirty to fifty baptisms were performed in a day.[36]

An independent assessment of the extent to which the Moravians apparently achieved their objectives appeared in the nineteenth century. It is found in an account by Joseph Sturge and a fellow Quaker of their visit to the West Indies in 1836–7. Sturge was well known as an exceptionally highly-principled Quaker politician. The two men reported at length on the Moravian mission in Antigua to which they estimated that 'nearly half the labouring population belongs . . . unless they forfeit their privileges by misconduct'.[37] Sturge and his companion attended a service at which they were impressed by the devout conduct and appearance of the large congregation. They also had the privilege of being allowed to observe at first hand

> the manner of exercising the discipline of the [Moravian] Church . . . which convinced us of real oversight is maintained . . . evenings in the week are set apart for the members to come to have 'a speaking' with the minister; . . . There is also, on each estate, a religious negro called a 'helper' who watches over members, and brings all delinquencies and disputes before the minister.

The Church's discipline, the Quakers concluded, was humane but respected.[38]

These observers had drawn attention to 'a religious negro called a "helper" '. Moravians had always enlisted the active assistance of the Church's lay members and nowhere was this more essential than overseas. Thus the missionaries' most 'faithful' converts were trained to be 'native helpers'. The missions in general could not have progressed without these men and women, and those in the West Indies were particularly dependent on them owing to the high rate of death and sickness among Europeans. Most of the 'helpers', the first of whom were appointed in 1738, were slaves living

---

33 This was the missionary George Schneller, writing from St Kitts, 23 Apr. 1791: BUL, Moravian congregation accounts.
34 Samuel Towle to C. I. La Trobe, 26 May 1794, MCH, letters from Antigua.
35 Henry Tschirpe and John Gunson to C. I. La Trobe, 26 June 1797, ibid.
36 E. W. Cröger, *Geschichte der erneuerten Brüderkirche*, iii, Gnadau 1854, 30.
37 Joseph Sturge and Thomas Harvey, *The West Indies in 1837: being the journal of a visit to Antigua, Montserat, Dominica, St Lucia, Barbados and Jamaica*, London 1838, 25, entry for 24 Nov. 1836 on Antigua.
38 Ibid. 18, 33, entries for 20, 28 Nov. 1836.

on plantations and some were skilled craftsmen or foremen, 'bombas', trusted by their masters. Their crucially important role is evident from the many references to them and their contribution in *Oldendorp's history*. They were responsible people with considerable influence among their own communities. The most spiritual and reliable were much more than intermediaries: they advised on the suitability of candidates for baptism and communion and, when the missionaries were short-handed, a frequent occurrence, they supervised the choirs. Some were also gifted evangelists.[39] 'Without these helpers they [the missionaries] could not take due care of so numerous congregations', the Elder, Johannes Loretz, reported in 1784 after his return from a visitation to the Danish islands where there were some thirty to forty 'helpers'.[40]

The majority of converts must have had a genuine desire to be and to remain members of a Moravian congregation, which meant to live within the Church's all-embracing system of discipline. This was usually exercised in public, with various levels of exclusion ending, finally, in expulsion as the last resort. A public display of discipline had more than one advantage. For instance, in 1755 when baptised slaves deserted a cruel master this was the opportunity for a missionary to explain Christian doctrine by example, taking his text from the Epistles: ' "Servants, be in subjection to your masters with all fear; not only to the good and gentle, but also to the froward." ' The whole congregation was told that, 'all those who adhere to the teachings of Jesus are there by duty-bound to endure all kinds of sufferings patiently, . . . to remain faithful to their masters . . . by running away [they] not only sinned against His holy ordinances, but they also brought shame on their entire religious community'.[41]

The majority of planters in the Danish islands, who originally had regarded the mission with suspicion and hostility, came to realise that that they could trust Moravians. Their confidence must have been reinforced in 1754 when missionaries warned officials as soon as they learnt of a plot by a large number of slaves in St Thomas to run away.[42] By 1764 missionaries were respected by planters and the conduct of their converts seems to have generally been considered exemplary. For example, in St Thomas the majority of slaves were being encouraged to receive religious instruction and they were given passes to attend chapel during the hours of curfew.

It is true that soon after the missions began the active support of a pious and prominent planter was secured in St Thomas. Further, there was a degree of backing from the government at home. Both were undoubtedly crucial. But it was results on the ground that mattered most. It was surely the mission-

---

[39] *Oldendorp's history*, 333, 418–19, 470, 541–50: homilies given by helpers appear at pp. 627–30.
[40] MCH, SFG minutes, 27 July 1784.
[41] *Oldendorp's history*, 494 (1 Peter ii. 18.)
[42] Ibid. 490.

aries' teaching and influence over their converts that enabled them to have *entrée*, as they now did, to the majority of estates.[43]

None of this would have been possible had the Moravian Church not found in the Scriptures justification for its acceptance of slavery as an institution. Moreover, the missionaries were instructed that as a general rule nothing good could come from interfering in relations between master and man. These aspects of the Church's doctrine and a deferential attitude towards the powers that be underpinned relationships within slave societies.

Teaching on slavery

Dedicated to the production of sugar in a plantation system and with inherently unstable and violent slave societies, the British and Danish islands in the Caribbean were governed by fear. Repressive laws and practices enabled small minorities of Europeans to dominate vastly superior numbers of slaves. Spangenberg and then Zinzendorf were made forcibly aware of these tensions during the later 1730s when they separately visited St Thomas. Each would also have heard at first hand of the traumatic experience of a major rebellion, earlier in the decade, in the neighbouring island of St John.[44]

It is against this background that Moravians learnt to accommodate themselves to the laws and customs of a slave society. Even before they were allowed to sail in 1732 from Copenhagen for St Thomas the first two missionaries had to accept that they would not be permitted, as they intended, to live as slaves.[45] They had to take their cue from Zinzendorf who, once the work was under way, consistently instructed them to obey the laws of the land, and warned them against giving offence by, for example, teaching slaves to read.[46]

Zinzendorf was almost certainly the first to make a definitive statement of the Moravians' teaching on slavery which did not change significantly when it was restated later by Spangenberg. In 1739, at the close of his brief, tumultuous visit to St Thomas, Zinzendorf had an address delivered to Moravian converts in the island. He was concerned that they remained true and that slaves did not seek baptism from false motives, such as in the expectation of gaining their freedom. He also disclosed his attitude to slavery. Zinzendorf seems to have accepted the truth of the curse of Ham. He admonished the blacks to be faithful to their masters, to be as diligent as though they were self-employed and to accept their status without question. 'You must know', he explained, that 'the Lord has made everything Himself – kings, masters, servant and slaves . . . everyone must gladly endure the state into which God

---

[43] Ibid. 557–8.
[44] Waldemar Westergaard, *The Danish West Indies under company rule, 1671–1754*, New York 1917, 121–78.
[45] *Oldendorp's history*, 272, 275–6.
[46] 'Instruction für die zu dem Samojeden gesandten Brüder 1736', in Zinzendorf, *Texte*, 40.

Plate 2. The Moravian mission station, Spring Gardens, at St John's, Antigua. Copper engraving from a watercolour by the missionary J. H. L. Stobwasser, reproduced by permission of the Unitätsarchiv, Herrnhut.

has placed him.' He also attempted to mitigate his stern message by suggesting some temporal consolation as well as hope of life in the next world: 'The blessed state of your souls does not make your bodies accordingly free, but it does remove all evil thoughts, . . . and everything which makes your condition of slavery burdensome.'[47]

After Zinzendorf's death there were a number of reasons why Moravians had to reconsider their acceptance of slavery. Plantations in the West Indies had been acquired by the Church over the preceding years, Spangenberg was uneasy that missionaries could be brutalised by the effect upon them of owning slaves[48] and there was the now sensitive matter of the public's perception. Further, it is likely that Quakers raised the pressing problem of slavery with Moravians in Pennsylvania where the two denominations were on excellent terms.[49]

In 1769 these issues came before the second of the reforming general

---

[47] Oldendorp's history, 363.
[48] Hamilton and Hamilton, History of the Moravian Church, 662 n. 79.
[49] For the Spangenberg–Benezet connection around 1755 see George S. Brookes, Friend Anthony Benezet, Philadelphia–London–Oxford 1937, 112.

synods. A minute suggests that the Church was concerned more by the consequences of owning slaves and plantations than by the rights and wrongs of slavery in principle. Moravians also feared that they might be suspected of using their property in the West Indies for financial gain, as their intentions in Labrador had been suspect in Britain. Synod gave particular attention to justifying the Church's ownership of estates in St Thomas and Jamaica, the amount of land on other islands not being considered sufficient to constitute plantations, and ruled that no harm could arise from the Church and missionaries owning small, well-managed plantations. 'A Plantation is in itself one of the most innocent and Natural Employments', similar to 'Husbandry in Europe', synod agreed. However, it was decreed that the only justification for the estates was as a means of support and security for the missions.

Missionaries kept slaves, 'according to the Custom' in the West Indies, and this was 'not thought wrong'. Their number, however, was to be no more than was essential for a mission's support and they were to be treated 'according to the rule of Paul' (a reference presumably to the precept, 'Masters render unto your servants that which is just and equal': Col. iv. 1). Nevertheless, the Church accepted that missionaries having oversight of slaves 'must . . . be sometimes severe with and suffer them to be punished'.[50] This should not come as a surprise. Moravians in North Carolina, for example, used to whip their children, white apprentices and slaves alike,[51] and similar practices certainly prevailed elsewhere. If need be, Moravians could resort to the New Testament, or to Spangenberg's *Exposition* to justify their use of 'corporal inflictions'.[52]

The 1769 directives concerning plantations and slave holding, although reviewed, were not revised during the remainder of the century, and were confirmed at a further synod in 1818.[53] Although troubled, the Moravian Church took a pragmatic view of its property in the West Indies; slaves and estates were necessary for the support of the missions. Moreover, slavery was neither contrary to Christian doctrine, nor to the laws of the land.

The most complete expression of Moravian teaching on slavery is found in Spangenberg's *Account of the . . . missions*. First issued in 1782, the appearance of the English translation of this work six years later coincided with abolition becoming a popular movement in Britain. Since 1774, when John Wesley first appealed to all true Christians to set slaves free,[54] most British evangelicals had come to believe that slavery was incompatible with

---

[50] For this and the paragraph above see MCH, general synod 1769, fo. 242. For further discussion on relations between masters and employees or slaves see Spangenberg, *Exposition*, 324–6.
[51] Susan M. Lenius, 'Slavery and the Moravian Church in North Carolina', unpubl. diss. Moravian College, Bethlehem, Penn. 1974, 99–100.
[52] Spangenberg, *Exposition*, 418.
[53] MCH, [general] synod 1818, paras 11–12 at pp. 276–7.
[54] John Wesley, *Thoughts upon slavery*, London 1774, 26.

Christianity.⁵⁵ The *New Spiritual Magazine* went further: it declared slavery 'contrary to the laws of God'.⁵⁶ This was not the Moravian interpretation of Scripture.

By the 1780s slavery was a matter of such international concern that an authoritative statement by the Moravian Church was surely required. There were its own members to consider in addition to the very people at home and overseas on whose goodwill its missions to slaves depended. It would have been inconceivable for the issue not to be addressed when Spangenberg prepared his closely argued missionary work for other Christians.

Spangenberg's acceptance of slavery as an institution was based on his interpretation of passages from the New Testament. In the belief that in apostolic times the majority of servants were slaves, he explained that 'no where' did the Apostles command owners to emancipate their slaves, citing the example of the runaway slave, Onesimus, whom Paul returned to his master. Moravians, Spangenberg explained, did not consider themselves justified in acting differently from 'the apostles of the Lord'.⁵⁷

Spangenberg not only stated his Church's doctrine, but also acknowledged the planters' genuine concern for their own security. In one of several passages in which he attempted to reassure them he wrote that:

> We will never omit diligently to set before the negroe slaves the doctrine which the apostles preached to servants. Servants in those days were almost universally slaves . . . it is of God, that one man is a master and another a slave, and that therefore they ought to acquiesce with the ways of God; nay, that their service, if done with faithfulness for the sake of Jesus, is looked upon as though they were serving our Lord Jesus Christ. This we have indeed done hitherto, and, God be praised, with good effect.⁵⁸

Nevertheless Spangenberg did allow himself to express sentiments of compassion for the slaves, 'under so hard a yoke, and under such bitter thraldom'.⁵⁹ By comparison, his *Instructions* to missionaries were brief and to the point. Two phrases are sufficient to illustrate this and the consistency with his previous work: slaves 'must be taught to be obedient to their masters', and learn to 'patiently submit' to their lot.⁶⁰ These statements were underwritten by the more general Moravian doctrine of respect for the powers that be and Spangenberg quoted St Paul's admonition: 'Let every soul be subject to higher powers.'⁶¹

Moravians taught converted slaves to respect authority at every level and

---

⁵⁵ Seymour Drescher, *Capitalism and antislavery: British mobilisation in a comparative perspective*, London 1986, 117.
⁵⁶ *New Spiritual Magazine* i (1783), 50.
⁵⁷ Spangenberg, *Account of the . . . missions*, 42–3. (For Onesimus see Philemon, 10–11.)
⁵⁸ Ibid. 42. Further assurances are given at p. 41.
⁵⁹ Ibid. 43.
⁶⁰ Spangenberg, *Instructions*, no. 56 at pp. 44–5
⁶¹ Ibid. (Romans xiii. 1). See also Spangenberg, *Account of the . . . missions*, 42.

to accept their situation in this world. These precepts would be repeated time and time again. In 1774 a *Litany for the use of the negroe congregations of the Brethren in the British dominions* was issued, in which prayers for all kings and princes, and for King George and the royal family are to be found. Guidance and protection was also sought for the 'dear Governors of the land wherein we dwell', so that all might live under these officials in peace, 'holiness and honesty'. The first in a series of invocations to address the particular circumstances of slave congregations was for 'those who are masters'. Pleas followed to 'make those that are servants faithful in all things, obedient to them that are their masters', that members would learn submission 'to every ordinance of man', and that their labour might be blessed. Finally, prayers were offered for the sanctity of marriage and for the safe delivery of children.[62]

Moravian teaching of respect for authority and subordination did not change and the missionaries' *Instructions* were not amended until 1836.[63] This continuity was reflected in some observations made in 1831 by a Captain J. F. Alexander FRGS whose account of his tour of the West Indies was published two years later, in the year that the British enacted emancipation. Alexander, a seasoned traveller and a former military man, accepted that emancipation would happen – granted gradually, he hoped. The conduct of Moravian missions in this and in all respects was much to his liking. He had the highest regard for Moravians, 'the best missionaries', whom he wished to see encouraged 'everywhere'. Their methods were 'judicious', whilst those of other denominations were 'quite the reverse'.[64] Missionaries from these other Churches needed to make an allowance 'for colonial customs' and endeavour to conciliate the proprietors. He censored, for example, a Presbyterian, a fellow Scot, for failing to teach slaves the 'duties of servants to masters' and 'to pray either for King . . . Governor, or any in authority'. Alexander concluded that this missionary compounded his errors by not coming to terms with a slave society. The man's righteous condemnation of planters' *mores*, which offended the whites, and his refusal to baptise bastards, which alienated the blacks,[65] dealt with what were difficult issues for many Christian missionaries in a manner quite unlike that of Moravians.

Moravian missionaries were indeed very discreet in expressing whatever personal views they may have held on slavery and how it was practised in the West Indies. The difference between them and other Protestant missionaries may first have come to light in the Danish islands where Royal Danish Lutheran missionaries had served since 1759. By the 1770s Moravians, it seems, were preferred. The Lutherans had been outspoken critics of the slave

---

[62] *Litany for the use of the negroe congregations of the Brethren in the British dominions*, printed for the SFG, London 1774, 7–11.
[63] Schattschneider, ' "Souls for the Lamb" ', 162.
[64] J. E. Alexander, *Transatlantic sketches: comprising visits to the most interesting scenes in North America and the West Indies*, London 1833, i. 106–7.
[65] Ibid. i. 103–5.

system[66] and the Danish government believed that there were civil advantages to be gained from the particular manner in which Moravians conducted their mission. In 1783, as part of a programme of reforms, a royal commission gave serious consideration to entrusting the slaves' education to the Moravians. The enquiry even suggested that it might be advisable for the Moravians to absorb the smaller Lutheran mission.[67]

The Moravian Church found slavery neither contrary in principle to the Scriptures nor incompatible with Christianity. In due course the majority of planters in the West Indies thus recognised that Moravian teaching supported rather than undermined slave societies. This was apparent first in the Danish islands and later in Antigua.

Moravians in Antigua, the 'gentry' and the 'better Sort'

The origin of the Moravian mission in Antigua is obscure, but what is certain is that it did not begin at the behest of absentee proprietors at home,[68] which is how the mission in Jamaica began. That mission, launched two years earlier, in 1754, arose from the urgent pleas of the pious brothers William Foster and Joseph Foster Barham, Sr, who, although resident in England, had inherited estates in the island. An extract from a letter of 1753 from Foster Barham to the Moravian evangelist John Cennick can be taken as representing the brothers' motives:

> I confess I am, and I hope ever shall be, uneasy in my mind, till some attempt is made for the enlightening of these poor souls – the negroes – in this part of the world [Jamaica], where Providence has cast my share of temporal blessings. . . . I cannot but persuade myself, that many good effects will arise from it.[69]

This rationale, with its hint that commercial benefits were among those anticipated, is to be found among other proprietors in Britain who later sought missionaries for their estates overseas.[70] Patronage from afar, however, did not assure missionaries of a welcome from managers in the West Indies where plantations were already notorious for absentee landlords. In 1815 the Moravian (Christian) Ignatius La Trobe, son of Benjamin La Trobe and by now secretary for nearly thirty years to the SFG in London, reviewed the attitude of planters towards his Church's missions. Of Antigua he wrote: 'In Antigua, some proprietors encouraged, & most of them were friendly to the

---

[66] Larsen, *Virgin Islands*, 85.
[67] Ibid. 93–4, 99.
[68] Nelson, 'Samuel Isles', 3–27. See also 'Retrospect of the mission . . . in Antigua', PA xxi (1853–6), 505–31.
[69] 'Retrospect of the mission . . . in Jamaica', ibid. 289n.
[70] Anne Claire Ince, 'Protestant missionary activity in five south Caribbean islands during slavery, 1765–1826', unpubl. DPhil. diss. Oxford 1984, 295.

cause & permitted their negroes to be instructed in the doctrines of Christianity.' Turning from the particular to the general he continued: 'I have heard it asserted by many of our missionaries in the islands . . ., that if only the *Proprietors* themselves lived on their Estates, the cause of religion would meet with more encouragement.'[71]

There is no doubting the justice of this observation; attempts made by some resident proprietors in Antigua to improve the management of their slaves were an important factor in the progress made by the mission during its formative years.

The Antigua mission began in 1756 when Samuel Isles, the British Moravian, arrived from the Danish islands where he had been serving. The shortage of missionaries was such that he began work with only his wife's assistance. They were later joined by other Moravians and in 1762 a chapel was built in St John's, the island's capital. The land for this well-chosen site was purchased by the Church so that the mission would have its own secure base which would not be dependent on a planter's goodwill. By the time of Isles's death in 1764 there were but thirty-six baptised converts, a number which had dwindled to fourteen five years later. Moravians attributed this lack of progress to a shortage of missionaries and the extreme poverty endured by them. There was some opposition from members of the white community, but this in itself was not sufficient to hold the mission back.[72]

When Isles had first arrived in Antigua George Thomas was governor and commander-in-chief of the Leeward Islands: earlier, as lieutenant-governor of Pennsylvania, he had shown himself well-disposed towards the Moravians.[73] Thus, when Isles presented his credentials, he was permitted to commence his work without further enquiry. As slaves were not allowed to assemble, Thomas advised him to find a proprietor who would permit him to preach on his plantation. This Isles succeeded in doing. For a period he lived on an estate owned by a William Dunbar who was himself anxious for his slaves' conversion. Dunbar made land available for a mission station, but events intervened which resulted in the chapel being situated in St John's. It was also during this period that Isles was befriended by the family of Nathaniel Gilbert, a leading member of the white community who, influenced by Wesley, also preached on the island from time to time.[74]

The Dunbars and Gilberts, like Thomas, were descended from some of Antigua's oldest families and principal proprietors. Until around 1775 some sixty-five such families owned all but a small proportion of this small island's

---

[71] C. I. La Trobe to Joseph Foster Barham, Jr, Sept. 1815, Barham papers, MS Clarendon Dep. c.378, bundle 1.
[72] For this and the preceding paragraph see Nelson, 'Samuel Isles', 3–27.
[73] G. H. Loskiel, *History of the mission of the United Brethren among the Indians in North America*, ii, trans., London 1794, 82. George Thomas (1718–74) was lieutenant-governor of Pennsylvania, 1738–47, and governor of the Leeward Islands, 1753–66.
[74] Nelson, 'Samuel Isles', 17–20. For Nathaniel Gilbert of Antigua (1721–74) see BDEB s.v.

intensively cultivated land and they dominated the colony's affairs. They were, in Richard Sheridan's word, the 'gentry' the majority of whom, even if not yet permanently resident in Britain, were nevertheless absent for prolonged periods.[75] Their estates were overseen by attorneys who were men of a similar background.

Thomas himself seems to have led the way in attempting to establish a rather more humane regime for the slaves; managers of his own estates were expected to care for their well-being.[76] In 1764 a pamphlet appeared in London which described the character of white society and the causes of 'irreligion' in the West Indies. This anonymous work, dedicated to Thomas as a token of 'unfeigned Esteem', may be regarded as referring to Antigua. The author believed that, as the islands had passed well beyond the pioneering phase, society was becoming a little more respectable. He claimed that 'not a few of our Planters . . . have mastered those domineering passions . . . [and] escaped the thousand Dangers that threaten those who live among slaves'. These men, among whom were the more responsible managers, tended to treat their slaves with 'proper Authority' and with 'Foreb[e]arance', thus gaining their loyalty.[77] They were the 'better Sort'. The author concluded that, compared with former times, the rather more civilised character of planter society gave grounds for optimism for the spread of religion which now, perhaps, could also be extended to slaves.[78] These observations, taken together with the idea of a 'better Sort', add a useful dimension to Sheridan's description of the gentry in Antigua.

Moravian Elders in Germany were well aware that progress in the West Indies was highly dependent on the goodwill of the planters, but in Antigua missionaries lost contact with these important men for a period. The mission was approaching its nadir in 1767 when one of the missionaries, acting on instructions, went out into the country from St John's and succeeded in meeting Francis Farley, one of the island's gentry, who gave permission for trial meetings to be held with his slaves on one of his estates. If successful the initiative could be extended to other properties under his control.[79] In the event there was no progress, but when he returned to the island from an overseas visit, Farley nevertheless commended the Moravians to other planters, notably to Samuel Martin, telling him that they 'preach a sound doctrine'.[80]

---

[75] Richard B. Sheridan, 'The rise of a colonial gentry: a case study of Antigua, 1730–75', *Economic History Review* 2nd ser. xiii (1960–1), appendix 1, pp. 355–7, 352–4.
[76] Walter Tullideph to Thomas, 8 Aug. 1745, 22 Sept. 1752, in Richard B. Sheridan, 'Letters from a sugar plantation in Antigua, 1739–58', *Agricultural History* xxxi (1957), 11, 23.
[77] *Discourse concerning the special causes of irreligion in the West Indies with the apparent symptoms of its decrease*, London [1764], 22–3.
[78] Ibid. 26–7, 35–6.
[79] William Balmforth to Johannes [von Watteville], 18 Nov. 1767, UA, R.15.D.b.15.a, no. 4. Francis Farley is identified in William Lister to Johannes, 17 Nov. 1767, ibid. no. 2.
[80] Balmforth to Watteville, 27 May 1770, ibid. no. 47. Farley's family had been in Antigua since 1688; he died c. 1780.

Farley and Martin were both leading proprietors in their own right and also acted as attorneys for others. They were intimate friends of long standing[81] and undoubtedly shared similar views on estate management. Their goodwill towards the Moravian mission was potentially very important indeed. In addition to owning some 500 slaves between them, it can reasonably be expected that they assisted missionaries in gaining access to twice that number on plantations for which they were attorneys. Farley, who was partner in an estate of more than 400 acres, with say 200 slaves, acted for a much larger property, having over 500 slaves.[82] Martin owned 600 acres with 300 slaves; but the substantial number of absentee proprietors for whom he acted has not been established.[83] It was, indeed, on Martin's estate that, after years of disappointment, the breakthrough occurred.

Born in Antigua in 1693, Samuel Martin in 1750 took over the family estate, Green Castle, some three miles from St John's where the mission station was situated, and turned it into a model sugar plantation. Renowned as the authority on plantation management, he received more requests from proprietors to oversee their estates than he could accept. Written for a younger generation of planters, his *Essay on plantership* made his principles, which were put into practice in Antigua by managers whom he had trained, known throughout the West Indies. Martin had also played a prominent part in the colony's affairs.

There seems indeed ample justification for the claim made by a lady from the Highlands that Martin was the 'loved & revered father of Antigua': visiting Green Castle in 1775, she found him to be 'high minded' and a 'considerate master'.[84] He taught in his *Essay* that blacks, being 'fellow creatures' created by God, 'ought to be treated . . . with humanity and benevolence'; moreover, their masters, if only from self-interest, should care for their well-being and set them a good example.[85] Martin was proud of his own record in this respect which, in his case, arose from more than the measures he took to be a successful and influential planter. He also was an intensely God-fearing man who at family prayers, he recalled, addressed the Deity with 'an awful countenance'.[86]

Although he saw himself as a Christian patriarch, it may not have been

---

[81] Samuel Martin to his son, Samuel, in England, 19 Aug. 1760, 25 Mar. 1761, letter books of Samuel Martin, ii, BL, MS Add. 41347, fos 51–2, 68.
[82] J. R. Ward, *British West Indian slavery, 1750–1834: the process of amelioration*, Oxford 1988, 63–6. Dr Ward kindly confirmed that Farley was attorney for Tudways through the 1760s and 1770s.
[83] For this and Martin generally see Richard B. Sheridan, 'Samuel Martin, innovating sugar planter on Antigua, 1750–76', *Agricultural History* xxxiv (1960), 128–37.
[84] [Mrs Shaw], *Journal of a lady of quality: being the narrative of a journal from Scotland to the West Indies, North Carolina, and Portugal, in the years 1774 to 1776*, ed. Evangeline Walker Andrews and Charles McLean Andrews, New Haven–London–Oxford 1934, 103, 262.
[85] Samuel Martin, *An essay on plantership: the seventh edition*, Antigua 1785, 1–4.
[86] Martin to his son Harry, *c.* 1770–1, letter books, v, MS Add. 41350, fo. 149.

until 1770 that Martin gave serious thought to the religious instruction of his younger slaves. He was on the lookout for a 'good young man' whose duties would include their religious teaching. Since he believed that the slaves could learn much through music, he wished them to be taught 'psalmody'.[87] Moravians, whom he met at this time, would certainly have supported the general idea.

The missionary who was to take advantage of the favourable disposition of Samuel Martin and Francis Farley was Peter Brown, a German-born Moravian who, together with his wife, had arrived in Antigua from Pennsylvania in 1769.[88] Moravians rightly attribute the development of the mission to this energetic and personable man who served on the island for twenty-one years until he retired, exhausted, in 1791.

At first Brown was so appalled by the mission's lack of progress, debts and the 'grinding' poverty all around him that had he not come at 'my Lord's bidding', as he wrote in May 1770, 'I should long since have quitted'.[89] Instead, he began to obtain entry onto plantations, sharing food with slaves in the fields and visiting them back in their quarters. He gained the confidence of both white and black communities and prospects for his mission soon changed dramatically for the better. At the end of 1771 the heart-warming news was circulated among congregations at home that: 'It seems as if after sowing in tears in Antigua for many years, that now a joyful Harvest is begun.' Brown had baptised his 'First fruit' on Farley's plantation,[90] meetings at Green Castle 'were quite filled with attentive hearers' and Martin himself was well disposed towards the mission.[91]

Had the missionaries displayed even a hint of the 'enthusiasm', which Martin thoroughly mistrusted, or expressed other than the most orthodox views on the rights of masters over their slaves, he would not have permitted them near Green Castle. Instead, the missionaries' visits were allowed to continue, but no longer under Martin's watchful eye. Sometime around the end of 1771 he sailed for England where he expected to end his days with his family.[92] His peace, however, was soon shattered by Lord Mansfield's judgement given in June 1772 in favour of James Somerset whose master had claimed the right to ship him back as a slave to Jamaica. Martin's shocked indignation at the effect of this ruling, and no doubt at the jubilation of the black community in London, was expressed in a letter to his eldest son, also Samuel, a member of parliament. Parliament, Martin urged, should have

---

[87] Martin to his son Samuel, 12 Apr. 1770, ibid. iii, MS Add. 41348, fos 109–10.
[88] Born 'Braun', he used the Anglicised version of his name in Antigua.
[89] 'Retrospect . . . Antigua', 511–12.
[90] Memorabilia and week 27, 1771, MCH, UEC minutes, 1770–4.
[91] 'Retrospect . . . Antigua', 513.
[92] Martin to [?], undated, letter books, v, MS Add. 41350, fo. 166.

'those people' deported to the islands with the intention of 'weaning them from the vilest idolatry . . . [and] restraining them from cruel behaviour'.[93]

Brown, in the meantime, reported that: 'The hour has at last struck for Antigua. . . . Oh what a fine congregation have we already on Col. Martin's plantation! We have thirty baptized, as many candidates for baptism, and about 150 hearers.'[94] By then he had been joined by Charles Shirmer who witnessed the 'great awakening on Martin's estates . . . the blessed consequences of which will ever be remembered'. The following year Shirmer left Antigua, but not before he saw 'Negroes flocking to the meetings from all quarters'.[95] An impressive nucleus of a much larger gathering was formed on Green Castle from where converts could walk to chapel at St John's and set an example to slaves who came on Sundays to market in the town.

By early June 1774 Martin was back in Antigua in good health, and 'no less thankful' to find that his slaves 'were in some measure reformed by an honest Moravian during my absence'.[96] It was important that he was satisfied by the missionaries' mode of teaching: 'I assure ye', he wrote to his daughter, 'the instructers [sic] of my Negroes have made such a reformation among them that delights my heart, and I shall continue the like Method of instruction without mystery or enthusiasm.'[97]

Brown's success on Green Castle should have given him much-needed confidence in the future of his mission. When he called on planters Martin's reputation and approbation surely assisted in opening up new opportunities. The right combination had at last come together to realise those heartfelt wishes so long expressed by bishops of the Established Church for the slaves' conversion. The prelude to making the model for the British of a mission to slaves in the West Indies began in Antigua on Green Castle, and was completed by Moravian missionaries working in the island.

In 1774, when news reached Europe from Brown that slaves came from sixty plantations to the chapel, which had been enlarged, the mission had some 1,500 catechumens.[98] The same year saw the beginning of the second mission station, situated in the south of the island where a pious planter was a particularly good friend.[99]

---

[93] Martin to Samuel, 10 July 1772, ibid. iii, MS Add. 41348, fos 153–4. For Samuel Martin, Jr (MP 1747–74) see Napier and Brooke, *The House of Commons, 1754–90*, 244. For the judgement and more see F. O. Shyllon, *Black slaves in Britain*, London–New York–Ibadan 1974, 108–10.

[94] 'Retrospect . . . Antigua', 513.

[95] Quotation from Charles Shirmer (1747–1827): extract from his 'course of life', Gracehill, Co. Antrim, [Moravian] Gracehill Diary, 22 June 1827, kindly copied by Mrs Rosalie White.

[96] Martin to the governor of North Carolina (his son Josiah), c. June/July 1774, letter book vi, MS Add. 41351, fo. 9.

[97] Martin to 'my dear daughter', 4 June 1774, ibid. fos 90–1.

[98] MCH, UEC 1770–4, minutes, week 16, 1774.

[99] 'Retrospect . . . Antigua', 514.

At St John's the need was now urgent for the mission to have its own cemetery where converts should be interred. Naturally the Moravians wished it to be located in the town, as near to the chapel and settlement as possible. The conduct of Christian funerals and the observance of Easter at a Moravian 'burial ground' were an essential part of both the Church's ritual and missionary methods. Converts could not possibly be allowed to continue with those customary obsequies found among the heathen.

Government officials in Antigua were almost certainly aware that the question of a cemetery in St John's for black people would raise contention among the town's whites. It was therefore a particular mark of the favour with which the island's leaders now regarded the mission that in 1775 the governor, Sir Ralph Payne, granted the Moravians permission to acquire land in St John's for that purpose. Payne, another of the island's landed gentry, like Thomas before him, also ensured that his slaves were well managed.[100] There were, nevertheless, objections to the cemetery which were not over-ruled until 1782 when the court in Antigua found in the Moravians' favour.[101] In the meantime the mission enjoyed the goodwill of Payne's successor, William Burt, also a West Indian proprietor and married to one of the Foster Barham sisters,[102] and continued to make good progress.

In 1782, the year before Porteus preached his missionary sermon in which he stressed the great progress being made by Moravians in the West Indies, missionaries in Antigua had around 3,000 'converts' in their care;[103] Moravian missions in the West Indies as whole, exactly fifty years since their launch, had more that 10,000 'converts', including catechumens.[104] The mission in Antigua, begun without British patronage from home, had initially made slow progress though not as a result of any considerable degree of opposition in the island. On the contrary, from the beginning some of the colony's most prominent resident proprietors, who included its governors, were well disposed. The Moravians' persistence, especially after the arrival of Peter Brown and with the encouragement of Francis Farley and Samuel Martin, meant that the mission was well established before the campaign at home against the slave trade forced planters onto the defensive. From 1788 this was a new factor tending to increase tension on the islands. At the same time the Moravian mission in Antigua was to play a small but nevertheless

---

[100] Ralph Payne, governor of Leeward Islands (1771–6). For his slaves see John J. Luffman, *A brief account of the island of Antigua: together with its customs and manners of its inhabitants, as well white as black, . . . in letters to a friend written in the years, 1786, 1787, 1788*, 2nd edn, London n.d. 124.
[101] MCH, 'Weekly Leaves', 1782, remarkable occurrences.
[102] William Mathew Burt was governor of the Leeward Islands 1776–81: BRO, MO 356, 7 Mar. 1781.
[103] According to Müller, *200 Jahre*, 355, the estimate from British islands for 1781 was 3,289. Progress on islands other than Antigua was negligible.
[104] Estimated total on British and Danish islands for 1781 was 10,328: ibid.

significant part in the early phase of the great debate on the slave trade which came to the fore in the late 1780s.

Porteus' contention that the conversion of the slaves at the hands of Moravian missionaries was in their masters' interest appears to have been justified. Moravians succeeded in building themselves into West Indian slave societies in a manner which gained the confidence of planters and the islands' governors. The Church's doctrine and methods enabled the missionaries to conduct their mission effectively among slaves, without alienating the masters. The missionaries' perception of their correct relationship with a slave society is evident from the loyal address that they presented to an incoming governor of the Leeward Islands in 1782: 'It was not our call to [inter]meddle in affairs of state. The particular duties of our profession will keep us much confined among the poor negroes, who will certainly become better servants and more useful members of society, as they receive the impression of the Gospel.'[105]

---

[105] *Antigua Gazette*, 3 Jan. 1782, cited in Oliver W. Furley, 'Moravian missionaries and slaves in the West Indies', *Caribbean Studies* v (1965), 15. Governor Thomas Shirely (1782–95) succeeded Burt who had died in 1781.

5

The 1788 Enquiry into the Slave Trade

From the late 1780s the issue of slavery, and the sense of almost national guilt which it engendered, quickened the pace of the missionary awakening. Public concern was not confined to the inhumane treatment of the slaves in the West Indies. It extended from the effects of an unrestrained and unregulated trade in slaves to the exploitation of 'Africa' itself. The notorious case of the slave ship *Zong* in 1783 did much to bring anti-slavery sentiments to the fore. Evangelicals in parliament and their followers in various denominations throughout the country were to play a leading part in a campaign to improve the lot of the slaves. In due course their efforts included promoting missions to blacks in Sierra Leone, as well as in the West Indies.

By the end of 1787 evangelicals and other serious-minded men and women had united with Quakers in leading a national campaign to persuade parliament to abolish the slave trade.[1] Its end, they expected, would force the masters to treat their slaves with humanity. Early in the following year William Pitt, prime minister since 1783, initiated a wide-ranging enquiry, at the highest level, into the trade. Conducted by a committee of the privy council, it took evidence from various witnesses who supported the claim made by Porteus in 1783 that the conversion of the slaves to Christianity was in the planters' interest. Converts, it was said, were apparently more moral and useful beings who could be treated better than other slaves. This encouraged the idea that the need to import slaves would gradually diminish. Continuance of the trade, however, was to be defended successfully on the grounds of broad economic and strategic considerations.[2]

The importance of the Moravian mission in Antigua will be apparent: evidence presented to the enquiry resulted in the Moravians being seen as the authority in the field. The example of their missions also encouraged leading men of the day in their belief that Christianity and civilisation could be extended not only to the slaves, but also to West Africa. The Moravians immediately began to receive more offers of assistance to establish new missions than they could accept.

Before turning to the enquiry itself it is necessary to introduce the British Moravian (Christian) Ignatius La Trobe and some leading abolitionists. It was La Trobe who successfully piloted his Church through the enquiry, and

---

[1] The London Meeting began its lobby in 1783: Roger Anstey, *The Atlantic slave trade and British abolition, 1760–1810*, repr. Aldershot 1992, 229–32.
[2] Ibid. 310–11.

his abilities and personality meant that its results for the Moravians were particularly favourable. This outcome could not have been predicted. There were moments when the Moravians' connections with abolitionists might, by association, have had an adverse effect on their missions in the West Indies.

(Christian) Ignatius La Trobe (1758–1836)

Ignatius La Trobe was well qualified to interpret the Moravian to the British world. Educated since his early teens by Moravians in Germany, where he remained and taught at their high school, he did not return to England until 1784. Elected a member of the SFG, he became its secretary three years later and in this capacity represented his Church and its missions to the British with considerable distinction for some forty-five years. Later, it was to him that founders of the new missionary societies turned for information and advice, while in the longer term he mobilised support in Britain for Moravian missions overseas.

Aged thirty in 1788 when the enquiry began, Ignatius was a most companionable man, a fine musician by any standard, and energetic in mind and body. He was also fortunate in having the benefit of his late father's 'very large circle of acquaintance'[3] who, significantly in this instance, included Bishop Porteus and Charles Middleton. Benjamin La Trobe's death in 1786 was preceded by his long illness at Teston, in Kent, where Middleton resided when in the country; it was from this period that Ignatius' long friendship and mutual confidence with Middleton had begun. Porteus meanwhile maintained his admiration for Moravian missions in the West Indies and his commitment to the reform of slavery soon had important consequences for Ignatius' future and for the Moravians' reputation.

When Ignatius La Trobe died in 1836 a Moravian wrote that:

> He was one of the few, whether viewed as a private man or as a public character. The Lord raised him up among us an eminent instrument for his work, particularly the spreading of the gospel among the Heathen. He preserved him in useful, & extensive activity, for an unusually long period of time.[4]

---

3   MCH, transactions with government, fo. 3, undated.
4   'Obituary' dated 6 May 1836 (photocopy from [Moravian] Fairfield congregation diary, Fairfield, Droylsden, Manchester, kindly supplied by Mrs Cooper). For Christian Ignatius La Trobe see *BDEB*, s.v. See also my article in Mason and Torode, *Three generations of the La Trobe*, 16–28.

James Ramsay, the Teston circle and the Moravians

In the course of his 1783 sermon before the SPG, Porteus disclosed that he was 'principally indebted' to the Revd James Ramsay (1733–89), who had served as a clergyman and doctor in the West Indies, for information on 'the state of the slaves'.[5] Although Porteus made it clear that slavery should be reformed, he was careful not to alienate the planters. Ramsay, on the other hand, was a pioneer abolitionist who first made his ideas known to the public in 1784 in two works published in England. His condemnation first of slavery, and then of the trade, deeply offended the planters overseas and proprietors and merchants at home.[6] Ramsay was also an important early influence on such leading abolitionists as Thomas Clarkson and Wilberforce:[7] Wilberforce almost certainly read his pamphlets before committing himself in 1787 to the abolition of the slave trade. Here again the evangelical Middletons provided the common link, this time between Ramsay, Wilberforce and Porteus. Porteus thought very highly indeed of the pious and cultured Lady Middleton and from 1786, by which time Ramsay was vicar of Teston, Wilberforce was a member of the Middletons' circle of evangelicals, known to Hannah More as the ' "Testonites" '.[8] It was evident from the beginning that Ramsay was familiar with Moravian missions in the West Indies.

When Ramsay returned to England from the West Indies in 1781 for the last time, he had experienced all aspects of slavery. In addition to his previous twenty years as clergyman and doctor in St Kitts, he had witnessed at first hand some of the worst horrors of the middle passage whilst serving, before his ordination in 1761, as a naval surgeon on a vessel commanded by Charles Middleton. On his return to England he was presented with the living at Teston, which was in the gift of a 'Mrs' Bouverie, the owner of Barham Court, with whom the Middletons lived when in Teston. And into that evangelical household, and also to Porteus, he introduced Benjamin La Trobe.[9]

But how did Ramsay himself become acquainted with La Trobe? Because the beginning of the Moravian mission in St Kitts had more or less coincided with Ramsay's departure for England, he first learnt of the Moravians from a mutual friend in the island. This was John Gardiner, a New Englander, who from 1768 until after the American revolution, was one of several 'high-calibre' lawyers practising in St Kitts where he and Ramsay became close friends. They were also political allies. Such was the controversy in which

---

5 Porteus, *A sermon*, 14n.
6 F. O. Shyllon, *James Ramsay: the unknown abolitionist*, Edinburgh 1977, 74.
7 Anstey, *Slave trade*, 248–51.
8 See Pollock, *Wilberforce*, 17, 49–52, for this and the paragraph below. See also Beilby Porteus, *A brief account of three favourite country residences*, London n.d. 4–16.
9 C. I. La Trobe, *Letters*, 18.

both men were embroiled[10] that there could be no question of Ramsay wishing to return to minister in that island again.

John Gardiner was another of those who, until they were acquainted with Moravians personally, were prejudiced against them. Before he left England in 1768 he had acted for John Wilkes, married a lady from Haverford West and practised on the Welsh circuit.[11] He therefore first gained his affectionate respect for the Moravians and their spirituality through the Moravian congregation and its minister at Haverford West.[12] By the time he sailed for the West Indies, he had become their 'hearty friend'. Indeed, before leaving he urged them to establish a mission in St Kitts with his assistance,[13] although a lack of resources meant that they were unable to take up his offer for some years. Later, when the first missionaries arrived in the island in 1777, Gardiner was their patron.[14]

Ramsay arrived back in England in that year, with no intention of returning to the West Indies. He planned to publish a book on slavery. Later in 1777 Benjamin La Trobe thanked Gardiner in a letter for 'introducing me to your worthy friend Mr Ramsay with whom I have had a couple of agreeable conversations'. Of Ramsay, Benjamin wrote: 'I feel his heart is humane and generous: He wishes much success to the missions; such characters are rare. I shall do my best to improve this agreeable acquaintance.' La Trobe expected that on his return to town Ramsay would, 'show me the book he has written about the negroes, and the methods to be pursued to make their state more bearable to themselves and more useful to Society'.[15]

Six months later Ramsay presented his bishop with a short 'Memorial', in manuscript, 'on the Conversion of the Slaves in the Sugar Colonies', 'suggesting motives for the improvement of the sugar Colonies particularly of the Slaves' whose rights as human beings were 'openly violated every day'. Ramsay had shown his plan to 'men of learning & piety in various ranks', and believed that 'the time approaches which will be favourable' for it to be brought 'to public notice'.[16] However, unable to obtain a living in England, Ramsay returned to the West Indies, this time as a naval chaplain, prudently leaving his 'book' unpublished. Benjamin La Trobe's description suggests that

---

[10] A. J. O'Shaughnessy, 'The politics of the Leeward Islands, 1763–83', unpubl. DPhil diss. Oxford 1987, 37. For Ramsay and Gardiner see ch. iv, esp. pp. 127–33.
[11] MCH, SFG minutes, 20, 22 Nov. 1768. For John Gardiner (1737–93) see *Dictionary of American biography*, s.v.
[12] MCH, Haverford West congregation diary, i, 16 Dec. 1767–6 June 1768. Pace O'Shaughnessy, 'The politics', 131, Gardiner was not yet the 'Unitarian' that he later became.
[13] MCH, SFG minutes, 20 Nov. 1768.
[14] 'Retrospect of the mission . . . in St Kitts for the past hundred years', *PA* xxx (1877), 227–8, 230, 236–7. For the complete account see pp. 225–67.
[15] B. La Trobe to John Gardiner, 18 Oct. 1777 (copy), MCH, letters from St Kitts.
[16] Memorial (signed James Ramsay, 18 Mar. 1778), suggesting motives for the improvement of the sugar colonies, LPL, Fulham papers, Leeward Islands, XX, fos 79–80.

it was an early draft of the first of his two 1784 works. This was some 200 pages long when printed.

In England once more in 1781 Ramsay brought with him letters for Benjamin La Trobe from missionary Gottwald in St Kitts. The link between Ramsay and Gottwald was to be of considerable importance for the Moravians during the slave trade enquiry. In 1786 Benjamin went to Teston with the express purpose of meeting Porteus who, according to Ignatius La Trobe, wished to discuss the slave trade. It was not to be for Benjamin was taken mortally ill on his arrival. From this period, however, his son, Ignatius, was frequently in the company of Ramsay and the Middletons.[17]

Ramsay's first publications and the Moravians

Ramsay's best-known work, his *Essay on the treatment and conversion of the African slaves in the sugar colonies*, was published in 1784 and was followed in the same year by his pamphlet, *An inquiry into the effects of putting a stop to the African slave trade and of granting liberty to the slaves in the British sugar colonies*. Moravian missions to the slaves are discussed in both works and at some length in the first. It was Porteus, apparently, who persuaded a reluctant Ramsay to publish the *Essay*.[18]

Although Ramsay stated in his *Essay* that his object was 'to get religion extended' to the slaves, he departed from the care which Porteus had taken to associate the conversion of the slaves with the planters' interests. Ramsay argued, for example, that slavery was uneconomic and, in a section entitled 'The obstacles that the Moravian missions have to struggle with',[19] that the tension naturally existing between master and slave inhibited the conversion of the slaves.

Ramsay was implicitly critical of the degree to which the Moravians, it seemed to him, compromised over slavery. He appears to have believed that the reason why they taught the slaves discipline and obedience was so that their owners 'may have no complaint against them [the slaves], while labouring to gain the *great point of general improvement*'.[20] Ramsay believed that, under these circumstances, slaves 'can acquire only an inferior kind of religion'. Nevertheless, such was the Moravian missionaries' 'success' (the word is Ramsay's) that he was forced to admit that it appeared 'to contradict my position that the present debased state of the slaves favours not religious improvement'.[21] In another section of his *Essay*, such a seemingly polemical

---

[17] C. I. La Trobe, *Letters*, 18–20.
[18] Thomas Clarkson, *The history of the rise, progress, and accomplishment of the abolition of the African slave-trade by the British parliament*, London 1808, i. 223–4.
[19] James Ramsay, *An essay on the treatment and conversion of the African slaves in the sugar colonies*, London 1784, 165. For the complete section see pp. 161–6.
[20] Ibid. 163. My emphasis.
[21] Ibid. 165–6.

statement as 'master and slave were natural enemies to each other',[22] was quite opposed to the Moravians' doctrine and potentially damaging to the planters' goodwill towards the missions.

There could be no doubt of Ramsay's purpose in his second publication, *An inquiry into putting a stop to the African slave trade*. In view of what he had written already, it may seem surprising that he found it necessary to revert to the Moravians once more. However, he wished to qualify, if not quite withdraw, his earlier doubts that missionaries, under the circumstances of slavery, could make real converts to Christianity. The Moravians' 'success', he now realised, was 'much more complete' than he had represented earlier. It was 'convincing proof that very considerable advances may be made among the negroes even in their present state'.[23] This revision in Ramsay's thinking was important. The position which he now adopted was similar to that of Porteus who did not believe that slavery in the West Indies and Christianity were incompatible.

Improvement or civilisation was central to the argument advanced by Porteus and Ramsay. They both appear to have been encouraged to adopt this stance by what they meant by the missionaries' 'success' in converting slaves to Christianity. Compared with Porteus, Ramsay may have placed even more emphasis on improvement. He found support in the example of Moravian missions for his argument against those who claimed that Africans were incapable of improvement. 'Is not all mankind as a species progressive', he asked in some notes, 'and have not various steps been gained even within living memory. . . . What were the Greenlanders before the Moravians missionaries went among them'?[24]

Ramsay's *Essay on the conversion of the African slaves*, followed by his advocacy of an end to the trade, enraged the planters. The very respectable circles in which he moved did not save him from being viciously attacked by the defenders of slavery and the trade. Compared to a bishop, Ramsay, a humble cleric, was a sitting duck. The planters had rather less reason to turn on Porteus who confined his efforts to securing the conversion of the slaves and reform and, moreover, long favoured gradual rather than immediate abolition of the trade.[25]

When Ramsay died in 1789 Porteus recorded in his diary that the 'obloquy' which he had aroused 'accelerated if not assisted his death'.[26] As 'poor' Ramsay wrote of himself two years earlier, 'I have long been considered as a

---

[22] Ibid. 173.
[23] Idem, *An inquiry into the effects of putting a stop to the African slave trade and of granting liberty to the slaves in the British sugar colonies*, London 1784, 9.
[24] Idem, manuscript (undated), James Ramsay papers, Rhodes House, Oxford, MSS Brit. Emp. S.2.
[25] In 1796 Porteus urged Wilberforce not to press for 'immediate' abolition: Anstey, *Slave trade*, 328. He himself moved to immediate abolition sometime before 1806: McKelvie, 'Anglican interest', 715.
[26] Porteus, diary, entry for 10 July 1789, Porteus papers, MS 2103, fo. 25.

marked man'.[27] The lesson would not have been lost on the Moravians. It seemed at one time quite possible that they would be associated in the minds of outraged planters with Ramsay and suspected of being dangerously well-informed supporters of abolition. This would have been particularly likely from the end of 1787 when the national campaign for abolition of the trade began to gather strength. Abolition became a very public cause and an intense political debate ensued.

Ignatius La Trobe and the beginning of the campaign against the slave trade

From early 1788 Ignatius La Trobe was frequently in the company of prominent abolitionists such as Ramsay. Indeed, he was personally in sympathy with their aims, although it was axiomatic that as a Moravian he should not meddle in politics. Inevitably the Moravians were drawn into the debate, but Ignatius' skilful handling of what was an issue fraught with danger for them resulted in the Church and its missions emerging with considerable credit.

The Middletons themselves were abolitionists. In 1788 Lady Middleton received what is now a famous token in recognition of being 'particularly forward in the business'. She was at the family's town house when Ramsay brought 'her a present from Mr Wedgwood, namely a bas-relief of a negro in a supplicating posture – with the inscription "Am I not a man & a brother" '.[28] Earlier it was at his wife's bidding in 1786 that Middleton wrote to Wilberforce urging him to take up the cause in parliament.[29] Ignatius was witness to both of these occasions.

Few of the Moravians' fellow evangelicals, if any, could have been other than abolitionists. Lady Middleton and 'Mrs' Bouverie both made donations in June 1787 when the Society for the Abolition of the Slave Trade was formed with the immediate object of promoting an enquiry by both houses of parliament 'into this inhuman traffick'. The wide appeal of its aims was immediately apparent although Francis Okely, the minister at Northampton, appears to have been the only well-known Moravian who overtly supported the abolition campaign when it was launched.[30] In 1787 the Northamptonshire Association of Baptist Ministers, having made its donation to the newly formed society, soon resolved to monitor events in parliament and ' "use all lawful means" ' to promote abolition.[31] A respectable

---

[27] Ramsay to Wilberforce, 1787, cited in Wilberforce, *Life*, i. 235.
[28] C. I. La Trobe, journal, entry for 31 Jan. 1788. Josiah Wedgwood (1730–95) was a founding member of the Abolition Society. Margaret Middleton died in 1792.
[29] C. I. La Trobe, *Letters*, 22. See also Pollock, *Wilberforce*, 53–4.
[30] *List of the society, instituted in 1787, for the purpose of effecting the abolition of the slave trade*, London 1787, 2, and 'Contributors'. See also Clarkson, *The history*, i. 286–8.
[31] Elwyn, *Northamptonshire Baptist Association*, 20.

cause at first, soon it was associated with dissent and fears of radicalism at home and slave uprisings overseas.[32]

Although an abolitionist at heart, as a Moravian Ignatius was embarrassed by the insistent requests for information from the ' "Testonites" '. This he discussed in January 1788 with one of the two principal Moravian ministers in Britain, Thomas Moore. Even though the proposal to abolish the trade was a political matter, Moore nevertheless concluded that abolition ought 'to be encouraged. But it would be by no means prudent to have the Brethren's name mentioned in the business, as that would give the opposition a handle to stir up all the Scandal [still associated with the Moravians] in their defence'.[33] Even more to the point, if Moravians in England were seen to be acting in support of the abolitionists, how would absentee proprietors, not to mention planters in the West Indies, react? At best the missionaries' reputation for discretion might well have been undermined and their work curtailed. For instance, there was surely a link between John Wesley's well-known condemnation of slavery and, in 1788, of the trade itself,[34] and Thomas Coke's reception in Jamaica a year later. Coke was mobbed and the new Wesleyan mission met with further riotous opposition, which the island's government apparently did nothing to prevent.[35] Moravian missions do not appear to have suffered a similar fate at this time anywhere in the West Indies. It is significant that in England Wesleyans had a very much higher public profile than the quiet Moravians.

Planters were alarmed and on the defensive. A letter of complaint from a 'Gentleman' in Jamaica, written in spring of 1788, reached Lord Hawkesbury, by then chairman of the enquiry into the slave trade. It concerned the 'clamour raised at home . . . by a parcell of most ignorant malicious & misinformed set of People . . . thro the Reveries of a Navy Doctor turned Presbyterian Pastor' – Ramsay, of course. This indignant gentleman also turned on the Quakers who on principle, he continued, did not defend their country;[36] an accusation that could also be levelled at Moravians.

From the islands came warnings that as a consequence of agitation at home on behalf of the slaves, rebellions were feared more likely. For instance, an attorney for the Foster Barham family's estates writing in 1788 from Jamaica, warned that 'if the people did not keep proper Watch over the

---

[32] Anstey, Slave trade, 273–8.
[33] C. I. La Trobe, journal, entry for 30 Jan. 1788. Thomas Moore was appointed co-helper in 1787 when J. G. Wollin succeeded Benjamin La Trobe.
[34] Anstey, Slave trade, 240.
[35] Peter Duncan, A narrative of the Wesleyan mission to Jamaica: with occasional remarks on the state of society in that colony, London 1849, 8–10, 16–17.
[36] Extract of a letter . . . Apr. 12 1788, Liverpool papers, BL, MS Add. 38416, fos 127–8. Like 'Methodist', 'Presbyterian' was term of ridicule when used by the duke of Bridgewater to describe Porteus who annoyed him: Wilberforce, Life, iii. 365.

Conduct of the Negroes [it] might prove very fatal'.[37] These fears appeared vindicated by the 'Dreadful Catastrophe', the rebellion of 1791 in San Domingue to which the author of a letter, also from Jamaica, referred Joseph Foster Barham, Jr. His correspondent hoped that the uprising would serve to restrain Wilberforce before his 'Intentions commit an Injury for which no suitable atonement [could] properly be made'.[38]

The Moravians must have been sensitive to the views of West Indian proprietors at home who, as a body, were influential and well represented in public life. The younger Joseph Foster Barham, who in 1789 inherited his father's estate, opposed immediate abolition of the trade and, elected to parliament four years later, made his views known to the House.[39] Samuel Martin, Jr, an MP until 1774, was now the head of his influential family, and the Moravians had particular reason to be grateful for his late father's paternal concern for his slaves. Opposed to abolition, Samuel, Jr, did not share Foster Barham's moderate views. Abolition, he wrote in 1788 to Hawkesbury, 'was that wild proposition' which Pitt was 'first' induced to favour 'by his friend Wilberforce's Methodism'.[40]

Ignatius La Trobe seems to have found himself, as a Moravian, caught between abolitionists, who were personal friends and supporters of the missions, and influential proprietors and apprehensive planters upon whose goodwill those missions depended.

The prelude to the first slave trade enquiry

In January 1788, when he anticipated an end to the slave trade, Ignatius assumed that the proprietors would encourage marriage between slaves in order to improve and 'continue the race'.[41] The tension that he must have felt about West Indian slavery more generally may have been relieved, to some extent, by his conviction of God's 'judgements against the poor African Nations for Crimes best known to him',[42] reasoning consistent with his Church's teaching. However, he identified himself with abolition when he discussed the now burning issue with John Newton, who had just published his *Thoughts upon the African slave trade*. In this he wrote of the trade as 'this

---

[37] John Vanheelen to Joseph Foster Barham, Sr, 23 June 1788, Barham papers, MS Clarendon Dep. c.378, bundle 1.
[38] Charles Rowe to Joseph Foster Barham, Jr, 6 Dec. 1791, ibid. bundle 2.
[39] Joseph Foster Barham was MP almost continuously from 1793 to 1822: R. G. Thorne (ed.), *The history of parliament: the House of Commons, 1790–1820*, London 1986.
[40] S. Martin to Hawkesbury, 3 Aug. 1788, Liverpool papers, MS Add. 38416, fo. 123. Martin owned property in 'ye Sugar Islands'. His brother Henry succeeded Middleton in 1789 as naval comptroller.
[41] C. I. La Trobe, journal, entry for 25 Jan. 1788.
[42] Ibid. entry for 19 Feb. 1788.

stain upon our National Character', but he was 'unwilling to give offence'.[43] Despite this explanation, which he repeated to Ignatius, Ignatius felt that Newton was pulling his punches. He was also aware of various telling 'anecdotes' that Newton did not wish to reveal from his slave-trade days. 'I differed from him', Ignatius recorded, 'for *we* wish to excite feelings of the utmost horror in the heart of the whole Nation against this complicated Work of Satan for the Destruction of Mankind.'[44]

Ignatius was more circumspect when, at Middleton's suggestion, Wilberforce called on him early in January 1788.[45] This was their first meeting and it marked the beginning of a long and fruitful connection for the Moravians. The 'projected abolition of the slave trade', Ignatius agreed, was a 'noble cause'. However, he was greatly comforted that 'Good came out of Evil': thousands of Africans, transported across the Atlantic, found in the West Indies 'eternal welfare ... in the knowledge of their Saviour as children of God, into whose liberty they were now translated'. Wilberforce shared 'these sentiments, but' he replied, they could not 'be a comfort nor hinder us from using our utmost endeavours to put a stop to it [the trade]'.[46]

Optimistic that the motion for abolition would be carried in parliament,[47] Wilberforce was already looking to Africa itself when he first talked to Ignatius. 'Africa', wrote his biographer, John Pollock, always 'had a large place in Wilberforce's thought.'[48] West Africa was topical. In 1787 Granville Sharp's plan for the relief of the black poor in London was put into effect when a party of more than 400 sailed for Sierra Leone. What Wilberforce wished the Moravians to consider anticipated some of the aims of the Sierra Leone Company, of which he became a director when it was formed in 1791.[49]

It was the idea of a mission settlement on the Guinea coast, such as the Moravians might be induced to establish, that Wilberforce wished to discuss with Ignatius. Their missionaries, he believed, could 'easily' make converts and teach Africans to 'plant Cotton & Indigo, articles much more valuable ... than Slaves' and to live in peace. By introducing 'Civilization & ... true Christianity', Wilberforce wished 'above all', Ignatius noted, to 'make some amends to this [the African] nation for the Cruelties hitherto inflicted upon them'.

His proposal, associated with a misapprehension about the Moravians, made it necessary for Ignatius to explain to him the essence of the Church's approach to missions and relations with governments. This was all the more essential in the light of Wilberforce's friendship with Pitt. Wilberforce

---

43 John Newton, *Thoughts upon the African slave trade*, London 1788, 1, 41.
44 C. I. La Trobe, journal, entry for 31 Jan. 1788 (my emphasis).
45 'Mr Wilberforce called', ibid. entry for 7 Jan. 1788.
46 Summary of meeting, ibid. entry for 25 Jan. 1788.
47 Anstey, *Slave trade*, 267.
48 Pollock, *Wilberforce*, 52.
49 The Sierra Leone Company and the Moravians are discussed at pp. 177–8 below.

suggested that the Moravians would, most probably, be granted favourable terms by the administration in the event of them agreeing to establish a mission settlement in West Africa. He further compounded Ignatius' embarrassment by drawing a parallel between Moravian missions and the 'success of the Jesuits of Paraguay'. With his mind focused on establishing mission settlements, Wilberforce's interest in the order is understandable, but it led to some 'plain speaking'. Ignatius explained that 'it had always been a maxim among the Brethren to keep out of all political business . . . never meddling in anything related to Government'. It was quite the reverse with the Jesuits whose wealth, he reminded Wilberforce, had also contributed to their downfall.[50]

Wilberforce's expectation that new forms of trading with Africa could replace slaving was also part of the abolitionists' economic argument. However, both Wilberforce and Ignatius most probably agreed that the establishment of a mission settlement should be deferred until there was peace on the coast, brought about by an end to the slave trade.

Before the end of January, they met again, this time at the Middletons' town house. But the large company present prevented them from continuing their discussions as they had intended. Moreover, as the abolitionists' earlier optimism was subsiding, there was little to be gained in the immediate future from pursuing the African idea. Around this time Pitt and Wilberforce agreed that more information was required about the trade and the ' "Testonites" ' were aware that an official enquiry was in the wind.[51]

Pressed by Ramsay, Wilberforce and others to provide information, Ignatius translated extracts for them from *Oldendorp's history* of the Moravian mission in the Danish West Indies. Whether these notes, or data from an estate in Jamaica which he also made available, assisted the abolitionists' case is immaterial. Although among good friends of his Church, Ignatius was coming close to meddling in what was not his proper business, and Ramsay's suggestion that he, himself, might publish pieces from *Oldendorp's history* showed how easily things could have got out of hand.[52] (The cautious Moravians did not publish *Oldendorp* in Britain, although it seems certain that they had intended to do so.[53]) The announcement in February that there was to be an official enquiry into the slave trade surely concentrated the Moravians' minds,[54] and it cannot altogether be a coincidence that ten days later the Church's principal ministers in Britain and Ignatius agreed that he should be rusticated. The Elders in Germany were advised that 'it would be

[50] C. I. La Trobe, journal, entry for 25 Jan. 1788.
[51] Ibid. entry for 31 Jan. 1788.
[52] Ibid. entry for 2, 3 Feb. 1788.
[53] For reference to *Oldendorp's history* 'now translating into English' see Spangenberg, *Account of the . . . missions*, 31.
[54] Established by order in council, 11 Feb. 1788: *Report of the Lords of Trade . . . slave trade 1789*, in *House of Commons sessional papers of the eighteenth century*, ed. Sheila Lambert, lxix, Wilmington, Del. 1975, 1.

better for himself, if he were elsewhere than in London on account of his numerous acquaintances here'.[55] However, directed by the Lot, the Elders replied in April that the proposal was not approved and that he must therefore remain in London.[56] As it turned out providence was proving kind to the Moravians.

Although a very respectable cause indeed, abolition was not an affair for Moravians to meddle in: it was too political and carried real risks for them. They were not taking counsel of their fears for their mission to slaves when they wished that their name should not be associated with the cause. Some years later, when he reflected on the 1788 enquiry and the Moravians' connection with it, Ignatius wrote:

> It struck me very forcibly, that if the Brethren were called upon to give any evidence concerning the Treatment of the Slaves in the West Indies, it might prove very injurious to our missions, by bringing upon us the ill will of the proprietors. . . . I therefore made such representations to Sir C Middleton, W. Wilberforce, the Bishop of London and others.[57]

By the end of December 1787 Beilby Porteus, now bishop of London and therefore with ecclesiastical oversight of the colonies in the West Indies, had been sworn in as a privy councillor.[58] He was to play a very active part in the subcommittee of the council which enquired into the slave trade and it was almost certainly at his initiative that the Moravians provided the enquiry with information on how their mission to the slaves was conducted. In the meantime they only narrowly prevented one of their missionaries from appearing before the committee.

The 1788 enquiry into the slave trade

Despite Ignatius La Trobe's misgivings, the enquiry into the slave trade turned out entirely favourably for the Moravians. It was important both at the time and for their further role in the missionary awakening, however, that he was on hand.

1788, indeed, with its focus on humanitarian issues overseas, was a significant year for the missionary awakening. The abolition campaign, the enquiry and the impeachment of Warren Hastings, which also opened that year, each brought to the fore long-simmering anxieties at home about native peoples in the empire and even beyond it. Of these, the issue of slavery, treatment of slaves and the state of peoples in Africa now became a subject of lasting

---

55 MCH, PHC, 20 Feb. 1788. He was to be sent to Yorkshire.
56 Ibid. 23 Apr. 1788.
57 MCH, transactions with government (fo. 4), n.d.
58 'Confirmed' bishop of London and sworn in as privy councillor on 7 Dec. 1787: Porteus papers, MS 2099, fos 169–70.

concern. Slavery in the West Indies was believed to degrade Africans to a status below that of human beings and to undermine the well-being of the British nation which condoned it.[59]

In the course of its proceedings the enquiry received reports of the good results obtained by the Moravian missions in the West Indies and most especially in Antigua. The Wesleyan mission, which had begun on that island more recently, also came in for honourable mention. Evidence presented suggested that slavery could to some extent be reformed from within by the conversion of slaves to Christianity. It seemed that converts became better workers and more moral beings. This was significant. Immoral conduct was associated with one of several explanations being canvassed for the islands' slave population failing to sustain itself. Impressed by the weight of testimony concerning the Moravians, the committee turned to them for a model of how missions to the slaves should be conducted. The Established Church and clergy in the West Indies, by comparison, were criticised for failing, apparently, to do anything for the slaves.

Established on 11 February 1788, the committee of enquiry was instructed to investigate 'the present State of the Trade to Africa, and particularly the Trade in Slaves'.[60] Lord Hawkesbury (1727–1808), president of the Board of Trade, was appointed chairman. The committee met for the first time on the following day when Pitt made 'some pertinent observations'. Henry Dundas, Porteus and John Moore, archbishop of Canterbury, were among the privy councillors present.[61] Porteus, rather than Moore, played an active part in the committee's work.

Hawkesbury, however, was the key figure. Competent, politically alert and very thorough, he opposed abolition, though concern for the slaves was a different matter. His position as chairman did not prevent him from accepting the Freedom of Liverpool later in the year, given 'particularly in gratitude', the borough's citation states, for his 'support for the African Slave Trade',[62] moreover, when he was advanced to an earldom in 1796, he took for his title earl of Liverpool. Porteus, in furthering his own aims for the unfortunate slaves, appears to have had no difficulty in securing Hawkesbury's co-operation both during and after the enquiry. The two men seem to have worked well together.

Porteus continued to value the example of the Moravians. As bishop of London, he used his apparent authority over the clergy in the West Indies in

---

[59] P. J. Marshall, 'The moral swing to the east and British humanitarianism, India and the West Indies', in K. Ballhatchet and J. B. Harrison (eds), *East India Company studies*, Hong Kong 1986, 69–74, 79–86.
[60] *1789 report*, in *Sessional papers*, lxix. 1.
[61] 12 Feb. 1788: Porteus papers, MS 2099, fos 169–70.
[62] Corporation of Liverpool to Hawkesbury, 8 Sept. 1788, and Hawkesbury to corporation (letter of acceptance), 12 Sept. 1788, Liverpool papers, MS Add. 41353, fos 169–70, 175. For this and further information on Hawkesbury see Dale H. Porter, *The abolition of the slave trade in England, 1784–1807*, Hampden, Conn. 1970, 44–5.

the spring of 1788 when he commended the example of the Moravians to them. This he did in a circular, requesting the clergy to attend, urgently, to 'The Instruction of the Negro Slaves in the principles of Morality & Religion'.[63] He also sought to enlist the goodwill of the islands' governors for the undertaking, sending them copies of the circular in which he reminded these officials of the crown that 'the best Christians make the best servants'.[64]

The West Indies were always the most important focus of Porteus' interest as far as missions were concerned and,[65] after the enquiry, he used his association with colleagues on the committee in an attempt to establish a new missionary venture in the region. Both Hawkesbury and Dundas were among the petitioners when the 'Society for the Conversion and religious Instruction and Education of the Negro Slaves in the British West Indies' received its charter.[66] The creation of this society in 1794 was entirely Porteus' doing. Dundas, one of the most influential of politicians, opposed immediate abolition. Nevertheless, in 1796 when he again defended the continuance of the trade, he could still describe it as 'founded upon injustice and inhumanity'.[67] By lending their support to the conversion of slaves to Christianity, Hawkesbury and Dundas added a further impression of respectability to their opposition to abolition on grounds of national interest.

Whatever might be said about the level of personal piety among other privy councillors, Porteus was not an isolated figure. It is likely that his wishes were taken into account prior to the enquiry's first meeting at which Hawkesbury read out some questions 'he had prepared'.[68] These 'Heads of Examination', listing more than fifty questions on which evidence was to be taken, include four related to missions and the religious instruction of slaves.[69]

Three days later, agents representing the islands in the West Indies were handed copies of the complete questionnaire.[70] These agents were also members of the West India Committee in London to which proprietors and merchants belonged, an influential body which was well represented in both

---

63 *A letter to the clergy of the West-India islands, by Beilby, lord bishop of London*, 2 Apr. 1788, London 1788.
64 Signed bishop of London, endorsed on reverse, West India governors, 22 May 1788, Fulham papers, Leeward Islands, XX, fo. 188.
65 McKelvie, 'Anglican interest', p. xii.
66 *Charter of the society for the conversion and religious instruction and education of the negro slaves in the British West India Islands*, proof copy, London c. 1794, LPL, papers of the Christian Faith Society, C.F.S./F3, fo. 148. See also McKelvie, 'Anglican interest', 584–624.
67 *Parliamentary history* xxxii (1818), col. 874, cited in Anstey, *Slave trade*, 310.
68 12 Feb. 1788: Porteus papers, MS 2099, fos 169–70.
69 Heads of examination proposed by Lord Hawkesbury to the Committee for Trade & Plantations on the 12 Feb. 1788, (copy), Liverpool papers, MS Add. 38416, fos 13–19, the four questions at fo. 16. The published version was similar to these; cf. pp. 18–21, in 'Paper A. Heads of enquiry transmitted to the Agents of the West India islands': *1789 Report*, in *Sessional papers*, lxx. 392.
70 15 Feb. 1788: Porteus papers, MS 2099, fo. 171.

houses of parliament.[71] Faced with the immediate requirement to defend their commercial interests at home and overseas, planters had resolved early in February to 'take such measures as necessary' to oppose abolition.[72] Among those deputed to undertake this task were Charles Spooner, agent for three of the Leeward Islands, including St Kitts, and John Brathwaite.[73] Brathwaite, agent for Barbados and lessee since 1783 of the SPG's Codrington estates in that island, was to be another of the petitioners on behalf of Porteus' missionary society.[74]

Spooner, it appears, was immediately effective. Within days of the agents first attending the enquiry he had convinced its members, Ignatius La Trobe understood, that abolition of the trade was 'impracticable'.[75] A year later, at a great gathering in London of the West Indian Committee, held on 19 May 1789, it was Spooner who received a vote of thanks for his 'unremitting exertions on this business'.[76]

In comparison, Ignatius charted a decline in the abolitionists' confidence.[77] From his perspective it must have seemed that the planters and their agents had seized the initiative and, later, that they were hi-jacking the Moravians. Early in June 1788 the missionary Gottwald arrived in London from St Kitts,[78] where he had served since the establishment of the mission. He was soon 'interrogated very closely' by Spooner who requested that he give evidence to the enquiry. All this, and Gottwald's connection with Ramsay, worried Ignatius very much indeed. He therefore secured from his superiors in London their agreement that, because in truth witnesses were not obliged to appear, it was best that Gottwald withdrew. When Spooner came round to Fetter Lane later that very day to deliver the summons he found, instead of his quarry, a note awaiting him. Written by Ignatius in the missionary's name, it explained that Gottwald had to absent himself on family business. This apparently satisfied Spooner and Ignatius 'was very glad thus to have hindered this mischief'.[79] Middleton approved of his prudent action. Ignatius, who himself now left town, received after his return from the

---

[71] Lillian M. Penson, *The colonial agents of the British West Indies: a study in colonial administration mainly in the eighteenth century*, London 1924, 243.
[72] Meeting of the standing committee of the West India planters and merchants, 7 Feb. 1788, Institute of Commonwealth Studies, London, West India Commitee archives, M. 915, minutes, fos 71–2, microfilm, 3.1.
[73] Penson, *Colonial agents*, 251–4, matches islands to agents.
[74] *Charter of the society*, LPL, C.F.S./F3, fo. 148. The spelling of Brathwaite follows the 1789 report, in *Sessional papers*, lxix. 299.
[75] C. I. La Trobe, journal, entry for 19 Feb. 1788.
[76] Institute of Commonwealth Studies, London, West India Commitee Archives, M. 915, minutes, 19 May 1789, fo. 99. It was recorded that 160 people were present.
[77] C. I. La Trobe, journal, entry for 19–25 Feb. 1788.
[78] MCH, FLD-26, 2 June 1788.
[79] C. I. La Trobe, journal, entries for 12, 13 June 1788. See also C. I. La Trobe to Porteus, 29 July 1788, MCH, transactions with government. For John Daniel Gottwald (1726–1805) see 'Memoir . . .', in *PA* xix (1849), 1–6.

' "Testonites" ' a large donation for the missions, twenty guineas: the SFG's treasurer was 'in ecstasy'.[80]

At the end of June Ignatius learnt that 'Mr Reeves', clerk to the enquiry, had commented that the committee's minutes were 'full of most excellent testimonies of the labour of the Br.[ethren] among the poor blacks, given by people he had least expected it from'.[81] Who were these unexpected witnesses and what was their evidence which prompted a clerk in Porteus' employ to note later against the relevant passages in the privy council's report: 'NB. Most of the Evidence here produced was given by persons who are *against* ye abolition of the Slave Trade'?[82] It seems to have come mostly, but not entirely, from agents and others representing the planters' interest.

In order to broaden the argument that it was already in the planters' interest to treat the slaves humanely, it seems that a concerted effort was made to use the example of the Moravian mission in Antigua as supporting evidence. Although Charles Spooner was not agent for Antigua,[83] he referred to the missionaries' 'great success' in that island, which he understood was attributable to their 'earnest and discreet Zeal'.[84] Agent John Brathwaite made no reference to the Moravians in Barbados, the island which he represented, preferring to speak of the

> Great advantages to the Interests of the Planters [which] have arisen from the Labours of the Moravian Missionaries in the Island of Antigua; and this Example is an Inducement to the Planters in other Islands to adopt the like Practice.[85]

In reply to questions concerning the work of missionaries, the official joint agents for Antigua expanded on Brathwaite's testimony.[86] There was, one stated:

> no particular religious Institution at Antigua for the Benefit of the Slaves; but they derive considerable Instruction from a Society of Moravians. . . . on account of the Zeal they show in teaching such Negroes as are Followers of them, who are now become very numerous, both His Majesty's Governors and the Planters have been well disposed to give Countenance and Encouragement to their [the Moravians'] laudable endeavours.[87]

---

[80] C. I. La Trobe, journal, entries for 23 June, 1 July 1788.
[81] Ibid. entry for 28 June 1788. For John Reeves (1752?–1829), a family friend and later first chief justice of Newfoundland, see *DNB*, s.v.
[82] This passage appears on back of extracts copied for Porteus from the enquiry's report: LPL, C.F.S./F3, fos 136–9, dated 21 Nov. 1791.
[83] Spooner's agencies included Grenada from where Governor Matthew also backed up his evidence *re* Antigua: *1789 report*, in *Sessional papers*, lxix. 375.
[84] Ibid.
[85] Ibid. lxix. 299.
[86] William Hutchinson and John Burton, ibid. lxix. 335. (Penson, *Colonial agents*, 252, lists Alexander Willcock as sole agent until 1790.)
[87] *1789 report*, in *Sessional papers*, lxix. 335.

The third of this sample of witnesses hostile to abolition was Dr James Adair, judge and resident in Antigua for more than twenty years, who was not, as Wilberforce politely phrased it, 'very favourable to my propositions'.[88] What makes Adair's evidence concerning the Moravians of interest is that he does not appear to have shown his true colours before the enquiry. Although in his reported testimony he spoke of their success in converting the slaves and its 'good Effects',[89] he elsewhere advocated that '*all*' slaves should attend the Established Church in the islands. One reason for this appeared in an undated pamphlet in which Adair singled out the Moravians for censure in language reminiscent of their earlier critics. Moravians, he alleged, were 'like the Romish missionaries . . ., who operate on the superstitions of . . . ignorant people . . . [and] trump a species of religion which has scarcely any resemblance to the plain precepts of Christianity'.[90]

If this remnant of old prejudices was aired before the committee, members were not impressed. Neither in its report, nor in that of the House of Commons' enquiry of 1790, is criticism of the Moravians' conduct to be found.[91] By comparison, the failure of the Established Church and the SPG to make any effective provision for the blacks in the West Indies was regretted and remarked upon by both enquiries.[92] Perhaps the bleakest report came from Jamaica. Despite admitting to the services of twenty clergymen in that island, the reply to the enquiry's question, 'Are Negro slaves or the children baptised' was, 'NO – very rarely.'[93]

Praise for the good effects of the Moravian missions did not come only from representatives of the West Indian interest. The enquiry also received favourable testimony on behalf of the abolitionists from the Revd Mr Stuart, for example, whom the indefatigable Thomas Clarkson commended to Hawkesbury as a man 'very willing to declare the cruel treatment of the Slaves'. A year earlier Stuart had confirmed to Porteus the veracity of Ramsay's similar allegations.[94] He had travelled extensively in the West Indies, seen for himself that slaves were treated more harshly in the British islands than in those belonging to Denmark, and attended meetings conducted by Moravians in St Croix, a Danish island. Stuart confirmed the general tenor of the evidence to the effect that Moravian converts were more

---

[88] 12 May 1789: *Parliamentary history*, xxviii (1816), col. 55.
[89] *1789 report*, in *Sessional papers*, lxix. 335. For James Adair see p. 327.
[90] James M. Adair, *Unanswerable arguments against the abolition of the slave trade*, London n.d., 221.
[91] 'Minutes of the evidence . . . committee of the House of Commons, representing petioners against abolition', in *Sessional papers*, lxxii. 24–5, 44.
[92] For example, Willcock's evidence ibid. 61. For the 1788 enquiry see Brathwaite *re* Barbados, and also Adair's letter, 3 June 1788, in *1789 report*, ibid. lxix. 299, 346.
[93] Ibid. lxix. 214 (question 18).
[94] Thomas Clarkson to Hawkesbury, 25 June 1788, Liverpool papers, MS Add. 38416, fo. 121. For the Revd Stuart–Porteus connection see Porteus papers, MS 2099, fo. 154, 13 Apr. 1787.

orderly and made better workers.[95] A Mr Gandy, a Quaker and for long a planter in St Croix, added that, since the mission was established, the 'treatment of the Negroes has been more humane'.[96]

Evidence presented by both sides left the committee apparently convinced that slaves could to some useful degree be reformed through the agency of missionaries. Spokesmen for the planters and for the abolitionists had confirmed Porteus' revelation of 1783 of the 'success' of the Moravian missionaries. Furthermore, the slaves' conversion was recognised by the planters themselves as being in their own interest. Here, at least, there was agreement: both sides of the great debate acknowledged the desirability of turning heathen slaves into Christians. But the committee did not stop here. As a result of favourable testimony concerning missions it now returned to the planters, and directly to the Moravians for the first time, and sought from those planters, whose slaves in Antigua had been converted, 'the fullest Information of the Effects produced . . . with respect to Behaviour'. This request led to further positive reports of an improvement in their conduct.[97] Porteus, in the meantime, agreed to obtain from the Moravians 'the methods employed by them in converting the Negro Slaves'.[98]

Early in July, therefore, Porteus explained to Ignatius that the committee, impressed by what it had learnt, wished to know how the Moravians achieved 'such success', and, in particular, how they were able 'to bring the believing negroes or other heathen into compliance with every christian order – teaching them sobriety, faithfulness, conjugal fidelity etc'. Pressed by Porteus, Ignatius reluctantly agreed to draft a treatise, suitable for the privy councillors, 'merely . . . [on] our mode of propagating Christianity. . . . We can never withhold such information as Government requires'.[99]

Ignatius soon had a draft available, which Middleton asked to see before it went any further: he seems to have been anxious that irreligious members of the privy council should not be provided with an opportunity to scoff at religion.[100] There followed two meetings with Porteus, who also made some amendments and additions, and at the end of July Ignatius sent him a revised version.[101] This is almost certainly the one, referred to below as the Moravians' 'submission', which Porteus commended to Hawkesbury a few

95 1789 *report*, in *Sessional papers*, lxix. 463.
96 Ibid. lxx. 361.
97 Reports from Entwistle and Gordon, ibid. lxix. 345–6.
98 His prior agreement is apparent in Porteus to Hawkesbury, 7 Aug. 1788, Liverpool papers, MS Add. 38223, fo. 128.
99 This paragraph is based on a meeting held on 3 July 1788 at the bishop's palace, Fulham: C. I. La Trobe, journal. McKelvie assumed that Porteus obtained the submission through Benjamin La Trobe (d. 1786): McKelvie, 'Anglican interest', 438.
100 C. I. La Trobe, journal, entries for 7, 9 July 1788.
101 Ibid. entry for 31 July 1788. See also C. I. La Trobe's covering letter to Porteus, 31 July 1788, MCH, transactions with government.

days later. In acknowledgement, Hawkesbury stated that he approved of it 'highly' and that 'it will make a very valuable part of our report'.[102]

During August the Moravians' submission was read at a meeting of the 'Lords of the Committee' who, Ignatius understood from Porteus, also approved of it 'highly'. They now wished to know 'what regulations' the Moravians thought should be introduced, so as to make available 'sufficient time to the Negro Slaves to receive Religious Instruction, and attend divine Service'. The Moravians replied that, 'if it was possible to make such Regulations on all Estates, as already have been made on some that the slaves might have, not only Sundays, but also the Afternoons on Saturdays, for their own use', this should be sufficient. The Church 'would ask for nothing more'.[103]

The reason for 'all' estates being included became apparent when Ignatius warned Porteus against privileges being limited to the missionaries' converts. Unless they were granted to every slave, he explained, they would 'make Hypocrites' of those who sought their conversion only in order to gain a temporal advantage.[104] 'Of course', Ignatius commented dryly in a typically Moravian note, but not to Porteus, it seems, 'we did not wish to prescribe anything, much less to complain of many difficulties laid in the way of the Missionary Efforts of our Brethren.'[105] He had impressed upon Porteus that it was absolutely essential for the Moravians themselves to be kept in the background. This was accepted; they were not called before the committee.

The Moravians' submission to the enquiry

The Moravians' submission appeared in 1789 as an appendix to the published report of the committee of enquiry under the title, slightly abbreviated, 'A short account of the endeavours of the Episcopal Church, . . . [of the] United Brethren, for promoting true Christianity amongst the heathen, particularly amongst the Negroes in the West India islands'.[106] Closely printed on three and a half pages, Ignatius La Trobe's treatise was a masterly distillation, taken without doubt from Spangenberg's missionary works. As the Elders received a copy with 'much satisfaction', before the committe's report was published, the submission can be taken as an authoritative statement of the Church's teaching.[107] Its importance for the committee was that it appeared to answer

---

[102] Porteus to Hawkesbury, 7 Aug. 1788, Liverpool papers, MS Add. 38223, fo. 128; Hawkesbury to Porteus, 9 Aug. 1788, Fulham papers, Leeward Islands, XX, fo. 191.
[103] Porteus to C. I. La Trobe, 13 Aug. 1788, and C. I. La Trobe to Porteus, 15 Aug. 1788, MCH, transactions with government.
[104] C. I. La Trobe, journal, entry for 1 Sept. 1788.
[105] The comment refers to the correspondence with Porteus (n. 103 above), MCH, transactions with government, fo. 8.
[106] 'Short account', in *1789 report*, in *Sessional papers*, lxix. 469–72.
[107] MCH, PHC, 8 Oct. 1788.

what the Moravians understood to be the enquiry's key question to them: how was it that they 'effected' among the slaves 'so great an alteration in their moral behaviour'.[108] This question arose from one of the central issues which had preoccupied the enquiry from the beginning: what impeded 'the natural Increase of Negro Slaves'.[109] It was due to 'Polygamy' and diseases attendant on the 'promiscuous use of women', Brathwaite explained in a typical and widely believed reply.[110] As a palliative he recommended the conversion of slaves and a Christian marriage for, with 'One Wife, the Negro is always better for it'.[111]

The submission included an account of the Moravians' teaching on 'morality' and marriage. In an extended section Ignatius explained and justified the Church's realistic doctrine which accepted that an existing polygamous association between slaves was not a bar to a Christian marriage. The question of polygamy, which 'caused no small Embarrassment to the Missionaries',[112] was also much on Ignatius' mind. A few days before he discussed the first draft submission with Porteus, Ignatius had a stiff encounter with Thomas Coke, the Wesleyan, who to his intense indignation accused the Moravians of condoning bigamy among slaves.[113] Ignatius almost certainly drew the issue to Porteus' attention.

Compared to the rather oblique phrases on moral conduct in the missionaries' *Instructions*, much more robust expressions appear in the submission. Here, readers were assured that 'behaviour not conformable to the Moral Law of God' was not tolerated by the missionaries. 'Drunkenness, Adultery, Whoredom, Sorcery', and more, were given as examples.[114] Sorcery, or rather *obeah*, African witchcraft, was a worrying phenomenon associated with poisoning in the islands on which the enquiry also requested and received information.

At the end of that part of the submission concerned with marriage, the elimination of 'heathenish' customs and discipline, Porteus had a paragraph inserted which served more than one purpose. It first confirmed that a bishop of the Established Church approved the Moravians' doctrine which reconciled existing polygamous relationships with baptism into the Church of Christ. Second, Porteus, anxious as ever to convince members of his Church of the missionaries' success in making real Christians, wished to back up his

---

108 Ibid. 23 July 1788.
109 No. 15, 'Heads of inquiry', in *1789 report*, in *Sessional papers*, lxx. 391 (appendix A).
110 Ibid. lxix. 293, 298; cf. Thomas Kerby's evidence to the Commons' enquiry of 1790, 'Minutes of evidence', in *Sessional papers*, lxxii. 6–9. Between 1792 and 1796 MPs tabled motions aimed at encouraging marriage and breeding: Porter, *Abolition*, 82–96.
111 *1789 report*, in *Sessional papers*, lxix. 293.
112 'Short account', ibid. lxix. 471; cf. Spangenberg, *Instructions*, no. 43 at pp. 36–7.
113 C. I. La Trobe, journal, entry for 23 July 1788. The encounter with Coke at Middleton's town house is described at length.
114 Cf. Spangenberg, *Instructions*, nos 29, 33, 41 at pp. 24, 28, 35, with 'Short account', in *1789 report*, in *Sessional papers*, lxix. 470.

confidence that slave converts learnt self-discipline. He therefore had inserted into 'his' paragraph: 'It is a Fact that at this present Time, some thousand Negroes in Antigua, and other islands, submit to them [the missionaries] with Willingness.'[115]

There appears to have been general agreement that slavery could be reformed through the slaves' conversion to true Christianity. Moreover conversion was considered an essential step towards improvement or civilisation. This in turn even made it conceivable that gradually slavery itself would come to an end. It was Edmund Burke who, when he considered this possibility, wrote to Henry Dundas in 1792 that he trusted 'infinitely more . . . to the effect and influence of religion, than to all the rest of the regulations put together'.[116] Burke's view of the way ahead was reinforced by consistent accounts of the beneficial effects of missionaries' endeavours. These came first from Porteus in 1783 and then from such widely divergent sources as Ramsay and the islands' agents.

The Moravians' pious friend William Knox, agent for Dominica, believed that if only the Established Church and government of the day had acted on the missionary proposals which he had made in 1768, at Archbishop Secker's request, 'much of the present outcry against the Slave Trade would have been prevented'.[117] A former under-secretary of state, Knox was not an abolitionist. He defended the trade in a letter addressed to Wilberforce, published in 1790, on the grounds that 'I never did or can consider it lawful, to purchase an African Negro, except to improve his state alive and hereafter.' Moreover, he regretted the failure of 'our church or state' to make any provision in the islands for slaves, or to assist those in 'the smallest degree' who did. 'I mean', Knox added, the Moravians in the West Indies and he cited their thousands of converts in Antigua.[118]

Evidence presented to the enquiry became subsumed into arguments advanced by both sides in the long abolition debates in the Commons that followed. It was Wilberforce who claimed in a major speech on 18 April 1791 that it was as a consequence of 'the happy effects of instructing the slaves in the principle of religion, . . . particularly in the Island of Antigua . . . [that] the planters themselves confessed their value, as property, was increased one third by their increased habits of regularity and industry'.[119] A year later, on 2 April a Mr Benjamin Vaughan, who had visited the West Indies recently, attempted to vindicate the planters. He claimed that Moravians 'had been of

---

[115] Compare the penultimate paragraph, ibid. lxix. 471, with C. I. La Trobe to Porteus, 31 July 1788, MCH, transactions with government.
[116] Edmund Burke to Henry Dundas, 9 Apr. 1792, in *The correspondence of Edmund Burke: VII: Jan. 1792–Aug. 1794*, ed. P. J. Marshall and John A. Woods, vii, Cambridge–Chicago 1968, 124.
[117] William Knox to Lord Chancellor Thurlow, 29 May 1789, in HMC, *Report on manuscripts in various collections*, vi. 203.
[118] Knox, *A letter from W. K. Esq. to W. Wilberforce*, 19–21.
[119] *The parliamentary register*, xxix, London 1791, 199–200.

the greatest benefit' in Antigua, and that 'many planters' now recommended the use of missionaries. He continued: 'Where religion was once instilled, there would be less punishment; more work done, and better done; more marriages, more issue, and more attachment to their [the slaves'] masters and to government.'[120]

But why were the Moravian Brethren, in particular, so acceptable to both sides; was it just a belief that missionaries were turning slaves into real and useful Christians? Politicians, proprietors, churchmen like Porteus, and such prominent evangelicals as Middleton and Wilberforce, learnt that the Moravians held ideas similar to their own about society and mankind. The Moravians' submission, compassionate but realistic, must have commended itself to these serious-minded men. On the one hand, attention was drawn to the enforced break-up of families and the 'Situation of the Children', which made it impossible for them to be educated,[121] whilst on the other, readers would have been in no doubt that a strict discipline and watch was maintained over converts. Converts were guided towards the adoption of a Christian walk and its accompanying conventions of civilised conduct. Baptism remained a privilege and the slaves continued to be taught to accept, as Christians should, their hard life on earth and obedience to those set in authority over them.[122]

Privy councillors, and the elite more generally, surely appreciated this part of the Moravian Church's doctrine. That Moravians shared their belief in Christians doing their duty in that station of life into which God had called them was explicit in the Moravians' submission and implicit in the testimony given to the enquiry. An ordered society was integral to British eighteenth-century thinking. Although Wilberforce, for one, wished to reform society, he had no wish to abandon its hierarchical order. To sustain that structure, he held authoritarian views, similar to those of the majority of men in his position.[123]

The enquiry established by Pitt in 1788 demonstrated that abolitionists and planters, who otherwise were opposed to one another, agreed that missions had a beneficial and humanising influence on slavery. Privy councillors appear to have been convinced that, although not complete, the Moravian model offered a significant way forward. Missions apparently made a more humane regime possible and held out hope that the current need for the trade would fade gradually away.

Moreover, Church Evangelicals and other serious-minded men and women had more than one reason to encourage the Moravians' work in the West Indies. For instance, although Moravians were legally Dissenters, they did not join with other Dissenters in the campaign for the repeal of the Test

---

120 Ibid. xxxii, London 1792, 197–8.
121 'Short account', in *1789 report*, in *Sessional papers*, lxix. 469, 471.
122 Ibid. lxix. 471–2.
123 Pollock, *Wilberforce*, 166–73.

and Corporation Acts, which was opposed by Wilberforce and the majority in the Commons.[124] Unlike the Wesleyans, Moravians were not a threat to the unity of the Established Church. In 1788, after an anxious Porteus asked him if John Wesley had yet ordained any ministers to remain in England, Ignatius observed 'I pity the poor Bishop who is a great patriot for the Church of England.'[125] Earlier, in 1785, the year that Wesleyans opened talks with Benjmain La Trobe concerning a possible coalition, it was his hope that the Moravians would in fact be the means of 'keeping good Souls in the established Church'.[126] Porteus to be sure was aware of the Moravians' over-riding respect for 'his' Church: this was a further reason for his favourable attitude towards them and he never wavered in having the greatest regard for their missionary work in the West Indies.[127]

The aftermath

Sceptical planters and government ministers, like Hawkesbury, were apparently now in favour of missions to a people, the slaves, whose needs, until the enquiry, Church and State had largely ignored. In the Commons Sir William Young and, from 1793, Charles Ellis were the principal spokesmen on behalf of the planters. They are also examples of absentee proprietors who wished to have their slaves placed under the care of missionaries. Young, a man of 'good sense' in Wilberforce's estimation[128], owned estates in Antigua and Tobago. Ellis's were in Jamaica and he would have known the Foster Barham family from childhood.[129] During the 1790s first Young on his own initiative, it seems, and then Ellis, prodded by Foster Barham, turned to the Moravians.

In 1792 Young made what was probably his first visit to the West Indies. He returned home with a 'High opinion . . . of the pious & useful endeavours' of the Moravians, 'founded on [his] Experience of the good effects of such missions on my Estates in Antigua'.[130] In a published account of his tour, Young also gave a generous description of a Moravian whose characteristic 'simplicity', he believed, enabled Moravians to 'assimilate' better with the

---

[124] Ibid. 154.
[125] C. I. La Trobe, journal, entry for 15 May 1788.
[126] B. La Trobe to UEC, 1 Feb. 1785, UA, R.13.D. 47.c. no. 494.
[127] (1807) Porteus papers, MS 2101, fos 154–62, cited in McKelvie, 'Anglican interest', 719.
[128] Young told Wilberforce that he preached on the 'Ten Commandments' to his slaves on Antigua: Wilberforce, *Life*, i. 360–1.
[129] For Charles Ellis and William Young see Thorne, *House of Commons, 1790–1820*. The Foster Barhams and Vassals/Hollands were related. Ellis was raised with Elizabeth Vassal.
[130] Copy of testimonial from William Young, 5 Nov. 1798, MCH, Tobago letters. William Young (1751–1821), does not appear to have made an earlier visit to the islands: *DNB* s.v.

slaves than could the clergy.[131] Young went on to invite the Moravians to establish a mission station on his Antigua property. His trustees, however, would not permit him to sell the freehold of even a few acres, so he offered land in Tobago instead [132] and he may later have joined with other proprietors who sponsored the mission in that island.[133]

In 1797 Young and Charles Ellis were the chief promoters in the Commons of a successful motion which, presented by Ellis, passed to assemblies in the West Indies responsibility for taking effective steps to 'diminish the necessity' of importing slaves whose 'moral and religious improvement' was the first measure urged upon the islanders. Foster Barham, who had entered parliament four years earlier, seconded the motion, believing it to be the way that slavery could be reformed and the trade brought to an end.[134] Wilberforce, in a stinging response, totally disagreed. Having no confidence in the humanity of the planters, he pressed for abolition first, adding that 'principles of policy, as well as of justice, were incompatible with slavery'.[135]

Around this time Barham began to mobilise some of his planter friends in the House to back an extension of the Moravian mission in Jamaica into their own estates. As a result a year later the Church agreed to meet the 'earnest applications of some Planters of consequence'.[136] Ellis participated fully in the project and when it was put to 'Mr Windham', William Windham, by now a trenchant anti-abolitionist, Barham pointedly reminded him of Ellis's successful motion to 'ameliorate the condition of our Negroes'.[137]

Various reasons can be advanced for Young, Ellis and the others deciding to back the Moravians. Consciences were pricked, it made sense of their stance on abolition and, following their success in the Commons, anti-abolitionists needed the islanders to give the appearance of acting positively. In addition, Barham could not have been alone in anticipating an end to the trade.[138] Faced with this worrying prospect, and the alleged economic advantages of the conversion of the slaves, proprietors had further reason to encourage the use of missionaries. Good stewardship of property should not

---

131 [William Young], *A tour through the several islands of Barbadoes, St Vincent, Antigua and Grenada, in the years 1791 and 1792*, London 1801, 283–4.
132 MCH, SFG minutes, 5 Nov., 3 Dec. 1793.
133 Tobago proprietor John Hamilton to [?] C. I. La Trobe, 9 Dec. 1799. A subscription list dated 8 Jan. 1800 names twenty-five estates supporting the mission, but the proprietors are not named: MCH, Tobago letters.
134 For this paragraph see *Parliamentary history*, xxxiii, London 1818, esp. col. 269, 6 Apr. 1797. For further details see cols 251–75.
135 Ibid. cols 277–8, quotation at col. 278.
136 MCH, SFG minutes, Aug. 1798.
137 Joseph Foster Barham, Jr, to William Windham, 22 Nov. 1800, Barham papers, MS Clarendon Dep. c.378, bundle 1. This bundle includes further references to Ellis's participation and to that of Bryan Edwards, Godfrey Webster and Barham's cousins, the Fosters. For Windham's opposition to abolition see Anstey, *Slave trade*, 357.
138 Joseph Foster Barham, Jr, to Charles Rowe, 5 Dec. 1792, Barham papers, MS Clarendon Dep. c.348

exclude care the labourers. It should by now have taken little imagination for these generally God-fearing British gentlemen with property in the West Indies to include their slaves in this habit of mind. While he was in Antigua Young showed that same paternal concern for slaves on his own estate which had been a notable feature of old Samuel Martin's management. The missionaries believed that Young was 'sincere' and noted that, before his departure, he 'made every regulation tending to the support and comfort of his negroes, and ordered that the old, infirm, and worn-out amongst these should receive an equal portion of provisions'.[139]

Proprietors opposed to abolition were not being inconsistent when they patronised Moravian missions. It seemed like good, commercial sense to do both. Further, it was politic for men in Hawkesbury's position, and for the planters, to be seen to be doing something for the slaves.

Porteus' axiom, enunciated in the context of missions to the slaves, that 'the best Christians make the best servants'[140] was more than an appeal to the planters' self-interest. It was also a widely held assumption which can be deduced, for instance, from brief notes kept by John Newton in January 1788 when the Eclectic Society discussed 'masters and servants'. Thomas Scott, later first secretary of the CMS and best known for his commentary on the Bible, was among members present. He favoured 'religious servants' as being 'Moral and orderly'; their 'duty, Obedience – Submission, Fidelity'.[141]

Abolitionists and their opponents had similar values and expectations in mind when they discussed the practical benefits to be derived from the slaves' conversion to Christianity. This is apparent from evidence given to the enquiry and from debates in the Commons. Both parties were also agreed on Moravian missions which exerted, indirectly, considerable influence on the thinking of all who wished to see slavery to a greater or lesser degree reformed. The manner in which the missions were conducted and the example of that in Antigua, in particular, seemed to offer a way forward.

The *Periodical Accounts* of Moravian missions

Largely as a result of the enquiry the Moravians now felt sufficiently secure in their standing to launch their first publication ever to give regular news of their work overseas: the *Periodical Accounts Relating to the Missions of the Church of the United Brethren Established among the Heathen*. Published in London from 1790, at roughly quarterly intervals, this journal was the last in

---

[139] PA i (1790), 196.
[140] Porteus to governors in West Indies, 22 May 1788, Fulham papers, Leeward Islands, XX, fo. 188.
[141] Eclectic Society notes, 7 Jan. 1788, John Newton papers, Firestone Library, Princeton, NJ. I owe this reference to Professor Bruce Hindmarsh. For Thomas Scott (1747–1821) see Balleine, *Evangelical party*, 113–20, 161.

the series of influential Moravian works to appear before the new missionary societies began to be formed later in the decade. Its publication was associated with the development of Ignatius La Trobe's role within the Church.

When, early in October 1788, the Elders of the Moravian Church expressed their satisfaction with the submission Ignatius had prepared for the enquiry, they also summoned him to Germany.[142] Towards the end of November he reached the Moravian settlement at Gnadenfrei, in Silesia, where the Elders were temporarily in residence. Although Ignatius was then ordained, his future position in the Church had not yet been decided and he was therefore somewhat apprehensive. His many interviews with the Elders began and ended with the venerable Spangenberg who, at their last meeting, advised him 'to put a mute on my violin in favour of the Cong.[regation]', ie the Moravian Church.[143]

During his visit he discussed with the Elders his proposal to have printed in England an appeal for urgently needed funds for the mission in St Kitts. Ignatius was now close to finding his calling. For the moment, as secretary of the SFG, he was well aware that the Church had considerable financial problems because of the cost of maintaining the missions. As a result a major appeal to the Moravian world was launched in the following year; 'extraordinary & liberal donations' were called for and provincial leaders were urged to 'air up' the Church's wealthy members and friends.[144]

Early in February 1789 Ignatius returned to London where he was to live for all but the last two years of his life. Despite earlier concern about his many acquaintances, he was authorised to renew and develop his contacts with the religious among the various denominations.[145] He soon called upon Porteus and resumed his friendly relationship with the Middletons.[146]

A few weeks after his first great abolition speech in the Commons that May, Wilberforce called on Ignatius.[147] He wished to discuss the slave trade. Ignatius, however, now made more attentive to his Church's affairs, raised with him the need for financial assistance towards building the first chapel in St Kitts. Wilberforce responded by making a generous donation on the spot, assuring Ignatius that he could 'always' count on his support, and advising him to write to his uncle, John Thornton. Thornton made substantial gifts to the SFG,[148] but his bounty was cut short by his death a year later.

'My success with Mr Wilberforce', Ignatius confided in his journal, 'kindled up the flame of Zeal for the furtherance ... of our missions within me & I

---

142 MCH, PHC, 8 Oct. 1788.
143 C. I. La Trobe, journal, entries for 20 Nov.–18 Dec. 1788 (from Gnadenfrei). The quotation is from the entry for 12 Dec. 1788.
144 MCH, UEC circular letters, 10 Aug. 1789.
145 MCH, transaction with government, (fo. 9.), n.d.
146 C. I. La Trobe, journal, entries for 20 Mar.–Apr. 1789.
147 Ibid. entry for 5 June 1789.
148 'Next day' Thornton gave first £10 and later £100: ibid. entries for 5–16 June, 14 Aug. 1789.

resolved to leave no stone within my reach unturned to be of service to them.' He went on to obtain from a well-disposed secretary to a charity a list of 'benevolent people' to whom he addressed an appeal, accompanied by an account of the missions. Feeling 'not much fit' for the role of fund-raiser, Ignatius wished that he possessed 'a 1/570 part of the collector's spirit possessed of my worthy and most valiant pattern, the redoubtable Dr Coke'. With more than £200 soon collected and 'still fishing for more',[149] he quickly overcame his inhibitions.

Ignatius La Trobe had now found his proper calling, not so much as a fund-raiser, but in the role of a quietly persuasive advocate and publicist for his Church's missions. He was to be the one to introduce a Moravian publication devoted to regular news from the mission field. Ever since 1769, when the British Moravians first made a similar proposal, it had been rejected,[150] but the Church now urgently needed to tap a new source of funds which could only be found in other benevolent Christians. Discussion with the charitably minded Lady Middleton had confirmed for Ignatius his 'opinion that we sh[oul]d. have printed a periodical Paper published by the Society ... with the newest Intelligence from our missions'.[151]

Thus in July 1789 Ignatius and the deputy chairman of the Brethren's missionary society, the SFG, recommended to the general synod then assembling in Germany the publication of a circular each quarter to give 'those worthy friends out of our Circle that take such a hearty & willing share in our Concerns of our missions ... the newest Account'. Distribution of manuscripts, it was explained, had for long proved to be an unreliable and inadequate means of circulating news.[152] In order to answer any lingering doubts as to the wisdom of a journal being published in England, the letter drew attention to an important consequence for the Moravians of the enquiry into the slave trade: 'The present laudable indeavours in this land to abolish [the] Slave Trade have occasioned more notice to be taken of our missions ... especially in Antigua ... our Saviour's Cause has been strikingly exalted amongst men.' Moreover, 'Gentlemen of consequence' had offered to assist the Moravians in establishing new missions in such 'different and distant parts as Tobago, New Holland & the Coast of Guinea'.[153] The Church's deep-seated aversion to publicity was overcome. Synod 'unanimously approved' the British Moravians' proposal[154] and, in the spring of 1790, the first number of *Periodical Accounts* was published in London.

The Moravians' submission to the enquiry made up the substance of the first number. Ignatius, of course, presented Beilby Porteus with a copy which

---

149 Ibid. entry for 6 June 1789.
150 MCH, SFG minutes, 31 Jan., 30 May 1769. For further details see PA ix (1823), p. iv.
151 C. I. La Trobe, journal, entry for 17 Sept. 1788.
152 To the Synod ... assembled at Herrnhut ..., 1 July 1789 (copy) letters written by the secretary, MCH, SFG letters.
153 Ibid.
154 MCH, resolutions of the synod, 1789, ch. 243, at 232.

is almost certainly that in the bishop's library.[155] Because Porteus had cajoled him into agreeing to the original, a bishop of the Church of England was a progenitor and, for once, 'an editor' of what became an influential Moravian publication. The main text was followed by a table from the submission, in revised form, recording the extent and progress to date of the missions world-wide (see table 1).

The submission reproduced in the *Periodical Accounts* proved to be a very acceptable introduction to Moravian missionary methods. Only 300 copies were produced at first, but such was the demand that a further 250 were made available well before the year was out and five years later a further reprint became necessary. In the summer of 1790 500 copies of the second number of the journal were printed and this became the normal print-run for the next few years.[156]

When they received their copies of the first number, members of the SFG prayed that 'our Saviour' would bless the *Accounts* and 'cause many that read it, to take an effectual part in the support of God in all parts'.[157] By the end of the year it seemed that these prayers were in the course of being answered. The journal was already gaining new friends for the society in its work overseas.[158]

If there was any one point since the crash of 1753 at which it could be said that the Moravians had a particular reason to be confident of their standing with the British, it happened as a result of the enquiry into the slave trade. There could no longer be any doubt that the Moravian Church had restored its good name. Its missions had played a large part in this outcome; the Church was now acclaimed for its work overseas.

This can be confirmed by reference to William Wilberforce's *Practical view of the prevailing religious system of professed Christians, in the higher and middle classes of this country, contrasted with real Christianity*, first published in 1797, which was an instant and lasting success, its influence extending well into the next century.[159] In this work Wilberforce aimed to contrast 'orthodox Christians' . . . defective scheme' with what he understood to be 'real Christianity'.[160] Despite the Moravians, 'not without reason' having in the past 'excited suspicions of the very worst nature', Wilberforce went so far as to hold them up as an example of what he meant by real Christians. They had, he stated, 'reclaimed their character and have perhaps excelled all mankind

---

155 C. I. La Trobe to Porteus, 7 Aug. 1790, MCH, transactions with government. (Copy in Porteus library shelved at B. P. 115, University of London Library.)
156 MCH, SFG minutes, 27 Apr., 17 Aug. 1790, 24 Feb. 1795.
157 Ibid. 27 Apr. 1790.
158 MCH, FLD-27, memorabilia 1790.
159 Pollock, *Wilberforce*, 145–55. According to Pollock (p. 147) 7,500 copies were sold in 1797 with translations and further editions following.
160 William Wilberforce, *A practical view of the prevailing religious system of professed Christians, in the higher and middle classes of this country, contrasted with real Christianity*, London 1797, 4.

Table 1
Extract from *Periodical Accounts* i (1790): 'the number of baptized in all Settlements of the Brethren among the Heathen, at the end of the year 1788'

In the Danish West Indies

St Thomas	(1732)+	2 stations	2,483
St Croix	(1733)	2 stations	3,669
St John	(1741)	2 stations	838
			6,990

In the British West Indies

Antigua	(1756)	2 stations	6,038
Jamaica	(1754)	(4 estates)	315
St Kitts	(1777)		147
Barbados	(1765)		20
			6,520

Surinam	(1735)	2 stations	c. 312
Sub-total West Indies and Surinam			(13,822)*
North American Indians (1740) now on north shore of Lake Erie			c. 200
Greenland	(1733)	3 stations	891
Labrador	(1771)	3 stations	63
Total			14,976

+ denotes year missions commenced

* These figures are lower than those in the submission in the enquiry's report. That number (16,045 for 1787) included catechumens and others on the missionaries' books. Figures in the table above, with minor exceptions, are of the baptised.[161]

in solid and unequivocal proofs of the love of Christ, and of the ardent, and active, and patient zeal in his service'.[162]

To support his claim, Wilberforce referred readers to evidence given to the 1788 enquiry by the planters' agents. By now well informed about how the Moravians conducted their missions, he went on to pay this tribute to the missionaries themselves. Theirs, he wrote, was 'a zeal tempered with prudence, softened with a meekness, soberly aiming at great ends by the gradual operation of well adapted means, supported by a courage which no danger can intimidate'.[163]

---

[161] PA i (1790), 16; cf. 'Short account', in *1789 report*, in *Sessional papers*, lxix. 472.
[162] Wilberforce, *Practical view*, 79–80.
[163] Ibid. 80.

6

Moravian Missionary Teaching and its Influence, 1792–1800

By 1790 the Moravian Church had restored its good name in England. It was now admired for its foreign missions by a broad cross-section of society, from the pious to the worldly, and the Church had gained the respect of ministers of the crown and officials.

A range of Moravian publications was available in English of which three, Cranz's *History of Greenland* and Spangenberg's two most recent works, his *Instructions* to missionaries and *Account of the . . . missions* described how the missions were conducted. All three were in an increasing number of hands and from 1790 were being supplemented by the regular appearance of the *Periodical Accounts*. Evidence could easily be deduced from the very first number of that journal that Moravian missionary activity was then more extensive than that of any other Protestant group.

By now many of the evangelicals who went on to establish the three great new missionary societies were personally acquainted with Moravians. They included Baptist ministers in the south Midlands, who were involved in the foundation of the Baptist Missionary Society; Thomas Haweis who was soon to join the founders of the London Missionary Society; Charles Grant, John Newton and members of 'his' Eclectic Society who together with Wilberforce's Clapham Saints were to found the Church Missionary Society. All these men, Dissenters and Church Evangelicals, are now associated with the beginning of the modern British missionary movement. Another is Thomas Coke whose contact with Moravians had begun in 1777, nine years before he led the Wesleyans' entry into the mission field. It may have been Coke himself who, in about 1785, initiated talks with Benjamin La Trobe in an attempt to form a 'coalition'. This idea did not commend itself to the Moravians who, Ignatius La Trobe confirmed, suspected Coke of seeking through their episcopate a valid ordination for Wesleyans. Discussions never got beyond preliminaries and it seems that the subject of missions was not raised.[1] It should be noted in passing, however, that, in the opinion of one authority, Clifford Towlson, it was 'at least probable' that the example of the Moravians stimulated the remarkable development of Methodist missions, a

---

[1] C. I. La Trobe, journal, entry for 23 July 1788. See also the '[Benjamin] La Trobe–Loretz correspondence', in Addison, *The renewed Church*, appendix E, pp. 194–224.

conclusion he reached after a wide-ranging survey of the interaction between Moravians and John Wesley and his movement.[2]

Moravian missionary thought and experience had by now been made generally available through the Church's publications and through personal contacts. It was to have a particular influence upon the founders of the Baptist and of the London missionary societies and also upon Melville Horne (c. 1761–1841), one of the first country members of the Church Missionary Society,[3] who was thus a bridge between that society and the Moravians (see chapter 7). His *Letters on missions*, published in 1794 and specifically addressed to the Protestant ministers of all British Churches, was a work second in time and significance only to William Carey's *Enquiry*.

The example of the Moravian Church

The launch of the BMS and of the LMS required much preparatory work. Their founders needed to combine and then engage the active participation of members from their own Churches in the cause. Although in the past there were doubts among some Protestants about whether Christians were obliged to work for the conversion of the heathen of the world overseas, this was no longer the issue that it once had been among, for instance, strict Baptists. It was now rather more a matter of persuading a sufficient number of British Protestants that foreign missions were not an impossibility. Leaders of the new societies believed that a new beginning was essential and that it should be made without delay. Before this could happen men who were ready to evangelise had to be found and funds mobilised in their support.

The Moravian Church showed English Protestants the way forward. It also provided founders of the BMS and LMS with the very necessary evidence with which to convince their followers that they too could maintain foreign missions, and be successful overseas. The publication in May 1792 of Carey's *Enquiry* was followed, in October, by the establishment of the BMS. It was then, and over the next few years, that missionary leaders from both societies repeatedly impressed upon their followers the remarkable and persistent zeal for missions displayed by the Moravian Church. Carey believed that it was the Moravians who had set other Christians the most encouraging contemporary example. Only their missionaries, and those of the Roman Catholics he conceded, provided him with the certainty that missions in widely different parts of the world were not a 'natural impossibility'. The progress being made by the Moravians greatly strengthened Carey's case against the

---

[2] Towlson, *Moravian and Methodist*, 182–3.
[3] For Melville Horne see *BDEB*.

argument that the time of the heathen had not yet come; 'for the success of the gospel has been very considerable in many places'.[4]

Similar statements were repeated time and time again. Confidence was vital. Moravian missionaries were credited with making real converts to Christianity and the scale of the Church's effort overseas seemed out of all proportion to the number of its members and its resources. All this was also presented as a cause for reproach and a spur to urge Protestants in other Churches forward. Knowledge of the Moravians' endeavours continued to fuel a sense of national guilt and leading missionary thinkers now expressed similar sentiments when they discussed the failure of their own Churches to evangelise overseas.[5] No one quotation is an adequate illustration of these several aspects, but that from the Northamptonshire Association's announcement of the formation of the BMS is very typical:

> The Moravian Brethren, have these sixty years past, sent missionaries to various heathen nations, and have discovered a zeal for the propagation of the gospel, which ought to provoke in all denominations of christians, a godly emulation. Their success has been remarkable.

In stressing the extent of Moravian missions, the circular specifically mentioned Greenland, the West Indies, North America, Labrador and the very recent announcement that the mission at the Cape of Good Hope was being revived; drawing on data from the Brethren's *Periodical Accounts*, it noted that the total number of converted heathen was about 15,000.[6]

It was David Bogue of Gosport, in Hampshire, a prominent Dissenter, who in 1794 said of the Moravians that relative to 'their number and substance', they had 'excelled ... the whole Christian world'. This statement appeared in an address in which he famously said 'We alone are idle.' Following the launch of the BMS he was attemptingt to shame Dissenters who practised infant baptism into action. The address was first published in the widely influential *Evangelical Magazine*. It was the first of a number of similar contributions later identified by the LMS as having had a key role in events leading up to that society's formation in 1795.[7] In due course Bogue became a prominent personality among the directors of the LMS.[8]

---

4   William Carey, *An enquiry into the obligations of Christians to use means for the conversion of the heathens*, Leicester 1792, repr. London 1891, 10–12, 36–7.
5   David Bogue, *A sermon preached at Salters-Hall, March 30 1792, before the correspondent board in London of the Society in Scotland ... for the Propagating Christian Knowledge in the Highlands and islands*, London 1793, before the Scottish SPCK. See also Melville Horne, *Letters on missions addressed to the Protestant ministers of British churches*, Bristol 1794, 36–7.
6   'An account of the Particular Baptist Missionary Society' (1792), reproduced in the *Baptist Annual Register* i (1790–3), 373.
7   'Address to professors of the Gospel', in 'An introductory memorial' to *Sermons, preached in London at the formation of The Missionary Society, September ... 1795: to which are prefixed, memorials respecting the establishment and first attempts of that Society*, London 1795, p. v.
8   For David Bogue (1750–1825) see *BDEB*.

Rowland Hill, the evangelical preacher who attracted an enormous following at his Surrey Chapel in London, was another. Hill had been much impressed around 1785 by letters from the Moravian Peter Brown about his work in Antigua.[9] During ceremonies attending the birth of the LMS, Hill preached a sermon at his chapel on 'Glorious Displays of Gospel Grace' in which he praised the Moravians, most especially for 'their amazing love of souls'. He also expressed the hope that the LMS might learn from them 'how they did good, that we may go and do good likewise'.[10]

It is not suggested that the written constitution of the LMS, or that of the other new missionary societies, owed anything directly to Moravian influence, rather, that these societies were formed was due in part to the example of the Moravian Church and its missions. It was surely for this reason that the BMS and LMS each named the Moravian Brethren in votes of appreciation.[11]

Once the two societies were in being, substantive matters of missionary theory and practice soon came to the fore. It was then that the influence of Moravian doctrine became apparent; certain key elements in the Church's teaching on mission – specifically the qualifications of missionaries, their manner of preaching the Gospel, and social and economic policies – became of critical importance.

The Moravian doctrine of mission

By 1790 Moravian doctrine of mission was available to missionary leaders and thinkers in Spangenberg's *Instructions* and *Account of the . . . missions.* Although the latter is the earlier work, it did not appear in England until 1788, three years after the *Instructions*.[12] These missionary works were not issued because there had been some recent change in doctrine or practice, for, as Spangenberg himself reminded Moravians in the *Instructions*, 'many points herein, respecting the work of God among the heathen, are to be regarded as the fundamental ideas of the late Ordinary [Zinzendorf]'.[13] David Schattschneider goes further, concluding as a result of his comparative study that Zinzendorf and Spangenberg should be considered 'co-authors' of the Church's missionary teaching.[14] It should also be noted that Spangenberg's

---

[9] Edwin Sydney, *The life of the Rev. Rowland Hill*, 4th edn, London 1844, 167–71. The first letter from Brown is dated 27 July 1785.
[10] *Sermons, preached*, 114
[11] The BMS on 12 Nov. 1793: Regents Park College, Oxford, AL MS, BMS committee minutes, I; the LMS on 25 Sept. 1795: [LMS] general meeting, London School of Oriental and African Studies library, CWM MS, board minutes, minutes of transactions 1/2.
[12] Spangenberg, *Account of the . . . missions*, preface dated 12 Dec. 1780; cf. idem, *Instructions*, p. iv, dated 14 Jan. 1784.
[13] Ibid. no. 71 at p. 54.
[14] Schattschneider, ' "Souls for the Lamb" ', 183–4.

great influence over the Moravian Church and its doctrine of mission did not end with his death in 1792. His *Instructions*, for example, were not modified until 1836.

By the 1790s Spangenberg was greatly respected by other Christians as the exponent of his Church's doctrine and founders of the new societies certainly consulted at least one of his missionary works. His *Account of the . . . missions* could be read not only as a Moravian work, but also as a very complete treatise on an evangelical approach to the conversion of the heathen. Whether there was anything else available in English at this time to match it must be very doubtful. (Although immensely influential, Edwards's inspirational *Life of David Brainerd*, for example, is in an altogether different category.) Leaders of the BMS and the LMS ensured that their societies' missionaries read Moravian works. They were on board the *Duff*, for instance, when she sailed in 1796 with the London society's first missionaries bound for the South Seas, and the LMS ordered that extracts were to be read every day.[15]

Schattschneider has established the 'Pauline roots' of Spangenberg's missionary teaching.[16] Its salient points are to be found in the first part of his *Account of the . . . missions*, the conversion of the heathen 'according to the scriptures', in which he establishes the foundation of Moravian missionary teaching and practice.

Spangenberg explains that although the first Apostles were men of humble origin, without 'philosophical knowledge', they were not illiterate and they were steeped, of course, in Christ's teaching. The parallel with the Moravians is apparent throughout and is reinforced in this instance by the example of Paul who, although brought up by a scholar, was trained as a craftsman, a tent maker. 'Paul's calling to labour in the Gospel', Spangenberg also observed, was 'attended with peculiar solemnity'.[17] The implication of this reference would have been well understood: Moravians were called into service overseas by the Lot, that is by their Saviour. Missionary leaders would certainly have known that the Church took all its important decisions in this manner.

Where Spangenberg turned to the preaching of the Apostles he noted, first, that the 'whole contents' of Peter's message was of 'Christ, the Messiah . . . and that He was the way to obtain salvation'.[18] The example of Paul, the model missionary, then assumes its importance. Whomsoever he addressed, it was always with 'simplicity'. Christ and the teaching arising from His death 'was the marrow and sap of Paul's preaching'.[19] As Paul declared that 'the word of the cross is in itself fraught with divine power', it did not need 'any

---

15 For the LMS see *EM* iv (1796), 384; for the Baptists see Andrew Fuller to John Sutcliff, 29 Apr. 1795, 29 Nov. 1802, 15 Dec. 1804 (Fuller's letters copied from various sources, AL typescript, 4/5/1). See also *Catalogue of books belonging to the mission library at Serampore*, [Serampore] 1804, 48, 79, 378–84.
16 Schattschneider, ' "Souls for the Lamb" ', 127–9.
17 Spangenberg, *Account of the . . . missions*, 12–13.
18 Ibid. 13.
19 Ibid. 16.

human argumentation in order to gain entrance', Spangenberg explained. Entrance into the heart, evangelicals would have understood. Paul also 'confirmed what he taught the heathen by his own example'.[20]

Concerning baptism, Spangenberg pointedly noted that the first Apostles, and Paul, 'little delayed' in granting it, 'when they [the heathen] received the word in faith'. He cited also the example of the Ethiopian eunuch who, when he affirmed to Philip that he believed with all his heart, was immediately baptised. It was significant, too, that the Apostles gave instruction after baptism. These remarks and the observation that the Apostles baptised as many as 3,000 in one day, may have been of some comfort to Moravians in Antigua who worried when they baptised between thirty and fifty. Spangenberg seems to have accepted that not all those who were baptised were in the first instance truly converted.[21]

It was at this point that Spangenberg quoted in his *Account of the . . . missions* the famous passage from the Gospel according to Matthew. He left readers in no doubt that Paul instructed his followers that they too were obliged to obey Christ's command to preach to all nations and to baptise them.[22] The sacred command had not ended with the Apostles.

It was very typical of Spangenberg and the Moravians that Paul, he noted, ordered 'strict observation of what the Synod had concluded'. In addition, all members of the Church were to be dressed and to conduct themselves in a seemly manner. Finally, 'where Paul found . . . persons who had grace and gifts, he made them his helpers'.[23] This also was the Moravians' practice.

The second part of Spangenberg's *Account of the . . . missions* illustrated, with anecdotes, early experiences in the field that contributed to the development of the Moravians' doctrine, or confirmed its effectiveness. The third and last part is the actual account of how the missions were being conducted. The same missionary teaching appears in the much less discursive, but more detailed *Instructions*. This work, published to mark the first jubilee of the missions, was addressed to all members of the Church at a time when more and more men and women of the right calibre were required to serve overseas.[24] One passage from it encapsulates the Church's long-standing doctrine of mission: 'A servant of Jesus seeks to gain the hearts of the Heathen for our Saviour; and if he obtains this, all other desirable things will be effected in them, through the grace of God.'[25]

Characteristics of the Moravian Church at home naturally had an important bearing on the development of its foreign missions. Of these fellowship,

---

[20] Ibid. 19–20; Philipp. iii. 17; iv. 8–9.
[21] Spangenberg, *Account of the . . . missions*, 22–3. For Antigua see Cröger, *Geschichte*, iii. 30.
[22] Matt. xxviii. 19–20; Spangenberg, *Account of the . . . missions*, 24.
[23] Ibid. 25.
[24] MCH, general synods, weekly accounts, 1764–89, 24–31 Aug. 1782.
[25] Spangenberg, *Instructions*, no. 23 at p. 19.

a Christocentric religion of the heart and a distinct and individual approach to the cure of souls were its most notable features. This and much more was central for all Moravian readers of Spangenberg's *Instructions*.

All who came forward as missionaries were volunteers. They were also members of a Church in which the majority, by now, would most probably have been raised from childhood. Spangenberg gave them practical hints on how to avoid even a risk of coercion. By far the most important part of his personal advice to would-be candidates was on steps towards self-knowledge. The Church wished to be assured that candidates were confident that they had a call from their Saviour before offering themselves.[26] A Moravian missionary was to know himself as 'A servant of Jesus', an expression constantly used by Spangenberg and fundamental to understanding the qualities that candidates ought to possess. Further necessary attributes were a mature temperament, in which a natural degree of zeal was balanced by patience, fortitude and an unshakeable trust in the Lord's providence. Little more needed to be said, except to remind Moravians that an abiding love for all mankind was especially requisite in the mission field.

Nor was there anything exceptional for candidates in Spangenberg's injunction that, as 'The Bible teaches, "Let every soul be subject unto the higher powers"; this [they were also to] maintain among the heathen'.[27] Experience in the field, as well as the Church's strict regulations, had taught Moravians to be obedient to the laws and authorities of nations wherever they settled.

Volunteers knew what was expected of them, that they were hazarding their lives; they also knew that participation in the missions by all Moravians at home was assured. Spangenberg explained this to other Christians in his *Account of the . . . missions*, citing, for example, prayers said every Sunday for the missionaries' preservation, 'as the apple of thine eye'. There was intercession, too, that all heathen nations might be visited by the Holy Spirit in the same way as those in the Moravians' care.[28]

Most members sent by the Moravian Church to serve overseas were so-called unlettered men, an important, modern precedent for the new missionary societies in England. Moravian missionaries did not receive a formal training in Christian doctrine, nor was their prime task to give the heathen extensive instruction in it. By comparison, the first missionaries sent to India from Halle were almost certainly scholarly men. Their emphasis was on translation of the Bible and the education of children.[29] Moravians, on the other hand, gave priority to a simpler approach; translating hymns for the

---

[26] MCH, harmony, ii, para. 727. See also Spangenberg, *Instructions*, nos 1–10 at pp. 1–9.
[27] This and the paragraph above are a compression of ibid. nos 55, 66 at pp. 44–5, 52–3, quotation at p. 44.
[28] Spangenberg, *Account of the . . . missions*, 55.
[29] Stephen Neill, *A history of Christian missions*, 2nd edn, Harmondsworth 1990, 194–6.

use of their congregations overseas. Where it was possible to 'school' children, they too learnt hymns.[30]

From the very beginning at Herrnhut the majority of Moravians were craftsmen[31] with a marked ability to establish themselves wherever they settled. They aimed at self-sufficiency, but their practice of communal piety did not mean that they lacked material incentives. All who could were required 'to earn their own bread'. The Moravian settlement at Bethlehem, Pennsylvania, however, in an exception to this rule, had practised community of goods until around 1760,[32] and in the mission field this practice was retained.

Spangenberg explained why it was essential for the whole mission's earnings and profits to go into a common 'cash account': the over-riding concern was that harmony should prevail within these small communities where, under circumstances of deprivation and frustration, envy and disagreements could too easily fester. None of the missionaries received a salary and they had always attempted to support themselves. Now, whilst some of them concentrated on preaching, others, their 'assistants', endeavoured to provide for the group by working, for instance, at their crafts. Spangenberg referred to these units, even if scattered over several sites, as 'one family'. He warned that were an individual to retain funds this would 'militate against his proper calling, and disturb that love and confidence which ought always to subsist among Brethren and Sisters on a mission'.[33] The Elders appointed both missionaries and superintendents overseas. On a large mission the superintendent, who might well have come from elsewhere, was given a brief to take control of local finance.[34]

The Church mistrusted on principle the use of interpreters even to explain the simplest of Christian concepts. Moravians were urged to preach by example, by 'their walk', until they had learnt to address the heathen in their own language. Their first approaches were to be such that the heathen, in Zinzendorf's colourful phrase, 'are often induced to think; hey! Whence comes these people!'[35]

Spangenberg's *Instructions* reminded Moravians that when they first actually preached to the heathen they were to 'confess before them, Jesus Christ as their Lord and Saviour; yea, as God overall'. They were to continue 'unweariedly preaching Christ and his sacrifice for us, until his gospel shall

---

[30] Spangenberg, *Instructions*, no. 39 at p. 33.
[31] Stewards of Zinzendorf's estate established the precedent: Guntram Philipp, 'Wirtschaftsleben', in Hahn and Reichel, *Zinzendorf und die Herrnhuter Brüder*, 320.
[32] Gillian L. Gollin, *Moravians in two worlds: a study of changing communities*, New York–London 1967, 17–18, 132, 149–64.
[33] Spangenberg, *Instructions*, no. 13 at pp. 11–12.
[34] See, for example, Christian Ludwig Rose, superintendent 1800–5: Krüger, *Pear tree*, 85.
[35] Spangenberg, *Instructions*, nos 19–20 at pp. 16–17. The quotation is from Zinzendorf, 'He who is a minister of the Gospel . . .', 1753, no. x, appendix 1, in Benham, *Memoirs of James Hutton*, 568.

kindle a fire in their hearts'.[36] Zinzendorf and in particular the early frustrating years on Greenland had taught patience and that attempts at converting the heathen to Christianity by argument or by proving the existence of God were fruitless. There, the crucial experience of the hearts of the heathen being opened 'especially' by descriptions of 'the sufferings and death of Jesus' did not come until after six long years.[37]

Thus St Paul's command to the Corinthians, ' "not to know any thing among you, save Jesus Christ and him Crucified" ', was central to the Moravians' doctrine. Spangenberg wrote in his *Account of the . . . missions* that 'the blood and death of Jesus must remain our diamond in the golden ring of the gospel'.[38] This evangelical approach to conversion was endorsed, in an extended footnote, by reference to those same non-Moravian authorities that had appeared twenty years earlier in Cranz's *History of Greenland*. The most significant by far, for British readers, was Edwards's *Life* of David Brainerd, the exemplary missionary to the North American Indians.[39] When Brainerd adopted their evangelical approach to preaching, the Moravians suggested that they had been the agent of God's purpose.

Whether or not this claim is justified may be disputed but it is incontrovertible that Edwards's account of Brainerd's spiritual journey and in particular his eventual success in converting some North American Indians to Christianity two years before his death in 1747 had an immense influence on the missionary awakening.

Of the link between Moravian methods of preaching and that of Brainerd nothing appears in Edwards's *Life*, and, indeed, Brainerd was directed by Presbyterians who were heartily opposed to the Moravians. However, he did begin his mission in 1742 in New York province at a time when the Moravians were entering the same field and establishing their settlements in Pennsylvania and he knew of their activities. In 1744 Brainerd himself moved to Pennsylvania where he lived for most of that year. It was only after he had crossed the border a year later into New Jersey that his 'marvellous success' began.[40] In June 1746, when Brainerd reflected on 'What amazing things God wrought in this space of time',[41] he concluded his report on those momentous days with:

> And, *first*, I cannot but take notice that I have in general, ever since my first coming among these Indians in New Jersey, been favoured with that assis-

---

[36] Spangenberg, *Instructions*, nos 18, 20 at pp. 15, 17.
[37] Idem, *Account of the . . . missions*, 60–1, quotation at p. 60.
[38] 1. Cor. ii. 2: ibid. 64, 68.
[39] Ibid. 70–1: Cranz, *History of Greenland*, ii. 425–6.
[40] Brainerd, journal, entry for 31 July 1745: Jonathan Edwards, *An account of the life of the late Mr David Brainerd, . . . to which is annexed: . . . : [from] his own diary . . . I. Mr Brainerd's journal among the Indians. II Mr Pemberton's sermon*, Edinburgh 1765, 163–4.
[41] Ibid. entry for 19 June 1746.

tance, which (to me) is *uncommon*, in preaching *Christ Crucified*, and making him the *centre* and *mark* to which all my discourses among them were directed.

God, Brainerd explained, had caused him to change his preaching so that he now sought to 'effect the *heart*'.[42] However, that Brainerd adopted his evangelical approach shortly after being a a close 'neighbour' of the Moravians in Pennsylvania is significant. Furthermore he would have known of them through his interpreter Moses Tattamy, a Delaware chief from north of Bethlehem who had been in contact with Moravians for some years before he met Zinzendorf in the area in 1742.[43] The Moravians were thus on sure ground when they stated, first in Cranz and later in Spangenberg's *Account of the . . . missions*, that 'We are well informed concerning that pious . . . indefatigable man', Brainerd. Even more significant was their observation that for

> as long as [Brainerd] continued the usual method of preaching . . . by connected arguments, he could effect nothing . . . but so soon as he took pattern by his neighbours, whose good success among the heathen he was an eyewitness of, and ventured straightway to preach to them simply the Saviour . . . such a large and quick awakening ensued that both he, and all the ministers of his persuasion who saw it were astonished, and forced to ascribe glory to God.[44]

Whatever the validity of the Moravians' 'claim', Brainerd's explanation for his God-given success in New Jersey was testimony to an evangelical mode of preaching.

Although the Moravians were selective and very cautious indeed before they would even consider any Christian becoming a full member of their Church,[45] the same constraints did not apply to the admission of heathen converts into the Church of Christ through baptism. There was no scriptural justification for delay. Baptism, the missionaries were taught, was a privilege to be granted once they had a 'true' impression that the gospel was working in the hearts of their candidates. Spangenberg advised that the 'custom' of prior catechising was not derived from the practice of 'Christ and his apostles; and besides, it occupies the mind, leaving the heart empty'. Baptism depended 'on

---

[42] Ibid. 423, 427. Italics are in the text.
[43] Moravians first met Moses Tattamy in 1734. For Zinzendorf and Tattamy see *The life of David Brainerd*, ed. Norman Pettit, in *The works of Jonathan Edwards*, ed. John E. Smith, vii, New Haven–London 1985, 254 n. 2. For Brainerd in Pennsylvania see 'appendix B', letter from the Moravian, M. S. Henry, historian of the Lehigh Valley, in Thomas Brainerd, *The life of John Brainerd*, Philadelphia 1856, 436–59. Henry traces Brainerd's movements. Evidence that David Brainerd and the Moravian Zeisberger ever met 'seems inconclusive': Richard A. Hasler, 'David Zeisberger's "Jersey connection" ', *TMHS* xxx (1998), 39.
[44] Cranz, *History of Greenland*, ii. 425–6; Spangenberg, *Account of the . . . missions*, 70–1.
[45] 'The Weal and Woe of the Unity' depended on who was admitted to communion: MCH, general synod 1764, resolutions, fo. 38.

the heart' and participation in communion on the 'right' understanding of the sacrament.[46]

The Church maintained and emphasised that care of the converted was an '*office of great trust*', for it 'has to do with souls'.[47] Readers of the *Instructions* were left in no doubt that baptism was only the first step towards making lasting conversions through 'Growth in the grace' and knowledge of the Saviour.[48] Great stress was placed on the missionaries' duty to lead 'all strayed sheep' back to their 'baptismal covenant'.[49] Exclusion was the last resort.[50] But, Spangenberg warned, customs and ideas which were part of a heathen's former life that were 'evil . . . must be rooted out'. Only customs consistent with Christian precepts could be allowed to continue.[51]

It was clear, incidentally, from the very first page of the *Instructions* that Spangenberg was addressing Moravian women as well as men. Missionaries' wives had a crucial but subsidiary role overseas: the same principles were followed as at home. The Church believed that members of the female sex would not 'open all their circumstances' to men and that 'some unsuitable, if not hurtful consequences' could arise, were men the only personal counsellors available.[52]

There can be little doubt that the Church's doctrine and practice of mission were generally observed by Moravian missionaries. Despite widely different circumstances, missions were conducted in the same manner. They were integrated within the Church and directed from the centre as part of the whole. The Church's authority was upheld everywhere by its members' beliefs, the use of the Lot by the Elders and the missionaries, and by a deeply rooted discipline. There were also universally established lines of reporting, supplemented by visitations from Elders or their nominees throughout the Moravian world. Nothing, humanly speaking, was left to chance.

Nevertheless it does not seem that the Elders dictated how a mission should evolve. For example, at the Cape of Good Hope, as Bernhard Krüger shows, the development of Genadendal into a recognisably Moravian settlement between 1793 and 1815 was not directed from Germany. It developed spontaneously on the ground in the way that seemed proper to the missionaries, who moved with great deliberation, constantly deferring to the Lot.[53] In Antigua, likewise, once the awakening among the slaves began in 1772, Peter Brown responded on his own initiative by baptising great numbers.

It is true, of course, that the formative period in the history of these missions occurred during wars which made communications, tenuous at best,

---

46 This discussion follows Spangenberg, *Instructions*, nos 27, 29, quotations at pp. 22, 25.
47 Ibid. no. 1 at p. 1.
48 Ibid. nos 32–3 at pp. 27–9, quotation at p. 27.
49 Ibid. nos 68–9, quotation at p. 53.
50 Ibid. nos 36–44 at pp. 31–8.
51 Ibid. nos 29, 33 at pp. 24–5, 28–9, quotation at p. 24.
52 Ibid. p. iii. See also nos 36–47 at pp. 30–7.
53 Krüger, *Pear tree*, 292–3.

Plate 3. Exorcism of four negro candidates for baptism. Woodcut reproduced from *Kurze, zuverlässige Nachricht von der, unter dem Namen der Böhmischen-Mährischen Brüder bekantent, Kirche Unitas Fratrum Herkommen*, n.p. 1757, by kind permission of the Unitätsarchiv, Herrnhut.

even worse. Missionaries were therefore left to their own devices to a greater extent than at other periods. Even so it is also notable that at the end of the Napoleonic wars it was the missionaries themselves who requested the first visitation to the Cape of Good Hope.[54]

Moravians at home and overseas addressed one another as 'brother' or 'sister'. This was much more than a convention; it was an expression of the enormous importance Moravians attached to a life led in Christian fellowship. They were members of the Brethren's Church, the Unitas Fratrum, their missions, the Brethren's missions. Samuel Greatheed of Newport Pagnell, a founding director of the LMS who knew the Moravians well, appreciated the unifying force behind these expressions. The Moravians, he said in a sermon preached in 1797 at Bedford, had

> vindicated the title they assumed: the *Unity of the Brethren*. Though dispersed, ... partly by Missionary labour, in every quarter of the globe; they are still one body, animated by one spirit; adhering to Jesus as their living head, and to each other as his members. But for this, ... what they have accomplished, would be incredible.[55]

---

[54] Ibid. 121.
[55] Samuel Greatheed, *General union recommended to real Christians, in a sermon preached at*

Plate 4. After baptism. Following the 'prostration' the newly baptised are raised and kissed by helpers from among their own nation. Woodcut reproduced from *Kurze, zuverlässige Nachricht von der, unter dem Namen der Böhmischen-Mährischen Brüder bekantent, Kirche Unitas Fratrum Herkommen*, n.p. 1757, by kind permission of the Unitätsarchiv, Herrnhut.

It is unthinkable that a rupture, such as happened between the BMS and its missionaries at Serampore in India after the loss of Fuller's wise counsel with his death in 1815,[56] could have occurred in the Moravian world. It would have been a denial of everything for which the Church stood. A similar situation would not have been allowed to develop, although individual missionaries, of course, left the Church for one reason or another. Unlike the Baptists, Moravian missionaries were neither in the employ of nor directed by a missionary society.

The influence of Moravian doctrine

It was apparent from the beginning that the object of the modern missionary movement was nothing less than global. Some of its first leaders therefore turned to the Moravians for the most complete model available to Protes-

Bedford . . . 1797, London 1798, 74. According to MCH, SFG minutes, Greatheed's regular donations to SFG commenced on 20 July 1790.
[56] E. Daniel Potts, *British Baptists in India, 1793–1837*, Cambridge 1967, 24–6.

tants, for that Church's religion of the heart, missionaries and institutions had proved their worth under widely different circumstances. Whilst the Inuit of Greenland and Labrador were a free and nomadic people, Africans in the Caribbean were slaves. The mission in India was 'the only one that has not succeeded like the others', a founding director of the LMS noted when he explained in 1795 the background to the formation of the new society.[57]

The Moravian Church had set important and useful precedents. Its missionaries were usually so-called unlettered men, the majority assisted by their wives, who had a defined responsibility for female converts. None of them received a salary and, to whatever extent was practicable, they collectively supported their mission. In 1792 about 140 men and women were serving across a broad mission field, at a cost to the Church itself of as little as around £3,000. Such mission statistics, though not financial details, were to be found in *Periodical Accounts*, whose editor, Ignatius La Trobe, willingly discussed Moravian missionary methods with his pious friends. Founders of the new societies must have been heartened to learn that the work could be conducted effectively, without a heavy reliance on funding from home.

The Moravian model was at the centre of many missionary leaders' thoughts when they considered for themselves how their societies' missions should be conducted. In the case of the Baptists, this can be inferred from Carey's *Enquiry* and confirmed by reference to his and other Baptist missionaries' correspondence from India with the BMS at home. From around 1796 Carey began to refer directly to how Moravian missions were conducted when he needed to explain in more detail to colleagues in England how he wished to develop his mission in India. Moravian influence on the LMS, on the other hand, was apparent immediately after that society's formation in 1795. It directors, who urgently needed to agree on how their first mission, that to the South Seas, should be conducted, immediately began to consider Moravian methods together.

Melville Horne (?1761–c. 1817)

There can be no doubt that Melville Horne's thinking was shaped generally, and in some instances quite specifically, by the Moravians. A grandson of Nathaniel Gilbert, whose family befriended the first Moravian in Antigua, Horne was a Wesleyan for a substantial part of his early life. Before he went overseas in 1792 to join his cousin, he had officiated at Madeley where he succeeded John Fletcher. The Bristol Moravians' record, dated 7 June 1792, of his visit to their city requires no further introduction: 'Br. Hartley became acquainted with a Church of England Clergyman, Mr. Melville Horne, who is

---

[57] Robert Cowie to his brother John, 8 Oct. 1795 (copy), CWM MS, Home Office extra 1/7/B.

going as Chaplain of the Settlement to Sierra Leone; having a very strong desire to preach the Gospel to the Negroes there.' It was in keeping with the development of Horne's thinking, revealed two years later in his *Letters on missions*, that he most probably sought out the Moravian minister in Bristol, John Hartley. Hartley, 'a lovely man among the Moravians', in Andrew Fuller's later estimation,[58] 'had much agreeable Conversation' with him and gave him 'Br. Spangenberg's Acc[ou]nt of the Brns. Method of preaching the Gospel among the Heathen; wh[i]ch he promis'd himself much pleasure & instruction in perusing'. Horne, the report continues, 'preached in the following weeks in many places, particularly in Mr Wesley's Room, in Bristol, was followed by very great crowds of hearers, & is truly a lively, & zealous witness of Jesus'.[59]

Horne completed his *Letters on missions* on his return from West Africa and they were published in Bristol in 1794. Despite his association with Wesleyans, they are a testimonial to Moravian influence and, specifically, to Spangenberg's great missionary pamphlet.[60] Many of his ideas were derived from the Moravian model. He used it as justification for his argument, backed up by his own experience in Sierra Leone, that missions ought to be manned by large groups of 'common men', men as united in their way of living together as in their manner of preaching to the heathen. He was convinced that it was essential, too, that their directors at home should be equally united on how the mission should be conducted.

Horne introduced his analysis of the Moravians by comparing them to the Jesuits, but without the suspected and invidious defects of that recently dissolved order. He went on to state that Moravians had 'laboured, and suffered, and effected *more than all of us* [Protestants]'.[61] A mission settlement as a basis for a Christian community, for which the Moravians as well as the Jesuits were famous, was an important part of his recommendations. Horne proposed that the first new British venture should be launched by not less than ten men acting as one mutually self-supporting unit overseas; half their number were to be pious laymen. Their whole establishment was to act as a 'seminary' from which the work could be extended in due course. He acknowledged that these ideas were not 'altogether novel'; the Moravians made great use of 'the piety of their lay brethren'.[62]

It is quite likely that Horne also took his suggestion of a 'seminary' partly from the Moravians. For instance, the successful launch of the Labrador mission had depended on two men, one of whom one had trained the other earlier in Greenland. The Labrador mission, itself an extension from Greenland, was also well known as having begun with one settlement which had

---

[58] Fuller to William Ward, 27 Oct. 1804, AL typescript, 4/5/1.
[59] BUL, BCD, 7 June 1792.
[60] Horne, *Letters*, nos 3, 7, 9 at pp. 34–7, 100–8, 135–6.
[61] Ibid. 34.
[62] Ibid. 43–4.

been established in 1771 by fourteen Moravians. This had by now been extended to three settlements. There were particular reasons for this mission being known in Britain: it was maintained by British Moravians with their own vessel sailing out of London, and other Christians gave their support through the SFG.

Horne understood that the economy with which Moravian missions were conducted, when compared with the cost of missions from other Churches, was a reason why they could be so extensive. This, and the scale of his own proposal, meant that missionaries capable of doing 'something' towards their 'own maintenance' were an 'indispensable necessity. The Apostles . . ., Jesuits, and the Moravians', he argued, 'have experienced the advantage'.[63]

There were limitations on the degree to which the Moravian model was appropriate for British Churches, two instances of which can be found in Horne's *Letters on missions*. The first related to married couples overseas. Although Horne appreciated the purpose underlying the Moravian practice, he came down in favour of single men from British Churches, at least in the beginning. His reason was revealing: the Moravians 'in this, and in many other respects, are a singular people . . . their women are educated in a way which render them fitter companions for missionaries than any other women in the world'.[64] In this he differed from Carey who had followed the Moravians in his *Enquiry* where he stated a preference for married couples and who had also thought that the missionaries, themselves, should be supported by others working at their crafts.[65]

The second was to some extent political. Horne was writing at a time in the 1790s when Dissenters in general and even Wesleyans on occasion, but with less justice, were suspected of harbouring dangerous political ideas.[66] Horne was sensitive to accusations such as these which, he recognised, might inhibit the development of new missionary endeavours. Compared to that of other Churches, Moravian discipline was for him 'severe and complicate' in contrast to ideas of personal liberty then prevalent in Europe. The discretion of Moravian missionaries was legendary; for they 'have never', Horne believed, 'provoked persecutions among the Heathen, nor incurred reproach among Europeans . . . by a turbulent spirit'. Wesleyans on the contrary, Horne feared, would be unable 'to steer clear of persecution, as the Moravians have done', although he anticipated that they too would succeed in the mission field.[67]

Missionary leaders in England recognised that Moravians were well integrated within their Church before being appointed missionaries. For as Samuel Greatheed, a director of the LMS, warned that society in 1796 'We

[63] Ibid. 44–5.
[64] Ibid. 68.
[65] Carey, *Enquiry*, 73.
[66] J. D. Walsh, 'Methodism at the and of the eighteenth century', in Rupert Davies and Gordon Rupp (eds), *A history of the Methodist Church in Britain*, i, London 1965, 302–4.
[67] Horne, *Letters*, 34, 37.

have not, like the Moravians, disciplined troops, but a hasty levy of irregulars . . . and are not to expect the subordination kept up in *their* missions.'[68] All the new missionary societies experienced difficulties of a disciplinary nature with some of the first men they sent overseas. The BMS, for example, was soon embarrassed by radically-minded missionaries who, contrary to instructions, meddled in politics. This became a repeated cause for concern for the society.[69]

Horne presented Moravian missionaries as the model for others to follow. They were 'men of ardent piety . . . entirely of one mind, as to the doctrines they teach, . . . and the discipline they exercise over their flocks'. His was a thorough appreciation not only of mission theory; he seems also to have understood what happened in practice. For instance, he was careful to note that the missionaries' 'scrupulous attention' to the Church's regulations had matured over the course of many years.[70] He seems to have been realistic about how much could reasonably be expected, at first, of new entrants into the mission field.

Horne urged that missionaries 'must . . ., possess a spirit truly catholick . . ., [and] serve the Church Universal', rather than their own denomination.[71] This passage echoes Spangenberg's warning in his *Account of the . . . missions* that 'the divisions in Christendom in so many parties' might well confuse the heathen and make their conversion less certain, adding that the Moravians on the other hand, who were 'neither for nor against this or the other party', were blessed when they learnt 'simply to preach Christ'.[72] Given the significance which Horne attached to the example of the Moravians, his thinking under this head may to some extent have been stimulated by them and by Spangenberg's warning. His plea certainly struck a welcome chord with the interdenominationally-minded founders of the LMS who, like the idealistic Thomas Haweis, shared his hopes.[73] They were to be disappointed.

Horne's role was thus that of a stimulating and widely respected missionary thinker whose *Letters on missions* must have added to the appreciations being made by missionary leaders of Moravian teaching and experience. His book not only influenced the formation of the LMS (indeed Thomas Haweis's

---

[68] Greatheed (on vetting candidates) to Haweis, 1 July 1796, letters to Haweis, ML, MS A 3024. For Samuel Greatheed (d. 1823) see John Morrison, *The fathers and founders of the London Missionary Society; with a brief sketch of Methodism and historical notices of the several Protestant missions from 1556 to 1839*, London–Paris n.d., 287–94.
[69] Basil Amey, 'Baptist Missionary Society radicals', BQ xxvi (1975–6), 363–71.
[70] Horne, *Letters*, 34–5.
[71] Ibid. 60.
[72] Spangenberg, *Account of the . . . missions*, 40.
[73] Wood, *Haweis*, 192–3, 238. See also W. R. Ward, *Religion and society in England, 1790–1850*, London 1972, 45.

review of it was an acknowledged catalyst[74]), but was read by succeeding generations of Baptist missionaries in India.[75]

The London Missionary Society

There was a significant difference between the Baptist and London missionary societies. Whereas the BMS was formed by a small, closely knit group of ministers, the LMS was established as 'The Missionary Society' by a large and diverse body of pious men who hoped to attract the support of Christians from across the denominations. It was soon evident that its founders were not as united as they should have been. They were quite unlike the Baptists in this and other respects.

No two men who had a prominent part in the affairs of the LMS could have been more different than Thomas Haweis, the evangelical clergyman, and David Bogue, the Dissenter, and tensions between them were evident from the beginning. Qualifications for missionaries, for example, were only one of the issues which divided them; Haweis suspecting, for instance, that personal and sectarian motives lay behind Bogue's advocacy of an academy for the preparation of missionaries.[76] In the event Haweis won the argument in the short term when he persuaded his colleagues to launch, without delay, their first venture, that to the South Seas.

The society's missionaries, that 'hasty levy of irregulars', totalling twenty-four souls, therefore sailed in 1796 without having been tutored in advance. Instead, their departure was preceded by an address delivered to them in July on behalf of the LMS by Dr Edward Williams, a minister from Rotherham, which confirms that the directors of the LMS shared with Haweis his great and well-known respect for Moravian missionary methods. Published by the society, as 'Counsels and instructions', Williams's address is substantially the same, and in many parts identical, to Haweis's *Missionary instructions*, also published in 1796.[77] In May a sub-committee of the LMS, established to draw up directions for missionaries, had considered a paper from Haweis which was either his *Missionary instructions* or a draft closely resembling the final version.[78] This seems to be confirmed by reference to a

---

[74] Lovett, *London Missionary Society*, i. 11–12.
[75] [Andrew Fuller], *Compiled by Andrew Fuller, memoirs of the late Rev. Samuel Pearce . . . with extracts from some of his most interesting letters*, Clipstone 1800, 130. See also *A catalogue . . . Serampore*, 36.
[76] T. Haweis, 'Autobiography', ML, MS B 1176, fo. 219. See also (undated) 'fragments of a diary', ML, MS B 1178, fo. 178; Wood, *Haweis*, 237–8.
[77] 'Counsels and instructions', in Henry Hunter and Edward Williams, *A sermon and charge delivered at Sion-Chapel, London: July 28, 1796, on the occasion of the designation of the first missionaries to the islands of the South Sea*, London 1796, 51–70. See also appendix 2.
[78] CWM MS, board minutes, 16, 24 May 1796, minutes of transactions 1/2. Two further papers from unnamed authors were also tabled.

postscript to the pamphlet in which Haweis introduced and commended to his fellow directors three letters from the Moravian Ignatius La Trobe, two written in November 1795, the third in February 1796. Rather than absorb their contents within the body of his own work, Haweis reproduced these letters in appendices because they 'contain hints so valuable and useful, . . . I think they will speak more forcibly by themselves; and I hope engage others of our brethren to pay a like serious attention to the subject, and produce something more complete for the instruction of our Missionary brethren'.[79]

The most recent of the three letters was a series of brief comments on each part of Haweis's *Missionary instructions*. Ignatius found nothing very material with which to disagree. His note on the first section can be taken as a fair representation of his views overall: 'Its whole contents are so excellent, and so much according to the experience of our missionaries, that I cannot possibly add any thing to them.'[80] His only qualification concerned Haweis's proposal to impress upon native peoples the superior capacity of Europeans by means of novelties: 'a magic lantern' and other instruments, for instance. His Church's missionaries had not attempted such an approach and it was one, Ignatius suggested, which was unlikely to gain their approval. Haweis accepted the warning; the relevant passage was not reproduced in the society's 'Counsels and instructions'.[81]

The origin of Ignatius La Trobe's letters is linked directly to a decision which had been taken in September 1795 at the first business meeting of the LMS: Moravian publications were to be 'laid upon the Table' and he was to be consulted. Directors, including Haweis, had several meetings with him and, before the year was out, 'his brotherly & affectionate' contribution to their deliberations was gratefully acknowledged.[82] One letter, the longest by far, answered eleven questions pertaining to the conduct of missions on which the society wished to be advised. These ranged from the qualifications of missionaries to the cost of the Moravians' Labrador vessel.

It was undoubtedly the same letter,[83] to which the Dissenting minister George Burder (1752–1832) referred a month later in a note to Haweis. One of the most respected of the society's founders and directors, Burder acknowledged 'The paper by Mr. La Trobe . . . [It] is most valuable, &, will, I trust, afford us great assistance . . . he exactly accords with the thoughts you have so frequently expressed.' Moreover, Burder continued, 'The success which has attended the Brethren, calls upon us to adopt their plan as our model.' Burder had copies made of this 'excel^t' paper for other ministers.[84]

---

[79] T. Haweis, *Missionary instructions, recommended to the serious attention of all . . . with an appendix, relative thereto, by the Rev. Mr Latrobe*, London 1796, 28–9.
[80] C. I. La Trobe to Thomas Haweis, 18 Feb. 1796, ibid. 'appendix no. I', 30.
[81] Cf. 'Fourth head' with 'appendix no. I', ibid. 18, 31.
[82] Quotations from CWM MS, board minutes, 28 Sept., 1 Oct., 9 Nov., 14 Dec. 1795, minutes of transactions 1/2.
[83] C. I. La Trobe to Haweis, 30 Nov. 1795, 'appendix no. III', 34–44.
[84] George Burder to Haweis, 23, 26 Dec. 1795, ML, MS A 3024.

Burder's father had been a deacon of the Congregational chapel in Fetter Lane, so Burder himself must have been aware of Moravians in London from his boyhood and seen their missionaries when they passed in the street. In 1803 he became pastor of the same chapel and remained there until his retirement twenty-four years later. Throughout that period he was the very influential secretary of the LMS.[85]

Haweis continued to canvass his colleagues. The next on his list may have been Joseph Hardcastle (1752–1819), the society's treasurer, whose opinion was much respected. A London merchant and Dissenter, who was also associated with Wilberforce's circle at Clapham Common, Hardcastle supported Moravian missions, which seem to have played a part in his own awakening. After Haweis had sent him 'Missionary hints & Mr La Trobe's paper', Hardcastle acknowledged them both with 'very high gratification'.[86]

Ignatius La Trobe's letters are written in his own style by a man who already had shown himself master of his subject. He had to be tactful in what he said to Haweis, but, when he warned him off ideas of impressing the heathen, he would have been well aware that Moravians were on their guard against making false Christians. Zinzendorf would have been appalled by Haweis's thinking and, in Spangenberg's words, 'Signs and wonders' were not to be found among the missionaries.[87] His advice to the LMS, which was promoted in a review of Haweis's *Missionary instructions* appearing in the *Evangelical Magazine*, was a further contribution to making Moravian missionary thought accessible to many.[88] What is more, the society continued to solicit his advice: for instance in 1796 on South Africa where the Moravians had recently renewed their mission.[89]

Qualifications of missionaries

On missionary qualifications the advice given by Ignatius to the LMS was again of crucial importance. In the course of their first business meeting in September 1795 the society's directors had agreed on 'Rules for the examination of missionaries'. They wished to be assured that 'No man' was selected unless 'he possess an eminent share of the Grace of God, and appears to have a call to this particular work'. A sub-committee of examiners was to be appointed; before a candidate could be accepted for service overseas all its members were to be unanimous on these points. Two rules which followed

---

[85] For George Burder see Morrison, *Fathers and founders*, ii. 81, 88–100.
[86] Joseph Hardcastle to Haweis, 2 Feb. 1796, ML, MS A 3024. For Hardcastle and the Moravians see Morrison, *Fathers and founders*, i. 303. According to SFG minutes annual donations from Hardcastle and his trading associates to the SFG commenced on 24 Feb. 1795.
[87] Spangenberg, *Account of the . . . missions*, 53.
[88] *EM* iv (1796), 259–60.
[89] C. I. La Trobe to Haweis, 8 Nov. 1796, ML, MS A 3024.

reflected Moravian thinking: 'It is not necessary that every Missionary should be a learned man. . . . Godly Men who understand Mechanic Arts, may be of signal use.'[90]

At the same meeting members resolved to consult Ignatius whose answers to questions relevant to the sub-committee's role supported these decisions. Ignatius began by carefully describing in his own words what constituted in the Moravians' belief a missionary's call, and explained how the Church attempted to satisfy itself that volunteers were confident of their calling. (The Elders in Germany, responsible for all appointments, depended on assessments made locally.) The LMS might have found the following advice in one sense reassuring. However, it also carried, by implication, an important rider and warning for every new missionary society:

> All seems, . . . to turn upon this, that we are first well assured, that those who offer, are *really children of God*. All our people (in our settlements more especially) are well known to the minister and other servants of the congregation, not only as to their public walk, but as to their private life and sentiments.

How were responsible Moravians able to satisfy themselves that candidates had come to a mature decision, guided by the Saviour, to serve His cause overseas? It was 'by a continual confidential intercourse',[91] those formal and informal opportunities presented by the Church's intimate and supportive discipline which was surely the crucial premise to Ignatius' advice. It was one that ministers of British Churches, accountable for assessing volunteers, overlooked at their peril. However, until they established academies or at least procedures for preparing and vetting candidates, the new societies must have found this advice difficult to follow in practice.

Richard Lovett, the historian of the LMS, believed that the society and its candidates were carried away in the beginning by enthusiasm for the South Seas venture. In their haste to get it underway the directors made too many inappropriate and ill-judged appointments in their first selections.[92] The BMS may have encountered similar but fewer problems. Fuller, the society's cautious secretary, explained to Carey in 1796 that it was not a lack of funds, 'but of *suitable characters*' which prevented reinforcements being sent to join him in India.[93] Such an attitude contributed to the resolution made by the BMS two years later concerning volunteers. They were to serve a probationary period, under a minister, before being appointed missionaries. A candidate placed in the care of Sutcliff later that year explained: 'They agreed I should come to Olney for a time, as well for my improvement in Knowledge, as that they might have some proof of my ability, before I was finally

---

[90] CWM MS, minutes of transactions 1/2, 28 Sept. 1795.
[91] C. I. La Trobe to Haweis, 30 Nov. 1795, 'appendix no. III', 37.
[92] Lovett, *London Missionary Society*, i. 46, 60.
[93] Fuller to William Carey, 9 Aug. 1796, AL typescript, 4/5/1.

accepted.'[94] Thus the BMS established a procedure that provided, amongst other opportunities, an intimate method for assessing candidates over time.

The LMS sought Ignatius' advice on whether it was prudent to send wives overseas from the beginning. This question was associated with the idea of a settlement being established straightaway. Where there was an element of doubt, Moravians usually sent single men in advance, Ignatius explained. However, as this did not seem to apply to the South Seas project, he cited examples of settlements being established at once. He also reminded the LMS why 'Missionaries' wives' rendered 'the most essential service in conducting the mission'.[95] In this instance Ignatius assisted the society in resolving an outstanding issue: at its meeting in November 1795, when directors reported on discussions with him, the LMS agreed that married men, accompanied by their wives, should be eligible as missionaries.[96]

The LMS posed five questions regarding the education and training of missionaries that might be thought necessary to prepare them for service overseas. Ignatius' reply reflected the Moravian Church's belief that nothing specific was required, providing always that the main condition concerning the call was met. He explained that 'previous tuition' in divinity was not necessary for Moravian men or women. All Moravians, and those destined to minister the Gospel most especially, would already have known their Bible and prayed for 'constant guidance of the Spirit'. Moreover, a missionary's preaching had always to be kept simple and to the main point, and a craft was of greater utility than 'theological learning' among non-Europeans.[97]

It could have been anticipated that Ignatius would discourage the LMS from looking to scholars for its missionaries. Two years previously he had advised the Baptists that 'Learning, and what the world calls accomplishments, we have not experience to be of much use.'[98] Taken out of context, this last statement appears ingenuous. But Ignatius left his readers in no doubt that missions did require some men educated to a level that would enable them to construct written languages where none had existed. Scholars undoubtedly possessed superior skills with which to acquire languages, but he nevertheless explained that 'those *called* the wise and learned', who had studied at some seat of learning, were seldom 'so well' suited 'for a mission to the heathen, as men brought up to a mechanical profession':

> But as mere civilization and improvement in various arts is not our immediate object, but the conversion of the heathens' heart to God; and we are told, and know, that man 'by wisdom knew not God'; we cannot admit the learned to have any advantage over the unlearned, in the work of a mission.

---

[94] Daniel Brundson, later missionary at Serampore, to M. J. Bedford, 30 Nov. 1798, AL, MS IN/2. For the BMS resolution see 20 Sept. 1798, BPA i (1800), 418.
[95] C. I. La Trobe to Haweis, 30 Nov. 1795, 'appendix no. III', 41.
[96] CWM MS, minutes of transactions 1/2, 9 Nov., 1795.
[97] C. I. La Trobe to Haweis, 30 Nov. 1795, 'appendix no. III', 38–9.
[98] C. I. La Trobe to John Rippon, 26 June 1793, *Baptist Annual Register* i (1793), 532.

To ensure that he was not misunderstood, Ignatius made two further points, the first being that some scholarly Moravians were in the field who, like the apostle [Paul]' laid 'aside all human wisdom' and thus made their own 'learning . . . useful in its proper place'; the second that few scholars were physically suited to the rigours of a missionary's life.[99]

Although Ignatius' letter was not the direct cause, the idea it expressed, that conversion through the heart, rather than civilisation and improvement, was the missionaries' first objective, soon resonated north of the border. Given the Protestant emphasis on 'The Book' and literacy, the question would surely have arisen somewhere. In May 1796 the assembly of the Church of Scotland debated whether the priority was 'civilisation' or conversion. On 27 May Dr John Erskine of Edinburgh, the leading advocate of the evangelical cause in Scotland, refuted the very idea that civilisation among the heathen was a prerequisite for their conversion. To support his case Erskine cited the example of the Moravians' experience in Greenland and commended Cranz's mission history to the attention of the assembly.[100]

The LMS also consulted Ignatius on how languages could most easily be learnt by missionaries. This was best achieved by these men living 'among the heathen and conversing with them daily', he replied, and the Church believed that there were advantages in this method for both sides. Moreover, although some of the more learned had prepared 'vocabularies and grammars', there was seldom time for newly appointed missionaries to study before taking up posts overseas. Until then, they usually continued in their normal course of duties at home, such as by working at their crafts.[101]

The burden of Ignatius La Trobe's advice was therefore that Moravians 'found mechanics of good sound understanding, and accustomed to bodily labour' to be the people most suited to missionary service.[102] All this was too much, or rather too little, for David Bogue. In April 1796, after receiving the Moravian's advice, Bogue urged his colleagues in a memorandum on India to find 'men of Talents'. He wished them to be 'able divines', with a capacity for languages, who had first studied at home. Bogue believed that however much 'plain men may be suited to the savage Greenlanders', they were 'by no means qualified to carry the Gospel to People so refined, ingenious & literary as the inhabit[ant]s of India'. He clinched his argument with the statement that

---

99 C. I. La Trobe to Haweis, 30 Nov. 1795, 'appendix no. III', 39–40.
100 *Account of the proceedings and debate, in the general assembly of the Church of Scotland, 27 May 1796, . . . respecting the propagation of the Gospel among the heathen*, Edinburgh 1796, 31, 35. For the development of the opposing view held by 'rational Calvists' see Ian Maxwell, 'Civilization or Christianity: the Scottish debate on mission methods, 1750–1835' (North Atlantic missiology project xii, 1996), typescript, 2–8.
101 C. I. La Trobe to Haweis, 30 Nov. 1795, 'appendix no. III', 42–3, 39.
102 Ibid. 40.

'Christ chose plain men but He gave them supernatural Endowments which are not now to be expected.'[103]

The Moravians were not unfamiliar with this issue. That most Moravian missionaries were indeed 'plain men' was not a barrier to the Church attaching the utmost importance to the acquisition of native languages, teaching literacy in the vernacular, and above all to the translation of hymns for the converts' use and edification.[104] Missionary leaders from other Churches would surely have been aware that Moravian craftsmen, like the missionary Jens Haven, spoke Inuit before he first went to Labrador and that Moravians had created a grammar and dictionary from the Greenlanders' difficult language.[105] Nor did the lack of a scholarly education prevent Moravians from appreciating Bogue's particular concerns with reference to India. For instance, when James La Trobe, a cabinet-maker, was in India he was by no means unaware of those cultural and religious differences between Europeans and the native people which inhibited the mission's progress.[106]

Bogue continued to be preoccupied with his conviction that missionaries ought to be trained before being appointed and in the course of 1796 he widened the scope of his argument. He turned his frustration on his fellow directors at the LMS who 'thought nothing more necessary for a mechanic than a serious Mind'. Bogue was insistent, first, that every man whom the LMS sent overseas should be endowed with 'considerable knowledge of the Doctrine of the Gospel', and second, that only those who had given proof of their faith and 'stability' over several years ought to be selected.[107] Moravians would have agreed with this, but they did not believe that any special preparation or new facilities were necessary in their own case. Their settlements at home were described in 1776 as 'proved seminaries' for missionaries, a view to which the Church tenaciously held. In 1818 a proposal for a training school was rejected by the general synod which decided to retain the Church's time-honoured ways of providing men and women for His service overseas.[108]

The new societies, however, could not continue without appropriate institutions. The Baptists developed their own procedures, based on candidates being placed under the supervision of ministers, while in 1800 directors of the LMS decided to establish an academy for the preparation of missionaries. However, as ' "The principal point" ' was that their ' "instruction must chiefly

---

[103] David Bogue, memorandum concerning missionaries in Surat, 7 Apr. 1796, CWM MS, South India general 1/1/A.
[104] Spangenberg, *Account of the . . . missions*, 50, 82–3.
[105] Marcella Rollmann, 'The role of language in the Moravian missions to eighteenth-century Labrador', UF xxxiv (1993), 58.
[106] James La Trobe at Patna to his niece, 1784 (copy), Lucy Torode collection.
[107] Bogue to 'Dear Sir', 28 Oct. 1796, CWM MS, home incoming letters (Home Office), 1/3/B.
[108] *Brotherly agreement*, vii; MCH, general synod 1818, resolutions, fo. 272.

refer to the heart"', the society did not depart from a central tenet of Moravian doctrine.[109]

Preaching the Gospel

Patience, if need be for years, and low expectations for the number of converts to be made overseas were integral to the Moravians' thinking. A 'time of waiting', Spangenberg had explained, was necessary for the missionaries to see 'whether there be here or there a person' who was being prepared through God's grace to 'hear and receive a word concerning Christ Jesus'. Spangenberg went on to cite examples of the missionaries' great 'patience to wait for the right time' for their first fruit to appear.[110] These were to be invaluable hints for founders of the new societies, the men they sent overseas and indeed for impatient supporters at home.

Horne described the Moravians' zeal for missions as 'calm, steady, persevering', and George Burder, in an important 'Address' published before the LMS was formed, associated these qualities with the early history of the Greenland mission.[111] There is much evidence that the well-known example of the missionaries' forbearance on Greenland made a great impression on the Baptists too. When Carey and Thomas left for India in June 1793 Baptists at home were warned that they should not despair if their 'utmost hopes' for conversions failed to materialise in a short space of time. Ministers recalled that in Greenland Moravians 'waited a considerable time before the seed they sowed ... began to promise a joyful harvest';[112] they also cited the experience of David Brainerd in North America. In August 1795 when Carey had been in India for less than two years, without a convert in sight, Samuel Pearce, a Baptist minister at Birmingham and his intimate friend, reminded him of the Moravians' similar experience. 'Be not discouraged ... if you do not succeed immediately', Pearce counselled, 'You know the Brethren laboured nearly six years without effect in Greenland; but they persevered.'[113] 'Persevere, we will Persevere', Carey replied.[114]

The example of Greenland was not only a source of consolation and encouragement: Pearce's 'You know' is all but confirmation that Carey had studied Cranz's *History of Greenland* before he went overseas. Alongside

---

109 Report of 'The committee appointed to draw up ... a plan for a seminary', 5 May 1800, in Lovett, *London Missionary Society*, i. 70–1.
110 Spangenberg, *Account of the . . . missions*, 51, 53.
111 Horne, *Letters*, 36: George Burder, 'An address' (April 1795), in *Sermons, preached*, p. xvi n.
112 'Address of the ... Northampton Association', BPA i (1800), 52.
113 Samuel Pearce to Carey, 27 Aug. 1795, in [Samuel Pearce], *Correspondence: containing extracts of letters from the late Mr Samuel Pearce, to the missionaries in India, between the years 1794 and 1798: and from Mr John Thomas, from 1798 to 1800*, London 1814, 49–50.
114 Carey to Pearce, 9 Nov. 1796, AL, MS IN/13, box 2.

Edwards's *Life* of Brainerd, it seems to have been considered essential reading for men who thought deeply about foreign missions. Pearce himself had for long been a keen student of missions when in October 1794 he volunteered his services. Two weeks earlier he was moved to record in his diary that 'The conduct and success of Stach, Boonish, and other Moravian Missionaries in Greenland, both confound and stimulate me. O Lord, forgive my past indolence in thy service.'[115] Matthew Stach and Frederick Bohnisch were two of three pioneers who made a resolution in 1735 that 'if even in ten years not one Greenlander should be converted, we would not allow our spirits to sink, but would endure to the end'. It was this pledge, or the complete account of their compact, both to be found in the *History of Greenland*,[116] that Pearce had recalled.

Cranz also recorded the events of 1738 in Greenland, when the missionaries' first convert was 'solidly awakened by the doctrine of Jesus's sufferings'. This confirmed for Moravians that the crucified Saviour should be at the centre of their preaching: they believed that this route to the heart, leading to conversion, had been revealed to one of their number through the intercession of 'the Holy Spirit'.[117] Ignatius drew their own account of these momentous days to the attention of the LMS,[118] just as earlier he had told Baptists of the Greenland experience.[119]

It is also worth noting that in that same work the suggestion first appeared, to be repeated *verbatim* in Spangenberg's *Account of the . . . missions*, that Moravians were the agents of God's providence when David Brainerd changed to 'their' evangelical manner of preaching.

Carey retained his particular respect for the Moravians which first made itself manifest with the publication of his *Enquiry*. His description of them six years later, as 'men eminent for godliness', was more than just a passing observation in the context of his reply to a letter from his old mentor at Olney, John Sutcliff.[120] A hint that he might adopt the Moravians' mode of preaching can be found in some of his earlier letters from India. He had been in India for a little over two years when he addressed peasants up country with the assistance, most probably, of an interpreter. Carey found it apparently 'easy to confound' their arguments, 'but', he reported to Fuller in 1796, 'My great Weapon is, and shall be Jesus Christ and him Crucified.'[121] Something of Carey's resolution and tribulations comes through in a letter to his 'dear

---

[115] Pearce, diary, 10 Oct. 1794, in [Fuller], *Memoirs of . . . Samuel Pearce*, 121.
[116] Frederic Bohnish (English spelling), 'Memoir', reproduced in Cranz, *History of Greenland*, ii. 469. For the complete account of the compact see ibid. i. 351–2.
[117] Ibid. i. 385–8 (in account of 2–18 June 1738). See also ibid. ii. 424.
[118] C. I. La Trobe to Haweis, 30 Nov. 1795, 'appendix no. III', 42.
[119] C. I. La Trobe to Rippon, 26 June 1793, *Baptist Annual Register* i (1793), 533.
[120] Carey to Sutcliff, 16 Jan. 1798, AL, MS IN/13, box 1.
[121] Carey to Fuller, 23 Apr. 1796, Carey's letters to Ryland, correspondence of William Carey and John Ryland, Northamptonshire Record Office, Northampton, MS, CSBC.9.

Sisters' written at this time. 'I try to speak of Jesus Christ and him crucified, and of him alone', he wrote, 'but my soul is often dejected to see no fruit.'[122]

In 1799, having apparently failed to make even one convert to Christianity, Cary joined the party of Baptist missionaries which had just arrived at Serampore. Among their number were Joshua Marshman and William Ward with whom he was to form the famous 'Serampore trio'. When they considered together how the gospel should be preached in India, they would draw on the example of the Moravians and their long experience in the field, together with that of David Brainerd's brief 'success'. Together the three men settled at Serampore with the intention of establishing a Christian missionary community based on the Moravian model.

Before their appointment to the mission Marshman had been under Ryland's guidance at Bristol and Ward, who intended to train for the ministry, had spent two years at the Baptists' academy at Halifax, near the renowned Moravian settlement at Fulneck.[123] Thus both men had had the opportunity of contact with Moravians during their probationary period. Ward's observation that the Moravians' 'child like temper' was 'one great reason' which enabled their missionaries to live together in 'brotherly love', may well have been based on personal experience.[124]

During their outward voyage they read Spangenberg's *Account . . . of the missions* and Cranz's *History of Greenland* and were greatly impressed. 'Thank you, ye Moravians', wrote Ward in his journal, 'you have done me good. If I am ever a missionary worth a straw, I shall owe it to you under our Saviour.' Marshman's thoughts ran in a similar vein after he had read Spangenberg's work.[125] Ward, perhaps the most thoughtful of the trio and certainly the closest to the Moravians in his thinking, believed that the Moravian pioneers in Greenland should be held 'in everlasting remembrance. Their testimony of the blood of Immanuel', he continued, 'will be the centre to which I shall be drawn'. It was surely reading this in Ward's journal, and his expressions of humility and 'brotherly love' engendered by the example of 'Moravian Missionaries',[126] that prompted some of Ryland's 'many tears' of 'pleasure'. These were due in part, Andrew Fuller reported, to Ward's evident 'attachment to . . . the spirit of the Moravians'.[127]

It was Ward who drafted at Serampore in 1805[128] the *Form of agreement: reflecting the great principles upon which the brethren of the mission at Serampore think it their duty to act in the work of instructing the heathen, agreed . . . October*

---

122 Carey to his sisters, 10 Apr. 1796, AL, MS FPC. E.20.
123 For Joshua Marshman (1768–1837) and William Ward (1769–1823) see *BDEB*.
124 AL, William Ward, missionary journal, i, entry for 22 June 1799.
125 Ibid. entry for 21 June 1799; Marshman to his father, 4 Sept. 1799, AL, MS IN/19A.
126 Ward, journal, i, 16, 22 June 1799.
127 Fuller to Ward, 13 June 1800, AL typescript, 4/5/1.
128 Ward, journal, ii, 5 Oct. 1805.

7, 1805. One clause in particular is a testimony to Moravian influence on Carey and his colleagues:

> Fifthly. In preaching to the heathen, we must keep to the example of Paul, and make the great subject of our preaching, Christ Crucified. . . . It is a well known fact that the most successful Missionaries in the world at the present day make the atonement of Christ their continued theme. We mean the Moravians. They attributed all their success to the preaching of the death of our Saviour.

The Baptists also confirmed that, like the Moravians, they would keep their first instruction of the heathen 'simple', care for and keep 'watch over the souls' of the converted, and labour constantly with 'patience'.[129]

There can be little doubt that Fuller and his fellow ministers at home, Ryland in particular for instance, were already in sympathy with the main thrust of this part of the *Agreement*. On the same day that the document was ratified by the missionaries at Serampore, Ward wrote in acknowledgement of a letter from Fuller that 'The crucified Sav. has been your theme so much lately'.[130] Moreover, it was not only the Baptists who justified their method of preaching by referring to the experience of 'the most successful Missionaries'. A similar phrase appears in the same context in the LMS–Haweis instructions of 1796.[131]

The approach adopted by Baptists and the London Missionary Society to the conversion of the heathen, which had originated in the Apostle Paul's instruction to the Corinthians, had now been endorsed in the field by the experience of Moravians and then by Brainerd's marvellous success. It is encapsulated in the words of the evangelical Ward who, following the Moravians, believed that Christ 'is the key that unlocks every thing'.[132] Founders of the new societies and the men they prepared for the mission field continued to recall the Moravians' experience. In 1815 Robert Moffat, later LMS missionary in Bechuanaland, was a student at the society's academy under Bogue's tuition. On the manner of preaching, Moffat noted that the Moravians 'began on the nature and perfections of God: afterwards they preached on the sufferings of Christ from which great effects followed'.[133]

---

[129] *Form of agreement: reflecting the great principles upon which the brethren of the mission at Serampore think it their duty to act in the work of instructing the heathen, agreed . . . October 7, 1805,* Serampore 1805, 6–7.

[130] Ward to Fuller (incomplete) acknowledgement of Fuller to Ward, 27 Oct. 1804, 7 Oct. 1805, AL, MS IN/16.

[131] 'Counsels', 58; reference to the 'most successful missions'.

[132] Ward to Fuller, 7 Oct. 1805, AL, MS IN/16.

[133] On preaching see typescript from [Robert] Moffat's original lecture notes of missionary lectures given by David Bogue', CWM, R8.

Social and economic issues

That Moravian missions were intended to be self-supporting encouraged Baptists in India, the BMS at home and the London society to adopt similar strategies. Their leaders also cited the example of the Moravians to meet objections from those who suspected that the integrity of men and missions could be compromised if missionaries had a dual role. Although, when these suspicions were first aired in the 1790s, such fears may have been exaggerated, they did not entirely go away. Early in the nineteenth century, when David Bogue, for instance, drew attention to the dangers that could arise from 'Blending other Employments with Missionary Labours', he hoped that the practice would soon be unnecessary.[134]

Moravian leaders, who had always attempted to mitigate the risks inherent in the Church's missionaries having to earn their keep, seem to have been reasonably confident that they had the balance about right.[135] In the early years many lessons must have been learnt, but later on the Church was quite open in drawing attention to opportunities for craftsmen to work in support of the mission settlement in India.[136] No system of selection could ever be perfect, but the motives of all Moravian candidates should first have been established before volunteers were considered by the Church's Elders. There were, moreover, controls exercised within the framework of each mission, while the practice of a community of goods was intended as a specific check on an individual's pecuniary ambitions.[137]

Against this background Ignatius La Trobe explained to the LMS in 1795 the various advantages which, in the Moravians' experience, accrued from missionaries as well as their lay assistants having useful employment. These were not confined to those economic benefits on which the whole Moravian project partly depended. Ignatius' discussion reflected both the Church's belief in a work ethic and that many Moravians were craftsmen. He explained that 'we think it good and profitable that Missionaries have something to do with their bodies, as well as their minds. It affords relief and variety, which even the most zealous and spiritual Missionary requires. . . . Nothing, undoubtedly, would be more detrimental . . . than a want of employ. . . . Of course', he concluded, even the work of a pious layman should 'never . . . interfere with his usefulness in . . . serving the mission in a spiritual way.'[138]

The LMS, which embraced the idea of sending craftsmen and men from

---

134 D. Bogue's lectures (I. Lowndes), Dr Williams's Library, London, New College collection, MS L14/9, fos 239, 249. Lowndes and Moffat were Bogue's students in 1815 at Gosport.
135 For example Zinzendorf (1733), in Spangenberg, *Leben*, iii/iv. 810–13; Spangenberg (1755), in Müller, *200 Jahre*, 331.
136 Letter . . . concerning the mission . . . in the East Indies, MCH, archive material relating to Bristol, pkt 4, 7 Aug. 1787.
137 Spangenberg, *Instructions*, no. 13 at pp. 11–12.
138 C. I. La Trobe to Haweis, 25 Nov. 1795, 'appendix no. II', 33.

the land to the South Sea islands, warned its missionaries that 'nothing would be more dangerous than a spirit of idleness'. Members of the first contingent were advised that they 'should have a community of goods' in the society's property, and that the 'produce' of their labours should 'come into a common stock'.[139]

In September 1795, when Thomas Haweis discussed options for the missionaries' conveyance to the South Seas, one of them was that the society should purchase its own vessel. Haweis may already have anticipated the objections which soon arose to the scale of the investment and from members opposed, it seems, to this religious institution taking on a commercial purpose.[140] In order to advance his proposal, therefore, and deal with such objections, Haweis again cited the example of the Moravians. Members of that Church owned the vessel which returned to Britain each year from the Labrador coast with produce acquired through barter with the Inuit. He understood that sales in London usually covered the mission's costs and that a dividend 'often' was paid.[141] As the Moravians were now greatly respected, their participation in trade to this extent for an evangelistic purpose was a commendation in itself. Directors of the LMS later agreed to the society's purchase of the *Duff*, a vessel of 300 tons costing nearly £5,000, and that she should return with freight from the Orient to defray the cost of establishing the mission. It may be noted in passing that unlike the Moravians the society does not seem to have been inhibited by a lack of funds. Within the first nine months of its existence the LMS had raised over £11,000,[142] an enormous sum by Moravian standards.

The example of the Moravians also enabled the BMS to answer its critics among Baptists in England in 1796 when it became known that Carey and John Thomas had taken employment in India. That they might do so was foreshadowed by Carey in his *Enquiry*. Moreover, the BMS 'in a sort' had agreed with the two men, before their departure, that it would be necessary for them 'to provide for themselves'.[143] The society could not then have anticipated, however, that Carey would take up a post as manager of an indigo factory and that Thomas was to be similarly employed. When this became known, Baptists in London objected, saying that they believed that missionaries could not pursue two objects 'of a different tendency'. In an unpublished letter the BMS soon warned Carey and Thomas that it too had

---

[139] 'Counsels', 66, 68.
[140] For this and the objection see Haweis's undated draft address to the directors of the Missionary Society, ML, MS 1961/2: Y 839, fos 234–55. For representations see Burder to Haweis, 26 Jan. 1796, ML, MS A 3024.
[141] For this and the previous paragraph see T. Haweis, 'Memoir on the most eligible part to begin a mission', 24 Sept. 1795, in *Sermons, preached*, 181.
[142] Lovett, *London Missionary Society*, i. 84.
[143] BPA i (1800), 93, referring to letters from India.

reservations concerning their participation 'in affairs of trade', but not to the point of prohibiting it.[144]

Discussion of this matter in the Baptists' *Periodical Accounts* included an extract of a letter from John Newton, a most respected friend. Newton met the London critics of the society and of Carey head on. He did not quarrel in principle with missionaries supporting themselves overseas and he cited the example of the Moravians. For as long as a man's motives were driven by a 'love of souls, . . . attention to business . . . will not hurt', Newton advised. He then made the crucial point about Moravians who found work overseas: 'they never *lay up*: they live upon a common stock'. They 'are excellent patterns for others', he added.[145] Newton confined his financial support to Moravian missions for 'there I seem to know what I am about', as he explained in 1795 to one of his many correspondents. 'I know their missionaries are eminently endued with a spirit of disinterestedness'. Nor did he disparage Carey for whom he soon developed an equal respect, and he made this known.[146]

However, Daniel Potts has suggested that what appeared to be a storm in a tea cup in 1796 left a taint of suspicion which led to the much later rupture between Serampore and the BMS.[147] Although indignant that his integrity had been questioned,[148] Carey, at the end of the year, turned his mind to how his mission could develop. In the first of two letters, he gave the BMS an outline of the 'advantages of a Christian Society'. Two benefits, in particular, which he identified, suggested that his ideas were influenced by the Moravians. First, the mission, he proposed, would be economically viable if missionaries and their helpers lived together in one community, with some of them being gainfully employed. Second, Carey envisaged that the whole group would 'add to the impetus of each particular soul'.[149]

In a much more detailed letter, Carey told Fuller that his proposal was 'similar to what the Moravians do', and he looked ahead to a future when he might be joined by up to eight families. He recognised that for this to be practicable the group had to be self-supporting. He also implored the BMS to send out 'more Missionaries'. He wanted them all to live and conduct themselves as one unit, for the wives to be 'as hearty in the Work as their Husbands', and to be governed by 'fixed Rules' of which one was to have 'nothing of our own but all the general stock'. 'The utility of this Community of Goods . . . will be obvious', Carey concluded.[150]

Eighteenth-century England had 'not forgotten' the experiments of the

---

144 BMS to Carey and John Thomas, Mar. 1795, AL typescript, 4/5/1.
145 BPA i (1800), 95–6. Newton is identified in the index to this volume.
146 Letter XXVII, 8 Oct. 1795, in John Campbell (ed.), *Letters and conversational remarks of the Rev. John Newton*, London n.d., 83–4. With reference to Carey see also letter XXXIII, 5 Apr. 1797, ibid. 100.
147 Potts, *British missionaries in India*, 14–15.
148 Fuller's note on Carey to BMS, 12 Jan. 1796, AL, MS IN/13 box 1.
149 Carey to BMS, 28 Dec. 1796, ibid.
150 Carey to Fuller, 16 Nov. 1796, ibid.

Anabaptists of Munster and others.[151] This may explain why the BMS could not decide on the 'propriety . . . of socializing families' in its first response, given in 1797, to Carey's ideas. Later that year Fuller wrote again to Carey: the BMS, he advised, now had 'nothing to object. The experience of the Moravians seems to sanction it'. This was the only reason given for the society's approval of Carey's plan. However, it could not be realised, Fuller noted, without 'more missionaries, and without some active amiable women amongst them'.[152]

The BMS seems to have been seized by Carey's ideas for a mission settlement based on the Moravian model that could sustain itself. About sixteen months later a large party including four carefully selected missionaries was assembled in England. Ward was the only single man among them and Marshman, like the others, was accompanied by his wife when they sailed in the summer of 1799 for India. Fuller had by then given Carey the good news of the society's intentions: 'Such a company we hope will strengthen your hands. . . . But now we apprehend you will find it necessary to form what you proposed, a kind of Moravian settlement; as otherwise we do not see how they can be supported.'[153]

By May 1801 the whole contingent together with Carey were settled at Serampore where they established their 'Christian Society'. A school had been opened and Carey had taken up his appointment at the College in Calcutta. The Baptists' total income from these sources alone, Marshman informed Fuller, was already about £1,000. Marshman also described how

> We are all united in one Society . . . one Common Stock . . . and we have entered into a solemn agreement that no Brother shall ever carry on any private trade; on the observation of this depends the very existence of the Mission; violate it, and, in such a country as this, the missionaries may get rich – but the mission dies.[154]

These thoughts were entirely in accord with Moravian teaching on which five years earlier Carey had based his recommendation for a Baptist mission settlement in India. The existence of the Moravian model seems to have been crucial to this proposal and Fuller's decision which sanctioned it. It was this that led to the foundation of the community at Serampore and the beginning of a progressive Baptist mission in India.

---

[151] J. D. Walsh, 'John Wesley and the community of goods', in Keith Robbins (ed.), *Protestant evangelicalism: Britain, Ireland and America, c. 1750–1950: essays in honour of W. R. Ward*, Oxford 1990, 26.
[152] Fuller to Carey, 18 Jan., 6 Sept. 1797, AL typescript, 4/5/1. Although the year of the first letter to Carey is unclear, the sequence leaves little room for doubt.
[153] Fuller to Carey, 25 Feb. 1799, ibid. Fuller to Revd J. Saffery, 1 May 1799, ibid. names the complete party.
[154] Marshman to Fuller, 2 May 1801, AL, MS IN/19A.

The example of the Moravian Church was one of the factors which inspired the formation of the Baptist and London missionary societies. Evangelical leaders, conscious that the failure of their own Churches to work for the conversion of the heathen to Christianity was no longer acceptable, gained confidence from the example, the perseverance and the scale of the Moravian missions and reassurance that their entry into the mission field was practicable. As the recognised missionary authority, the Moravian Church and its missionary teaching and practice was enormously influential. Significant aspects of the Moravian model were taken up by Baptists, by Melville Horne and by the LMS, while the Church's publications, alongside Edwards's *Life* of Brainerd, were the essential reading matter of the late eighteenth-century missionary.

7

The Beginning of the Modern Missionary Movement, 1800

The Church Missionary Society was founded in 1799, exclusively by Church Evangelicals; each denomination now had in effect its own missionary society.[1] The LMS had indeed been formed on an interdenominational basis, but most Church Evangelicals had remained aloof, and by a large majority. Thus in 1796 the respected Joseph Hardcastle of the LMS, and friend of both parties, failed to persuade members of Wilberforce's influential circle, the Saints, to associate themselves with it.[2] Largely in the hands of Dissenters, it was to become a Congregationalist society, and the very tiny minority of clergy prominent at first, such as Thomas Haweis, were 'irregulars'.

Political and ecclesiastical constraints were uppermost in the minds of those concerned and establishment-minded Church Evangelicals, Eclectics and their 'Clapham sponsors', who together formed the new society, initially called 'The Society for Missions to Africa and the East', on 'the Church principle'. The 1790s, in the aftermath of the French Revolution, were not a particularly favourable time to launch missionary ventures. In Britain political and social tensions ran high: evangelicals generally, still known as 'enthusiasts' and suspect, had yet to achieve respectability, and the hierarchy of the Established Church could not be expected to welcome an independent missionary society alongside the SPCK and SPG. One of the new society's first initiatives, therefore, was to seek the endorsement of the archbishop of Canterbury, John Moore, sending him an 'Account' of the society; Wilberforce led the delegation which canvassed his opinion. The archbishop's response being decidedly equivocal, the CMS hesitated until the summer of 1800 before embarking on what was to be a prolonged search, beginning in Britain, for missionaries.[3]

It was only then that the CMS cautiously came out into the open, circu-

---

[1] Wesleyan missions were controlled by the Methodist Conference from 1790 until 1813 when the Methodist Missionary Society was established: N. Allen Birtwhistle, 'Founded in 1786: the origins of the Methodist Missionary Society', *PWHS* xxx (1955), 25–9.

[2] Hardcastle to Haweis, 5 May 1796, Haweis papers, ML, MS A 3024.

[3] For this and the following paragraph see Elizabeth Elbourne, 'The foundation of the Church Missionary Society: the Anglican missionary impulse', in John Walsh, Colin Haydon and Stephen Taylor (eds), *The Church of England, c. 1689–c. 1833: from toleration to Tractarianism*, Cambridge 1993, esp. pp. 247–64. On Archbishop John Moore's response and the society's hesitation see also Hole, *Early history*, 58–60.

lating the 'Account' it had sent some twelve months earlier to Moore. Priority was given to forming 'a network' of well-disposed members of the Established Church, Melville Horne being among the first, through whom it was hoped to recruit candidates suitable for missionary service. It is against this background that the Moravians' good standing not only with Church Evangelicals but with the Establishment, too, needs to be taken into account.

The Church Missionary Society and the Moravians

Well before the formation of the CMS, the Moravians had consolidated their position with evangelical leaders and with the establishment and secured a valued place in British Christian society. The least dissenting of Dissenters, they had assiduously cultivated the goodwill of Church and State and were renowned for the very discreet conduct of their missions. It was probably for these reasons that they had gained the respect of Church Evangelicals in particular.

The beginnings of their connection during the 1780s with the founders of the CMS was described in chapter 3. Benjamin La Trobe had been a member of the Eclectics since 1783, Charles Grant, after his return to Britain from India in 1790, maintained friendly contacts with Moravians in London, while Wilberforce's considerable interest in Moravian missions had been evident from shortly before the 1788 enquiry into the slave trade. It is notable that in the latter's *Practical view* of 1797 he most warmly praised the manner in which they were conducted. As a respected leader of evangelical opinion, and as a member of the establishment, he must surely have taken the precaution of satisfying himself by perusing Spangenberg's *Exposition* of the Church's doctrine before he came out so publicly in favour of the Moravians.

The respect in which Moravians were held was apparent soon after the Sierra Leone Company received its charter in 1791, following the collapse of the settlement for the London black poor in Sierra Leone: many had died and the survivors drifted away. In 1792 the company applied to the Moravians for a 'Minister to conduct'[4] loyalists from Nova Scotia to Sierra Leone. Many of these were blacks from the southern United States, who, members of various denominations, 'loved their religion'.[5] Perhaps it was the Moravians' failure, for whatever reason, to take up the invitation that led to the appointment of Melville Horne as one of two chaplains to the colony, with such memorable, but unexpected, consequences. The CMS was in part the child of the Sierra

---

[4] MCH, FLD-27, 31 Jan. 1792.
[5] C. Fyfe, *A history of Sierra Leone*, Oxford 1962, 28–40, 55. See also A. F. Walls, 'A Christian experiment: the early Sierra Leone colony', in G. J. Cuming (ed.), *The mission of the Church and the propagation of the faith* (Studies in Church History vi, 1970), 108–16.

Leone Company:[6] ever since they had founded the company with Granville Sharp, Wilberforce, Henry Thornton (the chairman) and others had been attempting with varying success to engage missionaries, almost certainly beginning with the Moravians, to serve among people indigenous to Sierra Leone. It was undoubtedly as a result of Wilberforce's discussions in 1788 with Ignatius La Trobe concerning a mission settlement on the west coast of Africa that a year later the Moravian Church agreed to consider such a proposal in the event of a stable government being established. Between 1792 and 1795 repeated invitations were received to send missionaries to Sierra Leone, but these opportunities, like the first, were not taken up.[7] This could have been a set-back in relations but those founders of the CMS who were also connected with the company retained their regard for the Moravians. These gentlemen probably appreciated that, with the mission at the Cape being revived and commitments in the West Indies increasing, the Church's slender resources were fully extended.

The famous meeting of the Eclectic Society, which finally led to the formation of the CMS a month later, was held 18 March 1799 with John Venn, since 1792 rector of Clapham, leading the discussion. Charles Grant was present and Charles Simeon made a notably positive contribution. Venn and Simeon of course knew of Moravians from John's father and were well aware of Wilberforce's great respect for them.

Notes kept of the meeting are 'scrappy', but Venn is reported as saying that 'The nearer we approach to the principle of the ancient Church, the better. ... Success will depend, under God, on the persons sent on the Mission ... a mission should proceed from small beginnings.... Every Mission must support itself.' The editor of *Eclectic notes*, from which this passage is taken, states that Venn illustrated these 'principles' by '(1) The Primitive spread of the Gospel; and (2) By the Missions of the Moravians.'[8]

Venn and his colleagues would have been well aware of the history of Moravian missions and of how they had begun in 1732 in a very small way indeed in the West Indies on a self-supporting basis. Moreover, the juxtaposition of the primitive Church and the Moravians is not unexpected: the small, episcopal Moravian Church had for long been admired in Britain not only for the similarity of its rituals and practices to those of the primitive Churches, but also for its similar zeal and perseverence in spreading the Gospel.[9]

Venn demonstrated in the 1799 'Account' of the society, which he had

---

6   Hole, *Early history*, 16–18.
7   MCH, SFG minutes, 17 July 1792, 16 July 1793, 8 Sept., 1 Dec. 1795. The minute for 1 Dec. 1795 also refers to agreement in principle given by the 1789 synod to a mission in Sierra Leone.
8   *Eclectic notes; or notes of discussions on religious topics at meetings of the Eclectic Society, London ... 1798–1814*, ed. John H. Pratt, London 1856, 95–6.
9   Moravians 'seemed to embody the elusive spirit of the primitive church': John Walsh, ' "Methodism" and the origins of English-speaking evangelicalism', in M. A. Noll, D. W. Bebbington and G. A. Rawlyk (eds), *Evangelicalism*, New York–Oxford 1994, 27.

drafted, that he had absorbed Moravian experience in the field: 'It is evident', one passage reads in which episcopal ordination is discussed, 'that a Missionary, dwelling amongst savages . . . does not require the same kind of talents, manners, or learning, as are necessary in an officiating minister in England.'[10] He also rapidly identified what was to be the most difficult issue for the CMS – the recruitment of missionaries. It would be twelve years before the society would be in a position to send its first British-born missionaries overseas; and, in the meantime, it was not until 1804 that the society's first men, two German Lutherans, embarked for Sierra Leone, to begin the society's first endeavours overseas.

On the eve of their departure Henry Foster, a founding member of both the Eclectics and the CMS,[11] demonstrated in an 'Address' the emphasis that missionary leaders before him had placed on the example and conduct of Moravian missions. In terms not unlike those used earlier, Foster noted, for instance, the Moravians' disproportionate and 'noble' example which now, at last, was stimulating other Protestants to enter the field; had they in years past all followed that example and with the same degree of whole-hearted commitment 'the Heathen World' would not be in the state in which 'it now lies'. He went on to explain that the society was 'decidedly of the opinion, that a Missionary Settlement [in Sierra Leone], after the manner of the United Brethren [the Moravians], consisting of several Christians of both sexes, living as a small Christian Community . . . would promise more permanent and extensive success than any other scheme',[12] an opinion that men on the ground, advising the society, soon supported.[13]

From very beginning, therefore, the CMS turned to the example of the Moravians and, like the Baptist and London societies, drew on their practical experience. As the society developed its activities, this continued, as for instance in 1815 when the society decided to have its own vessel, the *William Wilberforce*, to service its West African mission.[14] At the same time the founders of the new society maintained their interest in the Moravian missions and continued to support them.

The Moravians and the modern missionary movement

The year 1800 marked the effective beginning of the modern missionary movement. Although it was not to be until the 1830s that it emerged as a great popular movement which, driven by publicity and allied to humani-

---

[10] 'Account of a Society for missions to Africa and the East', in Hole, *Early history*, appendix at p. 652.
[11] Henry Foster (1745–1844) in Hennell, *Venn*, 79–80.
[12] Henry Foster, 'Address', 31 Jan. 1804, in *Proceedings of the Society for Missions to Africa and the East Instituted by Members of the Established Church*, i, London 1801–5, 348.
[13] 'Report', 4 June 1805, ibid. 437.
[14] *Missionary Register of the Year* iii (1815), 228–39.

tarian causes, attracted large numbers of British candidates for service overseas and funds from masses of small subscribers,[15] a turning-point had been reached. Wesleyans, led by the vigorous Dr Coke were expanding their missions in the West Indies, the Serampore trio was at work in India, and the LMS had been established in a wave of publicity and had launched its mission to islands in the Pacific.

The Moravians were an integral part of the missionary movement in Britain and at the beginning made a substantial contribution to its character and the way it developed. In addition to giving the movement an air of respectability, through their example and long-standing reputation in the mission field, they were to some extent pioneers in three significant areas. The first was the importance they gave to publicity, in which the role of *Periodical Accounts* was of particular note, and the associated activity of fund-raising. The second was the degree to which the Moravian Church helped the movement gain an international dimension: by definition international itself, the Moravian Church assisted in the exchange of information throughout Europe and beyond and in the recruitment of non-British missionaries. The third lay in its contribution to the perception by government and officials that there could be civil and commercial advantages to be gained through the work of missionaries amongst native peoples.

Publicity and fund-raising

The successful development of the missionary movement would not have been possible without the active support and eventually the enthusiastic participation of the British public. Central to this mobilisation were two closely related activities: publicity, principally through journals with reports from the mission field, and fund-raising. Whilst the Baptist and London missionary societies were assisted mainly by Dissenters, the Moravians may have been more successful in attracting funds from Church Evangelicals.

Ignatius La Trobe retained a pivotal position in London as secretary of the SFG, and represented the Moravian Church and its missions to government. He edited *Periodical Accounts* and, by making good use of it, he acted in a very quiet way as the principal fund-raiser in Britain for Moravian missions.

Journals, it was said in the editorial that launched the *Evangelical Magazine* in 1793, were a 'powerful engine in the moral world' because of their influence in this age of philanthropy.[16] The Moravian *Periodical Accounts* was by then already among the publications in this category which became a driving force of the missionary movement. Its significance is two-fold: to the extent that it was the first missionary journal to appear at regular intervals and to be

---

[15] Brian Stanley, *The Bible and the flag: Protestant missions and the British empire in the nineteenth and twentieth centuries*, Leicester–London 1990, 78–80.
[16] 'Preface', EM i (1793), 1.

devoted entirely to missionary news, it was a model for similar publications issued later; it was also the platform for the promotion of Moravian missions, in themselves considered exemplary.

Publication of *Periodical Accounts* soon seemed providential for the Moravians themselves; for it was mainly through this journal that vitally needed funds were raised for the missions from other Christians in Britain. This was acknowledged by Ignatius in 1823 when he wrote that it was owing largely to *Periodical Accounts* that Moravian missions 'became known to the public, and to the religious in various denominations', noting that when the periodical first began to appear missions in general had yet to excite the public's attention.[17] Over its long life *Periodical Accounts* was the first of its kind to contribute to that publicity for missions upon which the growth of the missionary movement largely depended. The first series ran for 100 years at the end of which 365 numbers, just under one each quarter, had appeared. Its purpose, stated in the first number, was to give supporters in other denominations regular news of the missions, to stimulate interest in the work overseas, and to encourage all who prayed for the 'coming of the Kingdom of Christ, . . . [to] take an active share in its prosperity'.[18]

Within the context of Protestant missions, and as the least sectarian of Churches, the Moravian Church was then in a unique position to make such an appeal. The formation of the BMS was as yet two years away and it was not until 1795 that the establishment of the LMS excited much attention. Likewise it was not until the autumn of that year that *Periodical Accounts Relative to the Baptist Missionary Society* first appeared,[19] with the *Evangelical Magazine* becoming the official organ of the LMS in 1796. Thus, when it first appeared, the Moravian *Periodical Accounts* was a pioneering initiative. While the *Arminian Magazine* had since 1780 included within its pages occasional letters concerning the activities of Wesleyans overseas,[20] the strength of the Moravian journal was that it concentrated on the mission field to the exclusion of other topics of interest to the pious. It also was issued more frequently than the annual reports of the SPG and SPCK and its coverage was extensive. After the first and introductory number, largely taken up with the submission to the 1788 enquiry into the slave trade, *Periodical Accounts* began to assume its regular format. This consisted mainly of 'extracts of letters and diaries in the plain language of the Missionaries without additional observations'.[21] In view of the generous response to an appeal issued in 1789 for St

---

17 'Preface', PA ix (1823), pp. iii–iv.
18 'Advertisement', ibid. i (1790), p. iv.
19 Fuller to Pearce, 31 Oct. 1795, AL typescript, 4/5/1. The BMS then dropped the prefix 'Particular'.
20 For example, letters from Antigua published in the *Arminian Magazine* iii (1780), 387–9; xii (1789), 439–40. From 1798 the *Arminian* continued as the *Methodist Magazine*.
21 'Preface', PA iii (1801), p. vi.

Kitts (before the first issue of *Periodical Accounts*), it was appropriate that the first extract from a diary to be published included an account of the consecration of the chapel built in the island with funds raised.[22]

Periodical Accounts was subsequently used from time to time to launch other appeals in Britain for special assistance, for Antigua for instance.[23] When the St Kitts appeal was made there had been fears that it might be damaging to the work of the SFG but in fact it 'proved . . . more advantageous than hurtful to the cause of the Society by making it more *generally known*'. This minute, in Ignatius' hand,[24] illustrates that close link which always prevails between well-directed publicity and success in fund-raising.

Nevertheless, instances of lack of progress overseas were not withheld from readers: first reports from Labrador were brutally frank. These told of murders, though not among the missionaries' own people, exclusion of converts, and the destructive effect of encounters with European traders. 'It gives us pain', one station also reported, 'that we cannot even now mention any favourable change as to the course of our Esquimaux.'[25]

It surely mattered very much indeed to evangelicals in other denominations that they received evidence of real conversions, and extracts from diaries recorded instances of slaves in Antigua 'who departed this life, rejoicing in God our Saviour'. However, examples of 'backsliding' and consequent exclusion from a mission before, perhaps, a deathbed repentance, also appeared.[26]

News in brief from as far afield as Greenland, North and South America, the sub-continent of India, and the West Indies was a constant reminder of the extent of Moravian missions. Some nuggets of information, such as that given in 1791 of the decision to revive the long-abandoned mission at the Cape of Good Hope, carried portents of future significance.[27] The Cape was then under Dutch control, but as the wars with France progressed support for this mission became an additional British Moravian responsibility.

The introduction to the first number of *Periodical Accounts* reminded 'friends and well wishers' that the missions depended entirely on voluntary donations and on missionaries doing 'their utmost to earn something toward their own support'. A hint was also given that further funds from other Christians to finance the Church's effort overseas would be required.[28]

Unlike the reports of the two Anglican societies, neither financial statements nor lists of donors appeared in the Moravian journal and, despite

---

[22] 'Extract of a diary of the mission in St Kitt's, in 1789', ibid. i (1790), 17–19.
[23] 'Address to supporters', ibid. ii (1796), 174–7.
[24] MCH, SFG minutes, 2 Feb. 1790: his emphasis. Most SFG minutes from about 1787 are in C. I. La Trobe's hand.
[25] Hopedale, Labrador, 25 Aug. 1790, PA i (1790), 45–51.
[26] Ibid. 411–15.
[27] 'The latest accounts', ibid. 54–6.
[28] 'Preface', ibid. 7.

recommendations to the contrary, this continued. It took repeated requests from Wilberforce and Henry Thornton, who was to be treasurer of the CMS, before Ignatius was permitted in 1791 to show them in confidence statements of the central accounts of the missions department and of the SFG. Thornton, a man who must surely have recognised their poor financial state at a glance, had followed his late father in becoming a generous supporter. It was also at this time that the Revd Thomas Gisborne, convinced by his friends Wilberforce and Thornton that he was 'misinformed concerning the brethren', made a substantial donation.[29] Gisborne was a member of the Clapham Sect.

The Revd Basil Woodd (1760–1831), an evangelical of the Bentinck Chapel in London, proposed in 1795 that financial statements and names of benefactors should be published. His proposal, which he thought 'would be useful in making the . . . missions known and better supported', was not adopted. In a typically Moravian observation, Ignatius noted that 'Our Sav[iou]r has blessed the private applications.' Woodd may, however, have been the first of the clergy to plead the cause of Moravian missions in a sermon.[30] An Eclectic since around 1785 and a founding member of the CMS, he made a preaching tour on behalf of this society in 1813,[31] by which time sermons were a regular feature of the movement's fund-raising activities.

The charitably minded Woodd certainly had a point when he suggested publishing names of benefactors. A list compiled some time between 1794 and 1796 from SFG records would, for instance, have made impressive reading with the inclusion of Admiral James Gambier, Sir Charles Middleton, later Lord Barham, Wilberforce, Henry Thornton and Charles Grant, all of whom were soon to be associated together in the CMS.[32] Later, the pious Gambier became that society's first president.

These gentlemen were all Church Evangelicals, but financial assistance for Moravian missions came at this time from other denominations too. In particular large and exceptional donations were made in 1796: £20 each from the trustees of the *Evangelical Magazine* and from Andrew Fuller on behalf of the BMS. To these could be added £50 from the Missionary Society in Edinburgh on whose behalf Greville Ewing expressed 'most aff[ec]t[ionat]e concern for the welfare of the Brethren's missions'. Similarly, when £5 was received from Dr Thomas Davidson he reportedly added that were the abandonment of a mission in prospect, 'on account of the narrowness of our finances, they would rather afford some more assistance'.[33]

---

[29] See MCH, SFG minutes, 13 Sept. (donation of £100 from Henry Thornton), 11 Oct. 1791 (request to show accounts; donation of £31 10s. from Revd Thomas Gisborne). The accounts were in debit of c. £700 on 21 June 1791, ibid.
[30] Ibid. 8 Sept. 1795.
[31] For Basil Woodd see Balleine, *Evangelical party*, 61, 184, and Hole, *Early history*, 646.
[32] For these and other examples see MCH, SFG minutes, 1794–6.
[33] Ibid. 1 Nov. 1796.

According to John Campbell of Scotland, the formation of the LMS in London in 1795 'had a most *electrifying* effect on Christians of the north'.[34] But what had caused that particular munificence a year later from both sides of the border and expressions of concern for Moravian missions? In the answer to this question lies, perhaps, the most immediate explanation of why Moravians became so integral a part of the British missionary movement.

Both SFG and missions department accounts showed a deficit. Although now reduced, the SFG's debt at the beginning of 1795 was more than £1,000. Worse, with Holland over-run and Neuwied-on-Rhine, also the site of a Moravian settlement, twice sacked by the French, the missions department in Germany suffered many losses. Contributions to its funds in Europe were expected to decline.[35] It was as the result of what must have been a personal appeal made by Ignatius that in 1796 he raised some £500 for the missions department;[36] there was a close association between donors and the distribution network of *Periodical Accounts*.

Clearly, as by 1796 the effects of the war were being felt in Europe British evangelicals were unwilling to see Moravian missions falter for want of funds. War, it was said in 1819, had left Moravian centres in Europe, on which the missions largely depended, 'utterly impoverished.'[37] The spirit of generosity and solidarity within the missionary movement, engendered by the Moravians' plight, is well exemplified by the Baptist John Ryland who in 1813 wrote to a colleague: 'The Moravian missions I hear suffer a loss of 2,000£ a yr by the war on the Continent and are in distress. Let us vote them 100 guineas.'[38] A year later the CMS voted near double this amount 'to Moravian Missions . . . then in difficulty'.[39]

Looking back on this period Ignatius La Trobe noted that the missions in British colonies, which were to include the Cape of Good Hope, needed additional assistance from Britain and that those in Danish and Dutch colonies were forced to turn to the SFG in London for supplies. Mission expenses were also increasing at the very time that the Church's funds administered from Germany, never robust, were in decline. The outcome would have been 'not only appalling but ruinous', Ignatius wrote, had not members of British Churches, inspired 'Chiefly by the . . . *Periodical Accounts*', come to the missions' aid. Only British generosity and a sympathetic government enabled the missions to hold their ground.[40] The significance of his role at the inter-

---

[34] Robert Philip, *The life, times and missionary enterprises of the Rev John Campbell*, London 1841, 160. John Campbell (1766–1840) visited South Africa in 1812–13 on behalf of the LMS.
[35] MCH, SFG minutes, 27 Jan., 14 July 1795.
[36] Ibid. 12 July 1796.
[37] *First report of the London Association in Aid of the Missions of the United Brethren*, London 1819, 7.
[38] John Ryland to Saffery, 31 May 1813, AL MS, Reeves collection.
[39] Hole, *Early history*, 409.
[40] 'Preface', *PA* ix (1823–6), pp. vii–viii, ix.

face of the growing missionary movement was recognised by Wilberforce in a letter of 1815, describing Ignatius as 'the head and hand . . . of Moravian missions in England'.[41]

Circulation of the Moravian *Periodical Accounts*

Periodical Accounts was the first regular missionary publication to be associated with the new movement which began to stir public interest in missions. Within months of the first number appearing in spring 1790, Moravians in London observed that friends were being encouraged to support the cause and that new acquaintances were coming to its assistance. Two years later it was said that 'Circulation extends farther and farther'.[42]

A notebook has survived in which Ignatius La Trobe recorded the distribution between February 1797 and March 1801 of fourteen numbers of the journal (see appendix 3). Many well-known names from evangelical circles in Scotland as well as in England appear.[43] It can be assumed that with a few exceptions almost all non-Moravians identified were also regular contributors to the SFG. Luminaries of the Eclectic Society and of the Clapham Sect, all founders of the CMS, are among those named, including Josiah Pratt, secretary of the CMS from 1802 to 1824, and Charles Simeon, Fellow of King's College, Cambridge, both subscribers to the SFG.[44] Wilberforce himself took four copies of *Periodical Accounts*, one probably being for John Venn at Clapham, and after its formation the CMS also took the journal and obtained other Moravian missionary publications.[45]

The names of the LMS and of three new missionary societies in Scotland and individuals associated with them, like Bogue of Gosport and Greville Ewing, who published the *Missionary Monthly*, appear on the circulation list. John Rippon in London, editor of the *Baptist Annual Register*, was among Baptists receiving the Moravians' *Periodical Accounts* and he published information concerning the Moravians in the *Register*.[46]

The formation in 1796 of the Edinburgh and Glasgow missionary societies in Scotland was an early indication that the modern missionary movement would become a national movement. Approximately fifty copies of *Periodical Accounts* went north of the border, a considerable amount of financial

---

41 Wilberforce to Lord Caledon, 2 Mar. 1815 (copy), MCH, transactions of government.
42 MCH, memorabilia 1790, in FLD-22, -23.
43 See pp. 203–4.
44 Donations from Charles Simeon began to be recorded in the SFG minutes from 8 Jan. 1799. Josiah Pratt's annual 2 guineas began on 3 Mar. 1800.
45 Hole, *Early history*, 48.
46 Kenneth Ross Manley, 'John Rippon, DD (1751–1836) and the Particular Baptists', unpubl. DPhil. diss. Oxford 1967, 297.

support came back in return, and in 1802 Ignatius paid a visit to 'our friends in Edinburgh and Glasgow'.[47]

The distribution of *Periodical Accounts* among an influential circle of evangelicals at the University of Cambridge arose from Ignatius La Trobe's music-making in London with the extensive and pious Jowett family. Members included Henry Jowett of Magdalene, until he filled the place vacated in 1792 by John Venn in Norfolk, and John Jowett of Trinity Hall, Regius Professor of Law. Ignatius' friendship with the Jowetts led to an annual pilgrimage to Cambridge where he was warmly welcomed by his evangelical friends and where, until his death in 1813, John Jowett acted as collector for Moravian missions.[48] Isaac Milner of Queens', whose name is closely associated with that of Wilberforce and Charles Simeon, appreciated Ignatius' company and he too supported the missions.[49] Two Magdalene men now in New South Wales, Richard Johnson, the first chaplain, and Samuel Marsden at Parramatta, were among those overseas receiving *Periodical Accounts*. Moravians corresponded with both men. Marsden, in one letter, described the new colony in Australia as outwardly prosperous, but barren at heart.[50] He later launched the CMS mission to New Zealand.

A particular reason for Moravians having an apparently closer relationship with Church Evangelicals than with other Dissenters appears in Ignatius' explanation of how he gained the full confidence of his learned but critical friends in Cambridge. He won their trust because, as a Moravian, he could speak in honesty of, 'an undisguised and sincere friendship for the Church of England, a love for its episcopal order, a veneration for its liturgy . . ., and a hearty concurrence in its doctrines'. It was only this, Ignatius believed, that made frank exchanges on differences between their two Churches possible. 'But', he explained in a reference to the Moravian Church, 'as is generally the case, its missions attracted the chief notice.'[51]

Moravian missionaries found more than encouragement and edification in news of their brethren's work around the world which appeared in *Periodical Accounts*. One man, who wrote in this vein in 1812, added, 'I see plainly that in time to come, they will be a valuable history of the missions';[52] an observation which historians and scholars of other disciplines would endorse today.

The missionary movement had hardly begun when Ignatius recorded the distribution of *Periodical Accounts*, the print run of each number then being

---

[47] MCH, SFG minutes, 10 Sept. 1799, 11 Oct., 6 Dec. 1802.
[48] C. I. La Trobe, *Letters*, 6–11.
[49] Mary Milner, *The life of Isaac Milner . . . comprising a portion of his correspondence*, London–Cambridge 1842, 321–5, 334–8, 353–7.
[50] For Richard Johnson (Magdalene, 1780–4) see pp. 79–81 above; for Samuel Marsden see MCH, SFG minutes, 11 July 1797. See also J. D. Walsh, 'The Magdalene evangelicals', *Church History Review* clix (1958), 502–9.
[51] C. I. La Trobe, *Letters*, 10.
[52] Joshua Newby to C. I. La Trobe, 10 Feb. 1812, MCH, letters from Antigua.

around 500 copies. It is an indication of the vitality of the whole missionary movement that in 1834, when Ignatius retired, the circulation of the journal had increased six-fold.[53]

An international movement

The Moravian Church was now in regular contact from its centre at Herrnhut, in Saxony, with other evangelicals in countries across Europe, from Russia to Holland and on both sides of the Baltic. These links had grown stronger over the years through an international and interdenominational conference of evangelical ministers, Lutherans and Calvinists, which had met since 1756 under a Moravian chairman at Herrnhut. By 1800 some fifty ministers were participating.[54]

This pan-European evangelical network, linked together by correspondence, hastened the diffusion of the missionary movement outwards from Britain. It had a definite bearing on the beginning of the LMS mission in South Africa and it almost certainly paved the way for a fraternal exchange between that society and evangelicals in Europe.[55] Also, after the CMS failed to find suitable British candidates, a Moravian introduction led to the society engaging German Lutherans to serve as missionaries overseas.

From around 1795 the ministers' conference was being promoted to the English-speaking world; an account appeared first in Rippon's *Baptist Annual Register*, which urged a universal outlook, and a year later in the *Evangelical Magazine*.[56] Reports in English were also being disseminated by Moravians in Bedford, notably to Melville Horne, now at Olney, to the Baptist minister there, John Sutcliff of the BMS, and, among others, to Samuel Greatheed of the LMS.[57] In September of that year Thomas Haweis himself wrote to ministers assembled at Herrnhut, entreating their prayers for the newly established [London] 'Missionary Society'.[58]

It was also due to what seems to have been a Moravian initiative that this society was discussed when the ministers met a year later. The role of the British-born Moravian, Peter Mortimer (1750–1828), as secretary to the conference and translator, then led to further publicity being given in Europe

---

53 MCH, SFG minutes, 3 Jan. 1803; C. I. La Trobe, *Letters*, 52n.
54 Hellmut Reichel, 'Versuche in der Brüdergemeine zur ökumenischen Sammlung der Christen: die Aufnahme von Zinzendorfs Diasporagedanken und die Herrnhuter Predigerkonferenz (1750–1800)', UF xxix/xxx (1990), 188–97.
55 For example, [LMS] to L. C. Petzius in Sweden and to baron von S[c]hirnding in Saxony, 1799, Home Office extra, CWM MS, 1/1/F.
56 Information from C. I. La Trobe, 26 Mar. 1795, *Baptist Annual Register* ii (1794–7), 210–15: 19 Sept. 1796, EM iv (1796), 544.
57 BRO, MO 369, 25 July 1795. For the Bedford union of Christians see Ward, *Religion and society*, 48–50.
58 Reichel, 'Versuche in der Brüdergemeine', 192.

to the launch of the LMS.[59] That this society was founded on an interdenominational basis surely influenced the decision. In 1797, two years after the LMS published the account of its formation and sermons attending that historic event,[60] an edition in German appeared. It was translated by Mortimer and printed on the Church's press. Poor Mortimer! He was so greatly confused by the variety of English and Scottish denominations represented in the LMS that he required advice from England to make sense of them all. His analysis illustrated the predominance of Dissenters in the society. Mortimer raised the subscription for the German edition and he, no doubt, saw to its circulation.[61]

The Moravians' good relations on the continent with other evangelicals led to the recruitment by the LMS and CMS of missionaries from Europe, and this is particularly true of the Dutchman Dr Johannes van der Kemp, who in 1799 founded the LMS's first mission station in South Africa. It was owing to his visit in 1792 to the Moravian settlement at Zeist in Holland, and to the publicity later given in Europe to the society, that van der Kemp made contact with the LMS.

His first visit to Zeist followed the loss a year earlier, by drowning, of his wife and only child whom he had taken sailing: this horrific tragedy was the immediate cause of his evangelical conversion. It was also in 1792 that the Moravians renewed their mission at the Cape of Good Hope, then under the Dutch East India Company. Van der Kemp learnt at first hand from the Moravians of the renewal and of the revival around this time of their missionary society in Holland. In 1798 van der Kemp called on Ignatius in London and on his arrival at the Cape he consulted the Moravian missionaries at Baviaanskloof, known later as Genadendal, Vale of Grace. Moravians, van der Kemp's biographer concluded, 'were the first to guide him on his way to world mission'.[62]

An introduction effected by Ignatius led to German Lutherans being recruited by the CMS to serve as missionaries. The intermediary was Carl Steinkopf, who himself almost certainly had first learnt of the beginning of the missionary movement in Britain through the Herrnhut ministers' confer-

---

[59] C. I. La Trobe to Haweis, 19 Sept. 1796, EM iv (1796), 545.
[60] 'Introductory memorial' and sermons preached, 22–4 Sept. 1795, in *Sermons, preached*, esp. pp. xxiv–xxxiii.
[61] *Die Missions Societät in England: Predigten, gehalten in London, bei Errichtung der Missions-societät, am . . . Sept. 1795 . . .*, trans. Peter Mortimer, Barby 1797. The press and Moravian seminary were at Barby, near Magdeburg. For Mortimer's confusion see reference to Bogue's 'We are alone', ibid. 77; for denominations see pp. 72–4; for subscription see pp. ii–iii. Mortimer seems to have lived in Germany ever since he went to the Moravian high school at Niesky.
[62] Ido H. Enklaar, *Life and work of Dr. J. Th. van der Kemp, 1747–1811*, Cape Town–Rotterdam 1988, 44, and also pp. 27–31, 41–9. I am grateful to Professor Andrew Porter for bringing this work to my attention.

ence.⁶³ Steinkopf was secretary to a pious society at Basle in Switzerland until 1801 when he took up his new post in London as Lutheran pastor at the Savoy Chapel in London, and made contact with Ignatius La Trobe.

Ignatius had been approached by the CMS in its search for missionaries. Early in 1802 he introduced Steinkopf who then put the society in touch with the newly formed missionary academy in Berlin from where the CMS obtained its first catechists.⁶⁴ It is unlikely that the question arose of the Moravians themselves making men available; they were, as Baron von Schirnding, promoter of the Berlin academy, noted in 1798, 'hardly of a number to cultivate their own missionary field'.⁶⁵ This would have been well known in England.

A warm sense of fellowship linked Moravian missionaries passing through London with those of the CMS from Germany. For instance, when the SFG held a 'General Meeting' at Fetter Lane in November 1805 for its supporters, two Moravians destined for Surinam were present together with, '3 young missionaries from Berlin engaged in the Service of the Society for Missions to Africa & the East [CMS], by members of the established Church, & going to Africa. It was a lively meeting'.⁶⁶

The director of the missionary academy in Berlin from which the CMS recruited these and other young Lutherans was Johannes Jænicke; a Moravian minister in the city, Christian Frederic Cunow, was on the directing board. His presence is a sure indication that Moravian missionary thinking formed part of the syllabus.⁶⁷

'Civilisation' and relations with the state

A belief that missionaries were a potential force for civilisation and good order attracted the attention of government, and it was one that the Moravians seem to have represented, by now, in the official mind. The Moravians, themselves, had for long argued, and with success, that as conversion of the heathen to true Christianity brought in its wake the adoption of Western values of civilisation, foreign missions were in the national interest.⁶⁸ This proposition was stated in the Labrador submissions of the 1760s to government and its general acceptance was made manifest in Bishop Porteus' public endorsement of the mission in Antigua and in evidence given to the 1788 enquiry into the slave trade. The benefits of civilisation were

---

63 For reference to 'The German Brethren in Switzerland' already having information from Mortimer see Samuel Greatheed to John Eyre, 13 Feb. 1799, CWM MS, 1/6/A, home incoming letters (Home Office).
64 Hole, *Early history*, 75–83. For Carl Steinkopf (1773–1859) see *BDEB*.
65 von Schirnding to Haweis, 12 Dec. 1798, ML, MS A 3024.
66 MCH, SFG minutes, 4 Nov. 1805.
67 Johannes Jænicke to Carl Steinkopf, 8 May 1802, in *Proceedings*, i. 153.
68 B. La Trobe, *Succinct view*, 17; Spangenberg, *Account of the . . . missions*, 62–3, 102–5.

expressed in civil and commercial terms; converts, it was said, became obedient, loyal and useful citizens.

The new missionary societies followed the Moravians in making similar claims in their official pronouncements. The CMS, for instance, after the ringing statement of evangelical belief with which it introduced its 'Account' of the society in 1799, expanded on the 'substantial and durable' benefits of the Gospel with a vision of the 'benign' influence of Christianity: 'Fallen man becomes a new creature . . . wherever the Gospel is cordially received. . . . Civilization is promoted' and society improves.[69]

The idea of temporal advantages arising from missions continued to attract the official mind and the Moravians again provided the model. This was evident in a report by John Barrow in 1798 on his inspection of the Moravian settlement, Genadendal, at the Cape of Good Hope, made to the new governor of the colony, Lord Macartney. Earlier Barrow had accompanied Macartney on the embassy to China; neither man was naturally inclined to be well disposed towards Christian missions[70].

Moravians in London were always attentive to the importance of official appointments and their supporters knew that the mission was in a vulnerable situation before the British took over control of the Cape from the Dutch in 1795.[71] Under these circumstances the governor's countenance assumed an unusual degree of importance. In January 1798 Admiral Gambier commended the mission in a letter for Macartney in which he stressed the loyalty of Moravian converts in the West Indies who had been armed by the government, 'at a time when the islands were likely to be attacked by French plunderers and french [sic] principles'.[72]

Eight months later an order was issued at the Cape in Macartney's name authorising Moravians at Genadendal to build a chapel and to make other improvements. Permission to cut wood in the vicinity was a further valuable concession.[73] This favourable order had clearly been influenced by Barrow's report. It was the missionaries who undoubtedly impressed upon him that 'Their grand object is that of converting the Hottentots and other free people of colour to Christianity. But', Barrow added in terms which surely explained why both men approved of the mission,

> they [the missionaries] have done more. They have brought together three or four-hundred individuals of this wretched class of men and have taught them the . . . benefits arising from useful labour. . . . This institution may prove in

---

[69] 'Account', in Hole, *Early history*, 651.
[70] I am indebted to Professor P. J. Marshall for this information.
[71] No. 16, PA i (1790), 347–8. See also diary for 1795 by missionaries at the Cape, ibid. ii (1797), 3–33; Krüger, *Pear tree*, 61–75.
[72] Extract of a letter from Admiral Gambier to Lady Nepean which she transmitted to the earl of Macartney, Jan. 1798, MCH, transactions with government.
[73] By Command of his Excellency (copy), 10 Aug. 1798, ibid.

time a great advantage to the colony by instilling into the Hottentots a spirit of industry.[74]

Barrow, a pragmatist surely, noted the Moravians' priority of saving souls, but he came away believing that their approach to missions could also fulfil a civil purpose. Later, in 1805, he met Ignatius La Trobe in London. Had the first British occupation of the Cape continued, Barrow intimated, 'the intention of the English government [was] to give the Brethren a well wooded & watered Valley, for a [further] settlement'.[75] In the longer term mission settlements were recognised as being in the interest of the state and those of the Moravians 'flourished' under the British. Successive governors at the Cape encouraged new settlements with grants and 'protection' because they wished to see native people becoming industrious and peaceable, or in a word 'civilised'.[76]

Genadendal was also admired by visitors from missionary societies as the model of a Christian community of the converted. John Campbell, a visitor to the Cape in 1812–13 on behalf of the LMS, was lyrical in his praise; and, noting the Moravians' 'exertion to improve their people in civilization', he commented adversely in this respect on his own society's similar institution.[77]

Thus missionaries in the nineteenth century came to be accepted as useful agents of 'improvement' or 'civilisation' and their societies in Britain, like the Moravians before them, promoted the idea. In 1836–7 the secretaries to three missionary societies impressed upon a parliamentary committee that preaching the gospel was beneficial not only for native peoples but also for the nation at large. Commercial and civil benefits were among those cited. Nevertheless, the 'correct order' remained the introduction of Christianity overseas 'first'.[78]

During the early part of the nineteenth century leaders of the new missionary societies followed the example of the Moravians in their policy towards relations with government and Europeans overseas. At least until the 1820s, and as a matter of prudence and principal, the societies refrained from meddling in politics at home and attempted to restrain their men abroad from giving offence. This was essential at a time when Dissenters at home and missionaries abroad were suspected of spreading sedition. Each society also had its own particular reasons for adopting this policy. For instance, Andrew Fuller of the BMS was vigilant in his attempts to restrain politically minded

---

[74] Excerpt from John Barrow to Lord George Macartney, official report, in Maurice Boucher and Nigel Penn (eds), *Britain at the Cape, 1795 to 1803*, Houghton, SA 1992, 149–50.
[75] MCH, SFG minutes, 4 Nov. 1805. Barrow was at the Admiralty under James Gambier; Charles Middleton was First Lord.
[76] Krüger, *Pear tree*, 294.
[77] John Campbell, *Travels in South Africa: undertaken at the request of The Missionary Society*, London 1815, 10, 129.
[78] Stanley, *Bible and the flag*, 72, 157–60.

Baptists in India, where missionaries were on sufferance, from being present without a licence. If provoked, officials of the East India Company, who turned a blind eye to the Baptists' itinerant preaching, could have had them expelled. Even so Carey gathered facts on *suttee* which were used later to fuel the 1812–13 national campaign for legislation to force the Company to license missionaries. The societies, however, wisely left it to Wilberforce to lead an effective political lobby.[79]

As new entrants joined them in the mission field, the Moravians identified themselves with their cause. Their record of loyalty and discreet conduct at home and overseas meant that they were in a strong position to counter accusations of sedition made against Dissenters, such as those levelled indiscriminately in 1800 in a report sent to Henry Dundas by the governor at the Cape, and specifically against van der Kemp, the principal LMS missionary in South Africa.[80] Thus, in January 1806, when the British recaptured the Cape, the Dutch surrendered and Lord Caledon was appointed governor, Moravians at home were concerned to learn that Caledon apparently had an 'unfavourable impression of missions in general' and would not be in favour of those at the Cape. This led Ignatius La Trobe to ask Charles Greville, who assisted the Moravians in their business with government and officials, to include in his letter of commendation van der Kemp of the LMS and 'all the missionary establishments at the Cape'.[81]

The close and friendly connection between Moravians and Church Evangelicals, apparent in the 1780s, continued after the formation of the CMS, a society whose first objectives were influenced by its members' knowledge of the Moravians' approach to missions. Moravians contributed to the development of the modern missionary movement by stimulating the British public's interest in and support for missions, most notably through the publication of their *Periodical Accounts*, a pioneering initiative which the Baptist Missionary Society was the first to follow. At the same time they assisted the infant movement through their contacts with fellow evangelicals in Europe and by continuing to foster the goodwill and opinion of British administrators. Evangelicals of various denominations in England (and Scotland) who led the new missionary societies valued the Moravians as the most experienced partner in the great venture now beginning.

---

[79] Carson, ' "Soldiers of Christ" ', 76–82, 91–2; Stanley, *Bible and the flag*, 85–100.
[80] Governor George Yonge to Henry Dundas, 22 Oct. 1800, in *Records of the Cape Colony*, iii, ed. George McCall Teal, London 1898, 339–40.
[81] MCH, SFG minutes, 11 Aug. 1806. Charles Greville was to write the memorial.

Conclusion

To the *Unitas Fratrum* we look up with high respect and veneration as to the elder brethren in our Father's house in the cause of missions: LMS, 1799.[1]

[The Moravian brethren] . . . are an Episcopal Church, like ourselves: they have, amongst Protestants, taken the lead in the establishment of Missions, and are universally acknowledged as the brightest patterns of Missionary exertions: they have selected the places most difficult of access (Greenland – the coast of Labrador – the North American Indians and Cherokees – the West-Indian Islands among the Negroes – the Calmucs in Russia Asia – the Hottentots at the Cape, etc.) Their self-denial has been great, like that of the Apostles . . . their preaching simple (the cross of Christ) like theirs [the Apostles'] . . . their success wonderful . . . their economy most remarkable: Charles Simeon, c. 1824.[2]

This book has examined the contribution made in the second half of the eighteenth century by the international and evangelical Moravian Church to the missionary awakening in England, the awakening that in the last decade of the century led to the formation of the Baptist, London and Church missionary societies. The founders of these three societies, identified as being, broadly, evangelical Calvinists, came from a growing and increasingly influential cross-section of British society.

The development of a fraternal relationship between these evangelicals and Moravians in England was a particular feature, but 'party' allegiances should not be exaggerated. Benjamin La Trobe preached by invitation in Wesleyan chapels, Melville Horne was a Wesleyan when a Moravian in Bristol gave him a copy of Spangenberg's *Account of the . . . missions*, and Horne's subsequent *Letters on missions* were addressed to ministers in all British Protestant Churches. On the other hand, the Moravians' relations with John Wesley himself remained distant and tense. The example of the Moravians may have stimulated the 'remarkable development' of Methodist missions overseas, but their contribution to the beginning of these missions, whatever it was, belongs to those 'vital' early years of the evangelical revival around 1738.

Between 1760 and 1792 the Moravian Church gradually became the generally recognised authority in the field of foreign missions. This point had been reached when the Baptists established the first of the three new

---

[1] LMS (unsigned copy) to the ministers' conference assembled at Herrnhut, 22 Apr. 1799, Home office extra, CWM MS, 1/1/E.
[2] Charles Simeon, *Horæ homileticæ*, xi, London 1841, 314–15 n. f.

missionary societies. None of this could have been predicted in 1764 when, following the financial crisis and loss of credibility of the 1750s and the death of Zinzendorf, the era of Spangenberg began. The Moravians' commitment to expanding their foreign missions, then little known in Britain, and the reforms instituted were crucial to the Church's very future. The new Labrador project, by becoming a British Moravian responsibility, was of permanent significance for it caused the brethren in London to revive their missionary society, the SFG, as the platform from which the missions were promoted to other Christians. Simultaneously, a chronic lack of funds meant that the Moravians were, perforce, constantly drawing attention not only to their own missions but to the cause itself. Funds raised from other British Christians assumed ever more importance for Moravian missions.

Missionary ventures required a degree of official support and the Moravians showed how this could be encouraged without their becoming an instrument of state policy. They maintained an arms-length relationship with the civil authorities, cultivated their goodwill and, unlike the Jesuits, did not meddle in politics. That, as the Moravians claimed, converts from the heathen to Christianity were thought to make useful citizens, was an undoubted advantage in this process.

The Moravian Church, the least doctrinaire of Protestant Churches, was now 'the quiet of the land': it was a threat to no one, 'sheep stealing' was forbidden and its members were loyal and deferential. Brethren, like the personable and capable La Trobes, 'moved easily between denominations' and when necessary among the powers that be. The Church and its missions, for the two were as one, were well represented in Britain.

So, from the early 1780s the Moravian Church was gaining an increasing number of 'friends' in England who appreciated its simple, evangelistic beliefs. Attendance at its chapels, where accounts of the missions could be heard, was notable and Spangenberg's *Exposition* was an influential and welcome statement of the Church's doctrine.

Personal contact between Moravians and other Christians was of great importance. John Newton's fruitful connection with Benjamin La Trobe, and that of Ignatius with the ' "Testonites" ' are examples. Newton and Thomas Haweis, also an intimate friend, were at the centre of overlapping networks of evangelicals, and were early advocates of the Moravians' exemplary work overseas. Both men played pivotal roles in the missionary awakening: Newton, for instance, for his role in the formation of the Eclectic Society and Haweis as the principal channel of Moravian influence within the London Missionary Society.

The 1780s were important years for the missionary awakening and for the Moravians' growing reputation; Bishop Porteus' missionary sermon of 1783 and the 1788 enquiry into the slave trade were landmarks in these respects. Porteus rested his case, that the lot of slaves could be improved in the West Indies, on evidence from Moravian missions in the islands, particularly in Antigua. It was largely due to Porteus, and to rising alarm at the state of the slaves, that these missions came to the attention of the serious-minded in England.

Moravian doctrine enabled the missionaries to build themselves into slave societies, while 'gentry' still resident in the 1770s in Antigua played a part in the 'breakthrough' in that island. All that Porteus claimed was confirmed by the 1788 enquiry into the slave trade. Missions were seen as being central to the reform of slavery, the enquiry turned to the Moravians for the model and prominent absentee proprietors, out of enlightened self-interest, sought the services of their missionaries.

By 1790 the Moravians held a secure position among the pious and with the establishment and their missions were enjoying the patronage of a growing number of Church Evangelicals, among whom were future founders of the CMS. They were also in receipt of more invitations to establish new missions than they could accept. Wilberforce first raised with the Moravians the possibility of a mission settlement in West Africa in 1788, three years before the Sierra Leone Company was established. Charles Grant and the cause of 'India' played a critical role in the thinking that led to the formation of the CMS. Grant's link with the Moravians began in the 1770s in Calcutta when he was almost certainly one of those 'principal gentlemen' who encouraged the Moravians to establish a mission settlement in Bengal. The awakening might well have taken a different course had the court of the East India Company at home, to whom the Moravians applied in 1778, been willing to admit their missionaries into Bengal.

The adoption by the Northamptonshire Association of Baptists of an evangelistic theology illustrated the over-riding importance for the missionary awakening of evangelicalism and its penetration amongst Calvinistically inclined denominations. By the early 1790s there were, it was claimed, more than 300,000 Calvinists holding 'evangelical principles' and the Moravians estimated that they themselves were 'known to and more or less connected' with between 500 and 600 'faithful ministers of the gospel [evangelistic ministers]' in England.[3] This number could well have included Baptists in the Northamptonshire Association who, beginning with the younger John Ryland of Northampton about ten years earlier, were on friendly terms with Moravians. It now seems certain that, before they established their society, Ryland and his colleagues in the BMS, and this includes William Carey, the author of the ground-breaking *Enquiry*, studied Moravian missions. The clergyman Melville Horne evidently did so before he compiled his famous *Letters on missions*.

The table appended in 1790 to the first number of the Brethren's *Periodical Accounts* was evidence of the sheer range and progress of Moravian missions since they had begun in 1732. The Church's record was unmatched by any other group of Protestants. However, it was well known within evangelical

---

[3] Samuel Benade's report from London, in BRO, MO 967, minutes of the ministers' conference, Herrnhut 1792.

circles that it had hardly a sufficient number of missionaries available to fill existing places, let alone to take on new, 'speculative' opportunities such as those in 'Botany Bay' and Sierra Leone. Indeed, it was, and for long remained, a source of wonder that such a small Church, with about 10,000 communicants at home, could send so many into the mission field.

While Johannes van den Berg, in his influential investigation into the missionary awakening in Britain, acknowledged that the 'heroic work of Herrnhut' was admired by 'spiritual leaders in Britain', he did not believe that the Moravians had 'a direct influence' on the awakening.[4] However, it seems that he was not aware that Horne and founders of all three new missionary societies studied Moravian missions. The Moravian Church in fact made a direct and powerful contribution to the missionary awakening in England, as evidence relating to the periods both before and after the formation of these societies compellingly demonstrates. David Cranz's *History of Greenland* and Spangenberg's authoritative *Account of the . . . missions*, with their comprehensive explanations of Moravian missionary teaching, supported by examples from the field, proved immensely influential and complemented Edwards's inspirational *Life* of David Brainerd. Cranz's book was almost certainly the most widely read Moravian work in evangelical circles and can now be considered as a classic of the missionary awakening.

The Moravian contribution was also of a very practical nature. There was, first, the mere fact of Moravian missions, their progress and the Church's record of success in apparently making true converts to Christianity. From the mid 1780s the example of the small Moravian Church acted as a very acute stimulus on the awakening, as evangelicals gave vent to their sense of guilt and outrage at the relative failure of the British to take the Gospel to the heathen overseas. Apparent in Newton's missionary sermon of the early 1780s, founders of all three societies expressed similar sentiments time and time again as they acknowledged that the Moravians' endeavours were out of all proportion to their numbers. The extent and progress of their missions, moreover, supported Carey's global vision.

At the same time accounts of the missionaries' experience in Greenland made a very deep impression. Their patient persistence, without reward in terms of conversions, proved to be a most valuable object lesson for entrants new to the mission field; their circumspection was admired not only by missionary leaders and Horne, but by the thoughtful William Ward, Baptist missionary and and one-time radical, who fervently wished to model his conduct on the Moravians.

But the Moravian Church did much more than merely stir the missionary awakening. Melville Horne and the Baptist, London and Church missionary societies drew heavily on Moravian missionary teaching and experience and each of the societies adopted important Moravian practices. This was

[4] J. van den Berg, *Constrained by Jesus' love: an enquiry into the motives of the missionary awakening in Great Britain . . . 1698–1815*, Kampen 1956, 125.

apparent in the discussion of the manner of preaching, on sending so-called unlettered men into the field, on their qualifications and on whether or not they should be accompanied by their wives. There were, of course, differences in emphasis and detail, arising partly from a recognition that men and women from British Churches did not have the same experience as Moravians raised in their settlements at home. Nevertheless, George Burder's observation to Haweis seems to have expressed a generally held opinion: 'The success' of the Moravians, he wrote of the newly established LMS, 'calls upon us to adopt their plan as our model.'[5]

The perception that missions should be self-supporting and that settlements were the ideal establishment provide further very telling evidence of Moravian influence as the Baptists' own words at home and from Serampore, overwhelmingly prove.[6] What is more, although Moravian mission settlements were seen as model communities of industrious and pious converts to Christianity, missionary leaders followed the Moravians in believing that their 'priority' was to preach the crucified Saviour and to save souls.

The Moravian Church made a significant contribution to the missionary awakening in England owing to its record across a broad mission field, backed up by a thoroughly worked-out and documented doctrine of mission. The Church, through its presence in Britain and its pan-European connections, was also an early contributor to the vitality of the modern missionary movement, assisting with publicity and the recruitment of missionaries. Founders of the three societies were conscious of their debt to the Moravians whose missions gained immeasurably, in the longer term, from being an integral part of the missionary movement in Britain. Two things above all else made it possible for the international Moravian Church to play so significant a role in the missionary awakening. First, that it was an evangelical Church and that evangelical spoke to evangelical; second, that there was a British Moravian community in England.

The driving impulse in late eighteenth-century England to launch foreign missions from these shores to convert the heathen to Christianity arose from developments in theology, the increasing spread and penetration of evangelicalism. This study has confirmed, what has for long only been suspected, namely, that the Moravian Church should be numbered among the important contributors to the missionary awakening in England.

---

[5] Burder to Haweis, 23 Dec. 1795, ML, MS A 3024.
[6] For an earlier and similar conclusion see Stanley, *Baptist Missionary Society*, 39–40.

APPENDIX 1

The Numerical Strength of the Moravian Church, 1822

The small size of the Moravian Church, upon whose members its foreign missionary effort largely depended, was to make a great impression on missionary thinkers in England. Comparative statistics for different periods have not been established, but those published for the year 1822 can be taken as a reasonable guide for the period covered in this book when some growth in membership occurred. In 1822 there were 16,125 members of the home Church in Europe, Britain and North America. At the same time some 33,000 converts to Christianity and catechumens were in the care of 171 missionaries and their wives. The numbers for members and converts include children.

It would be misleading not to draw attention also to the religious societies to be found right across the continent of Europe which were supervised by Moravians. In 1824 the total number recorded as members of these societies was 79,000 approximately half of whom were in Lithuania and Estonia. The purpose of these societies was confined to edification and they made rapid progress for a period of about thirty years from 1760.[1]

---

[1] Holmes, *United Brethren*, ii. 353–62. For these societies in general see Hamilton and Hamilton, *History of the Moravian Church*, 191–2; for those in the Baltic states see Ward, *Protestant evangelical awakening*, 144–55.

APPENDIX 2

A Comparison of Texts

A comparison of the text of the London Missionary Society's 'Counsels and instructions'[1] with that of Thomas Haweis's *Missionary instructions*, both published by T. Chapman of Fleet Street, London, in 1796, indicates that Haweis, influenced by his knowledge of Moravian teaching, provided most of the material. Texts from 'Counsels' illustrate issues addressed by Haweis in his *Missionary instructions*.

Passages from 'Counsels' identical to those in Haweis's *Missionary instructions* are reproduced in roman; phrases or words in Haweis not found in 'Counsels' are in bold. Changes to punctuation are not identified. The headings (which do not appear in either text) refer to themes discussed in chapter 6.

Fellowship

'Counsels', I, opens with a five-paragraph exhortation which is not found in Haweis. The remaining ten paragraphs follow the 'first head' in his *Missionary instructions*. Opening passages to some of these paragraphs (which are not numbered in the original) confirm that they originated with Haweis:

> para 6: [**The first and most important injunction is,**] 'Live together in love and union.' Ye are brethren, but being men, are encompassed about with infirmities. Bear and forbear: . . .
>
> para 7: We [I] request it solemnly, we [I] adjure you in the Great Master's name, 'Love one another out of a pure heart fervently;' . . .
>
> para 8: Your own examples must preach as powerfully as your words. But if ever bitter envyings and strife arise, you will put an effectual bar to [**in the way of**] your own usefulness, and defeat the great purpose of your Mission. . . .
>
> para 9: [**Be patient with one another . . .**] You will be very differently qualified, and in some things there can be no competition between you. . . .[2]

Manner of preaching

The key paragraph in 'Counsels', II, follows exactly the 'second head' in Haweis, *Missionary instructions*, with one possibly notable exception:

> *How* are they to teach, whether in discoursing publicly, or in private conference, will hardly admit of doubt:- The Bible, and experience of the most suc-

---

[1] 'Counsels and instructions', in Hunter and Williams, *A sermon and charge*, 51–70.
[2] Cf. 'Counsels', 52–3; Haweis, *Missionary instructions*, 3–5.

cessful Missions, assure us, that the great doctrine of Atonement must be the corner stone. (The glory and the humiliation of Jesus),³ [**A crucified Jesus**], and every thing relative to the deliverance from sin by him and death by him must make the ground work. . . .⁴

The paragraph which follows in 'Counsels' is identical to that in Haweis, but the succeeding one has typical minor amendments and omissions. An example is taken from the opening sentence:

Affect not [**Avoid all**] subtleties and deep points of controversy, either among yourselves or with the natives.[**Never dispute.**] Wave as much as possible what would lead to questions, rather than godly edifying.⁵

Communal life, the work ethic and community of goods

How much of your time the necessary attention to your provision and maintenance will require, cannot be known till you get there; [**I think no great deal of it will be required; though**] labour is rather to be courted than refused, as nothing would be more dangerous than a spirit of idleness.⁶

Whilst every brother possesses the property he chooses [**chuses**] to carry with him, as an individual – as a Christian Society they should have a community of all goods provided by the Society's funds, of the produce of their lands, and of their several labours, all this should come into a common stock. . . .⁷

Impressing the heathen

Ignatius La Trobe warned Haweis against novelties. This was not mentioned in 'Counsels', although a hint of Haweis's thinking survived:

During the time also that our several handicraftsmen are at work . . . [**probably**] the natives will crowd with curiosity around them: all readiness to instruct them should be shewn. . . .⁸

At such seasons there will be a favourable opportunity to address the natives . . . and to mingle divine subjects of instruction with lessons of information. [**and the anvil, and the chisel . . . become real handles to our discourse. I confess my most sanguine hopes of the natives' conversion are from mechanic Missionaries.**]⁹

(David Bogue, with India rather than the South Seas in his sights, might well have winced when he read this last passage from Haweis's *Missionary instructions*.)

---

3 Not in Haweis, *Missionary instructions*.
4 Cf. 'Counsels', 58; Haweis, *Missionary instructions*, 8.
5 Cf. 'Counsels', 59; Haweis, *Missionary instructions*, 8.
6 Cf. 'Counsels', 66; Haweis, *Missionary instructions*, 11.
7 Cf. 'Counsels', 68; Haweis, *Missionary instructions*, 14.
8 Cf. 'Counsels', 67; Haweis, *Missionary instructions*, 12–13.
9 Cf. 'Counsels', 67–8; Haweis, *Missionary instructions*, 13.

APPENDIX 3

Distribution of the Moravian Periodical Accounts, Feb. 1797–Mar. 1801[1]

C denotes a member of, or an individual connected with, the Clapham Sect
E denotes a member of Eclectic Society

Recipients resident in London unless otherwise stated

1. Founders and first associates of the CMS[2]
Bacon, John, sculptor, d. 1799 **E**
Barham, Lord (Sir Charles Middleton) (Teston, Kent) **C**
Cardale, William, solicitor
Cecil, Revd Richard **E**
Dikes, Revd Thomas (Hull)
Dixon, William (Lambeth)
Edwards, Revd Edward (King's Lynn)
Elliott, Charles **C**
Fearon, Devey, MD
Foster, Revd Henry **E**
Gambier, James, admiral
Grant, Charles **C**
Hoare, Henry, banker
Johnson, Revd Richard (NSW) (also listed under missionaries)
Jowett, John
Martin, Ambrose, banker
Newton, Revd John (three copies) **E**
Pratt, Revd Josiah **E**
Simeon, Revd Charles (King's College, Cambridge) **E**
Stillingfleet, Revd James (Hotham, Yorks)
Thornton, Henry **C**
Wilberforce, William (four copies) **C**
Wilkinson, Revd Watts (Hoxton)
Wilson, William
Woodd, Revd Basil **E**

---

[1] This material is incomplete and provided for example only. It has been extracted from MCH, A table showing to whom & when the Periodical Accounts ... were distributed by the secretary of the Society for the Furtherance of the Gospel.
[2] These have been identified by reference to Hole, *Early history*, appendix A at pp. 621ff.

2. Other notable members of the Established Church
Barham, Joseph Foster, Jr
Barrington, Shute, bishop of Durham
Fitzgerald, Lady Mary
Gisborne, Revd Thomas C
Harpur, Lady Frances (2 copies) (sister of Charles Greville who advised Moravians)
Milner, Dr Isaac (Queens' College, Cambridge)
Milner, Joseph (Hull) (d. 1797)
Porteus, Beilby, bishop of London
Serle, Ambrose
Sharp, Granville
Stillingfleet, Revd James (Worcester)

3. Baptists
Rippon, John
Ryland, John (Bristol) also for 'Mr Carey'

(Copies presumably reached Andrew Fuller and John Sutcliff from those sent to the Moravian centre at Bedford. Sutcliff also forwarded Moravian publications on to Serampore, India.)

4. Directors of the London Missionary Society
Bogue, David (Gosport)
Eyre, Revd John (Homerton)
Greatheed, Samuel (Newport Pagnell)
Hardcastle, Joseph (6 copies)
Haweis, Revd Thomas (Northampton)
Hill, Revd Rowland

5. Missionary societies
London, Edinburgh, Glasgow, Perth, Stirling
(BMS and CMS not listed)

6. Non-Moravian missionaries overseas
Johnson, Revd Richard (NSW)
Marsden, Revd Samuel (NSW)
Ringletaube, William (Calcutta) (Ringletaube was in close connection with the Moravian Church before becoming an SPCK missionary and from c. 1799 an LMS missionary in India.)
van der Kemp, Johannes (Cape of Good Hope)

7. Some Scottish worthies
Davidson, Dr Thomas (Edinburgh)
Ewing, Greville (Glasgow)

Haldane, James (Edinburgh)
Haldane, Robert (Edinburgh)
Hunter, Andrew, professor of Divinity (Edinburgh)
Plenderleath, Robert (Edinburgh)

Davidson and Plenderleath were later president and treasurer, respectively, of the Edinburgh Association in aid of Moravian Missions.

8. Miscellaneous

The thirty-three copies of *Periodical Accounts* sent to the city of York, in addition to those sent to the Moravian settlement at Fulneck in Yorkshire, may be attributable mainly to Quakers.

Ignatius La Trobe's Cambridge friends took eight copies.

The fifty copies sent to to Bethlehem, Penn., suggests that *Periodical Accounts* was used by the Moravian missionary society in the USA to promote the cause among English-speakers. (German was still the main language in the settlements.)

Bibliography

Unpublished primary sources

MORAVIAN

Bedford, Bedfordshire Record Office (BRO)
Archives of the Bedford St Peter's Moravian Church (MO)
    Congregation diaries
    Elders' conference minutes
    Minutes of the ministers' conferences at Herrnhut

Bristol University Library (BUL)
Special collection, DM 451
Archive of the Maudlin Street, Bristol, Moravian congregation
    Congregation diaries
    Elders' conference minutes
    Weekly accounts from the synods

Herrnhut (Germany), Unitätsarchiv (UA)
Account of B. La Trobe's last illness
General synod of 1789, supplement and protocol
UEC correspondence with Antigua
UEC correspondence with British congregations

London, Moravian Church House (MCH)

British province
Provincial helpers' conference minutes
Provincial synods, 1765, 1766, 1771

Church as a whole
Copies of letters and reports [to UEC], 1787–93
General synods, 1764, 1769, 1782, 1789, 1801, 1818
General synods, weekly accounts, 1764–89
Harmony of the four synods, 1764–82
Interim conference, 1762
UEC circular letters, 1760–1860
UEC minutes, 1770–4
'Weekly Leaves', 1768–1831

Fetter Lane, London
Congregation diaries

Elders' conference minutes
Extracts from the London archives

Missions
Letter concerning . . . the mission . . . in the East Indies, 7 Aug. 1787, material relating to Bristol, packet 4
Letters from West Indies, separate parcels, A3

SFG
Correspondence
Labrador voyages, miscellaneous, 1770–1851
Minutes of the Brethren's Society for the Furtherance of the Gospel among the Heathen, 1766–1831 (incomplete) (also on microfilm)
Sundry papers
Table of distribution of *Periodical Accounts*

Miscellaneous
Haverford West congregation diary I, 1763–8
Letters to B. La Trobe, parcels 3–4, A3
John Newton letter (extract), 23 Dec. 1780, folder B, A3; also in letters (copies), A. C. Hassé
Transactions with government: copies of original correspondence, C. I. La Trobe

Pudsey (Yorks), Moravian Church, Fulneck
Official correspondence, UEC [and others] to Fulneck elders' conference

NON-MORAVIAN

Cambridge, Cheshunt College Foundation, Westminster College (CFWC)
Countess of Huntingdon papers, series F
Welch collection, typescripts from other archives

Leominster, Lucy Torode collection
Extracts from Br. James La Trobe's correspondence

London, British Library (BL)
Hamilton and Greville papers
Hardwicke papers
Liverpool papers
Samuel Martin papers.
Oriental and India Office collection
    Index to court minutes.
        Miscellaneous correspondence

London, Doctor Williams's Library, New College collection
David Bogue's lectures

London, Friends' House Library
Correspondence, 1767–8 Benezet/SPG, MS Box 5. 22(1)

London, Institute of Commonwealth Studies
West India Committee archives, M. 915 (microfilm, 3.1)

London, Lambeth Palace Library (LPL)
William Bull papers
Christian Faith Society papers
Fulham papers, Leeward Islands, XX
John Newton papers
Beilby Porteus papers: notebooks (transcript), diary

London, Public Record Office (Kew) (PRO)
CO 194 Colonial office records, Newfoundland and Labrador

London, School of Oriental and African Studies
Council of World Mission (CWM)
London Missionary Society
    Board minutes, minutes of transactions
    Correspondence
    Home incoming letters
    Home Office extra
    South India general, 1796–1812
    Typescript from [Robert] Moffat's original lecture notes of missionary lectures given by David Bogue, 1815, R8

London, Wellcome Institute Library
Sir Joseph Banks, journal of a trip to Holland, 1773

Manchester, John Rylands University Library (JRUL)
MS Eng. 1244 C. I. La Trobe journal, 1788–9

Northampton, Northamptonshire Record Office
Correspondence of William Carey and John Ryland

Oxford, Angus Library, Regent's Park College (AL)
BMS committee minutes, i
BMS home, A. Fuller's correspondence, 1793–1815
Typescript copied from various sources . . . Fuller's letters prepared by E. A. Payne, 4/5/1
William Carey, journal, letters to BMS Committee, letters to his relatives
Correspondence of Daniel Brundson
Correspondence of Joshua Marshman
Correspondence of William Ward
Reeves collection
William Ward, missionary journal, 1799–1811 (draft typescript by E. Daniel Potts)

Oxford, Bodleian Library
Barham papers, MS Clarendon Dep. c.357–91, c.428–32

Oxford, Rhodes House
James Ramsay papers

Pennsylvania, Pennsylvania Historical Society
Thomas Penn papers

Princeton, NJ, Firestone Library
John Newton papers

Sydney, NSW, Mitchell Library, State Library of New South Wales (ML)
Thomas Haweis papers: autobiography, miscellaneous papers 1788–96, correspondence

Published primary sources

Moravian publications in English, 1760–1800
1767
Cranz, David, *The history of Greenland: containing a description of the country, and its inhabitants; and particularly, a relation of the mission carried on for above thirty years by the Unitas Fratrum.* . . ., trans., London 1767
1768
A candid declaration of the Church known by the name of Unitas Fratrum, relative to their labour among the heathen, London 1768 (rev. version of 1740 original)
1769
J. H. [James Hutton], *A letter to a friend in which some account is given of the Brethren's Society for the Furtherance of the Gospel among the Heathen; Stated rules of the Brethren's Society for the Furtherance of the Gospel* (in one pamphlet), London 1769
1771
La Trobe, B., *A succinct view of the missions established among the heathen by the Church of the Brethren or Unitas Fratrum in a letter to a friend*, London 1771
1774
[Hutton, James], *A brief account of the mission established among the Esquimaux Indians, off the coast of Labrador, by the Church of the Brethren or Unitas Fratrum*, London 1774
Litany for the use of the negroe congregations of the Brethren in the British dominions, London 1774
1775
[Spangenberg, A. G.], *A concise historical account of the present constitution of the Unitas Fratrum; or Unity of the evangelical Brethren, who adhere to the Augustan Confession*, trans., London 1775
1776
The brotherly agreement and declaration touching the rules and orders of the Brethren's congregation in London, London 1776 (internal document)

1780
Cranz, David, *The ancient and modern history of the Brethren; or a succinct narrative of the Protestant Church of the United Brethren or, Unitas Fratrum, in the remoter ages, and particularly in the present century*, trans., London 1780

1784
Spangenberg, A. G., *An exposition of Christian doctrine, as taught in the Protestant Church of the United Brethren, or, Unitas Fratrum*, trans., London 1784

1785
Spangenberg, A. G., *Instructions for members of the Unitas Fratrum who minister in the Gospel among the heathen*, trans., London [1785]

1788
Spangenberg, A. G., *An account of the manner in which the Protestant Church of the Unitas Fratrum, or United Brethren, preach the Gospel and carry on their missions among the heathen*, trans., London 1788

1790
Periodical Accounts Relating to the Missions of the Church of the United Brethren Established among the Heathen (journal, 1st ser. approximately quarterly from March 1790)

1794
Loskiel, G. H., *History of the missions of the United Brethren among the Indians in North America*, trans., London 1794

1796
Spangenberg, A. G., *An exposition of Christian doctrine* . . ., 2nd edn, Bath 1796

Other Moravian

Acta Fratrum Unitatis in Anglia: report from the committee to whom the deputies of the United Moravian Churches . . . was referred: together with some extracts of the most material vouchers and papers . . ., London 1749

Benham, Daniel, *Memoirs of James Hutton: comprising the annals of his life and connection with the United Brethren*, London 1856

First report of the London Association in Aid of the Missions of the United Brethren, London 1819

Hahn, Hans-Christoph and Hellmut Reichel (eds), *Zinzendorf und die Herrnhuter Brüder: Quellen zur Geschichte der Brüder-Unität von 1722 bis 1760*, Hamburg 1977

Kurze, zuverlässige Nachricht von der, unter dem Namen der Böhmischen-Mährischen Brüder bekantent, Kirche Unitas Fratrum Herkommen . . ., n.p. 1757

La Trobe, C. I., *Journal of a visit to South Africa in 1815 and 1816 with some account of the mission settlements of the United Brethren, near the Cape of Good Hope*, London 1818, facsimile edn, Cape Town 1969

────── *Letters to my children: written at sea during a voyage to the Cape of Good Hope in 1815*, London 1851

Memorial days of the renewed Church of the Brethren, trans., Ashton-under-Lyne 1822

[Okely, Francis], *Supplement to the short sketch of the work carried on by the Moravian Church in Northampton . . . respecting the erection of the chapel* . . ., London–Aylesbury 1888

C. J. A. Oldendorp's history of the mission of the evangelical brethren on the Caribbean islands of St Thomas, St Croix and St John, ed. J. J. Bossard, Barby 1770; trans. and ed. Arnold R. Highfield and Vladimir Barac, Ann Arbor, Mich. 1987

Spangenberg, A. G., *Leben des Herrn Nicolaus Ludwig Grafen und Herrn von Zinzendorf und Pottendorf*, Barby 1773–5, repr. Hildesheim–New York 1971

Zinzendorf, N. L. von, *Texte zur Mission, mit einer Einführung in die Missionstheologie Zinzendorfs*, ed. Helmut Bintz, Hamburg 1979

New missionary societies and founders

Bogue, David, *A sermon preached at Salters-Hall, March 30 1792, before the correspondent board in London of the Society in Scotland . . . for Propagating Christian Knowledge in the Highlands and islands*, London 1793

Carey, William, *An enquiry into the obligations of Christians to use means for the conversion of the heathens*, Leicester 1792, repr. London 1891

Catalogue of books belonging to the mission library at Serampore, [Serampore] 1804

Form of agreement: reflecting the great principles upon which the brethren of the mission at Serampore think it their duty to act in the work of instructing the heathen, agreed . . . October 7, 1805, Serampore 1805

[Fuller, Andrew], *Compiled by Andrew Fuller, memoirs of the late Rev. Samuel Pearce . . . with extracts from some of his most interesting letters*, Clipstone 1800

Greatheed, Samuel, *General union recommended to real Christians, in a sermon preached at Bedford . . . 1797*, London 1798

Haweis, Thomas, *Missionary instructions, recommended to the serious attention of all . . . with an appendix, relative thereto, by the Rev. Mr Latrobe*, London 1796

—— *An impartial and succinct history of the rise, declension, and revival of the Church of Christ: from the birth of our Saviour to the present time*, London 1800

Hunter, Henry and Edward Williams, *A sermon and charge delivered at Sion-Chapel, London: July 28, 1796, on the occasion of the designation of the first missionaries to the islands of the South Sea*, London 1796

Die Missions Societät in England: Predigtent, gehalten in London, bei Errichtung der Missions-societät, am . . . Sept. 1795 . . ., trans. Peter Mortimer, Barby 1797

[Pearce, Samuel], *Correspondence: containing extracts of letters from the late Mr Samuel Pearce, to the missionaries in India, between the years 1794 and 1798: and from Mr John Thomas, from 1798 to 1800*, London 1814

Periodical Accounts Relative to the Baptist Missionary Society, Clipstone 1800, 1801

Proceedings of the Church Missionary Society for Africa and the East, ii–iv, London 1806–10

Proceedings of the Society for Missions to Africa and the East Instituted by Members of the Established Church, i, London 1801–5

Ryland, John, *The work of faith . . . the life and death of the Reverend Andrew Fuller*, London 1816

—— *Pastoral memorials: selected from the manuscripts of the late Rev. John Ryland, D.D., of Bristol: with a memoir*, London 1826, 1828

Sermons, preached in London at the formation of The Missionary Society, September . . . 1795: to which are prefixed, memorials respecting the establishment and first attempts of that Society, London 1795

Sidney, Edwin, *The life of the Rev. Rowland Hill*, 4th edn, London 1844

Official publications

Acts of the privy council of England: colonial series, v–vi, ed. James Munro, London 1912
Canadian archives: documents relating to the constitutional history of Canada, 1759–91, ed. Adam Shortt and Arthur G. Doughty, Ottawa 1918
Documents relative to the colonial history of the state of New York: procured in Holland, England and France, ed. E. B. O'Callahan, Albany, NY 1856–87
English historical documents, ed. David C. Douglas, IX: *American colonial documents to 1776*, ed. Merril Jensen, London 1955
Historical records of New South Wales, ed. F. M. Bladen, ii, Sydney 1893
House of Commons sessional papers of the eighteenth century [slave trade], lxvii–lxxiii, ed. Sheila Lambert, Wilmington, Del. 1975
In the privy council: in the matter of the boundary between the dominion of Canada and the colony of Newfoundland in the Labrador peninsula, London [1926–7]
Journals of the commissioners for trade and plantations [1750–3], London 1932; [1764–7], London 1936; [1768–75], London 1937
Parliamentary history of England from the earliest period, to the year 1803, xxxiii [1797], London 1818
Parliamentary register; or, history of the proceedings and debates of the House of Commons, xxix–xxxii, London 1791–2
Pennsylvania archives (1st series): selected and arranged from original documents in the office of the secretary of the commonwealth by Samuel Hazard, Philadelphia 1852–6
Records of the Cape Colony, iii, ed. George McCall Theal, London 1898
Royal instructions to British colonial governors, 1670–1776, ed. Leonard W. Labaree, New York 1967

Newspapers and periodicals

Arminian Magazine
Baptist Annual Register . . . including sketches of the state of religion among different denominations . . . at home and abroad
Christian Observer
Critical Review
Evangelical Magazine and [from 1813] *Missionary Chronicle*
Gentleman's Magazine
London Chronicle
Missionary Register for the Year (1813–16)
Monthly Review; or Literary Journal (1749–89)
New Spiritual Magazine; or Evangelical Treasury
Northampton Mercury
Periodical Accounts Relating to the Missions of the Church of the United Brethren Established among the Heathen
Periodical Accounts Relative to the Baptist Missionary Society
Public Advertiser
Public Ledger

Contemporary books, journals etc

Abstract of the charter and of the proceedings of the Society for the Propagation of the Gospel in Foreign Parts, London 1771, 1783

Account of the designs of the associates of the late Doctor Bray: with an abstract of their proceedings, London 1789

Account of the Naval and Military Bible Society, from its institution in 1780 to Lady-Day 1804, London 1804

Account of the proceedings and debate, in the general assembly of the Church of Scotland, 27 May 1796, . . . respecting the propagation of the Gospel among the heathen, Edinburgh 1796

Account of the Society for Promoting Christian Knowledge, London 1763, 1772

Adair, James M., *Unanswerable arguments against the abolition of the slave trade, with a defence of the proprietors of the British sugar colonies*, London n.d.

Alexander, J. E., *Transatlantic sketches: comprising visits to the most interesting scenes in North America and the West Indies*, London 1833

Barrow, John, *An account of travels into the interior of southern Africa, in the years 1797 and 1798*, London 1801, 1804

Boswell, James, *The correspondence and other papers of James Boswell relating to the making of the 'Life of Johnson'*, ed. Marshall Waingrow, London 1969

Boswell's life of Johnson, ed. G. B. Hill, New York n.d.

Boucher, Maurice and Nigel Penn (eds), *Britain at the Cape, 1795 to 1803*, Houghton, SA 1992

Bull, Josiah, *Memorials of the Rev. William Bull, . . . compiled chiefly from his own letters, and those of his friends, Newton, Cowper and Thornton, 1738–1814*, 2nd edn, London 1865

Burke, Edmund, *The correspondence of Edmund Burke, VII: Jan. 1792–Aug. 1794*, ed. P. J. Marshall and John A. Woods, Cambridge–Chicago 1968

Burney, Charles, *The letters of Dr Charles Burney, I: 1751–84*, ed. Alvaro Ribereiro, Oxford 1991

Campbell, John, *Travels in South Africa: undertaken at the request of The Missionary Society*, London 1815

Cary's new map of England and Wales [with] all the direct and principal cross roads, London 1794

Cecil, Richard, *The works of Richard Cecil, MA, with a memoir of his life*, ed. Josiah Pratt, London 1838

Charter of the society for the conversion and religious instruction and education of the negro slaves in the British West India islands, proof copy, London c. 1794 [LPL, C.F.S./F3]

Clarkson, Thomas, *The history of the rise, progress, and accomplishment of the abolition of the African slave-trade by the British parliament*, London 1808

Coke, Thomas, *A extract of the Rev. Dr Coke's journal from Gravesend to Antigua in a letter to the Rev. J. Wesley [together with] A continuation . . . in two letters*, London 1787

—— *A journal of the Rev. Dr Coke's third tour through the West Indies in two letters to the Rev. J. Wesley*, London 1791

[Cussons, George], *Memoirs of Mr George Cussons of London . . . extracted from his diary*, London 1819

Discourse concerning the special causes of irreligion in the West Indies with the apparent symptoms of its decrease, London [1764]

Eclectic notes; or notes of discussions on religious topics at meetings of the Eclectic Society, London . . . 1798–1814, ed. John H. Pratt, London 1856

Edwards, Jonathan, *An account of the life of the late Mr David Brainerd, . . . to which is annexed: . . . .: [from] his own diary . . . I. Mr Brainerd's journal among the Indians. II Mr Pemberton's sermon*, Edinburgh 1765

────── *The life of David Brainerd*, ed. Norman Pettit, in *The works of Jonathan Edwards*, ed. John E. Smith, vii, New Haven–London 1985

Enquiry into the causes of the alienation of the Delawares and Shawanese Indians from the British interest . . . together with the remarkable journal of Christian Frederic Post, by whose negotiations, among the Indians on the Ohio, they were withdrawn from the interest of the French, London 1759

[Mrs Flannigan], *Antigua and the Antiguans: a full account of the colony and its inhabitants*, London 1844

[Gibson, Edmund), *The bishop of London's letter to the masters and mistresses of families in the English plantations abroad; . . . May 19, 1727*, London 1727

HMC, *Fourteenth report: the manuscripts of the earl of Dartmouth, X: American papers*, ii, London 1895

────── *Report on manuscripts in various collections*, vi, Dublin 1909

────── *Manuscripts of the earl of Egmont, Viscount Perceval: diary of the first earl of Egmont (1730–47)*, i, ii, London 1920, 1923

Horne, Melville, *Letters on missions addressed to the Protestant ministers of British churches*, Bristol 1794

Howell Harris's visits to London, trans. and ed. Tom Benyon, Aberystwyth 1960

Hume, John, *Sermon preached before the incorporated Society for the Propagation of the Gospel . . . at their anniversary meeting . . . 1762*, London 1762

Hurd, Richard, *Sermon preached before the incorporated Society for the Propagation of the Gospel . . . at their anniversary meeting . . . 1781*, London 1781

Knox, William, *A letter from W.K. Esq. to W. Wilberforce, Esq.*, London 1790

Life and a selection of letters of the late Rev. Henry Venn, ed. Henry Venn, London 1839

List of the society, instituted in 1787, for the purpose of effecting the abolition of the slave trade, London 1787

Luffman, John J., *A brief account of the island of Antigua: together with its customs and manners of its inhabitants, as well white as black, . . . in letters to a friend written in the years, 1786, 1787, 1788*, London 1789

Lysaght, A. M., *Joseph Banks in Newfoundland and Labrador, 1766: his diary, manuscripts and collections*, Berkeley–Los Angeles 1971

Martin, Samuel, *An essay upon plantership: the seventh edition*, Antigua 1785

Milner, Mary, *The life of Isaac Milner . . . comprising a portion of his correspondence*, London–Cambridge 1842

Montagu, Mary, *The complete letters of Lady Mary Wortley Montagu, 1752–62*, ed. Robert Halsband, Oxford 1965–7

Newton, John, *Thoughts upon the African slave trade*, London 1788

────── *The works of the Rev. John Newton*, London 1808–9

────── *Letters by the Rev. John Newton . . . including several never before published*, ed. Josiah Bull, London 1869

────── *Letters and conversational remarks of the Rev. John Newton*, ed. John Campbell, London n.d.

[Okely, Francis], *Seasonably alarming and humiliating, animating and exhilarating truths respecting the nature of Christ's passion; . . . in a metrical version . . . from the works of . . . William Law*, London 1774

[Pennant, Thomas], *Arctic zoology*, London 1784, 1787

Philip, Robert, *The life, times and missionary enterprises of the Rev. John Campbell*, London 1841

Porteus, Beilby, *A sermon preached before the incorporated Society for the Propagation of the Gospel . . . at their anniversary meeting . . . 1783*, London 1783, rev. 1784

―――― *A letter to the clergy of the West-India islands, by Beilby, lord bishop of London*, London 1788

―――― *An essay towards a plan for the more effective civilization and conversion of the negroe slaves on the trust estate in Barbadoes . . . first written in the year 1784, and now considerably altered*, London 1789

―――― *A brief account of three favourite country residences*, London n.d.

Ramsay, James, *An essay on the treatment and conversion of the African slaves in the sugar colonies*, London 1784

―――― *An inquiry into the effects of putting a stop to the African slave trade and of granting liberty to the slaves in the British sugar colonies*, London 1784

Rimius, Henry, *A candid narrative of the rise and progress of the Herrnhuters, commonly called Moravians*, London 1753

Römer, L. F., *Nachrichten von der Küste Guinea*, Copenhagen–Leipzig 1769

[Mrs Shaw], *Journal of a lady of quality: being the narrative of a journal from Scotland to the West Indies, North Carolina, and Portugal, in the years 1774 to 1776*, ed. Evangeline Walker Andrews and Charles McLean Andrews, New Haven–London–Oxford 1934

Simeon, Charles, *Horæ homileticæ: or discourses digested into one continued series, and forming a commentary upon every book of the Old and New Testament*, ix, London 1841

Smollett, T., *The history of England from the revolution to the death of George II*, Edinburgh 1805

Sturge, Joseph and Thomas Harvey, *The West Indies in 1837: being the journal of a visit to Antigua, Montserat, Dominica, St Lucia, Barbados and Jamaica*, London 1838

Terrick, Richard, *Sermon preached before the incorporated Society for the Propagation of the Gospel . . . at their anniversary meeting . . . 1764*, London 1764

Thornton, John (ed.), *Bogatzky's golden treasury: a reprint of John Thornton's edition of 1775, with critical notes hitherto unpublished by John Berridge*, ed. Charles P. Phinn, London 1891

Voyage of the Resolution and Discovery, 1776–80, ed. J. C. Beaglehole, Cambridge 1967

Warburton, William, *A sermon preached before the incorporated Society for the Propagation of the Gospel . . . at their anniversary meeting . . . 1766*, London 1766

Wesley, John, *Thoughts upon slavery*, London 1774

―――― *The journal of the Rev. John Wesley*, ed. Nehemiah Curnock, standard edn, London 1938

―――― *The letters of John Wesley*, ed. John Telford, London 1960

―――― *The works of John Wesley: journal and diaries, V: 1765–75*, ed. W. Reginald Ward and Richard P. Heitzenrater, Nashville, Tenn. 1993

Whitefield, George, *An expostulatory letter, addressed to Nicholas Lewis, Count Zinzendorf*, London 1753

―――― *The works of the Reverend George Whitefield*, ed. John Gilles, London 1771

Wilberforce, Robert I. and Samuel Wilberforce, *The life of William Wilberforce*, London 1838

——— *The correspondence of William Wilberforce*, London 1840
Wilberforce, William, *A practical view of the prevailing religious system of professed Christians, in the higher and middle classes of this country contrasted with real Christianity*, London 1797
Wilson, Thomas, *The works of . . . Thomas Wilson*, iii, in *The life of . . . Thomas Wilson, D.D., lord bishop of Sodor and Man*, ed. C. Crutwell, Bath 1784
[Young, William], *A tour through the several islands of Barbadoes, St Vincent, Antigua and Grenada, in the years 1791 and 1792*, London 1801

Works of reference

Blackwell dictionary of evangelical biography, 1730–1860, Oxford 1995
Compact edition of the dictionary of national biography, Oxford 1975
Dictionary of American biography, London–Oxford–New York 1931
Dictionary of Canadian biography, iv, Toronto–Buffalo–London 1979
Namier, Sir Lewis and John Brooke (eds), *History of parliament: the House of Commons, 1754–90*, London 1964
Thorne, R. G. (ed.), *The history of parliament: the House of Commons, 1790–1820*, London 1986

Secondary sources

Abbey, C. J., *The English Church and its bishops, 1700–1800*, London 1887
Addison, William George, *The renewed Church of the United Brethren, 1722–1930*, London 1932
Amey, Basil, 'Baptist Missionary Society radicals', BQ xxvi (1975–6), 363–76
Anderson, Gerald H., *The theology of Christian mission*, London 1961
Anstey, Roger, *The Atlantic slave trade and British abolition, 1760–1810*, Aldershot 1992
Balleine, G. R., *A history of the evangelical party in the Church of England*, London–New York–Toronto 1933
Barham, F. Foster, *The Foster Barham genealogy*, London 1844
Basye, A. H., *The lord commissioners of trade and plantations, commonly known as the Board of Trade, 1742–82*, New Haven 1925
Bellot, Leland J., *William Knox: the life and thought of an eighteenth-century imperialist*, Austin, Tx–London 1977
Bennet, J. Harry, *Bondsmen and bishops: slavery and apprenticeship on the Codrington plantations of Barbados, 1710–1838*, Berkeley–Los Angeles 1958
Birtwhistle, N. Allen, 'Founded in 1786: the origins of the Methodist Missionary Society', PWHS xxx (1955), 25–9
Brainerd, Thomas, *The life of John Brainerd*, Philadelphia 1856
Brooke, John, *King George III*, London 1985
Brookes, George S., *Friend Anthony Benezet*, Philadelphia–London–Oxford 1937
Brown-Lawson, Albert, *John Wesley and the Anglican evangelicals in the eighteenth century*, Edinburgh–Cambridge–Durham 1994
Carey, S. Pearce, *William Carey DD*, London 1923
Carter, Harold B., *Sir Joseph Banks, 1743–1820*, London 1988

Clarke, W. K. Lowther, *A history of the SPCK*, London 1959
Cnattingius, Hans, *Bishops and societies: a study of Anglican colonial and missionary expansion, 1698–1850*, London 1952
Cochrane, J. A., *Dr Johnson's printer: the life of William Strahan*, London 1964
Cröger [Croeger], E. W., *Geschichte der erneuerten Brüderkirche*, Gnadau 1852–4
Daily watchwords 1998: the Moravian text book with almanac, London 1998
Davey, J. W., *The fall of Torngak, or the Moravian mission on the coast of Labrador*, London 1905
Davies, Rupert and Gordon Rupp (eds), *A history of the Methodist Church in Great Britain*, i, London 1965
Davis, David Brion, *The problem of slavery in western culture*, Ithaca–London 1969
—— *The problem of slavery in the age of revolution 1770–1823*, London 1975
Doerfel, Marianne, 'John Hartley, an eighteenth-century British headmaster of a German public school', *British Journal for Eighteenth-Century Studies* xii (1989), 145–64
Drescher, Seymour, *Capitalism and antislavery: British mobilisation in a comparative perspective*, London 1986
Duncan, Peter, *A narrative of the Wesleyan mission to Jamaica: with occasional remarks on the state of society in that colony*, London 1849
Ehrman, John, *The younger Pitt*, London 1996
Elbourne, Elizabeth, 'The foundation of the Church Missionary Society: the Anglican missionary impulse', in John Walsh, Colin Haydon and Stephen Taylor (eds), *The Church of England, c. 1689–c. 1833: from toleration to Tractarianism*, Cambridge 1993
Elwyn, T. S. H., *The Northamptonshire Baptist Association*, London 1964
Embree, Ainslie T., *Charles Grant and British rule in India*, London 1962
Enklaar, Ido H., *Life and work of Dr J. Th. van der Kemp, 1747–1811*, Cape Town–Rotterdam 1988
Freeman, Arthur J., *An ecumenical theology of the heart: the theology of Count Nicholas Ludwig von Zinzendorf*, Bethlehem, Penn.–Winston-Salem, NC 1998
Frost, Alan, *Convicts and empire: a naval question*, Melbourne–Oxford–Wellington–New York 1980
Furley, Oliver, W., 'Moravian missionaries and slaves in the West Indies', *Caribbean Studies* v (1965), 3–16
Fyfe, C., *A history of Sierra Leone*, Oxford 1962
Gad, Finn, *Gronlands historie English (The history of Greenland)*, II: *1700–82*, trans. G. C. Bowden, London 1973
Gollin, Gillian L., *Moravians in two worlds: a study of changing communities*, New York–London 1967
Goveia, Elsa, *Slave society in the British Leeward Islands at the end of the eighteenth century*, New Haven, Conn.–London 1965
Hall, Neville A. T., *Slave society in the Danish West Indies*, Baltimore–London 1992
Hamilton, J. Taylor and Kenneth G. Hamilton, *History of the Moravian Church: the renewed Unitas Fratrum, 1722–1957*, Bethlehem, Penn.–Winston-Salem, NC 1983
Hasler, Richard A., 'David Zeisberger's "Jersey connection" ', *TMHS* xxx (1998), 37–53
Hassé, E. R., *The Moravians*, London n.d.

Haykin, Michael A. G., *One heart and one soul: John Sutcliff of Olney, his friends and his times*, Durham 1994

Hennell, Michael, *John Venn and the Clapham Sect*, London 1958

Hindmarsh, D. Bruce, *John Newton and the English evangelical tradition between the conversions of Wesley and Wilberforce*, Oxford 1996

Hole, Charles, *The early history of the Church Missionary Society for Africa and the East to the end of AD 1814*, London 1896

Holmes, John, *History of the Protestant Church of the United Brethren*, London 1825, 1830

Hutton, J. E., *A history of the Moravian Church*, London 1909

—— *A history of Moravian missions*, London n.d.

Jenkins, R. T., *The Moravian Brethren in north Wales: an episode in the religious history of Wales*, London 1938

Kerr, R. E., 'A letter from the Rev. Benjamin La Trobe to Miss Mary Bosanquet', *PWHS* xx (1935–6), 88–93

Kroyer, P., *The story of Lindsey House*, London 1956

Krüger, Bernhard, *The pear tree blossoms: a history of the Moravian mission stations in South Africa, 1737–1869*, Genadendal, SA 1966

Langford, Paul, *A polite and commercial people: England, 1727–83*, Oxford–New York 1992

Larsen, Jens, *The Virgin Islands story*, Philadelphia 1950

Lehmannn, E. Arno, *It began at Tranquebar*, trans. M. J. Lutz, Vepery, Madras 1956

Lewis, A. J., *Zinzendorf the ecumenical pioneer: a study in the Moravian contribution to mission and unity*, London 1962

Lovett, Richard, *The history of the London Missionary Society, 1795–1895*, London 1899

Macintosh, Neil K., *Richard Johnson: chaplain to the colony of New South Wales: his life and times, 1755–1827*, Sydney 1978

Marshall, P. J., 'The moral swing to the east: British humanitarianism, India and the West Indies', in K. Ballhatchet and J. B. Harrison (eds), *East India Company studies*, Hong Kong 1986, 69–95

Martin, Roger H., *Evangelicals united: ecumenical stirrings in pre-Victorian Britain, 1795–1830*, Metuchen, NJ–London 1983

Mason, John and Lucy Torode, *Three generations of the La Trobe family in the Moravian Church*, Newtonabbey, Co. Antrim 1997

Morris, Henry, *The life of Charles Grant*, London 1904

Morrison, John, *The fathers and founders of the London Missionary Society; with a brief sketch of Methodism and historical notices of the several Protestant missions from 1556 to 1839*, London–Paris n.d.

Müller, Karl, *200 Jahre Brüdermission*, I: *Das erste Missionsjahrhundert*, Herrnhut 1931

Neill, Stephen, *A history of Christian missions*, 2nd edn, Harmondsworth 1990

Nelson, Vernon H., 'Samuel Isles, first Moravian missionary on Antigua', *TMHS* xxi/1 (1966), 3–27

Northampton group of Moravian chapels and preaching houses, London–Aylesbury 1886

Nuttall, Geoffrey F., *The students of Trevecca College, 1768–91*, Denby n.d.

Orchard, Stephen, 'Evangelical eschatology and the missionary awakening', *Journal of Religious History* xxii (1998), 132–51

Oussoren, A. H., *William Carey, especially his missionary principles*, Leyden 1945

Pascoe, C. F., *Two hundred years of the SPG, 1701–1900*, London 1901

Payne, E. A., *The prayer call of 1784*, Edinburgh 1942

────── ' "William Carey, especially his missionary principles", by Dr A. H. Oussoren', *BQ* xxii (1946–8), 165–7

────── 'Doddridge and the missionary enterprise', in Geoffrey F. Nuttall (ed.), *Philip Doddridge*, London 1951

────── 'Carey and his biographers', *BQ* xix (1961–2), 4–12

Penson, Lillian M., *The colonial agents of the British West Indies: a study in colonial administration mainly in the eighteenth century*, London 1924

du Plessis, J., *Christian missions in South Africa*, Cape Town 1965

Podmore, C. J., 'The bishops and the Brethren: Anglican attitudes to the Moravians in the mid-eighteenth century', *Journal of Ecclesiastical History* xli (1990), 622–46

────── *The Moravian Church in England, 1728–60*, Oxford 1998

Pollock, John, *Wilberforce*, London 1977

Porter, A. N., *Religion and empire: British expansion in the long nineteenth century, 1780–1914* (inaugural lecture, King's College London), London 1991

Porter, Dale H., *The abolition of the slave trade in England, 1784–1807*, Hampden, Conn. 1970

Potts, E. Daniel, *British Baptists in India, 1793–1837*, Cambridge 1967

Price, Richard, *Alabi's world*, Baltimore–London 1990

Ragatz, L. F., *The fall of the planter class in the British Caribbean, 1763–1833*, New York–London 1928

Reichel, Hellmut, 'Versuche in der Brüdergemeine zur ökumenischen Sammlung der Christen: die Aufnahme von Zinzendorfs Diasporagedanken und die Herrnhuter Predigerkonferenz (1750–1800)', *UF* xxix/xxx (1991), 176–98

Rican, Rudolf, *The history of the Unity of the Brethren: a Protestant Hussite Church in Bohemia and Moravia*, trans. C. Daniel Crews, Bethlehem, Penn.– Winston-Salem, NC 1992

Rollmann, Marcella, 'The role of language in the Moravian missions to eighteenth-century Labrador', *UF* xxxiv (1993), 49–64

Sayer, Edwin A., *These fifteen pioneers of the Moravian Church*, Bethlehem, Penn.–Winston-Salem, NC 1963

Schlenther, Boyd S., ' "To convert the poor people in America" ', *Georgia Historical Quarterly* lxxvii (1994), 225–56

Schulze, Adolf, *Abriss einer Geschichte der Brüdermissionen*, Herrnhut 1901

Seymour, A. C. Hobart, *The life and times of Selina, countess of Huntingdon*, London 1844

Sheridan, Richard B., 'Letters from a sugar plantation in Antigua, 1739–58', *Agricultural History* xxxi (1957), 3–23

────── 'Samuel Martin, innovating sugar planter on Antigua, 1750–76', *Agricultural History* xxxiv (1960), 126–55

────── 'The rise of a colonial gentry: a case study of Antigua, 1730–55', *Economic History Review* 2nd ser. xiii (1960–1), 342–57

Shyllon, F. O., *Black slaves in Britain*, London–New York–Ibadan 1974

────── *James Ramsay: the unknown abolitionist*, Edinburgh 1977

Skarsten, R., 'Erik Pontoppidan and his asiatic prince Menoza', *Church History* l (1981), 33–43
Smith, George, *The life of William Carey, shoemaker and missionary*, Everyman edn, London–New York n.d.
Stanley, Brian, *The Bible and the flag: Protestant missions and the British empire in the nineteenth and twentieth centuries*, Leicester 1990
—— *The history of the Baptist Missionary Society, 1792–1992*, Edinburgh 1992
Stoeffler, F. Ernest, *The rise of evangelical Pietism*, Leiden 1965
Tibbut, H. G., 'Joshua Symonds, diarist', *Bedfordshire Magazine* iv (1953–5), 338–42
Towlson, Clifford W., *Moravian and Methodist: relationships in the eighteenth century*, London 1957.
van den Berg, J., *Constrained by Jesus' love: an enquiry into the motives of the missionary awakening in Great Britain . . . 1698–1815*, Kampen 1956
Vickers, John, *Thomas Coke: apostle of Methodism*, London 1969
Walls, A. F., 'A Christian experiment: the early Sierra Leone colony', in G. J. Cuming (ed.), *The mission of the Church and the propagation of the faith* (Studies in Church History vi, 1970), 108–16
Walsh, J. D., 'The Magdalene evangelicals', *Church History Review* clix (1958), 499–511
—— 'Methodism at the end of the eighteenth century', in Rupert Davies and Gordon Rupp (eds), *A history of the Methodist Church in Great Britain*, i, London 1965
—— 'The Cambridge Methodists', in P. Brooks (ed.), *Christian spirituality: essays in honour of Gordon Rupp*, London 1975
—— 'John Wesley and the community of goods', in Keith Robbins (ed.), *Protestant evangelicalism: Britain, Ireland and America, c. 1750–1950: essays in honour of W. R. Ward*, Oxford 1990
—— ' "Methodism" and the orgins of English-speaking evangelicalism', in M. A. Noll, D. W. Bebbington and G. A. Rawlyk (eds), *Evangelicalism*, New York–Oxford 1994
Ward, J. R., *British West Indian slavery, 1750–1834: the process of amelioration*, Oxford 1988
Ward, W. R., *Religion and society in England, 1790–1850*, London 1972
—— 'Zinzendorf and money', in W. J. Sheils and Diana Wood (eds), *The Church and wealth* (Studies in Church History xxiv, 1987), 283–305
—— *The Protestant evangelical awakening*, Cambridge 1992
Weaver, Glenn, 'Moravians during the French and Indian War', *Church History* xxiv (1955), 239–56
Welch, Edwin, *Spiritual pilgrim: a reassessment of the life of the countess of Huntingdon*, Cardiff 1995
Westergaard, Waldemar, *The Danish West Indies under company rule, 1671–1754*, New York 1917
Whiteley, William H., 'The establishment of the Moravian mission in Labrador and British policy, 1763–83', *Canadian Historical Review* xlv (1964), 29–50
—— 'Governor Hugh Palliser and the Newfoundland and Labrador fishery, 1764–8', *Canadian Historical Review* l (1969), 141–63
Wickwire, F. B., 'John Pownall and British colonial policy', *William and Mary Quarterly* 3rd ser. xx (1963), 543–54

Williams, Glyndwr, *The British search for the North West Passage in the eighteenth century*, London 1962
Wood, A. S., *Thomas Haweis, 1734–1820*, London 1957

Unpublished theses etc.

Brunner, Daniel L., 'The role of Halle Pietists in England (c. 1700–c. 1740) with special reference to the SPCK', DPhil. diss. Oxford 1988
Carson, Penelope S. E., ' "Soldiers of Christ": evangelicals and India, 1784–1833', PhD diss. London 1988
Doll, Peter M., 'Imperial Anglicanism in North America, 1745–95', DPhil. diss. Oxford 1989
Evans, Ronald Paul, 'The life and work of Thomas Pennant (1726–98)', PhD diss. Swansea 1993
Hayden, Roger, 'Evangelical Calvinism among eighteenth-century British Baptists with particular reference to Bernard Foskett, Hugh and Caleb Evans and the Bristol Baptist Academy, 1690–1791', PhD diss. Keele 1991
Hiller, J. H., 'The foundation and the early years of the Moravian mission in Labrador, 1752–1805', MA diss. Memorial University, Newfoundland 1967
Hindmarsh, D. Bruce ' "I am a sort of middle-man": John Newton and the English evangelical tradition between the conversions of Wesley and Wilberforce', DPhil. diss. Oxford 1994
Ince, Anne Claire, 'Protestant missionary activity in five south Caribbean islands during slavery, 1765–1826', DPhil. diss. Oxford 1985
Lenius, Susan M., 'Slavery and the Moravian Church in North Carolina', diss. Moravian College, Bethlehem, Penn. 1974
McKelvie, Graham D., 'The development of official Anglican interest in world mission, 1783–1809, with special reference to Bishop Beilby Porteus', PhD diss. Aberdeen 1984
Manley, Kenneth Ross, 'John Rippon, DD (1751–1835) and the Particular Baptists', DPhil. diss. Oxford 1967
Mason, J. C. S., 'The role of the Moravian Church during the missionary awakening in England, 1760 to c. 1800', PhD diss. London 1998
Maxwell, Ian, 'Civilization or Christianity: the Scottish debate on mission methods, 1750–1835' (North Atlantic missiology project xii, 1996), typescript
O'Shaughnessy, A. J., 'The politics of the British Leeward Islands, 1763–83', DPhil. diss. Oxford 1988
Phillips, I. Lloyd, 'The evangelical administrator, Sir Charles Middleton at the Navy Board, 1778–90', DPhil. diss. Oxford 1974
Podmore, Colin John, 'The role of the Moravian Church in England, 1728–60', DPhil. diss. Oxford 1994
Rees, S. E., 'The political career of Wills Hill, earl of Hillsborough (1718–93) with particular reference to his American policy', PhD diss. Aberystwyth 1976
Roxborough, William John, 'Thomas Chalmers and the mission of the Church with special reference to the rise of the missionary movement in Scotland', PhD diss. Aberdeen 1978

Sangster, P. E., 'The life of the Rev. Rowland Hill (1744–1833) and his position in the evangelical revival', DPhil. diss. Oxford 1964

Schattschneider, David A., ' "Souls for the Lamb": a theology for the Christian mission according to Count Nicolaus Ludwig von Zinzendorf and Bishop Augustus Gottlieb Spangenberg', PhD diss. Chicago 1975

Stead, Geoffrey, 'European Pietism in Yorkshire: the origin and early development of the Moravian settlement at Fulneck, 1742–90', PhD diss. Leeds 1994

Terpstra, Chester, 'David Bogue, DD, 1750–1825', PhD diss. Edinburgh 1959

Index

Page numbers in *italic* refer to plates/map. Moravian missionaries appear by name under missionaries, Moravian.

Account of the . . . missions (Spangenberg), 67, 88, 146; cited, on Brainerd, 151, 152; on slavery, 103–4; compared with *Life* of Brainerd, 147–8; influence of, 157, 169. *See also* Moravian missionary teaching
act of parliament: to encourage Moravians to settle in American colonies (1749), 8–9, 10
Adair, Dr James, of Antigua, 130
Adams, Capt. Sir Charles, 35, 53
Adby, Revd William, 78
African princes, 57, 58
agents, colonial, *see* West India Committee
Alexander, Du Pré, second earl of Caledon, *see* Caledon
Alexander, Capt. J. E., 105
Anabaptists, 174; Moravians compared to, 10
Anglican Church, *see* Established Church
Antigua: character of white society in, 108; 'gentry of', 107–8; Moravian mission in, 8, 91, 95, 153, 194–5, and beginning of, 106, 107, progress of, 108–9, 110–13, 142, and Sturge on, 99; Wesleyan mission in, 126. *See also* slave trade, 1788 enquiry into
Arctic zoology, 68
Arminian Magazine, 181

back-sliders, treatment of, 97, 99, 153, 182
Bacon, John, 78, 202
Banks, Joseph, 52–3
Baptist Annual Register, 185, 187
Baptist Missionary Society (BMS), 59, 159, 172, 191–2; candidates of, 163–4; and Carey's plan for a 'Moravian' settlement, 173–4; founders of, 73, 84–5, 87–9; and Moravian missions, 88, 145, 183, 184, 195; rupture with Serampore, 155, 173

Barbados, Moravian mission in, 26, 129, 140, 142. *See also* SPG
Barham, Joseph Foster, Sr, 69–70, 106; and family of, 70, 81, 136
Barham, Joseph Foster, Jr, MP, 203; and abolition, 122, 137; and support for Moravian mission in Jamaica, 70, 137
Barham, Lord, *see* Sir Charles Middleton
Barrow, John, 190–1
Bedford, 54, 69, 70, 81, 85, 86, 187; and Baptists, 88
Bellot, Leland J., 56
Benezet, Anthony, 92
Bengal, *see* Calcutta, Patna, Serampore
Berlin: missionary academy in, 189
Bethlehem, Penn., 31, 150, 151, 204
Bogue, David, 160, 203; address by, 145; on qualifications of missionaries, 165–6
Böhler, Peter, 45
Bosanquet, Mary, 77
Botany Bay, 78–9, 80; and Moravians, 80–1
Boughton, Thomas, 86–7
Bouverie, 'Mrs', 116, 120
Brainerd, David, 87, 167; changes manner of preaching, 151–2; and Moravians on, 151, 152. *See also Life* of
Brathwaite, John, 128, 129, 133. *See also* slave trade, 1788 enquiry into
Brethren's Society for the Furtherance of the Gospel (SFG), 44–5, 183; and Labrador mission, 46–8, 50–1, 158, and Spangenberg's letter, 47–8; publicity for, 49–51, 65, 180–1, 182, and fund-raising, 51–2, 54–5; revival of, 28, 44–6, 47, and constitution of, 49; subscribers to, 52–3, 88, 183–4, 185–6
Bristol, 14, 44, 57–8; Horne's visit to, 156–7; Moravian chapel in, 51
British West Indies, 90–1; Moravian mission in, 8–9, 18, litany used, 105, loyalty of converts, 190, number

baptised, 142. *See also* Antigua, Barbados, Jamaica, St Kitts, Tobago
Broughton, Revd Thomas, 55, 56
Brown, Revd David, 83
Bull, William, 70–1, 72–3
Burder, George, 161–2, 144, 167
Burke, Edmund, 134
Byron, Capt. John, 39

Calcutta, 81, 82, 174
Caledon, Lord, 185n., 192
Cambridge, University of, 185, 186, 202, 203, 204
Campbell, John, 40
Campbell, John, of Scotland, 184, 191
Cape of Good Hope, 15, 19; LMS mission at, 188, 192; Moravian mission at, 153, 182, 188, 190–1
Cardale, William, 63, 202
Carey, William, 84–5, 167, 192; conversion and missionary awakening of, 86–8; and Moravian influence, 173–4; takes employment in India, 172. *See also* BMS, *Enquiry into the obligations of Christians*
Carleton, Guy, 40
Carteret, Mrs B., 55
Carteret, John, first Earl Granville, *see* Granville
Cavendish, Mrs Anne, 55
Cecil, Revd Richard, 73, 74, 78, 202
Cennick, John, 63, 106
Chelsea, 53, 55; and Lindsey House, 39
Childs, Thomas, 55
Christian Observer, 10
Church Evangelicals, 62, 79, 143; relations with Moravians, 135–6, 177, 186, 195. *See also* Clapham Sect, CMS
Church Missionary Society (CMS), 78, 183; 'Account' of, 176–7, 178–9, 190; and Moravians, 179, 184; recruits missionaries from Germany, 179, 188–9; and Sierra Leone Company, 177–8, 179. *See also* Eclectic Society
Church of England, *see* Established Church of England
Church, primitive, 76, 178
Clapham Sect, 78, 176, 183, 202–3
Clarkson, Thomas, 116, 130
Codrington estates, *see* SPG
Coke, Revd Thomas, 57, 58, 121, 133, 140. *See also* Wesleyans
community of goods: BMS agrees to, 173–4, and Marshman on, 174; and LMS, 172; and Moravians' practice of, 150, 173
conversion and civilisation, 189–91; CMS on, 190; Moravians on, 32, 35, 164–5; Porteus on, 92–3, 119; priority of, 164–5, 191; Ramsay on, 119; Wilberforce on, 123
Cranz, David, 17, 20–1
Critical Review, 43, 66
Culworth (Northamptonshire), 85, 86, 87
Cunow, Christian Frederic, 189
Curtis, Lt Roger, 38–9

Danish West Indies: Moravian mission in, 17, 18–19, 20, 22, 100, number baptised, 142; Royal Danish Lutheran missionaries, 105–6. *See also* St Croix, St John, St Thomas
Dartmouth, earl of, 42, 55, 69; and Moravian mission to Labrador, 32, 35–6, 39–40
Davidson, Dr Thomas, 183, 203
Discourse concerning the special causes of irreligion in the West Indies, 108
Dissenters, 60, 135–6, 177; and LMS, 176, 188; suspect, 158, 191–2
Dodd, Dr William, 76–7
Duff, 147, 172
Dundas, Henry, 126, 127, 192

East India Company (EIC): and Baptists, 192; and Moravians, 81–4
Eclectic Society, 78, 135, 202–3; and formation of CMS, 178–9
Edinburgh Missionary Society, 183, 185–6, 203
Edwards, Jonathan, 87. See also *Life of David Brainerd*
Egmont, earl of, 41, 42
Ellis, Charles, 136–7
Enquiry into the obligations of Christians to use means for the conversion of the heathen, 84, 87, 144–5, 172
Erskine, Dr John, of Edinburgh, 165
Esquimaux, *see* Inuit
Essay on the treatment and conversion of the African slaves, 117, 118
Established Church of England, 90, 95, 176; criticised, 130; Moravians' respect for, 65–6, 136
evangelical Calvinists, 59, 61–2, 68, 75, 84; journals for, 73–4, 94; numbers of, 73
Evangelical Magazine, 73–4, 145, 180, 183,

187; Moravian publications reviewed in, 74–5
Ewing, Greville, 183, 185, 203
Exposition (of doctrine, Spangenberg), 66–7, 72–3, 74–5, 103; Benjamin La Trobe's preface, 72, 75
Eyre, John, 74

Farley, Francis, 108–9, 110
Fetter Lane, 162; Moravians in, 50, 63, 70, 80, and attendance at chapel, 51, 77–78, and missionaries from CMS, 189
Fletcher, Revd John, 7, 156
Form of agreement: reflecting the great principles upon which the brethren of the mission at Serampore think it their duty to act . . ., 169–70
Foster, Henry, 78, 179, 202
Foster, William, 69, 106
Fuller, Andrew, 73, 84, 88, 169, 170, 183; on a Moravian settlement, 173–4. *See also* BMS
Fulneck (Yorkshire), 63, 169

Gad, Finn, 21
Gambier, Admiral James, 183, 190, 202
Gardiner, John, 116–17
Genadendal, *see* Cape of Good Hope
Gentleman's Magazine, 43, 67, 93–4
Georgia, 56, 57
Gibson, Edmund, bishop of London, 91
Gilbert, Nathaniel, of Antigua, 107, 156
Gisborne, Revd Thomas, 183, 203
Glasgow Missionary Society, 185–6, 203
Grant, Charles, 178; in Calcutta, 62, 81; his missionary proposal, 83; and Moravians, 83–4, 183, 202
Granville, Lord, 55
Greatheed, Samuel, 154, 158–9, 187, 203
Greenland, Moravian mission in, 5, 17–19, 20–1; New Herrnhut, 21–2, 22; progress of, 21–2, 142. *See also History of Greenland*
Greenlanders, 20–1, 94, 119, 165
Greville, Charles, 52, 192
Guinea Coast (West Africa), 26, 123–4. *See also* Sierra Leone

Halle: missionaries from, 5, 55–6, 149
'Happy' deaths, 98, 182
Hardcastle, Joseph, 162, 176, 203
Harris, Howell, 50, 55
Hartley, John, 156–7

Hassé, Bishop E. R., 24
Hastings, Selina, countess of Huntingdon, *see* Huntingdon, countess of
Haweis, Revd Thomas, 61, 68, 74, 159–60, 203; admiration for Moravians, 75–6, and commends their missionary methods to LMS, 160–3; disagrees with Bogue, 160; and ministers' conference at Herrnhut, 187; and mission to South Seas, 62, 172
Hawkesbury, Lord, 121, 126, 131–2, 136
HMS Niger, 35, 53
Herrnhut, Saxony, 7, 13, 20, 150; ministers' conference at, 187, 188–9; missionaries from, 18, 25–6
Hill, Revd Rowland, 69, 146, 203
Hill, Wills, first marquis of Downshire, *see* Hillsborough
Hillsborough, Lord: and mission in Labrador, 32, 33, 37–8; well-disposed towards Moravians, 38, 56
History of Greenland, 41, 53, 55, 151, 152; commended in Scotland, 165; influence of, 74, 167–8, 196; Newton on, 71; and North-West passage, 44; publication of, 17, 42; reviews of, 42–3; John Wesley on, 43–4
Horne, Melville, 74, 144, 156–7, 177; contrasts Moravians with Wesleyans, 158; and Moravian missions, 156–8, 159–60, 167; receives copy of Spangeberg's *Account of the . . . missions*, 157. *See also Letters on missions*
Huntingdon, countess of, 55, 57, 77
Hurd, Richard, bishop of Lichfield, 60, 77
Hurlock, Philip, 53
Hutton, James, 29, 33, 56, 64; his connections, 52, 77; and SFG, 45, 47

improvement, *see* conversion and civilisation
Inquiry into the effects of putting a stop to the African slave trade, 118, 119
Instructions (for missionaries, Spangenberg), 67, 81, 105, 146, 153
Inuit, 28, 29, 30, 34–5; atrocities against, 36; Mikak, 36–7; Moravians' fears for, 40–1
Ireland, James, of Bristol, 57–8

Jamaica: clergy in, 130; Moravian mission in, 69, 137, 142, and origin of, 106;

rebellion feared, 121–2; Wesleyan mission in, 121
Jænicke, Johannes, 189
Jenkinson, Charles, first earl of Liverpool, see Hawkesbury
Jesuits: Moravians compared to, 55, 68, 124, 157
Johnson, Revd Richard, 79–81, 186, 203. See also Botany Bay
Johnson, Dr Samuel, 52, 76
Johnson, Sir William, 30
Jowett family, 186

Knox, William, 56–7, 134
Krüger, Bernhard, 15, 153

Labrador, Moravian mission in, 13, 18, 34–5, 145; and the SFG, 28, 46–9, 52; and British policy, 29–30, 30–1; commended to privy council, 35, 38; orders in support of, 33–4, 39–40; negotiations for, 29–30, 32–3; progress of, 142, 182
La Trobe, Benjamin, 45, 47, 57, 76–7; joins Eclectic Society, 78; lobbies EIC, 82–3; meets Middleton, 79; and Newton, 62, 70, 71, 194; and Porteus, 66–7, 116; and Ramsay, 117–18; sketch of life, 63–4; on Wesleyans 136
La Trobe, (Christian) Ignatius, 10, 106, 133, 136, 191, 192; and abolitionists, 120, 121, 122–5; advice to Baptists, 164, and to Haweis/LMS, 162–3, 164–5, 171; assists CMS, 188–9; finds his calling, 139–40; introduces *Periodical Accounts*, 140; sketch of life, 115; Wilberforce on, 185
Law, William, 85, 86
Legge, William, second earl of Dartmouth, see Dartmouth
Letters on missions, 74, 154–60; significance of, 144, 157, 159–60
Life of David Brainerd, 87, 147, 151, 168, 196
Litany for the use of the negroe congregations of the Brethren in the British dominions, 105
Livius, George, 81–2, 83
London, 10, 37; Bentinck Chapel, 183; Castle and Falcon, Aldersgate, 78; port of, 50; St Mary-le-Bow, 60; St Mary Woolnoth, 69; Savoy Chapel, 189; Surrey Chapel, 146. See also Chelsea, Fetter Lane, Whitehall

London Missionary Society (LMS), 59, 74; and Church Evangelicals, 176; considers qualifications of missionaries, 162–4, and Bogue's dissent, 165–6; consults Ignatius La Trobe, 161, 165, 171; divisions within, 160; establishes academy, 166–7; foundation of, 145–6; links with Europe, 187–8; purchases the *Duff*, 172. See also Cape of Good Hope, van der Kemp
Lovet, Richard, 163

Macartney, Lord George, first Earl Macartney, 190
Magdalen College, Oxford, 10
Marsden, Samuel, 186, 203
Marshman, Joshua, 169, 174
Martin, Samuel, of Antigua, 108–10, 111
Martin, Samuel, Jr, MP, 110, 122
Melville, Viscount, see Henry Dundas
Middleton, Sir Charles, 79, 80, 120, 131, 183, 202; and Ramsay, 116
Middleton, Lady Margaret, 120 and n., 140
Mikak, see Inuit
Milner, Isaac, 186, 203
missionaries: dual role of, 158, 171, 172–3; and politics, 123–4, 158–9, 191–2; and trade, 32, 172
missionaries, Moravian: models for others, 159, 172, and of perseverance, 167–8; mortality of, 26–7; numbers of, 23–4, 65, and shortage of, 24, 80, 148, 189; self-sufficient, 25, 26, 150, 171–3; volunteers, 24, 26, 149, 171, and Spangenberg's advice, 149–51, 153
missionaries, Moravian: individuals: Frederick Bohnisch, 168; Peter Brown, 110, 111, 146; Christian Drachart, 33, 34, 38; John Daniel Gottwald, 118, 128; John Grassman, 83–4; Jens Haven, 29, 30, 45, 166, and appears in 'Esquimaux Dress', 51; Samuel Isles, 107; James La Trobe, 83, 166; Frederick Martin, 96; Frederick Post, 31; Matthew Stach, 168; David Zeisberger, 31, 51
missionary awakening, 59–61, 61–2, 68, 94; and guilt, 60–1, 94; and *Life* of Brainerd, 147, 151; and prayer, 62, 87; and slave trade, 125; stimulated by Moravians, 143–6
Missionary instructions (Haweis), 160–1, 162, 200–1

INDEX

Missionary Society, The, *see* London Missionary Society
modern missionary movement, 155, 176, 179–80, 185–6, 186–7; publicity for, 179–81
Moffat, Robert, 170
Monthly Review, 66–7
Moore, John, archbishop of Canterbury, 126, 176
Moravian Church: *Ancient and modern history* of, 7, 66, 71; 'brotherly agreements', 13, 14; *Candid declaration* of, 46; choir system, 20, 21, 97; constitution of, 11–12, 14–15, and *Concise historical account* of, 65; doctrine of, 12, derided, 9–10, and errors acknowledged, 12, 72; Elders of (UEC), 28, 42, 108, 132, 139, and role of, 6, 12–13, and visitations by, 25, 45; funds, lack of, 10–11, 12–13, 25, and for missions, 26, 47–8, 182–4, and British generosity, 183–4, 184–5; 'heathen festivals', 24–5, 91, 78; hymns of, 10, 43–4, 149–50, and hymn-theology, 21; the Lot, 14–16, and deferrals to, 16, 17, 28, 125; love feasts, 48, 50–1; mission of, 16, and missions part of, 25; missions department, 12, 26, 47, 183; publications by, 16–18, 50, 64–8, 74; recognition of, 8–9, 10; reputation of, 10–11, 56, 71, 130, and restored, 63–4, 141–2; respect for Church and State, 8, 9, 13–14, 65–6, 149; revival of, 6–8; 'Weekly Leaves', 25. See also *Exposition* (Spangenberg)
Moravian missionary teaching, 24, 146; on baptism, 148, 152–3; on native languages, 150, 165–6; on preaching, 20, 147–8, 150–2, 164–8, 170; on qualifications of missionaries, 164–5; on role of women, 153; its Pauline roots, 147–8; on self-preparation, 149. *See also* community of goods
Mortimer, Peter, 187–8

Nain (Labrador), 38
'native helpers', 99–100, 148
Naval and Military Bible Society, 77–8
Newfoundland, Indians of, 36
New Herrnhut, *see* Greenland, St Thomas
Newport Pagnell (Buckinghamshire), 70, 85, 154

New Spiritual Magazine, 94, 104
Newton, Revd John, 80, 85, 122; advises BMS, 173; his circle, 68–70; and B. La Trobe, 70; his missionary sermon, 60–1; on Moravian doctrine, 73, and publications, 71–2
North American Indians, 30–1; Moravian mission to, 23, 51, and Loskiel's *History*, 74
Northampton, 77, 85, 86, 87
Northamptonshire Association of Baptist Ministers, 59, 62, 85, 120; prayer call issued by, 87

Okely, Francis, 77, 85, 86–7, 88, 120; and John Ryland, Jr, 87
Oldendorp, C. G. A., 22
Oldendorp's history, 22–3, 96, 98, 100, 124
Olney (Buckinghamshire), 69, 84, 85

Pal, Krishna, 84
Palliser, Commodore Sir Hugh, 29–30, 33–4, 44; and the Inuit, 29–30, 36–7. *See also* Labrador, Moravian mission in
Palmer, Revd Thomas, 80
Paris, Treaty of, 29
Patna, 83
Payne, Sir Ralph, 112
Pearce, Samuel, 167–8
Pennant, Thomas, 67–8
Perceval, John, second earl of Egmont, *see* Egmont
Periodical Accounts Relative to the Baptist Missionary Society, 173, 181
Periodical Accounts Relating to the Missions of the Church of the United Brethren Established among the Heathen, 88, 138–9, 140–1, 145, 180; circulation of, 185–7, 202–4; contents, 181–3; extract from (number baptised), 142; and Porteus, 140–1; significance of, 180–1
Pietism, 5, 6, 24; and Danish court, 19. *See also* Halle
Pitt, William, the younger, 78–9, 114, 126; and Wilberforce, 78–9, 123–4
polite society, 50, 51, 52–5
Pollock, John, 123
Pontoppidan, Eric von, 17–18, 20
Porteus, Beilby, bishop of London, 67, 83, 90–1, 125, 140–1, 203; cites example of Moravians, 93–5, 126–7; establishes missionary society, 127; sermon before the SPG, 92–5; and *Plan* for slaves,

227

94–5; and 1788 slave-trade enquiry, 126, 131, 133–4
Potts, E. Daniel, 173
Pownall, John, 31–2, 34, 45–6. *See also* Labrador, Moravian mission in
Practical view of the prevailing religious system of professed Christians, in the higher and middle classes of this country, contrasted with real Christians, 141–2
Pratt, Josiah, 185, 202
Proclamation of 1763, 29, 31
proprietors, *see* West Indian planters

Ramsay, James, 116–20; enrages planters, 119–20
Remarkable journal of Christian Frederic Post, 31
Rimius, Henry, 10, 71, 74
Rippon, John, 185, 203
Royal Danish Lutheran Missions, 5, 17, 23; compared with Moravian missions, 19, 23, 105–6. *See also* Tranquebar
Royal Society, 53
Ryland, John, Jr, 69, 73, 84, 87; and Moravians, 87, 88, 169, 184, 203

St Croix, 130, 142
St John, 142; slave rebellion in, 101
St John's (Antigua), 107, 108, 112; Moravian mission station at, 102
St Kitts, 116–17, 139, 142; and Moravian chapel in, 182
St Thomas: Moravian mission in, 5, 19, 95–7, 100–1, 142
San Domingue, 122
Schattschneider, David, 146, 147
Schirnding, Baron von, 169
Scotland, 73, 184, 185–6; Church of, 165
Scott, Revd Thomas, 138
Seasonally alarming and . . . exhilarating TRUTHS, 86
Secker, Thomas, archbishop of Canterbury, 42, 92
Serampore: Baptists at, 84, 155, 169, 174; Moravians at, 82, 84
Sharp, Granville, 178, 203
Shuldam, Molineux, 38–9
Sierra Leone, 157, 179; Company, 177–8
Simeon, Charles, 70, 178, 185, 202; cited, 193
Skelton, Dr Philip, 56
slavery: issue of, 90–3, 103–4, 125–6; and Lord Mansfield's judgement, 110; Moravians and, 97, 100, 101–6, 135;

reform of, 93, 134, and amelioration, 137. *See also* slave trade
slave trade, 91–2, 93–4; abolition of, 114, 118–24, 128; debated in Commons, 134–5, 137; and 1788 enquiry into, 124, 125–6, 127–32, 194–5, and Moravians, 129–30, 140–1, and their submission, 132–4; justified, 114, 123, 134–5
Smollett, Tobias, 43
Society for the Abolition of the Slave Trade, 62, 120
Society for the Conversion and Religious Instruction and Education of the Negro Slaves in the West Indies, 127
Society for Missions to Africa and the East, *see* CMS
Society for Promoting Christian Knowledge (SPCK), 55, 60
Society for the Propagation of the Gospel (SPG), 30, 51–2, 60, 130; and Benezet, 92; Codrington estates, 90, 92, 128, and Barbados committee, 94; sermons preached before, 60, 91–3
Solander, Dr Dan, 53
South Seas, 62, 79; and LMS, 147, 163, 171–2
Spangenberg, August Gottlieb, 5–6, 7, 17, 98, 102; in England, 45–6; and SFG, 44–5, 47–8; on visitations, 25; visits St Thomas, 101; works by, 66–7, 72–3, 74; and Zinzendorf, 24, 146. *See also* Moravian missionary teaching
'speakings', 98–9
Spooner, Charles, 128, 129
Steinkopf, Carl, 188–9
Stoeffler, Ernest F., 6
Strahan, Andrew, 64, 66
Strahan, William, 64, 66
Sturge, Joseph, 99
Succinct view (of Moravians missions), 50, 65, 92
Surinam, 23, 142, 189
Sutcliff, John, 84, 88, 168, 187, 203
Sydney, Lord, 40
Symonds, Joshua, 69, 70

Tattamy, Moses, 152 and n.
Test and Corporation Acts, 135–6
'"Testonites"', 121, 194
Thomas, Sir George, 107–8, 112
Thomas, John, 167, 172–3
Thornton, Henry, 178, 183, 202
Thornton, John, 54–5, 70, 77, 139

INDEX

Thoughts upon the African slave trade, 122
Tobago, 136, 140
Towlson, Clifford W., 143–4
Townsend, Thomas, first viscount Sydney, *see* Sydney
Tranquebar, 5, 23; Moravians at, 55

van den Berg, Johannes, 196
van der Kemp, Dr Johannes, 188, 192, 203
Vaughan, Benjamin, MP, 134–5
Venn, Revd Henry, 52, 55, 68, 69
Venn, John, 70, 178–9

Warburton, William, bishop of Gloucester, 91–2
Ward, William, 169–70, 174, 196
Watteville, Johannes von, 96–7, 98
Wedgwood, Josiah, 120
Wesley, Charles, 57
Wesley, John, 57, 66, 103, 121, 136, 193; on Cranz's *History of Greenland*, 43–4
Wesleyans: and Horne, 157, 158; missions of, 121, 126, 193; and Moravians, 57–8, 136, 143–4
West India Committee, 127–8
West Indian planters: absentee, 106–7; encourage Moravian missions, 93, 94–5, 100, 106–7, 131, Ignatius La Trobe on, 106–7; oppose abolition, 121, 122, 128, and vindicated 134–5; oppose missions, 19, 91, 121
Whitefield, George, 10–11, 62

Whitehall, 28; and sentiments of humanity in, 29, 40, 41
Wilberforce, Mrs Hannah, 62
Wilberforce, William, 83, 176, 178; and Botany Bay, 78–9; and Moravians, 80, 123–4, 139–40, 183, 185, 202, and their character, 141–2; opposes amelioration of slave trade, 137; on slaves' conversion, 134. *See also* slave trade
Wilks, Matthew, 74
William Wilberforce, 179
Williams, Dr Edward, of Rotherham, 160
Wilson, Thomas, bishop of Sodor and Man, 91
Wombwell, George, MP, 82
Woodd, Revd Basil, 183, 202

Young, Sir William, 136–8

Zeist (Holland), 53, 188
Zinzendorf, Count Nicolaus Ludwig von, 5–7, 12, 15, 23; his 'Blood and Wounds' theology, 20; his 'First fruits' idea, 95–7, 98; hymns by, 10; his instructions to missionaries, 17, 18, 23, 150; and Spangenberg, 24, 146; on status of slaves, 101–2; on visitations, 25; visits St Thomas, 19, 101
Zong, 114

ERRATA

Amendments and corrections please to:
J.C.S. Mason,
The Moravian Church and the Missionary Awakening in England 1760-1800

A. Footnotes
The full text of the original footnotes appear below, with the actual changes or additions shown in bold and underlined.

Page 9, Note 15, (addition to last line)

> For the act being carried by missionaries to Antigua (1756) see Vernon H. Nelson, 'Samuel Isles, first missionary on Antigua', *THHS* xxi/1 (1966), 9; to Tortola (1759) see *C.G.A. Oldendorp's history of the mission of the evangelical brethren on the Caribbean islands of St Thomas, St Croix and St John*. ed. J.J. Bossard, Barby; trans. and ed. Arnold R. Highfield and Vladimir Barac, Ann Arbor, Mich. 1987**, 606-607.**

Page 44, Note 81, (correction in line three)

> May 1778, Prince William Sound: *The voyage of the Resolution and Discovery, 1776-1778*, ed. J.C. Beaglehole, pt 1, Cambridge **1967**, 349-51. For Pickersgill (1776) see Glyndwr Williams, *The British search for the North West Passage in the eighteenth century*, London 1962, 184-5.

Page 80, note 116, (addition to line in actual text)

> Newton to Bull, 27 Oct. 1786, MS 3095, fos 196-7**, LPL.**

Page 80, note 119 (spelling correction)

> Protokoll des **Synodus**, 1789, R.2.B.48c. no.47

B. Index

New entry (shown in bold)
Page 228,
> **Quakers, Anthony Benezet, 92; Sturge and Harvey on Moravians in Antigua, 99**

John Mason, 3 Dec. 2010

www.ingramcontent.com/pod-product-compliance
Ingram Content Group UK Ltd.
Pitfield, Milton Keynes, MK11 3LW, UK
UKHW021318180426
11947UKWH00015B/1309